VIBRANT WITH WORDS

Vibrant with Words: The Letters of Ursula Bethell

Selected and Edited by Peter Whiteford

Victoria University Press

VICTORIA UNIVERSITY PRESS
Victoria University of Wellington
PO Box 600 Wellington
http://www.vuw.ac.nz/vup

First published 2005

National Library of New Zealand Cataloguing-in-Publication Data

Bethell, Ursula, 1874-1945.
Vibrant with words : the letters of Ursula Bethell / selected and
edited by Peter Whiteford.
Includes bibliographical references and index.
ISBN 0-86473-504-9
1. Bethell, Ursula, 1874-1945—Correspondence. 2. Poets, New
Zealand—Correspondence. I. Whiteford, Peter. II. Title.
NZ821.2—dc 22 [B]

Published with the assistance of a grant from

creative nz
Arts Council of New Zealand Toi Aotearoa

Printed by Astra Print, Wellington

CONTENTS

ACKNOWLEDGEMENTS

My first and greatest debt is to those who have preserved the letters from which this selection is drawn. The majority of the letters are now to be found in public repositories, but some are still in private hands, and I am particularly grateful to have been allowed access to those. Diana Bethell and Connie Summers have been very generous with their time and knowledge, and with allowing me to reproduce papers in their care, and I am pleased to be able to acknowledge their help. The late Robert Erwin, who took over the role of literary executor from Lawrence Baigent, graciously replied to my enquiries, in spite of his own poor health, and willingly agreed to the publication of the letters.

The Macmillan Brown Library in the University of Canterbury has the principal collection of Ursula Bethell's papers, and these include drafts of letters she wrote, letters that had presumably been returned, and all the letters to Kathleen Davies (née Taylor), which Mrs Davies added to the Bethell archive; the Hocken Library in Dunedin holds the letters to Rodney Kennedy, Charles Brasch, and Toss and Edith Woollaston (which are included in the Brasch archive); the Alexander Turnbull Library in Wellington holds the papers of Sir John Hall, Monte Holcroft, and J H E Schroder, together with the lesser collections of letters to Johannes Andersen, W F Alexander and Pat Lawlor. The letters to Eileen Duggan are held in the Archdiocesan Archives of the Catholic Church in Wellington. One letter to Edith Woollaston is held at the National Museum Te Papa Tongarewa in Wellington (printed by permission of Philip Woollaston). Finally, the Bodleian Library, Oxford, holds the papers of the publisher Sidgwick and Jackson, which include Bethell's letters to Frank Sidgwick. I am grateful for permission to reproduce all these letters, and am indebted to the librarians and the staff at these libraries for considerable assistance. I am particularly grateful to Max Broadbent and Jeff Palmer at the Macmillan Brown, and to Stuart Strachan and Anna Blackman at the Hocken Library.

A number of colleagues at Victoria University have offered timely advice and help, and I am grateful to Jean Anderson, Tony Angelo, Bill Manhire, Paul Millar, Arthur Pomeroy, and Peter Russell, and most particularly to Vince O'Sullivan, who has provided enormous help through his knowledge of Bethell, through his continued interest in the project, and through the example of his own scholarship. Beyond Victoria, I have received very welcome help from Jill Trevelyan, who curated an exhibition on the life of Ursula Bethell at the National Library, from Stephen Harris at the University of New England, Fr. Justin Taylor of the École Biblique in Paris, and Tim Parkin, at the University of Queensland.

I am also very grateful to a number of people who responded to my enquiries, among them Felicity Groom, Arthur Mayhew's granddaughter; Clive Whitehead, of the University of Western Australia; Rob Bolton, Chairman of the Church Lads' & Church Girls' Brigade Historical Group; Rev. Hugh Wybrew, Canon of St Mary Magdalene's, Oxford and Alan Palmer, historian of that parish; the archivist at the Wellcome Institute; and Gerry Evans of Wellington.

A number of research students have worked on Ursula Bethell under my supervision, and I am pleased to acknowledge the work of Charlotte Elder, Samantha Lentle, and Anne Holleron. I am also grateful to Charlotte for her preliminary transcriptions of the Kennedy letters.

I am grateful to Victoria University of Wellington for granting me a period of research leave during which this book could be completed, and for monetary grants to cover some copying and travel. I am indebted to Fergus Barrowman at the Victoria University Press; and I am once again grateful to my English department colleagues for leaving me (mostly) undisturbed.

Finally, I owe a special debt to family members – to Chris and Gaye in Christchurch, for their generous (and frequent) hospitality when I worked at the Macmillan Brown, to Gerry, who readily discussed Bethell's spiritual reading with me, and especially to Anne, Phillipa, Nick and Ben, for their support and encouragement over many years.

Introduction

In his introductions to the *Collected Poems* of Ursula Bethell (1985 and 1997), Vincent O'Sullivan draws our attention in a number of ways to the essential privacy of this striking woman. There is, most obviously, her decision to publish under the hastily-assumed pseudonym, Evelyn Hayes; there is the forcefulness of her letter to Frank Sidgwick, affirming the 'positive passion' with which she clung to 'private anonymity;' there is the confession to Rodney Kennedy of her inability to 'understand how people part with their privacy so readily;' and there is, as O'Sullivan notes, the surprisingly unrevealing quality of 'poems that seem so personal.'[1] That reluctance to promote herself is confirmed in many of the letters printed here. When she offers biographical details, as she does to a surprising number of correspondents, she does so with an insistence on their privacy. The notion that at some future time there might be an edition of her letters, or a full-length biography, would no doubt have drawn from her an injunction like that of Henry James to Lucy Clifford: 'burn my letter with fire or candle (if you have either! Otherwise wade out into the sea with it and soak the ink out of it).'[2]

And yet, she offers a glimmer of hope to a would-be biographer or editor. Her words to Kennedy quoted above are part of a wider comment: 'Being a Victorian I can never understand how people part with their privacy so readily. That is, private people. The great, who are in the public eye, *have* to do so.' Similarly, writing to Pat Lawlor, she seeks to have him remove all biographical detail from an article he had written, arguing that 'chat or surmise about a writer' does not help 'to place a book,' but then acknowledging that it is 'a different case' with 'an established author.'[3] Ursula Bethell would never have thought herself great, or even have claimed for herself an established reputation, but her importance in New Zealand literature cannot be denied. A letter from Charles Brasch to John Schroder, inviting the latter to contribute some

---

[1] O'Sullivan's two editions have different introductions. I have drawn on both of them in these remarks.

[2] Quoted in a review of Philip Horne (ed.), *Henry James: A Life in Letters,* by Bernard Richards, *Essays in Criticism* (April, 2001), 271.

[3] The letters to Kennedy and Lawlor are printed below.

memory of Bethell to the soon-to-be-launched *Landfall*, includes the following reflection: 'Miss Bethell was a friend – & guide & philosopher – to so many of the young & aspiring in so many fields, & also to others not so young, that any future social historian of this period will be bound to regard her as an important figure whatever his opinion of her as a poet.'[4] In addition, the careful preservation of letters by so many, including Bethell herself, and their lodging within public archives argues for their wider dissemination.[5] As an illustration, the letters to Kathleen Davies were deliberately deposited in the Macmillan Brown Library, where they could be made available for the use of future scholars because, in Mrs Davies' words, 'they are the journal of a rare soul, much tormented.'[6] Without doubt, Bethell is a figure 'in the public eye,' at least in the public that attends to New Zealand literature, and in the absence of a full biography, these letters provide the greatest insight into the life and thought of this remarkable woman, whose prominence among New Zealand poets, and whose influence within the New Zealand cultural scene of the 1930s and early 1940s, is becoming increasingly acknowledged. Indeed, the letters go some way towards exemplifying Thomas Jefferson's famous comment of 1823, that a person's letters constitute 'the only full and genuine journal of his life.'

Regrettably, and perhaps inevitably, the letters can offer only a partial insight rather than a 'full journal,' for we are constrained by what has been lost. At first sight, the absences are striking. There are no letters here to her sister Rhoda, whom she admired and loved, or to her close friend Ruth Mayhew, the recipient and addressee of some of the poems in *From a Garden in the Antipodes*, or to Arthur Mayhew, to whom she was, if anything, even closer, and whom she often describes as the 'godfather' of her first volume. Nor is there any letter to the dearest friend, Effie Pollen, with whom she spent ten happy years ('the happiest years of my life') in her cottage on the Cashmere Hills. If any such letters have been preserved, they are not yet available in public repositories.[7] Those absences, if not countered, are at least mitigated to some degree

---

[4] Alexander Turnbull Library. MS-Papers-0280. (Dec. 4, 1946.)

[5] In an undated fragment, Schroder confessed to Bethell that he had 'kept very carefully all letters in which you referred to your poetry' with the express intention of depositing them within a public archive. He continued, 'Does this intention disturb or displease you.... If so, be sure I shall abandon it.' We may assume that Bethell did not object.

[6] The words are in a letter from Kathleen Davies to Max Broadbent, Jan. 27, 1980, accompanying the gift of the letters, and held with the Bethell papers.

[7] Certainly there appears to be nothing relevant in the papers of Ruth Head (deposited with those of Sir Henry Head in the Wellcome Library), and my correspondence with the family of Arthur Mayhew suggests there are no extant letters.

by the frequent references to Arthur, to Rhoda, and to Effie in the letters that are extant. (Surprisingly, there are considerably fewer references to Ruth.) There can be no doubt of the importance of each of them, in different ways, to Ursula Bethell.

Other gaps, too, emerge. There is none of her correspondence to D'Arcy Cresswell, Helen Simpson, Blanche Baughan, Arthur Prior or Denis Glover, and almost nothing to Eric McCormick, to Toss or Edith Woollaston, or to Lawrence Baigent.[8] Again, all of these people had important places in her life; they appear often as characters in the letters we do have, but too infrequently as recipients in their own right.

In spite of these inevitable losses and gaps, however, we are fortunate to have an extensive archive of her letters (preserved in some cases by good luck, in others by sound judgement) that together cover much of her life, both in chronological terms, and in terms of her varied interests. The earliest of the letters was written a few days before she turned seven, the last of them dictated a few days after she turned seventy, and just a few months before she died.

Some selection has of course been necessary, and I have tried in this to do justice to the richness of her life and the variety of her interests.[9] Although I have naturally been drawn by those letters that reflect on her own writing or on poetry in general, those that most fully chart her intellectual growth, or her emotional or spiritual life, and those that reveal the breadth of her reading, I have also included trivial and domestic details, which can be equally revealing of circumstance or of temperament; and I have not sought to eliminate all repetition, for the fact that a particular concern emerges in letters to three or four, or that a turn of phrase, or Biblical or literary allusion recurs often has its own significance. My desire has been to allow her letters to tell the story of her life, by attention both to the critical events and equally to the recurring matters that together give a life its pattern and shape.

One further remark about the process of selection deserves to be made. The letters as published here may seem to betray a rather curious 'clustering' in respect of individual recipients. Thus, there are several letters in succession to John Hall, to Frank Sidgwick, and to John Schroder, and later to Rodney Kennedy, to John Summers, and to Kathleen Taylor. In part, this may be an accident of preservation

[8] Some measure of what has been lost can be gauged from the numbers of letters that have survived *from* Cresswell (32), Prior (32), McCormick (42), Edith Woollaston (29) and particularly Toss Woollaston (90).

[9] This selection represents about one third of what is extant in terms of individual items. It is more difficult to quantify in terms of overall length, in part because Bethell's letters varied from the briefest of notes to letters running over many pages.

(especially in the earlier years), but it is not an artificial product of the editorial process. On the contrary, publication of all the letters would make this clustering all the more striking. For it seems apparent that part of Bethell's personality involved her forming a strong, sometimes exclusive and overpowering relationship with an individual, and each new friendship had, for her, something of the intensity of an infatuation.

* * *

In the first of her extant letters to Holcroft, Bethell acknowledges that she is 'very much concerned with *words*' and then adds the vivid image, 'I listen to them, try them – ring them on the counter so to speak.' That concern with words is part of the natural interest of the poet, but it is also part of a lifelong affection for words, a love of language, that informs the poetry just as it does the correspondence. 'Ah, telos, telos – It wd. be fun to have access to the great N. E. D. Words were all our daily delight in those days,' she wrote to Schroder of her time in Oxford, where she boarded with the family of the lexicographer, A. L. Mayhew (Sept. 15, 1932), and she indulges in a variety of word games in her letters with Sidgwick, mimicking Effie Pollen's Irish accent, or her mis-spellings, or indulging in Latin jokes. At the same time, words themselves are a recurrent subject of the poetry of *From a Garden in the Antipodes,* from the 'plain words' of the opening 'Foreword,' through the 'lovely-sounding names' of 'Catalogue,' the 'wonted word out of the past' that is invoked in 'Primavera' and the 'good word' quoted in 'Time,' to the concluding 'Dirge' which closes by proposing to 'say no word more.' The difficulties of finding the right word are acknowledged in 'Alpines,' which confesses itself inadequate to 'perpetuate ... By means of any hieroglyph / The deep, the living azure of the dark blue gentian.' But the effort remains, the effort to name, to voice, to echo, to tell, for words, as we are informed in the aptly titled 'Name,' are the permanent accompaniment without which the gardener were solitary. In that poem, the gardener welcomes her morning silence, for 'the silence is vibrant with words.' That sense of the pulsing vitality of language appears as much in Bethell's letters as it does in her verse, and it seemed to provide a fitting title for this selection.

* * *

Reviewing a volume of the letters of William Wordsworth, James K. Baxter remarked that one of the reasons for reading the letters of a great poet is 'the hope of discovering some part of the circumstantial scaffolding of his poems.'[10] These letters do, indeed, provide such clues – the acknowledgement that the title of *Time and Place* was a deliberate response to Browning's poem 'Never the Time' is one simple example[11] – but 'circumstantial scaffolding' is a suitably ambiguous phrase, and Baxter is wise enough not to suggest that we turn to the letters only to elucidate the poems. Indeed, it would diminish Ursula Bethell to think of her letters in such a way. She is indignant when a reviewer of *Time and Place* writes 'E. H. knows no schoolmistress but her garden,' declaring to Rodney Kennedy that the garden was 'a brief episode in a life otherwise spent – far otherwise' (Sept. 14, 1936). These letters fill in some of the details of just how otherwise that life was spent; where the life has already been told in broad outline,[12] they add colour and humour, and intellectual, spiritual and emotional depth. At times, they do so in ways that are remarkably revealing. Allen Curnow suggested, in the introduction to his Caxton anthology, that her verse reads like a published correspondence; on the contrary, publication of the correspondence allows us to see the clear differences between the two, and the frankness of some of the correspondence reinforces just how guarded she was in her verse.

The collection begins with exactly the sort of charmingly inconsequential letter a young child might write, but the slightly later letter to her English Grandmamma, and those she wrote home from Oxford and Nyon already reveal recurrent aspects of her character; her wit, her keen eye for and occasional impatience with the minor foibles of others, her little snobberies, her very English-ness, and her love of language can all be seen. The letters home from Oxford give a small glimpse into the intellectual society she might have enjoyed there; a fuller picture can be found in the fascinating memoir of Arthur Mayhew, in which he describes the 'mid-Victorian houses, girt with limes and chestnuts,' and remarks on the family's dwelling within 'a road rich in Professors.' Mayhew notes that 'almost opposite us were Walter Pater and his sister ... almost next door Tom Arnold' and later observes that Lewis Carroll was a frequent guest at their tea-table. He never mentions the young New Zealand girl who stayed with them for two years, but his memoir is revealing of the milieu into which she had been introduced. The impact of such an environment in these formative years can readily

---

[10] Quoted in *Spark to a Waiting Fuse,* ed. Paul Millar, p. 20.

[11] See the letter to Woollaston, July 10, 1936.

[12] Brief biographies can be found in Holcroft's monograph, in O'Sullivan's introductions, and in the *Dictionary of New Zealand Biography* (DNZB), although they do not always agree in detail.

be imagined, and it is little wonder that Bethell felt herself drawn back to England's cultural richnesses in later years.[13]

When she returned to New Zealand from her Swiss finishing school in 1892, fluent in French and competent in German (she uses both, sometimes a little affectedly, in her correspondence), she became involved in various kinds of 'good work,' in particular with the recently established Boys' Gordon Hall. Her letters to the movement's patron, the former Premier, Sir John Hall, reveal a poised and self-assured young woman, committed to social work, and having found her métier in working with young boys, with whom she appears to have had a natural rapport.

As she revealed much later, however, that social work masked a keen homesickness for the more sophisticated culture of England, and however much she applied herself, New Zealand could not long hold her. By 1896 she was back in England, accompanied by her brother and another friend, at liberty to travel extensively around the English countryside. Again her letters reveal an assured young woman, confident of her place 'in the social scheme of things,' and 'sure of moving about befriended in any country.'[14] Financially, she enjoyed independence and security (although later world events would rob her of some of that security), and she was able to spend time in Germany and Switzerland studying music and painting. But she was, in Vincent O'Sullivan's apt phrase, a 'true daughter to social responsibility,' and she felt some unease at such a leisured lifestyle. By the end of the century she had returned to London, setting aside her involvement in the arts for a renewed commitment to charitable work with the Church of England.

It is a very different voice that emerges, however, in the letters from this period to the Dundee social activist, Mary Walker. Bethell by this time was engaged in working in an Anglican community in East London, in the midst of a poverty and deprivation for which her privileged life in New Zealand had done nothing to prepare her. Somewhat paradoxically, though, it is not the poverty and squalor that is so dispiriting, but the 'fecklessness' of her tiresome and boring house companions, in whom she finds, at times, a sanctimoniousness that she despises. She is attracted by a more contemplative life with the London Deaconesses, but appears unwilling to embrace the loss of personal liberty that such a commitment would entail. It seems that the anxieties she expresses in these letters to Mary Walker mask a deeper uncertainty about her

[13] Mayhew's memoir (see bibliography) was virtually unknown until recently. I am grateful to Clive Whitehead for drawing it to my attention.

[14] The phrases occur in a letter to Brasch, July 31, 1941.

commitment to the religious way of life. Ultimately ill health decided her future for her: a life-threatening bout of pneumonia forced her away from London to recuperate in Santa Cruz, and then in New Zealand.

The next twenty or more years of her life, which continued to be divided between England and New Zealand, are scarcely represented at all in the letters that have survived: a lively *jeu d'esprit* written on board ship to her cousin, Dorothea Reader; a fascinating revelation (albeit to a very young nephew) of the lifestyle of the English in India just before the outbreak of the Great War; and a couple of examples of what we might call her business letters, one to a young woman disappointed that her fiancé had enlisted in 1915, and another disapproving of some apparent impropriety in the workings of a weaving studio. Some details to fill in these years are included in the biographies noted above, but all too little is known of this part of her life. The absence of letters from the period is telling, but there are clues in later letters which point to at least two significant occurrences.

Although she had returned to New Zealand for a much-needed period of convalescence in 1903, still there was the call of England, and her next departure in 1904 was intended to be a permanent one; she wrote to Sir John Hall of making her 'final farewell' to the Colony. This time, however, it may not have been just the English culture that attracted her; from vague hints in later letters, it appears she returned to England with the intention of marrying and settling there. In none of those hints does she name her husband-to-be,[15] beyond the single initial 'A,' but she does provide other identifying details about the man she calls her 'sweetheart.' He was born in the early 1870s, briefly attended Oxford University, but left in some disgust at the privileged lifestyle of the 'gilded youth;' he shared with Bethell a fondness for poetry, which he would read aloud to her; around 1904 or 1905 he declared himself unable to go ahead with their marriage because of his ill-health; and he died (rather later, it would seem, than his health had led him to expect) in 1939. A note in some papers added to the Bethell archive[16] records information supplied by Kathleen Davies that Ursula Bethell had intended to marry 'the brother of Lady Head.' This cannot be Arthur (who completed his degree at Oxford, and did not die until 1948), but it may well be an older brother, Arnold Mayhew.[17] Eldest of the Mayhew sons, he was born in 1873 and died in 1939, having been a canon at St.

[15] In a letter to Kathleen Davies she reveals that she was not formally engaged, but implies that a form of betrothal had taken place.

[16] The papers have been donated by Felicity Holland, niece of the young woman who is the subject of Bethell's 'little requiem' poem; see the letter to Sidgwick, Nov. 4, 1929.

[17] Actually named Anthony Arnold, after his father.

Alban's Cathedral and later at Salisbury Cathedral.[18] Like Bethell, he never married, but his occupation within the Church would certainly have fitted well with Bethell's interests. He clearly had some interest in poetry: the Macmillan Brown Library holds a copy of Palgrave's *Golden Treasury* (1896) which is inscribed 'Ursula Bethell d.d. A.A.M[19] x.6.96.' Moreover, his name occurs in a letter to Bethell from Arthur who relates, with some trepidation, that he [Arthur] has shown *From a Garden in the Antipodes* to Arnold, who greatly admired the verse. It is difficult to avoid the impression that Arthur writes as circumspectly as he does, conscious that any mention of Arnold's name must still be done with care and tact.

The other significant event followed hard on the heels of this great disappointment. Writing to John Summers in 1939, Bethell revealed that it was just at this time that she first met the younger New Zealand woman, Effie Pollen, whose 'tender sympathy [at Bethell's loss] was amazing.' How they met is not known, but after her arrival in England, the 'shy, frightened' Effie Pollen was invited to live with Ursula, her mother and sister, who had a home together in Hampstead. (Had they, too, gone to England expecting to celebrate Ursula's marriage?) Bethell describes her as 'désouevrée': literally, the word may mean unemployed or idle; perhaps the suggestion here is of one at a loose end. At this stage, Ursula was keeping house for her mother and Rhoda while the latter was training as a nurse; no doubt she welcomed some help with housekeeping duties, for as her letters from the late 1930s reveal, she was not someone who readily settled to domestic chores. Then after three years Effie Pollen returned to Wellington; and Ursula Bethell returned to Christchurch the following year, where she involved herself in further parish work.

By 1913 she was again ready to leave New Zealand, returning eventually to England after a stay of several months in India (where Arthur Mayhew was prominently involved in colonial administration and education). She spent the Great War in London, working in a variety of voluntary occupations, before returning to New Zealand after the Armistice. Effie Pollen's father, a medical doctor, had recently died, after the influenza epidemic of 1918 (Mrs. Pollen had died many years earlier), and so Bethell again invited her to come and share her home, offering her 'the shelter she needed.' Initially, that home was with Bethell's mother at 47 Webb St. (the house Bethell later gifted to the Church of England), but in 1924 she bought the bungalow that she named Rise

[18] See Whitehead 1997: 73 (fn. 8).

[19] The initials preclude any identification with Arthur, whose second name was Innes.

Cottage,[20] which she shared for the next ten years with Effie Pollen. But of these years, too, the epistolary record is largely silent.

Then, abruptly, in 1929 there is a cable to Arthur Mayhew, accepting the offer from Sidgwick and Jackson to publish *From a Garden in the Antipodes.* And from that point on, we are comparatively well served, with letters covering every year from then until her death in 1945.

The first voice to emerge from these years, perhaps not unexpectedly, is that of the writer in conversation with her publisher. It is a voice that is by turns excited at the prospect of publication, deferential to the wishes of the publisher, and justifiably proud at seeing herself in print, but always there is a sense of self-assurance and sophistication as she engages in witty, literate exchanges with Sidgwick or later with Schroder. (These letters incidentally seem to confirm Robert Erwin's contention that *From a Garden in the Antipodes* was the only book formally published under the pseudonym Evelyn Hayes, and the Evelyn Hayes who wrote the much inferior verse in *The Glad Returning* and *The Haunted Gallery* is not to be identified with Bethell.[21]) And just as the letters from this period provide us with evidence about Bethell's 'writerly' life, so too do they reveal something of her domestic life, its daily routines, its cares, and above all its simple pleasures that were shared with Effie Pollen.

In the same period, though, a somewhat different voice can be heard in the letters to Monte Holcroft. She had taught Holcroft in her Sunday School classes years before, and it was probably impossible for her to set aside that tendency to instruct, to direct the younger man in his studies, and in the course of his life. Such direction, such intense interest in his life appears to have been too much for Holcroft (not a young man, after all, but in his early thirties) and he wrote distancing himself from a relationship that seemed overpowering. It was a pattern that would be played out in similar fashion with others – later letters to Toss Woollaston, to Rodney Kennedy, to John Summers, and to Eric McCormick all give evidence of occasional tensions as Bethell's interest in their lives proved too controlling. It was a tendency she acknowledged, struggled against, and regretted; its effect on these relationships can be seen in an occasional stiffness or an apologetic tone, and can be guessed at from the occasional extended silences.

In 1934, the happiness of life at Rise Cottage was shattered when Effie Pollen, younger than Bethell by some five years, died suddenly after

[20] The name derives from the family's estate, Rise Park, in Yorkshire.

[21] Erwin, Robert. 'Ursula Bethell and Evelyn Hayes : a misattribution?' *Landfall*, v. 31, no. 2 (June 1977), 156-162.

a brief and painful illness. Ursula Bethell was devastated, and as is sometimes the way with grief, she needed to tell of Effie's death, and of her own shock, over and over again. She does so repeatedly in these letters, just as she must have done in life. At each telling, the emphasis is slightly different, but they are all alike in revealing just how she felt – 'a tree struck by lightning – dead.' The remaining ten years of her life were deeply affected by this loss, and few letters from the period do not contain some residual note of sorrow. Charles Brasch (who met her in 1938) recalled that she spoke 'as if out of some abyss of remoteness and sorrow,'[22] and she wrote as she spoke, from the same barren and empty place.

There has, especially in recent years, been much speculation about the nature of the relationship between the two women. An age that can scarcely imagine any love as being non-sexual has perhaps predictably sought to read a sexual element into their friendship. Holcroft quoted a letter in his monograph in which Bethell described the relationship as 'prevailingly maternal' (Jan. 3, 1935), but that description has been called into doubt by some readings of Bethell's life and poetry. If the words to Holcroft are to be doubted, then so are those to a number of others – to Brasch, to Summers, to Kathleen Taylor (in letters reproduced below) and to Rodney Kennedy, to whom she wrote (in an undated fragment) 'the last love was maternal which means so unspeakably much to a woman.' When Bethell reflected on the relationship, as she did frequently, it was always in these terms. Effie Pollen 'was to me,' she wrote to Brasch, 'all the children I might have had' (July 27, 1938). The poignancy of these repeated expressions makes it scarcely credible that they are a subterfuge, deflecting attention from a lesbianism Bethell could not acknowledge, or that she failed to recognise for what it was. There is ample evidence in the letters that both the love and the shattering grief were real, and there is equally convincing evidence about the nature of the relationship. Perhaps, too, there is a difference to be noted in Bethell's use of words, for she was always very careful about her use of language. She readily calls Effie Pollen her 'darling;' indeed, after the latter's death, that diminutive is the commonest term of endearment she uses. But it is worth noting that it is not a term reserved exclusively for Effie Pollen; she uses it, too, of Kathleen Taylor, Paul Gabites, John Summers, Eric McCormick, and Merlin Davies (towards all of whom she adopted, at times, a decidedly maternal attitude), not to mention her nephew, Richard, and the Blackheath cat, Christopher. But the word

[22] See Brasch's memoir, *Indirections* (1980), p. 303.

'sweetheart,' by contrast, the term she uses when referring to the man she wished to marry, is reserved exclusively for romantic relationships.[23]

After Effie Pollen's death, Bethell sold Rise Cottage and moved to a small (and to her mind quite inadequate) flat in the house she had formerly owned, but had recently gifted to the Church of England. It was used as a centre for the training of Deaconesses, and much as Bethell approved in principle of such a training scheme, in practice she found living amongst the students trying. There is certainly no evidence that she found it a stimulating intellectual environment. She missed Effie, she missed their home and her garden, she missed the spectacular views from the Cashmere Hills, and she missed the invigorating air. She longed to get out of the city as much as possible; she felt oppressed by it, stifled, and she attributed her indifferent health to the damp Christchurch climate. In fact, given how much she is associated with Anglophile Christchurch in the literary consciousness (the city has very much adopted her as its own), it comes as something of a surprise to read the vehemence with which she repeatedly expresses her dislike of 'the trivial city.' For Canterbury and North Canterbury she retained warm feelings (although she found any return to Akaroa painful), but for the city itself she has rarely a kind word in these years.

What did bring some joy to the final years of her life was the friendship of a circle of young people, and the opportunity to help them in their lives. There is, for example, a wholly new vitality in her correspondence as she becomes involved in the plan to provide a painting scholarship for Toss Woollaston, and there is a positive glee as she shares with Brasch the intrigues she had developed to hide his involvement. She established a particular rapport with Rodney Kennedy, whose own thoughtfulness and sensitivity to her grief struck a special chord with her, and whose sometimes mordant wit she relished. She established a quite different relationship with Charles Brasch, based on their common experiences of Europe, their interest in philosophy and their mutual love of languages. She is more reflective when writing to Brasch, and more inclined to disclose biographical details, emboldened to do so, perhaps, by his distance abroad. Whatever misgivings Brasch may have had about her poetry (and the letter to Schroder quoted above suggests there were some), he was very taken with her as a person, describing her in a letter to Woollaston as 'to me, the centre of things, [having] the wisdom of experience, the innocence of goodness, & great

---

[23] Nor should the ambiguity of gender in her pseudonym be mis-construed; the letter to Sidgwick makes clear that posing as 'an elderly gentleman' was a conscious subterfuge to avoid recognition in the close social circle within which she moved in New Zealand.

knowledge,' and attributing his decision to return to New Zealand to her urgings.[24]

In Bethell's letters to John Summers there is an engaging range of voices. At times, she was very much the spiritual director Brasch imagined her to be;[25] at other times, her role was more that of an adult education tutor (the combination strongly suggestive of von Hügel's *Letters to a Niece*). But when she abandoned the role of director, she wrote as friend and confidante, delighted to accept from Summers the pet name, Felicity, which had associations for her with one of her favourite authors, Traherne, and also with Arthur Mayhew, whose daughter bears that name.

With all of them she shared an interest in music and philosophy, and especially in literature and art, inadequate though she professed herself to judge or comment on modernist work. With all of them, too, she debated, with no little anxiety (and always with a glance towards what her family might think), an uneasy commitment to pacifism in a country preparing for war. And to all of them she communicated her own continued concern for matters of religion, encouraging first Holcroft and later Summers towards a study of theology, expressing misgivings about the impact of the Oxford Group on Woollaston, and sharing a great variety of books, practical and theoretical, about mysticism and prayer, about Christian ethics and social justice, and about Scholastic philosophy and aesthetics. As much as anything, these letters make clear just how important religion – its language,[26] its beliefs and its daily practices – was to Ursula Bethell, and in so doing they confirm the judgements of Vincent O'Sullivan and, more recently, Lawrence Jones, about the significance of traditional Christianity in her poetry.[27] Traditional her Christianity is, but it is also noticeably eclectic and catholic, being informed initially by her mother's Presbyterianism, and later by her own experiences of Anglo-Catholicism in Oxford and of Church of England social action in London, her readings of medieval English mystics such as Richard Rolle and Julian of Norwich, and of seventeenth century English divines, her familiarity with Spanish mystics such as John of the Cross and Teresa of Avila, her fondness for the Quaker John Woolman, and her knowledge of French Catholic writers,

---

[24] Woollaston archives, National Museum of New Zealand Te Papa Tongarewa, CA 000457/1/5. Oct. 11, 1945.

[25] See Brasch's *Indirections* (1980), pp. 302-03.

[26] See, for example, how often she directly quotes, or indirectly alludes to Biblical phrases.

[27] O'Sullivan's remarks are to be found in his introductions; those of Jones are in *Picking up the Traces* (2003), pp. 142-44.

such as the classical authors Jacques-Bénigne Bossuet, Jean-Pierre de Caussade and François de Sales and the contemporaries Jacques Maritain and Léon Bloy.[28]

The final group of letters, certainly the most personal and revealing of all, are those written to Kathleen Taylor, and later to Kathleen and her new husband, Merlin Davies. The friendship with Kathleen Taylor, some forty and more years her junior, is something Bethell describes as miraculous; on a number of occasions she draws comparisons between Effie and Kathleen, and in the protective love she showed for the latter we sense something of how she felt for the former.

Particularly moving is a series of letters she wrote to the Davies when they were on their honeymoon. Worn down by constant ill-health, in the grip of a cancer that she knew nothing of, she was also emotionally wrung out by the sudden juxtaposition of the bliss she experienced in witnessing their marriage and the dreadful loneliness she faced with the ensuing departure of two who had rapidly assumed a great importance in her life. It is not exaggerating to suggest that being left alone in this way brought about an emotional and spiritual crisis for her, almost as threatening as that brought on by Effie Pollen's death. The letters she wrote record her anguished attempts to resolve this crisis, and record at the same time (as she reflects on their union) her final shattering recognition of what had been denied her when her own anticipated marriage did not eventuate. Neither the 'consecrated virginity' that she experienced in the Anglican community, nor the surrogate motherhood that she felt characterised some of the relationships of her later years could adequately replace that 'fundamental deprivation' (see the letter to Kathleen Davies, Jan. 1-4, 1944).

The very last letters, some of them dictated when she was unable to write, have a poignancy all of their own as she welcomed the news of her impending death, and communicated that news to her many friends. It was news that she felt able to welcome for it enabled her to prepare herself properly for death, tidying up life's loose ends, and accepting the spiritual counsel of her 'domestic chaplain,' Merlin Davies. There is an awareness, in these last letters, of a 'story come to its end,' as she wrote in the final poem of 'By the River Ashley.' The cancer is a good illness; she knows that 'the hour is dark,' and to the 'Divine Picnicker by the lakeside' she is ready to say 'Come.'

That apparent calm resignation masks the suffering that attended her final weeks, a suffering that is revealed in a poignant note from

[28] Some of these authors she would probably have known through an anthology of mystical writings.

Helen Simpson to Toss Woollaston, who writes, a month after Ursula's death, that 'the last afternoon I can't yet look back upon with anything like calm.' She affirms that Bethell 'kept an amazing measure of mental power & alertness to the very last,' and reflects that this alertness 'deceived us ... into believing she was more, & more constantly herself, so that the unhappiness, which I'm afraid there was no mistaking, seemed possibly more tragic than it need have done.'[29]

* * *

Read together, the letters of the final ten years of her life have often a sense of yearning about them. Bethell yearned for Home, and is often tempted to sell everything and return to 'loved and lost London' (indeed, she had planned to make such a move from the late 1920s), but is discouraged from doing so by financial concerns. Remaining in New Zealand, whether by election or force of circumstance, she yearned for company, for friendship, and for love, for however much she enjoyed and was stimulated by the lively circle of artists, musicians and writers, none of them really could provide her with the love and spiritual companionship she felt was lacking in her life. It was only finally with Kathleen Taylor that we sense she discovered a friendship even remotely like that she had had with Effie Pollen. And no sooner had she achieved such a loving friendship, than it appeared to be taken from her, first by Kathleen's marriage to Merlin Davies, and then with the announcement of their intention to leave for England.

Equally, as she grudgingly acknowledged that she would never return Home, she yearned for a home. The flat in Webb St. held little appeal for her (except at the very last when Kathleen Taylor boarded there), and she longed for a place that would allow her to reconstruct something of the pattern of life at Rise Cottage, and to reconstruct its memories. She had several opportunities to shift from Webb St., but increasingly lost the confidence needed to make any major move. In her heart, she no doubt knew there could be no second Rise Cottage, but the longing for something like it remained, as all these longings did.

For throughout these years, she was restless. Perhaps she was always restless, apart from the brief interlude at Rise Cottage. She wrote a biographical note to Pat Lawlor that suggested her many journeys between New Zealand and England were brought about by particular circumstances, not by restlessness (Sept. 2, 1940), but there is more

[29] Woollaston archives, National Museum of New Zealand Te Papa Tongarewa, CA 000457/1/5. Feb. 13, 1945.

conviction in her undated confession to Eric McCormick: 'I don't belong anywhere in particular – I've dodged to and fro [...] I have not been able to settle' (c. Oct. 1941). On the surface, this appears to be another statement of her sense of separation from her true homeland, or indeed from any place she might call home. It speaks of a double exile, from New Zealand and from England. But beneath that surface, I suggest, Bethell means something more.

In one of the Garden poems, 'Elect,' the rose 'Pilgrim' is admired for its 'beautiful name,' and in keeping with the connotations of that name, she refuses to pamper the rose; she plants it 'in a difficult place, / In the pathway of the east wind.' It is fitting that Bethell should admire this pilgrim rose, and see it as a symbol of election, for the traditional Christian image of life as pilgrimage had a special significance for her. She adopted, as a personal emblem, the scallop shell traditionally associated with the shrine of St James at Compostella, the symbol so beloved of English pilgrims. She quotes often from Bunyan's *Pilgrim's Progress*, and she speaks more than once of her desire to compile an anthology or daybook of extracts on the notion of life as pilgrimage. The sense of exile that can be discerned in her poetry and in her letters, then, includes not just the note of expatriation from a loved homeland, but also the traditional religious idea that, for the *exules filiae Hevae,* life is a journey to another home. Bethell's literary papers include an undated cutting from the *Times Literary Supplement* that expresses a view she must have shared: 'it is precisely because man is not master of his fate, because he is a powerless pilgrim in a mysterious universe ... that art and religion were born. The true poem is always a miracle. It springs, at the right crisis, from the poet's way of life and habit of thought. For a moment he has a vision of overmastering truth and beauty around him.'

The letter to Frank Sidgwick (Dec. 30, 1934) in which Bethell revealed her grief after Effie Pollen's death includes the poignant sentence: 'I shall not want another home on this planet.' It is a striking reminder of how much joy was to be found in the years at Rise Cottage, joy that was perhaps only otherwise approached in her childhood immersion in the natural world by the river Ashley, within sight of Mt. Grey. But at the same time it epitomizes the pilgrim's yearning for another home outside of this mysterious universe, beyond a merely fugitive beauty. It is that yearning, captured and stilled for a moment in the miracle of a poem, that is at the heart both of Bethell's poetic experience and of her spiritual life, and that echoes through so much of her correspondence.

Editorial Note

The text attempts to reproduce as accurately as possible what Bethell wrote, without pretending to a facsimile reproduction. Many of the letters are reproduced in full, but some have been edited to omit less significant material. Such omissions are shown by an ellipsis in square brackets, placed within the line when the excision is of a phrase or sentence, or placed on a separate line if the excision is of one or more paragraphs.

For the most part, Bethell's hand is clear and legible; on the rare occasion when a word or phrase has defied interpretation, the word 'illegible' appears in square brackets. I have ignored words and phrases that have been crossed out or overwritten, except on a few occasions where they serve to clarify Bethell's thinking. Words added by her above or below the line are inserted in the text where appropriate. Occasionally, Bethell glossed her own letters with asterisked marginalia; these are also included at the end of the relevant paragraph. Postscripts and afterthoughts are conventionally placed at the end of a letter, although Bethell sometimes wrote them at the head or lengthways in the margins. Words I have added to clarify meaning are also in square brackets.

Bethell's emphases are for the most part confined to a single underlining, which is rendered here in italics; double underlinings are printed in small capitals. Abbreviations occur extensively in the correspondence; these have been retained as she wrote them, except when their expansion is not obvious. Abbreviated names are identified in footnotes unless their identity is clear from the context.

The text has been emended as lightly as possible: I have inserted a closing bracket or quotation mark where one has been forgotten, and silently corrected any very obvious slips of the pen, while preserving stylistic idiosyncrasies (such as the very frequent omission of an apostrophe from it's, or the spelling 'havn't') Examples of dittography are silently omitted. In matters of punctuation, Bethell shares with Mansfield a fondness for a dash where one might expect a comma or a full stop. I have come to feel that some of the 'feminine dashes' (see her letter to Sidgwick, Nov. 4, 1929) can be replaced with a full stop without any damage (a following upper case being a reliable guide), and have lightly emended her punctuation.

Bethell was also a little idiosyncratic in her dating of letters: many are fully dated, but she sometimes omits the year, and at times she provides only a day, or dates a letter according to religious feasts. The layout of dates has been standardized, but such quirks as "King's Birthday" or "Vigil of S. John the Baptist" have been preserved. Dates enclosed within square brackets are editorial, and are preceded by a query if conjectural.

Sometimes, a letter begun on one day may not be completed for several days, and there may even be letters to another correspondent intervening. For the sake of simplicity, these letters have been entered at the date they were begun.

The annotations at the foot of each page are intended to identify people, events, and allusions where these might add to the reader's understanding; it has not been possible (nor would it be desirable) to identify every such reference. However, I have annotated rather more fully than might otherwise be expected, given the absence of a full biography. Johnson's desire, expressed in his *Preface to Shakespeare*, to be 'neither superfluously copious, nor scrupulously reserved' in his notes and glosses seemed an admirable goal, but even as he declared it, Johnson recognised that 'it is impossible for an expositor not to write too little for some, and too much for others. He can only judge what is necessary by his own experience; and how long soever he may deliberate, will at last explain many lines which the learned will think impossible to be mistaken, and omit many for which the ignorant will want his help.' No doubt the annotations here will strike some in the same way, but I trust that the help offered will outweigh any intrusion.

References to Bethell's *Collected Poems* in the notes are to Vincent O'Sullivan's editions, which provide a more accurate and complete text than that of the 1950 collection.

CHRONOLOGY

1874	Mary Ursula Bethell born in Horsell, Surrey, 6 October (St. Faith's Day).
1876	Arrived in New Zealand with parents, Richard Bethell and Isabella (née Lillie). Birth of second child, Marmaduke.
1877	Richard Bethell purchased Pahau Pastures, near Culverden in North Canterbury.
1879	Birth of third child, Rhoda.
1881	Family moved to Rangiora.
1885	April 30, Richard Bethell died of pneumonia.
1887	Family shifted to Christchurch.
1887-88	Attended Christchurch Girls' High School.
1889-91	Attended Oxford Girls' High School, England. Boarded with Mayhew family, becoming lifelong friend with Ruth (later Lady Head) and Arthur.
1891-92	Attended finishing school in Nyon, Switzerland.
1892	Returned to New Zealand. Spent three years teaching Sunday school and performing social work.
1894	Involved in Boys' Gordon Hall. Friendship with Sir John and Lady Rose Hall dates from this time.
1896	Returned to England (via Switzerland and Italy), touring with brother (Marmaduke) and friend. Visited paternal uncle's estate, Rise Park, in Yorkshire.
1897-98	Studied music and painting in Germany and Switzerland. Rhoda Bethell also in Switzerland at this time.
1898	Undertook social work in London with Lady Margaret Hall Settlement.
1899	Joined Anglican community, Women Workers for God (the Grey Ladies); met and later worked with Mary Lucy Walker of the Dundee Social Union.
1901	Holidayed in Switzerland over summer. Suffered serious attack of pneumonia. Left Grey Ladies at end of year.
1902	Left England. Spent several months in Santa Cruz, California, recuperating from pneumonia.
1903	Arrived back in New Zealand, living mostly in Christchurch.

1904 Returned to England via USA. Further involvement in social work. Travelled widely. Anticipated marriage called off. Met Effie Pollen, who lived with Bethell, her mother and sister in Hampstead.

1907 Death of Sir John Hall.

1908 Effie Pollen returned to New Zealand (Wellington).

1909 Bethell returned to New Zealand.

1910 Purchased house at 47 Webb St., Christchurch. Involved in parish work.

1913 Returned to England, via Java and India.

1914 In Switzerland at outbreak of war; returned to England. Worked in London at variety of occupations – Cub mistress, night waitress, information officer.

1919 Returned to New Zealand after Armistice.

1924 August, bought Rise Cottage (10 Westenra Terrace) in Cashmere Hills, where she lived with Effie Pollen. Began writing poetry.

1926 Made last visit to England (6 months) with Effie Pollen. Hospitalized in Sydney on way home for operation to nose, eyes and cheeks.

1927 Began submitting poems to Australian journal, *The Home*, using pseudonym Evelyn Hayes. Death of Isabella Bethell.

1929 *From a Garden in the Antipodes* published in London. 'By Evelyn Hayes.' Correspondence with Frank Sidgwick dates from this time.

1931 Began extensive correspondence with J H E Schroder, literary editor of *The Press*, who had reviewed *From a Garden*. Met Toss Woollaston, who gardened for her at Rise Cottage.

1932 Met and began corresponding with D'Arcy Cresswell (none of her letters have survived).

1933 Began correspondence with Monte Holcroft. Friendship with Archdeacon Whitehead dates from this time.

1934 August: Cresswell proposes that Robert Lowry publish a booklet of her verse; September: outline of *Time & Place* arrived at with Cresswell's advice. Effie Pollen died 8 November after brief illness. Sold Rise Cottage and moved into house in Webb St., known as St. Faith's House of Sacred Learning. (Had earlier gifted the house to the Anglican church as a centre for training deaconesses.)

1936 *Time & Place* published in Christchurch. 'By the author of *From a Garden*.' Extensive correspondence with Rodney Kennedy dates from about this time.

1938 Visited Wellington, met Eric McCormick. Correspondence with Charles Brasch begins. Involved in organising painting scholarship for Woollaston, funded largely by Brasch. Submitted unpublished poems to McCormick for comment in preparation for *Day & Night*.

1939 January: correspondence with John Summers begins. February: visited Woollastons at Mapua. June: hospitalized in Wellington, suffering from influenza and dilated heart. Revises selection for *Day & Night*; October: *Day & Night: Poems 1924-1934* published in Christchurch. 'By the author of *Time and Place*.'

1940 McCormick invited her to comment on the manuscript of his centennial survey, *Letters and Art in New Zealand*.

1941 Met Kathleen Taylor (later Davies). Extended winter holiday at Kaikoura. Brasch offers her an annual allowance, which she declines.

1942 Reads and comments on Holcroft's manuscript of *The Waiting Hills*.

1943 Kathleen Taylor residing at St. Faith's House. Met Allen Curnow. November: St. Faith's House of Sacred Learning closes. December: Kathleen Taylor marries Merlin Davies.

1944 Ill health recurrent complaint in letters. Hospitalized in January and again in April. May 7 diagnosed with inoperable cancer. May 8 moves to private rest home. Agrees to publication of *Collected Poems* (which did not appear until 1950). Continues working on 'River Ashley' sequence.

1945 Dies 15 January; buried with parents at Rangiora Church of England Cemetery.

List of Illustrations

The illustrations between pages 162 and 163 are all reproduced from material held in the Macmillan Brown Library, at the University of Canterbury, except that of Effie Pollen, which is reproduced from the *Evening Post* of November 10, 1934. The captions and dates reflect information available in the Macmillan Brown archive.

I am very grateful for permission to include them here.

THE LETTERS

I: 1881–1923

TO ISABELLA BETHELL – OCTOBER 2, 1881

Colham

My dear Mother

I think you must be busy, packing up the things to go away from Glenmark,[1] and have you made up your mind if your going to live in Rangiora.[2] I am getting on with my music. What does Rhoda look like in her Granny-bonnet, I am sure she is a dear little thing in it, love to Rhoda and Mamy[3] and for you.

I am your loving child
Ursula

Private collection.

TO MRS LILLIE – OCTOBER 9, 1887

Armagh Street, Christchurch

My dear Grandmamma

I have found time to-night to write a short letter. You know that I go to school now,[4] so there is nothing very interesting to tell about as it is term time, however as the other day (the 6th of this month) was my birthday, I think I will tell you how I spent it. I did not keep it on the very day, but on the Saturday after, I took two of my friends, with

---

[1] Richard Bethell had been looking after Glenmark Station (at Hurunui, in North Canterbury) in 1881 while its owner, G. H. Moore, was away in England. Glenmark (which the Tasmanian Moore had purchased in partnership with Isabella Bethell's father, Dr John Lillie) was reputed to be one of the largest and most valuable freehold estates in the country.

[2] Richard Bethell's own estate, Pahau Pastures, was considerably to the north of Rangiora, at Culverden (near Hurunui). Finding it too remote, Isabella Bethell preferred to live at Rangiora and the estate was leased.

[3] Marmaduke Bethell was born in 1876; Rhoda in 1879.

[4] When living at Rangiora, Ursula Bethell had received her education from a governess. In Christchurch, she initially attended Mrs Crosby's School, then in 1887 began studying at Christchurch Girls' High School.

another younger for Rhoda, down to one of our "sea-side resorts" – New Brighton.

New Brighton is, I think, about 4 miles from town; you go to it by tram, the journey is over a sort of sandy plain most of the way, and as the gorse is nearly in full bloom, the sea-breeze was beautifully fresh as well as very sweet with the scent of the gorse.[1]

Pure gorse is, I believe, very much more beautiful than what you see in England, so you may imagine what a lovely sight the golden belt [is], about the width of 5 ordinary hedges, in some places a great deal wider, for they do not trim the hedges down there, I suppose they are glad to have the sandhills covered.

I think New Brighton must be *very* different to the Brighton of England. Ours is a plain beach (it extends 40 miles) backed by Sandhills; "New Brighton" is a cluster of houses in one part; there are ponies to hire; & a row of forms along the beach are the conveniences; this is our "fashionable watering-place"!

Of course there are no bathing machines, & where you bathe (in the summer only) your dressing rooms is a "behind a sandhill"; you have to run down from your sandhill, & if the tide is not very high this is a good way; your clothes are kept from being blown away by being buried in the sand; I do think splashing about in the open breakers must be much nicer than bathing-machines.

Those ponies that are to hire are my delight as I have no animal of my own now; & if you had been on New Brighton Beach at 12.30 P.M. Saturday afternoon last you would have beheld a spectacle! Imagine three young persons – bare-headed – bare-legged – bare-armed – you would only have discovered the sex of one from her flying petticoats (that was me!) for the other had on a gymnasium suit, so you see I used the expression "young persons" advisedly.

Imagine these two characters aboard two ponies tearing up & down the beach! (Dear me – I'm afraid I will shock you!!)

Later on the pony-man asked me to try one that was not accustomed to a side-saddle, oh! how it did kick up at first! I was nearly off.

(23rd) I had to leave off writing the other night to go to bed, but I will go on with my letter now.

After that we two equestrians had to stop our performances as our purses were emptied. Then we had something to eat – & nothing very much happened until we had to start home.

---

[1] Bethell's attitude to New Brighton was not always as favourable. Years later, she described it to Charles Brasch as 'a most repulsive spot ... seldom have I seen a more revolting pleasure resort' (March 1, 1943).

The "short letter" has turned out to be quite a long one, (for me) but I must stop now, I don't know when you will get this, for I think the last mail has just gone.

I am afraid this is a dreadfully untidy letter, the writing is very bad, but I have so much fast writing to do at school, for in most things they give us a sort of lecture & then they give us "notes" to take down in a book which we learn from, this fast writing has got me into a careless way. I should be glad if you could pass this on to some of my aunts as it would save me writing.

And now, dear grandmamma, with much love, I remain

Your affectionate grand-daughter
Ursula

Private collection.

TO ISABELLA BETHELL – JULY 25, 1889

18 Bradmore Rd, Oxford[1]

My dear Mother

[...]

A great many of our passengers left at Plymouth – amongst them Miss Menzies – no one was very sorry – she has done an immense amount of harm during the voyage. She went about talking about the kind things she had done – & always making a fuss about religion – & yet everybody saw she was the most selfish vain old thing possible. How funny it is how a person's character comes out on a voyage. And yet Miss Maude[2] who never said a word about religion or anything of that sort did a wonderful lot of kindness in a quiet way & instead of doing Christianity harm she was working for it.

Plymouth was very, very pretty – though we did not see it well for it was pouring with rain – we steamed out about 6:30. The next morning the fourth officer came down & roused us up at six to look at land and at some immense men-of-war steaming down the channel. You know there is going to be a wonderful naval review[3] – hundreds of English men-of-war – & the German Emperor will be present with ten German men-of-

---

[1] The address of the Mayhew family, with whom Bethell stayed while attending school at Oxford. Theirs was a large mid-Victorian home situated in the leafy suburbs just to the north of the city centre.

[2] Sybilla Maude (who later founded the Nurse Maude Association in Canterbury) had chaperoned Bethell on the voyage from New Zealand. See *DNZB* II. 321-22.

[3] Spithead was the scene of numerous naval reviews in the 19th century; this one, held in the first week of August, marked the visit of Kaiser Wilhelm II.

war. I thought the ships that we saw splendid & the turret ships & the torpedo-boats are the most evil looking things. Oh – I forgot [to] mention that we saw the Eddystone Lighthouse splendidly – what a wonderful building it is.[1] I was dressed a little before seven on Tuesday morning & went on deck. It was raining very much but the sea was very calm & we had a very good passage up. I just missed seeing an interesting sight – there was a large waterspout seen just before I went on deck. It was very funny weather for the middle of Summer – but the pilot said they had been having perfect weather until a few days before. We were very near land & I saw a great many interesting places on the coast – Beachy Head – Brighton – Eastbourne – Hastings – & many others. We passed the Isle of Wight in the middle of the night or I should have seen that too. By the afternoon I had most of my things packed up – melancholy work. We were in the river at about five. Such a wonderful amount of shipping I could hardly have imagined anything like it. We saw the boat that had taken the Shah of Persia up the river on his last visit to London[2] – it was painted up with the Persian colours – I saw training-ships – & warships – & trading-ships – & colliers – & barges – and Pacific ships, & Indian ships, & yachts & boats by thousands. We only stopped a very little time at Gravesend & no one got off. It was raining hard most of the time & London was under a mist so I could not see much of it. We docked at about half past eight – Mrs. Majors & Mrs. Findlay were waiting on the quay & were at once clasped in their loving husbands' arms & carried off to their cabins. Most of the passengers left that night but Miss Maude & I decided to stay till next morning it was so late & so horribly wet & cold. The captain & his wife left that night but the poor officers had to stay on board – there was a policeman in front of the bullion room all night too.[3]

Macmillan Brown Library. MB 558. C1.

---

[1] A new lighthouse had been built by James Douglass on the Eddystone Rocks in 1882 to replace the famous Smeaton's Tower. Bethell may be referring to the Douglass Tower, or to the older edifice, since Smeaton's Tower had been dismantled and re-erected on Plymouth Hoe. Both were widely admired for their engineering ingenuity.

[2] Nasir ad-Din, Shah of Persia, had been touring Great Britain through most of the month of July, 1889.

[3] The remainder of the letter has not survived.

TO ISABELLA BETHELL – [? 1890/91]

[18 Bradmore Road, Oxford]

[...]

[1]'We went together to the afternoon service at St. Barnabas'[2] the church which Mrs. Soulsby[3] often attends, & to which I had never been before – & to which I shall not be longing to go again. What wd. you have said to it! The Altar with a gorgeous canopy over it & seven red lamps always burning before it – & many candles & crucifixes. The clergyman decked out to a degree – he was robed & unrobed several times during the service by two little acolytes who always stood by him – & he looked like the pictures of Roman Catholic Priests. While singing a hymn they marched round the church – many men clothed in red holding banners & crucifixes – & then a boy with incense which filled the church! Choir & acolytes & the clergyman! But I have no time to dwell upon this subject. I think my godmother seems very nice – a stalwart lady & disposed to see everything thro' rosy spectacles. We went to see a Mr. Wilson, brother to the Warden of Keble who lives not far from here & mentioned my name. Mrs. Wilson immediately said "does she belong to the Bethells of Rise, for if so she is a sort of cousin of mine" & Mr. Wilson said "I wonder if she is any relation to my old friend Richard Bethell of Exeter College."[4] Of course my godmother was very excited &

---

[1] The beginning of this letter has been lost. Bethell's comment at the end of the letter suggests it should be dated some months after her arrival in Oxford – perhaps late 1890 or early 1891.

[2] Reflecting the impact of the Tractarian Movement, St. Barnabas' Church in Jericho (consecrated in 1869) was famous for its elaborate, ritualistic services. The following account from *Kilvert's Diary* (ed. William Plomer) closely resembles Bethell's letter: 'The clergy and choir entered with a procession, incense bearers and a great gilt cross, the thurifers and acolytes being in short white surplices over scarlet cassocks and the last priest in the procession wearing a biretta and a chasuble stiff with gold. The Magnificat seemed to be the central point in the service and at the words "For behold from henceforth all generations shall call me blessed" the black biretta and golden chasuble (named Shuttleworth) advanced, was 'censed' by the thurifer, then took the censer from him and censed the cross, the banners, the lights and the altar, till the Church was in a fume. At least so Mayhew said. I myself could not see exactly what was done though I knew some ceremony was going on. It appeared to me to be pure Mariolatry' (III. 319). Coincidentally, the Mayhew mentioned is A. L. Mayhew, at whose home Bethell was staying.

[3] Principal of Oxford Girls' High School. Although it had only been established in 1875, the school already enjoyed a considerable reputation.

[4] The estate of Rise Park, at Holderness, County York, together with Watton Abbey, belonged to William Bethell, the older brother of Ursula's father, Richard (of Exeter College). In a letter to Sir John Hall (Oct. 11, 1896), she records a visit to Rise Park with her brother, Marmaduke.

she took me to lunch there on Tuesday; when I discovered Mrs. Wilson to be a third cousin – a descendant of the Clitheroes. Do you know anything of these Wilsons? They are, of course well known in Oxford. They seem very nice especially Mr. Wilson, he told me how father once drove him to the Goodwood from Shopwick.[1] Isn't it funny I should discover them after being here so long?

[...]

Important.

Please stamp your next letter with two 3^{d} stamps and the next with a fourpenny & a 2^{d}, as I want them for Charlie Warren's collection.

Please give my love to Rhoda and everyone

with much love
yr affectionate daughter
Ursie

Macmillan Brown Library. MB 558. C1.

TO ISABELLA BETHELL – [APRIL, 1891]

[18 Bradmore Road, Oxford]

[...]

[2][I] was the only one to go to early service with Mrs. Mayhew. "I am afraid poor Janet[3] will not see another Easter" she said sadly to me as we went along, "and I shall lose you too soon" – how I have become grafted into this family. I dread leaving – I suppose you have heard already of the next year's arrangements, which Mrs. Soulsby has made so suddenly. It will be delightful to go to Switzerland.[4] Mrs. Soulsby has behaved very strangely lately, I must say. I would not mention only I am afraid she may give you a false impression. As far as I can make out she wanted me to go right away straight from the Infirmary but as no one would have me, she proposed that I should simply come to Mrs. Mayhew to disinfect, then go off: Just giving Mrs. M. all the bother & trouble only to lose me at once – Mrs. M, knowing too how cut up I should be to [be] hurried off in this fashion, naturally objected; she proposed that I should stay for the summer term, which is simply delightful in Oxford with

[1] Shopwyke is on the outskirts of Chichester; the reference to 'the Goodwood' is presumably to the well-known racecourse nearby, at that time privately owned by the Duke of Richmond.

[2] This letter, too, is acephalous. The date is suggested by the closing remarks about snow in April.

[3] Janet Mayhew died June 20, 1891, at the age of nineteen.

[4] Bethell attended a finishing school near Nyon (in the predominantly French-speaking canton of Vaud), bordering Lake Geneva, for the academic year 1891/92.

boating & everything, & thus complete the school year. Mrs. Soulsby told her view of the matter in a letter to me at the Infirmary in which she said she considered that Mrs. M. had charged too much for my board, & therefore was "making a hard fight to keep me as long as possible"!

I was very vexed & hurt at this idea; after all Mrs. M.'s kindness to say such a thing to me. I have not lived in this house two years for nothing: Mrs. Mayhew is a lady, & not a mercenary one; besides the Mayhews are not paupers! The very idea of trying to make money by me is too preposterous – Mrs. Mayhew mentioned to me that both Mr. M. and she were surprised & hurt by letters they had had from Mrs. Soulsby.

I am very much surprised at Mrs. S. saying this, for generally I respect her wise judgement & nice feelings, & warmly admire her great kindness & consideration; I am very sorry that any unpleasantness should have arisen on my account towards one for whom I have so much affection as Mrs. Mayhew. She has been a kind mother during my stay here, & no less have her children been brothers & sisters: you will like to read some of her letters to me in the Infirmary when I come home.[1]

However, I believe that Mrs. Soulsby has since been very pleasant, & has apparently rather regretted her conclusions – so that you will not say a word of this to her or anyone – will you? Of course I said nothing to Mrs. Soulsby.

[...]

What *do* you think is going to be my *autumn* dress this year. The same brown check which Miss Crosby made for me when I left New Zealand! The stuff is not a bit worn out – it has gone to be cleaned & will be done up with brown velveteen. My dress for summer afternoons will be a *very* thin greenish woollen material – trimmed somehow with dark green narrow ribbon – velveteen. I'll enclose a pattern if not overweight. And oh! I have the sweetest new dressing gown. It is most aesthetic – a dull green colour – with a pattern like this. Sort of palm leaves. Pure wool, made like this.[2] Dear me, my drawing gives no idea of its elegance – that kind of collar is faced with soft green liberty silk – & the cuffs, the girdle, which goes under that front flappy part & fastens at the side with a knot & tassel – is of silk cord – (thick). The colour is splendid for not showing dirt – & this elegant article only cost 21/. (reduced) – no more than an ordinary ugly one.

Oh, what astounding news that was in the last letter I got in the Infirmary, of the burning down of Glenmark. Just think, that mansion –

[1] These letters have not survived.

[2] Bethell included two rudimentary line drawings here.

that palace – vanished.[1] What a loss! I hope that they will buy their things in New Zealand henceforth. How characteristic of Miss Moore to rush in and save her canaries! [...]

Oh, I must just tell you what I have been doing since I have been home – I don't know when you will get such a long letter as this again! On Easter Sunday evening I went to Cathedral with the Lloyds. They had "I know that my Redeemer liveth" – it was most splendidly sung by a boy with a lovely voice. Mr. Lloyd said afterwards that he thinks it the most difficult anthem to sing ever written. Professor Skeat, the great Cambridge Philologist has been staying here. He is in great excitement because he has discovered among the MSS at the Bodelian a new poem of Chaucers – & an edition of the Canterbury Tales which he believes have not been found before.[2] On Monday he took me over the Bodelian[3] – it was very interesting to go with him. I enjoyed the old MSS very much, and saw the famous autograph copy of the Ormulum – quite unique.[4] The illuminating of those books is something wonderful.

On Monday afternoon I went to tea at the Wilsons. On Tuesday Mr. Sankey took Janet & me out for a drive in his Victoria – he would insist on our sitting on the proper seat while he sat on the tiny little one which is opposite to it. He made us stay to lunch & then we went home in one of the new hansoms – they are very large, with a speaking tube to the driver – looking glass – box of matches & place for cigar ends at the side. He is a kind man. In the afternoon I took the youngest French class at Mr. Lynam's,[5] because Aunt Lizzie was away. It was great fun: little boys are so delightfully naughty – & so terribly ignorant of French – one spelt "victoire" – "victwor"!

---

[1] Moore's house at Glenmark Station was burned to the ground in February, 1890. It was a large and ostentatious property, reputedly having cost some £90,000.

[2] Walter Skeat was professor of Anglo-Saxon at Cambridge University, founder of the English Dialect Society, and editor of many Old and Middle English works. The 'new poem' refers to Chaucer's ballade 'To Rosemounde,' extant in a single manuscript, Bodl. MS. Rawl. poet. 163. It was first printed by Skeat in *The Athenaeum*, April 4, 1891. However, it is not possible to identify the edition of the *Canterbury Tales* referred to here. It is not mentioned in Skeat's brief note on 'Rosemounde.'

[3] The spelling may be a simple error for Bodleian, but it may reflect a late-nineteenth century pronunciation (1st syllable rhyming with 'goad').

[4] The Ormulum, Bodl. MS. Junius 1, is a late 12th century series of Gospel homilies in English verse, running to several thousand lines. Its author, Orm, an Augustinian canon, composed it for his brother, Walter. Its primary interest, though, is not literary but linguistic, for Orm devised his own semi-phonetic spelling system and idiosyncratic script to indicate vowel quantities and other points of pronunciation.

[5] This must refer to the Oxford Preparatory School, founded in 1877, and run for many years by the Lynam family. It is situated on the northern outskirts of Oxford University (very near the Mayhew's house). The school is now known as The Dragon School.

I have been writing in Janet's room this morning – she seems brighter today. Yesterday I scoured the market for some mushrooms, which she seemed to fancy. Poor girl, she never goes to sleep till one or two a.m. – & coughs terribly in the night.

The weather is dreadfully cold – snow in April – & not a sign of buds on the trees. I am comforted by some lovely new – – (Private, don't read aloud) combinations which are woven and fit closely. [...]

I must make the Cherubic Arthur[1] run with this to the post. I have run it very close.

I am sure I have omitted many things I wanted to say – but stop I must.

With love to all
yr loving Ursie.

Did I tell you how delighted the girls were with the Maori bags?

Macmillan Brown Library. MB 558. C1.

TO ISABELLA BETHELL – [? OCTOBER, 1891]

[Nyon, Switzerland]

[...]

[2]We are having terribly bad weather; at the beginning of the week snow was on the mountains of Savoie, & even on the Juras; consequently it has been very cold. Also for 4 days at the beginning of last week & again today the rain is pouring in torrents. It is a pity for the time of the vendanges has come.[3] There is distress all about the country. I have taken to my new autumn & winter dress. What do you think it is? My New Zealand tweed resuscitated – with brown velvet sleeves, yoke, & band round the bottom; it is most "comme il faut"[4] & *becoming* & new; it must be splendid material. Here I regard all that I can see of myself with satisfaction! I wish they would begin warming the house – I am shivering with cold.

---

[1] Arthur Innes Mayhew was the sixth of seven children in the Mayhew family. Born in 1878, he was educated at Winchester then at New College, Oxford. Later, he had a distinguished career as an educational administrator in India, taught Classics at Eton, and then served in the Colonial Office in Whitehall, again in the field of educational administration. Arthur Mayhew remained a particular friend of Bethell's; he was instrumental in gaining publication for her first volume of poetry, and his name occurs frequently in her correspondence.

[2] The beginning of this letter has been lost.

[3] The timing of the 'vendanges' (that is, grape harvest) suggests a date in October.

[4] Fr. Literally 'as it is necessary'; here, proper, appropriate.

Alas! My dear mother my principal dissipation at present is dentistry for though the oracle at Nyon declares my teeth to be a very good sort, he says they are terribly spoilt by anaemia (this word is not spelt right I know but I hope it is recognisable). He has done two already – but several are decayed above & around the stopping, & he will have to take the stopping out of one. One or two will mean gold I think – & from [what] I remember of them when they were done before – I dread the second edition. I believe my visits to the torturer will extend to the new year for each time the tooth has to be "écartée"[1] so as [to] be able to be got at. This separating is a painful business – especially as mine are close together. I have such a business every evening; first there is the cleaning of the teeth; then with hair on end I take a pointed instrument & twist a bit of cotton wool on its end, then a little bottle with a red label "Carbolic acid" concentrated, poison. I take the damp cork & dab the cotton wool on to it – which is quite enough for the purpose; then I smear it cautiously on the 2 teeth to be treated & cake them over with camphorated chalk: then comes a tremendous business of rinsing out my mouth. Then I have to adjust the indiarubber between the teeth to [be] separated, and then I put more chalk in my mouth! He says I ought to do this last often as it is good for the teeth. I am so thankful he is a good dentist – & he is so careful not to give more pain than necessary, (so different from the rough Oxford dentist) & doesn't say in that idiotic fashion – "Now, I'm not going to hurt you in the least" as so many do. He says my teeth ought to be very good & not give trouble when once I am nineteen or twenty.

But enough of my teeth. I will turn to fleas. We have had such a plague of them. Scarcely a night passes that I do not have a grand hunt. I have been three times successful. Then in the day time I often undress & search. One morning I felt a creature at me, & said (very cunningly) to Madame "Pardon, Madame, mais puis-je chercher quelque chose!"[2] She thought I meant a pen or pencil – but the "quelque chose" in my mind was the animal – I found it & consigned it to a watery grave. I have caught 7 or 8 altogether this term, not to count those disappeared in other ways, and one still at large in my room. And it is the same thing in the other rooms. Not very pleasant.

A new mistress has come in the place of Mademoiselle Pagon. She is quite old and is a Madame. She has been much at Paris – & tells us which is the present Paris fashion for pronouncing a word. The people here have naturally not got the pronounced French accent but the French is

---

[1] Fr. 'Separated, spread out.'

[2] Fr. 'Excuse me, Madame, but may I look for something.'

very pure – better than at the other end of the lake, I believe. The German accent of the girls is hideous – but I don't think I shall get it, for after all I am not so much with them. Madame says that I have nearly lost my English accent – tho' of course it isn't perfect yet. I find one has to be a little affected in pronouncing French – because the French sounds are not natural to an English voice. I always used to think Ruth[1] spoke very affectedly in French – but now I see she was right – & Madame says she speaks extremely well.

I believe a new girl is coming into my room today or tomorrow: therefore I mourn & weep. She is a German, but I hear something about her being the daughter of a "baronin",[2] so perhaps she will be a little more refined than some of the girls here. Now I am coming near to the end of my letter. It gets colder & colder.

The time is passing by ... soon it will be Spring & I will fly away. Oh happy prospect, I involuntary cry although the life here is happy enough.

With love to all & much to yourself.
Yr loving Ursula.

Macmillan Brown Library. MB 558. C1.

TO THE MAYHEW FAMILY – [?1891/92]

[Nyon, Switzerland]

A Plaint from the Ewelamb[3]
(To be read, meditated on, & acted on by all the family)

What is Life Without a Letter?

Oh me sisters and me brithers
Listen to the distant cry
Of the poor Ewelamb who withers
In Mont Blanc's vicinity.

---

[1] Ruth Mayhew was another of the family with whom Bethell formed a particular friendship. Born in 1866, she was educated at Oxford University (without being able to take a degree). She taught at Oxford High School, and in 1899 became Headmistress of Brighton High School for Girls. In 1904 she married Henry Head, a prominent physician and neurologist (knighted in 1927). With her brother Arthur, she remained a close friend of Bethell, and it was to Ruth that many of Bethell's Garden poems were addressed (see letter to Frank Sidgwick, July 15, 1929).

[2] Ger. 'A baroness.'

[3] This was the first of several light-hearted letters written in verse; an undated copy is preserved in Bethell's papers.

Know ye how that joyous gladness
Inexpressible delight!
Letter for me! Banish sadness
Suddenly the day is bright.

The bell at 4 o'clock that ringeth
For the bread & chocolate
Sometimes, too, a letter bringeth
Oh how eagerly we wait.

In a corner take the letter
Bread & chocolate also take
Munch & read – why, sure no better
Tastes the English tea-cake!

Three or four times read it duly
Read the choicest bits again
Read the whole thereof, now, newly,
Fold it with regret & pain

Put it safely in its cover
In the pocket, so, with care;
From time to time there feel it over
To be sure that it is there.

And when brown & tattered place it
In a small elastic band,
With others like it, worn, effacèd,
Written in many a diverse hand.

But if, alas! in vain one stirrèd
Expectations – "None today" –
Turn away with hope deferrèd
Disappointed turn away.

Take the bread, & take the tiny
Round hard piece of chocolate;
Water it with tears so briny
Mourn this hard & dreary fate.

While the Germans, choc'late biting

Ope their packets broad & fat
Stamped with "Reichpost" – scrawly writing
Oh my friends! – consider *that*!

"What is life" – the Ewelamb crieth –
"Without a letter!" It is sad . . .
Take a pen, ere that tear drieth
Write to Ewelamb – make her glad!

Note at the time. "Poetic license paints the anguish at not receiving letters rather strong – Also chocolate never tastes like English tea even when reading a letter".

Macmillan Brown Library. MB 558. L5.

TO SIR JOHN HALL – OCTOBER 17, 1894

235 Gloucester St W. ChCh.

Dear Sir John Hall[1]

The Committee fully understand that as you are absent from town for the greater part of the year you will be unable to take an active part in the working of the Gordon Hall; but we feel that the assurance of your interest in this work will stand us in great stead, and we know that your advice & help will be most valuable to us.[2]

Mr. Bevan Brown & Mr. Chrystall have consented to become Vice-Presidents, and I should be glad to know if you approve of our asking Mr. G. J. Smith (Member for Christchurch) to be a third; he is generally spoken of as a very upright man, and, I believe, is a favourite with the people; he has moreover already given us a little help in the past. We are anxious to get this matter settled in order to have our report printed.

---

[1] Sir John Hall (1824-1907) emigrated from Hull, England, in 1852 and became a prominent runholder and provincial leader in North Canterbury. He entered national politics in 1855 and became Premier in 1879 after defeating Sir George Grey. Hall was one of the most significant conservative politicians of the 19th century, but paradoxically was at the same time a champion of the liberal cause of female suffrage. His involvement with Bethell relates principally to the development of the Gordon Hall, but he and his wife Rose subsequently became regular correspondents and friends. See *DNZB* I. 172-74.

[2] The Boys' Gordon Hall was a charitable organisation set up (as the Annual Report notes) 'to provide amusement and instruction for the working boys of Christchurch of from twelve to eighteen years of age, for their physical, mental, and moral improvement.' Sir John Hall was the patron.

There are at present two vacancies on the Committee, but we shall have to wait till next year in order to see what fresh workers present themselves before electing new members.

I have just heard from Mr. Vincent (the proposed Manager) who is still suffering considerably from Influenza; he tells me that he intends going into the country for three weeks' change after "Show Week"; that upon his return he would be able to assume management of the Hall, & that as soon as he is well enough he will visit the Hall as frequently as possible. Our position therefore is this – The present workers must carry on the Hall for about another four weeks, during that time a meeting must be arranged between Mr. Vincent & the Committee in order that they may decide whether to appoint him or not. In the event of his appointment it will be the next duty of the Committee to collect his salary – the sum proposed was £50 – & Mr. Vincent will take entire charge of the work & make it his business to reorganize it so as to make a fresh start next year.

I am
Faithfully yours
Ursula Bethell
Hon. Sec.

Alexander Turnbull Library. MS Papers 1784-208.

TO LADY ROSE HALL – NOVEMBER 11, 1894

235 Gloucester St W. ChCh.

My dear Lady Hall[1]

I was thinking of writing to you when your letter came, in order to tell you about Susan, the wayward maiden. She is safely packed off to a most desirable farm-household near Kaiapoi. Miss Weston, the daughter of the house, was for a time sub-matron at St Mary's, so she is experienced in dealing with this sort of girl. I heard of the place through Miss Fanny Torlesse[2] & cannot be sufficiently thankful that things have turned out so. It was high time the child left the town & I only hope she will stay where she is.

My perplexities are resolving themselves gradually. It's really very like the pig that wouldn't go over the style story! As far as I can make out, the landlord won't make the alterations because it would be too costly & raise the rent too much. Therefore Mother will wait for another

---

[1] Bethell wrote often to Lady Rose Hall (née Dryden), but this is the only letter that has survived, preserved among her husband's papers.

[2] Possibly the author of *Bygone Days* (London, 1914). See *DNZB* I. 547.

house, & will see no necessity to promote a holiday just now. As Rhoda has only been doing nominal lessons lately I think she will hold out till the usual ones. No invitation has come from Wanganui so I presume they are going to wait till another term – as this one is so full of examinations. I am rather sorry not to get away in dusty December – still it is very necessary for me to be here for the purpose of funds-collecting some time in the summer. Of course the landlord *may* relent & the call to Wanganui come & all this be over-turned but I think I may safely say that I shall be able to come in January at the time that suits you best. How delightful it will be!

Please tell Sir John that I shall be only too happy to mount any photographs for him – work neatly executed – design & ornamentations a speciality of the firm! But I must make a study of adhesives first. That starch was not altogether satisfactory.

As to the Hall – it is closed, I am thankful to say. I was not present at the last Committee Meeting – having gone to Lyttelton for the closing night of the Club there. [...]

It was great fun at Lyttelton comparing notes between the "Town Push" & the "Lyttelton Gang". They were quite as noisy as mine, & some looked much wilder, but they are not so desperately *blasé* as most of ours. I there made acquaintance with Mr. Seager, who promised to come & give conjuring to our boys next year. He said he was going to Hororata[1] one day after the New Year to show Magic Lantern in the *Town Hall*. I said I might perhaps be there too.

Yes, that was a terribly sad week. Two years ago I was in Folkestone for All Saints Day. I recollect the service so well because they had just had the news of the wreck of the "Pommerania" several Folkestone residents being among the drowned.[2] It seemed like a repetition of it on that day this year[3] – only the disaster seemed to be brought still nearer home.

Just room to say goodbye.

I am affectionately yrs
Ursula Bethell

Alexander Turnbull Library. MS Papers 1784-209.

---

[1] Hororata was the nearest township to Hall's substantial holding, Terrace Station, on the banks of the Rakaia river.

[2] The name of this vessel is difficult to read. A vessel named the S. S. Pommerania was indeed wrecked off Folkestone, with the loss of 50 lives, on Oct. 23, i. e. just before All Saints Day, but it occurred in 1878, not (as this letter would imply) in 1892.

[3] This must refer to the sinking of the S. S. Wairarapa on Oct. 29 off Great Barrier Island, in which 135 passengers and 20 crew lost their lives.

TO SIR JOHN HALL – MARCH 17, 1895

Gloucester St West.

My dear Sir John

Lady Hall was kind enough to bring the beautiful draughtsboard yesterday; it is really too good for them altogether & I must only allow it to be used as a reward of extreme virtue.

Our opening really went off very well; the Mayor entered into the thing well, the Bishop was most felicitous & the boys seemed delighted with Mr. Seager.[1] The boys were in full force & it now rests with Mr. Vincent to keep up their interest.

I hope that when you are able to visit the Hall things will be going on in an equally satisfactory manner.

With many thanks for the game.

I am
Yours most sincerely
Ursula Bethell

Alexander Turnbull Library. MS Papers 1784-211.

TO SIR JOHN HALL – NOVEMBER 27, 1895

Gloster St W

My dear Sir John

I enquired of Mrs. White of Wanganui concerning the red gum I told you of: she writes to say – "The scarlet-flowering gum 'eucalyptus ficifolia' would no doubt do well in Canterbury in a *well-sheltered* spot: they are quite easy to grow & flower in about 3 years from the seed. The Warratah (Telopea speciosima) & Embothrium coccineum are equally beautiful shrubs & flower young."[2]

As you are interested in current social movements at Home I thought you might like to look at the papers I am sending you; they are sold at a penny a number & are a venture of the Christian Social Union & edited by Adderley.[3] They seem to me to be very clear &

---

[1] The Gordon Hall had re-opened on March 15. Bethell invited Sir John to chair the opening, but he was unable to attend.

[2] The fondness for Latin botanical names that O'Sullivan comments on (*Collected Poems,* p. 102) can be seen already here.

[3] The Christian Social Union was founded in Oxford in 1889 (a time when Bethell was still at school there) by Brooke Westcott, Henry Scott Holland and Charles Gore (later a controversial appointment as Bishop of Worcester). James Adderley, another friend of Gore, was also a prominent early member. The CSU published a wide range of material,

comprehensible to the people – without in the least being *written down* to them – and, as a rule, very moderate in tone. But I see they find it difficult to make it suit all classes of people – addressing themselves at one time to working men, & at another to shareholders. They can be obtained through White the bookseller here, but the numbers I send you are already bespoken.

I am glad to say Mr. Vincent has obtained work. He has charge of Friedlander Bros. Wool-Store at Addington.

I enclose with the papers a couple of pens Lady Hall said she would like to have.

I find a great deal to be done these last days & hard to think of everything.

With my love, dear Sir John

Sincerely yours
Ursula Bethell

Alexander Turnbull Library. MS Papers 1784-214.

TO SIR JOHN HALL – JANUARY 16, 1896

S. S. PrinzRegent Luitpold

My dear Sir John

I am delighted to be able to set your fears at rest with regard to our fate on board this vessel. We are in charming quarters – I'm sure on no French boat could more be done for one's comfort. We came on board with many misgivings – particularly about the fare – but these speedily vanished. First satisfaction was our cabin – clean & airy – with every conceivable attention to our bien-être.[1] Next, the stewards – whose extreme respectability almost awed us at first, until one discovered their boundless good nature for which no request seems too irksome. Then, the meals, which we had heard were the weak point of this line – & renewed satisfaction. Some of the dishes are certainly strangely continental – but all the food is delicately cooked, scrupulously clean, & served in a refined way. All the arrangements are under the control of a chief-steward – the most amiable of beings – who pays heed to one's every wish. Tea & ice water are to be had in unlimited quantities – there are punkahs in the saloon – & double awnings on deck. Judging from our treatment in this class, I should think the steerage here must be superior to the second class on the Orient line. Miss Vaughan, who, in previous

---

but Bethell may be referring to *Goodwill*, a monthly magazine that Adderley edited from 1894-1910.

[1] Fr. 'Well-being.'

voyages has scarcely had one day free from "malaise" is wonderfully well – & indeed has constituted herself head nurse of the invalids. I am afraid these are all very materialistic observations – but really I am most anxious to say all the good I can of this line.[1]

The Captain is a very portly & imposing old gentleman, who quite won my heart by the fatherly advice on the subject of my health which he gave me on finding me prostrate with a headache the other day. He makes a most particular inspection of the ship every day – (we never saw the Captain of the Orient boat the whole way out). Unfortunately we hear that a martinet is concealed behind all this paternal bonhommie – the iron hand behind the velvet glove! It is rumoured that he does not hesitate to order the officers into retirement for the slightest offence. Hence doubtless the excellent discipline of the ship, but I fear he is not a favourite.

The stewards are men of talent, & we have a string & a brass band. Yesterday was the 25th Anniversary of the Unification of the Empire[2] – or something of that kind – & so in the evening there was a procession around the decks & martial music was played.

Our crossing from New Zealand was boisterous, & we suffered greatly. The one pleasant recollection of that part of the journey is a brief peep at Hobart – a dear little place. Unfortunately we had only 3 hours there in the evening & bad weather or we should have so much liked to make an expedition in the environs. We had to content ourselves with supper at a very nice hotel you may be acquainted with – Heathorne's is I think the name! In Melbourne we had only time to do some shopping & then took to the train. The journey to Adelaide was interesting in many respects – but the country anything but attractive. Everything was completely parched – hardly any grass struggling through the bricky earth – & that brown & dried up. The dusty gumtrees or leafless sheoaks gave no relief to this dreary & arid scene, & the sky seemed to repeat the prevailing colour, being covered with hard metallic clouds, which did not in the least suggest thoughts of moisture. No doubt we saw it at the worst time, but I could not help feeling thankful that my lot had not been cast in Australia. One curious thing I noticed was the number of ruined buildings to be seen from the train – some with the stone walls standing & the roof open to the sky – others merely

[1] The line in question was the Norddeutscher Lloyd line (Bremen) which began operating a service to Australia in 1886.

[2] The unification of the German Empire after the defeat of the French in the Franco-Prussian war (1870-71). Kaiser Wilhelm I was crowned Emperor at Versailles on Jan. 18, 1871.

a chimney beside a heap [of] stones – this adding greatly to the desolate aspect of the country.

The railway stations struck us as wretched badly planned, badly managed, & extremely dirty but the people were, with hardly an exception, most good natured & obliging & their manner was certainly condescending & friendly rather [than] respectful, but one had not the heart to resent it.

Adelaide did not prepossess us – it was if possible more burnt & dried up than anything that went before & left one with a sensation of unquenchable thirst.

I forgot to mention our fellow passengers – who are all quite respectable – & if some are rather vulgar, we console ourselves in thinking what sort of people we *might* have been thrown with. By far the nicest of them is an old lady, Mrs. Pickett, a theosophist, who is bound for India to perfect herself in her faith. There is an Afghan Mohammedan, going to Mecca, they say. There are two parsons in our class – one Anglican & the other Baptist – (at our Sunday Service the prayers will be read by the former & the sermon preached by the latter – with mixed hymns!) There is a Canadian doctor of a very sceptical turn of mind – so there are some very lively discussions to be had at times – I assure you.

We shall soon be having what is called afternoon tea – tho' we have forsaken tea in favour of something cooler – since unlimited lemon squashes may be had gratis. Your biscuits accompany this refreshment – and are greatly appreciated.

A day or two will bring us to Colombo. Then I shall rejoice to feel the first stage of our voyage accomplished, for however comfortable we may be, I am always happier on terra firma; this hot weather, too, is very trying – & headaches prevent my doing anything at all for the greater part of the time.

My next news, if all goes well, will be from England. I look forward with increasing eagerness to seeing that dear country again – & also to finding New Zealand mails soon after arrival, when I hope my people will give me tidings of all friends out there – that is, if my mother has not also left the country. Mr. Wilson gave me very sad news just before I left, & spoke also of renewed anxiety on Mr. George Hall's account – but I hope the next reports will be better.[1]

I hope also to hear in time that others are struggling with the difficulties of the Boys' Hall – struggles which yet one looks back to with

---

[1] George Hall was Sir John's brother, who had followed him out to New Zealand in the 1850s.

so much gladness afterwards – and indeed, who could be altogether despairing when encouraged by such kind help & sympathy as you were always ready to give me, & for which, dear Sir John, I feel I have never adequately thanked you. I can't tell you what a difference kindness like yours makes to one (for life doesn't always go on oiled wheels) – it is the greatest encouragement. How glad I shall be if ever I am able to be of the slightest service to you while in England – & hope you will always tell me if there is anything I could possibly do.

Je vous prie de saluer bien affectueusement de ma part Lady Hall.[1] Miss Vaughan also wishes to send her love to her.

I must not end without apologising for the very untidy appearance of this letter – the ship shakes so much at times that it is impossible to hold one's pen steadily – but I am glad to have been able to achieve any sort of a letter whatever. May I venture to remind you of the promised *photograph* before I say good-bye?

Yours most truly
Ursula Bethell

Alexander Turnbull Library. MS Papers 1784-217.

TO SIR JOHN HALL – MARCH 23, 1896

Government House Chatham.

My dear Sir John

I have just come down from London where I was careful to do your commission at the stores. I am afraid the result is not altogether satisfactory; it being the end of the season there were only two furry footmuffs – one a huge black thing, cost 4 guineas, & the other in patterns of such a vulgar description that I am sure you would not have tolerated it inside your study. It was therefore apparently a choice between your having cold feet throughout the coming winter & sending one of this other kind, leather outside, & with can for hot water. I chose the latter alternative, thinking that if you don't care for it in your room, it might be useful in the carriage.[2] I met with no better success concerning the warm soles – they had none so thick as the pattern in stock; however I left it with them as they promised to procure some exactly the same & forward them with the muff. They were in the Auxiliary Stores, & as the Army & Navy deposit does not count for the

[1] Fr. A traditional, formal salutation: 'Please give my kind regards to Lady Hall.'
[2] Hall's reply suggests the foot muff was greeted rather unenthusiastically.

other Stores, I had some difficulty in arranging about the payment – but it is all right now.

[...]

We are enjoying ourselves immensely here – it is so amusing to see the soldiering going on all round. There is a regiment of Scots in these barracks – & they are pretty to look at. I also enjoy hearing the pipers, but everyone does not agree with me on that point. On one side this house looks out over the barrack square – on the other there may be seen the Medway, Rochester Cathedral, & a good many smoking chimneys, quite a picturesque sight. England seems to me more & more delightful every day – far surpasses my recollections – rosy though they were. Just now the spring flowers are beginning to come out & the weather is quite warm. We shall stay here for some time, then most likely to Maidstone or Brighton, then to London for first week in May, then perhaps to Cambridge, Oxford for Eights week,[1] Malmesbury, then several places in Yorkshire – that is our programme as at present sketched. All our wanderings have been without accident so far, & we hope for equal good fortune in the future.

[...]

My brother & I had a few days in Switzerland en route, but the weather was too cold for it to be as pleasant as usual. During the week we spent in Genoa however, the weather was perfection, & I enjoyed myself immensely poking about in old churches & galleries. I suppose Genoa is one of the least interesting of Italian towns & yet one finds it to be much more interesting than most people imagine when one reads about it & finds out the old bits that the hurrying tourist does not generally see.

[...]

Hororata (as inadequately set forth in my sketches) is universally admired. I have to explain that every house & garden in New Zealand is not as pretty as that. The lambhorns are also appreciated. Will you please give the enclosed to Lady Hall.[2] Je vous prie de me rappeler au bon souvenir de tout le monde chez vous.[3]

Believe me, dear Sir John
Affectionately yours
Ursula Bethell

Alexander Turnbull Library. MS Papers 1784-218.

---

[1] Eights Week is the main annual rowing event at Oxford University. It takes place during the 5th week of Trinity Term in May.

[2] There is nothing to indicate what the enclosure might have been.

[3] Fr. Another formal salutation: 'Please give my best regards to everyone at your home.'

TO SIR JOHN HALL – OCTOBER 11, 1896

18 Bradmore Road Oxford.

My dear Sir John

It was delightful to have your letter and those photographs besides. How splendid they are, especially that of you. I could not wish for a better picture of you & it is particularly nice that it should be taken in that familiar corner of your own verandah. Thank you a hundred times. I shall always delight in having it.

Your account of this new enterprise at what used to be the Addington Gaol interested me greatly.[1] It ought to be very useful. I do hope it may work successfully – it seems to be sure of sound management – I wish I could say the same of a Christchurch Boys' Club – but any such scheme must evidently be given up until the right man appears to take it in hand – and so one must say to oneself "Pacienza"! I am sure no one, dear Sir John, no one could wish *you* to do more in these matters than you have. I am sure one's only anxiety would be lest you should too often deny yourself that rest & country life the right to which you of all people have earned.

[...]

It seems but the other day when I sent off my last letter to Lady Hall – & how much ground I have been over since then!

Yorkshire, Derbyshire, Northumberland. Our relations were indefatigable in their efforts to provide [us] with something fresh to do & see – in Northumberland there was something special to do every afternoon! We investigated the Roman remains at Chollerford – we saw the Hexham Agricultural Show – (what a quaint & interesting old town is that) – saw my cousin's electric works in Newcastle & his newly invented torpedo boat[2] – went down to Durham – when I saw that Magnificent Cathedral for the first time. I had never pictured myself anything so massive, so truly strong & impressive. I should like to take New Zealanders visiting England for the first time to Westminster Abbey then to Durham – those two alone would be worth the voyage here & back.

While staying at Newton Ryme near York we made what was to us a most interesting expedition to see Rise the family house. We went by

---

[1] The Salvation Army Prison Gate Brigade was established in June 1896 on land that was originally part of the Addington Gaol. It served as a halfway-house for former prison inmates. See *The Press*, June 13, 1896.

[2] It is not clear what Bethell is referring to here; the date of the invention of the torpedo boat is disputed, but they were certainly being produced for the British Navy 20 years before she wrote this.

way of Hull & Beverley – so now I have seen those towns of which I have so often heard you speak. We drove from Beverley to Rise & saw the Holderness country to advantage. Rise is an ugly – but comfortable & extremely large House – the park however was pretty & I found the deer especially attractive – I revelled in gazing at the few portraits of our ancestors that grace the staircase. I don't know why this should give one so much pleasure, but it does! The house was undergoing painting & papering, so we went on to spend the night with a cousin, Sir Henry Boynton at Burton Agnes. I think it may be likely that you know this beautiful house with its exceptionally fine oak staircase. It's quite a privilege to live in such a house – I wish we could have stayed longer. I will not write out the long list of all the places we went to – Ripon, Bolton Abbey, Fountains Abbey, & so on – But we saw a great deal of Yorkshire. Then we were in London. Then in Kent, where the hop-picking was going on. Picturesque from a certain distance. A nearer sight of these poor wretches from the slums working away at their holiday work, was saddening enough. However they are not uncared for by their employers – on the estate where we saw them at work, open air services (mostly music) are held for them in the evening – & city missionaries or district visitors come down to move about among them.

Then my brother went off to Switzerland, & I came to Oxford. I have been here nearly all the time since the beginning of September & have been very happy with old friends.[1] Oxford seems to grow more & more beautiful & I like being in no place so well as here. The weather has been kind until the last week or so, since when regular autumn storms have set in, & we have said good-bye to sketching & boating. The beautiful red mantle of Virginian Creeper that covered most grey walls a few weeks ago has now altogether vanished & the leaves are beginning to fall from the trees. Still my travels do not end here for a few days ago – on Michaelmas Day in fact – we went down to Winchester to see the youngest boy who is a scholar at the College. Of course you know Winchester – isn't it a charming place – (really my supply of adjectives has been so severely taxed during all these travels that I should be glad to see nothing new for a year at least!) We "did" the College, & saw the Cathedral, mounting even to the top of the Tower, whence the view well rewarded our fearful climb – and in the afternoon we walked out to St Cross & were entertained by a dear old "Brother" – and altogether thoroughly enjoyed ourselves. Then my brother & I went on for a night to Southhampton, & while there drove in the New Forest, which I had often wished to see.

---

[1] As the address indicates, Bethell was staying with the Mayhews.

My brother is now in London & sails for New Zealand this week. He has seen a great deal of England, and I think is quite ready to settle down to steady work in his native land.[1]

These are of course interesting times. This difficult Armenian question – the Czar's visit – Lord Rosebery's resignation – these things are eagerly talked about.[2] Naturally you have the main facts in the telegrams & this mail will bring you the details of the speeches that have been made. I was fortunate enough to be here when Canon Gore addressed a meeting on the subject of Armenia – he is always well worth listening to – & one has not that privilege so often in Oxford now that he has been installed at Westminster.

The hand of a spoiler is at work in Oxford; they are pulling down the pretty old cottages in Holywell in order to build hideous but rent-producing tenements. Some of the workers – people who have lived in these cottages for years – cannot afford the higher rent & so have to migrate to the "East End" – thus swelling the number of the poor in one particular quarter of Oxford & emphasizing that sharp contrast between the well to do & the badly to do parts of this town. Carfax Church has been demolished. This is a change for the better for that corner between the High & Cornmarket street was perilously narrow.

I am planning to spend the winter in Germany – in Dresden most likely – but first I am going to see my sister in Switzerland & stay with a friend at Le Lôcle in Neuchatel. For some reasons I shall be glad enough when this flitting about is over & I am able to settle down to some work & become perhaps a more useful member of society than I am at present.

I am writing as well to Lady Hall by this mail. I was so very sorry to hear of her being so far from well, but hope that her stay at Sumner will really have done her good. Of course Sumner must be much warmer than Hororata & Lady Hall will have been spared the cold winds – but I am sure she must have been sorry to leave the Hororata home for so long a time.

You are good enough to ask me whether there is any N. Z. paper I should like to see. I have seen the Weekly Press once or twice as my mother has it sometimes, but I should much like to see a number of the Church News sometimes if you really would send me one on

---

[1] The *DNZB* (IV. 57) suggests that this 'contact with English gentry had a lifelong effect' on Marmaduke Bethell, who subsequently became an active social leader in the Amuri County.

[2] The events referred to here are the atrocities suffered by the Armenians at the hands of the Turks; the visit of Czar Nicholas II to Paris; and the resignation of Rosebery first from his position as Prime Minister and then as leader of the Liberal Party.

occasionally. No more space so I must say goodbye. Always, dear Sir John

Affectionately yours
Ursula Bethell

Alexander Turnbull Library. MS Papers 1784-220.

TO MARY WALKER – [? NOVEMBER 9, 1899]

Greyladies,[1] Blackheath Hill, S. E.

My dear Mary[2]

[...]

Many thanks for your letter – but you are doing far too much – now please don't follow the fashion & break down. I am wondering how your tea has gone off today. Isn't the state of things you describe in yr. letter to Miss Hall a disgrace to Xtians! But the human heart is vile & stubborn as I am going to show presently.

[...]

I won't refuse anything now which seems to be a "call" but don't feel in the least as if I could be of any use to anyone – so you had better think twice & thrice before calling me![3] I assure you I'm a prey to the evil one & merged in despair about my own doings & horrible hatred of my fellow creatures. Alas what right have I to be trying this sort of work – when my heart is so evilly disposed towards my fellow Xtians. And as for Lorrimore Square. When I go near that house I feel a loathing of all goodness & a wild desire to go off & be an utter pagan like Ruth – it has the most shocking effect on me – & what a silly & weak creature I must be for it doesn't seem to render others thus desperate. Oh how tiresome it is to have an irritable temper & a heart the size of a green pea.

However when I'm with the boys I really am quite happy what tho' a useless whited sepulchre, pour le reste.[4] Am very busy helping with one

---

[1] The Grey Ladies, also known as the Women Workers for God, was an Anglican settlement based in London performing a variety of social work. Although not formally a religious order, the women did wear a grey and black religious habit.

[2] Mary Lily Walker (1863-1913) was a leading social activist in Dundee. A brilliant university scholar, she was attracted to the work of the Dundee Social Union from its foundation in 1888. From May 1898 to May 1899 she was with the Grey Ladies in London, where she met Bethell. Most of Bethell's letters to her are imperfectly dated, and even the sequence is uncertain. However, the context suggests they were all written after Walker returned to Dundee. This first letter is headed Thursday 9th.

[3] When she returned to Dundee, Walker revitalised the DSU, which had been struggling to retain voluntary workers. She invited Bethell to join her in her work.

[4] Fr. 'For the rest.'

thing & another – Miss Vaughan & her club – & then have shopped with Miss Tregarthen for her room at Lorrimore wh. she is going to do up. I look at her with an anxious eye. Can't think why she doesn't go melancholy mad. How I should like to poke a pin into Miss Utterton's sanctimonious self-satisfaction. Sweet Xtian feeling this!

[...]

Rhoda writes splendid letters with droll accounts of their doings. I miss her much – & what a convenient outlet she was for ill humour.

[...]

Now I have a gas-fire in my room. Its a beast, but its a most convenient beast. I hate it while recognising its advantages. Must go to bed. Now don't you overdo it & come to a bad end. No wonder you feel overburdened at times – but think what you have accomplished already!

Yours ever
Ursula M. B.

Macmillan Brown Library. MB 558. C.11.

TO MARY WALKER – [1899]

At the Parish

My dear Mary,

I must not delay to thank you for your timely letter. It really was very helpful & your advice is Gospel truth. Already before it came I had got a step on the way, because the Vicar offered me the Brigade Boys & it came over me that it was no good trying to do this from Bkheath. So I had a talk with Miss Yeatman & we arranged that if I do take over these boys I am to try the experiment of living down in Southwark at St Mary's, for a month after Easter. So there goes my room you see – & really I don't want to cling to anything. The only thing that troubles me is the thought of "Lorrimore" wh. has always been a stumbling block – I see myself turning into one of those dirty looking depressed draggletailed uninviting people. The first step to their saintly state has been taken! This is only half serious, please. I really feel happier now I am making no more bargains – but I am terribly tired, & no mistake. Yesterday I was seized with weeping for no reason & could not stop for an hour – it quite takes away one's self-respect.

I am very doubtful about accepting this new plan. I don't think I am capable of coping with them – they are spoilt already & I am too feeble. I am to see the Vicar tomorrow & I suppose I shall do what he tells me.

Miss Yeatman does not seem very favourably disposed towards the Dundee plan. I don't know why. I think she thinks I should pine so far from England perhaps I should. But that doesn't matter. I should like to come as you feel I should be a comfort (I don't deserve half the affection which Heaven sends me) but really I'm afraid you wouldn't find me of much use & I'm not going to say what I should like or shouldn't for fear of making bargains. I'm *sure* you will get someone & I am *sure* your work will get on all right. But it seems to me this last year of the century is to be a waiting one for the nation & for lots of people in it.

Thank you very much indeed for your consoling letter – I confess the future seems grey and silent, but then the body is aweary of this great world.

I will write again when I have seen the Vicar.

Your affecte friend
Ursula

Macmillan Brown Library. MB 558. C.11.

TO MARY WALKER – APRIL 4, [1900]

My Parish Perch

Private & Confidential

My dear Mary,

I dry up my tears (literally) in order to write the letter you demand. I know I have kept you waiting a shameful long time – but I was partly bothered & partly busy. I do seem to be busy & the days chock full but the result is nothing whatever. Also I knew you were suited with a helper & so no longer in need of a letter of consolation.

Inwardly I am at my wits end: the conviction of my pointlessness & uselessness grows on me daily. What is the use of trying to be a parish worker & love your parishioners when you hate your house companions to distraction. I am sure I try to get used to them but its no good, those tiresome untidy feckless old Greyladies irritate me without ceasing. No doubt they are most good & excellent but they are too boring for words. And the untidyness of the house gets more & more annoying & the chapel services instead of helping irritate still more. Of course I know I oughtn't to be thinking of myself but of how sad it is that Miss Yeatman is going etc. So I do & think it is most sad – but I get irritated in spite of not thinking.

Then down here things don't grow. How presumptuous I was to offer to do boys. What qualifications have I? none whatever. I can't teach or originate or anything. The parish certainly is wretchedly unorganised – no two bits of work run together – no co-ordination or growth. It makes it very hard. When I began to expound this to my curate, he proceeded to tell me under seal of secrecy that the C. L. B. Captain[1] is going – & if so the C. L. B. may have to be broken up, & he would like me to have all the junior boys & work in a certain amount of drill, etc. This certainly wd. make me feel less superfluous – but I don't believe I ought to undertake it. It is a sort of temptation to further presumption.

The other day I went to see The London Deaconesses[2] again & always come away with qualms. Their house is so neat & quiet & their chapel so beautiful. They look so clean & fresh & healthy & are so sure of their methods. I believe I shall have to end up there. I am beginning to think I have not given up enough. I have clung to things too much. I have now my own room which I love, & this little parish room which is a sort of ideal to me & I think they ought to be given up. I expect if I had really knuckled under & not held out for my liberty I should not have this feeling of utter helplessness – They attract me in every way. But then when I think all this I remember that I might hate them as I hate Greyladies & where should I be then. Also should I ever be a good parish worker I do loathe all their dirt & decrepitude so much. And then I remember spring & the country & pictures & music & liberty & wonder whether I could ever settle down to doing without it all.

But the training – that surely would make me different. I think the greylady system is perfectly silly & I believe half of them are quite incapable. How wd. an army get on without discipline – they don't learn their job by simply running out to be shot at.

But I am frightened by remembering that I cannot stand small disagreeables – how should I stand a long training if I run away from All Saints House. I never go to meals there now the whole place makes me feel so utterly ill. But if I can't stand that should I stand greater hardships. How[ever] I really think the Deaconesses would be clean. My conscience gives me no peace & the heavens seem silent & all I know is that I am miserably incapable & useless.

---

[1] Church Lads' Brigade – an Anglican movement founded in 1891 by Walter Gee. Its object was 'the advancement of Christ's Kingdom among lads of all classes, the promotion of reverence, discipline, self-respect, and all that tends towards true Christian manliness.' Boys were occupied with drill work, ranks, rifle shooting, marching and gymnastics, and Church attendance was compulsory. Each parochial unit was known as a Company, its officer in charge being known as the Captain.

[2] This may refer to the London Diocesan Deaconess Institution, an organisation of lay women working for the church in London, or to a smaller group within that institution, the Deaconess Community of St. Andrew, which was more formally constituted as a religious community. The later remarks about doing away with liberty may indicate the second of these.

[...]

Oh dear I know I am not playing the game but I believe I am only fit to be a looker on & see how badly they do it! What is the use of telling the Lord one is ready to do His will – when one knows perfectly well that if His will were for one to go to Lorrimore Square one couldn't face it.

Now I must get something to eat so farewell.

Quelle bête de lettre.[1]

Yours ever
Ursula

Macmillan Brown Library. MB 558. C.11.

TO MARY WALKER – [APRIL 14], 1900

Easter Eve — Greyladies, Blackheath Hill, S. E.

Dear good nurse of my body & soul

Here comes a photograph of your patient to greet you at Easter. It gives me rather a wicked expression which is right.

I did sympathise with you so in your ministerial troubles it is horrible when the services one depends upon for support turn out to be nothing but irritating. I do hope you have found some compensations. I have kept an inadequate Holy Week – being too poorly to fly out to services much – but yesterday went to the 3 Hours at St. Saviours where we had Mr. Otley. It was much the most helpful service of the kind I have ever been to – not at all emotional but very helpful & simple & practical, & much of what he said went right home to me. I must try to make notes of what I remember.

[...]

Oh I have such a rhume de cerveau[2] – too much for any thought. Miss Hall is gone to Newcastle. Had a talk with my Vicar who said everyone there was just as low [as] myself & I was drinking the common cup, & wants me to attempt the boys. So I said I wd. make the experiment after a holiday & from Southwark, but could not do it from here. I look at my room with such regretful eyes.

It is good of you to think of sending me a book – right glad will it make me. I *have* got the 1st Vol. of Romans & my godmother always promised me the II. She seems rather to have forgotten but she may send it yet. Well, dear Mary I hope you will have a happy Easter & that some

---

[1] Fr. 'What a beast of a letter.'

[2] Fr. 'A head-cold.'

hopes for yr. work will shortly spring up out of a wintry & barren ground. You must hold the fort & at last we shall hear of the "relief of Dundee."[1] As for me I am quite tongue tied & brain & heart-tied about my future. Blindfolded am I, but not near such an infidel as a week ago.

Adieu
Ursula

Macmillan Brown Library. MB 558. C.11.

[TO MARY WALKER – JULY 1901.]

Buffet de la gare. Perroy. Vaud. Suisse

[...][2]

Well, thank you very much for your letter of sympathy – I can hardly now think of Christopher without tears – he was such an altogether darling – I can't bear to think of St. Mary's without him. Why can't I feel the same deep affection for human beings! One can't manufacture a sentiment like that with however great efforts!

If ever the soul of an animal revealed itself – it was in those last weeks – Well I hope he is trotting about with Origen and S. Francis of Assisi and S. Jerome and S. Blaise and John Woolman now – & that they understand how round and furry he was when he had a body. Ah me how much of interest there is to live for in the other world.

[...]

Macmillan Brown Library. MB 558. C.11.

TO SIR JOHN HALL – DECEMBER 5, 1901

St Mary's 85 Union St. Borough.

My dear Sir John

I was going to write you a word of farewell today & now I must add to it my hearty thanks for your kindness. I feel that South London has really no claim on you & so my personal gratitude is all the stronger. The help is particularly welcome as I have made myself responsible for the salary of the Gymnastic Instructor this winter in addition to all the many expenses which meet me in my work. I am going to hand over one Pound

---

[1] British action to relieve the besieged town of Mafeking had begun just days before this letter was written.

[2] Much of this letter has been carefully cut away. Christopher was a pet cat; in a postcard to Walker, Bethell describes him as 'nearer to me than anybody else at Blackheath.'

to Miss Vaughan for the Girls Club & I know she will be most thankful for it.

But even more cheering is your interest and sympathy, dear Sir John, & you must let me thank you for that again. I quite hope to show you the Boys Club next time you come – Please God it will have borne better fruit by then.

Did I seem narrow in my outlook on religious work here. Three years pretty steady work & observation have taught me a great deal & showed me some of my mistakes. One of the saddest things to think of is the amount of mistaken effort & ignorant wasting of forces that goes on around here, but perhaps the knowledge of this makes the toiler take too mistrustful an attitude sometimes.

I am writing late at night, having spent the morning in the Police Court waiting to give evidence about a case of theft in this house, in the afternoon went to a Temperance meeting, visited some of my people, lectured a small boy, went to have a look at the Club, & then for an hour or so began to instruct a bigger boy in the Christian Faith and so the days go by.

I should have liked to be able to see you off tomorrow, but it is impossible & no doubt many of your friends will be there. I can only wish you a calm & pleasant voyage, and another one back again before too long.

I cannot remember whether you have had any photograph of me since I put on my uniform & have hunted about for one, only finding this very bad snapshot which I enclose as a sort of Christmas card,[1] and to remind you a little of your

grateful & affectionate
Ursula Bethell

Alexander Turnbull Library. MS Papers 1784-246.

TO SIR JOHN HALL – MARCH 29, [1904]

The Pines. Featherston Wairarapa.

My dear Sir John

I want to thank you once more for coming to say good-bye to me, & for your kind present, & for all your kindness. I left with my mother to be sent to you a photograph which was done not long ago & which some people think good. I don't think you have one of me & it may serve to bring me to your memory sometimes.

[1] Now held in the ATL photographic archive.

My sister & I are having a quiet pause here before my final farewell to the Colony.[1] Once more goodbye, dear Sir John; May you have a happy Easter Festival.

Always affectionately yours
Ursula Bethell

Alexander Turnbull Library. MS Papers 1784-259.

TO DOROTHEA READER – JULY 19, 1904

At sea.[2]

Cousin Doff, I greet you well!
'Spite the ocean's damnèd swell
(In poetry, that word is used
Two syllabled, it is excused)
My state of health remains at par
Save for a vestige of catarrh
(Anxious thing, catarrh, at sea
Where kerchiefs cannot washèd be!)
Hale in body and in brain
Tasting – (or the rest is vain)
The joys of a *contented mind*[3]
May these lines my cousin find.
Your letter, Doff, is my delight;
I praise you much that you did write
In such a full & vivid way,
(I read it several times a day).
By this letter-writing zest
May you *often* be possest!
Have my postcards dropping in
Testified that mid the din
And bustle of my travel hurry
I thought upon my cousin furry?
First there was the tedious ocean
Where I took your Daddy's potion
(One *must* make the rhyming matchy
Or I would have called it cachet).

---

[1] At this point, Bethell clearly intended to leave New Zealand for good.

[2] This letter to Bethell's cousin, Dorothea Reader, was written as she returned to England via the United States, where she had earlier recuperated from the pneumonia that threatened her life in 1901-02.

[3] The allusion is to John Wesley's 'O for a thankful heart' (Hymn LI).

At San Francisco on the bay
Next I made a little stay,
(Long ago the Friars came,
Called the harbour by this name
For their sweet Saint Francis' fame).
Very busy there was I,
Tired, & in perplexity,
(Which route should I patronize?
How much baggage? Of what size?
Should I pause at such a spot?
Et caetera – it matters not).
Gladly then I sought a rest
On a silent mountain's breast –
Skyland's dear umbrageous orchard
Welcomes her, the city-tortured, –
There, by kind friends entertained
A happy octave I remained.
Onwards then by South Pacific
Railway at a pace terrific.
Santa Barbara I viewed
And next day my way pursued
Unto big Los Angeles,
Gardens full of green palm-trees –
Groves of luscious oranges –
Weather was too hot to please.
West, then, through South Californy
Through the desert bare & tawny
Where the cactus grows so Thorny
(I was sometimes almost suffy-
-cated by the car so stuffy.)
Who would wish to be the owner
Of the wastes of Arizona?
Yet the Indian who dwells there
Thinks it, doubtless, strangely fair
Thinks his mud hut very tony
Scours the sand on fleetest pony
Loves his lonesome Arizony –
Perhaps he doesn't think at all
My knowledge of the man is small
– (His basketwork and necklaces
Move me, though, to ecstasies) –
A little nonsense pray forgive

It brightens up my narrative!
Many from the train alight
At Williams in the dead of night:
Northwards thence they will be hurled
To th'eighth wonder of the world –
Colorado's grandest Cañon:
But I have no blithe companion
To nerve me up to the exertion
Needful for this fine excursion –
What is more, I cannot spare
Money for the railway fare.
Now please take a map & find
La Junta – (pronounced "*H*unta", mind,)
Where I took another train
Upwards from the level plain
To high Colorado Springs
Where Pike's Peak its summit flings
To the clear remotest sky.
There the eagle used to fly
There the Indian used to creep,
Noiseless, from the rocky steep.
Indians, eagles, fled away
Now the miner has his day,
And a thousand villas stand
On the healthy table-land.
Now farewell ye gentle friends!
Farewell, heights whose purple blends
With the russet of the rocks,
On I haste me where the flocks
And herds of Kansas farmers graze
In fields with flowers all ablaze.
Hereabouts I may not tarry
– On to the extraordinary,
Vast, renowned St. Louis Fair,
Where assembled thousands stare
At the world's collected riches.
But the Fair's a pleasure which is
Tiring more than any pleasure,
So I leave this hoard of treasure
Longing for a land of leisure:
This I find in sweet Kentucky –
Ah, the traveller is lucky

Who traverses these rolling fields
Where the blue grass region yields
Food for fleet horse or fat cattle.
Here they fought full many a battle
When in dreadful civil strife
Brother took his brother's life.
At Louisville and Lexington
I break my course, then hurry on
Up the wooded Alleghany
Range, whence, cold and turgid, many
Rivers flow, all crammed with lumber.
At a mountain inn I slumber.
Next I make my pleasant quarters
By the Proud Potomac's waters.
Washington! thou noble town
Justly great is thy renown!
Noble are thy shady streets
Where the loit'ring stranger meets
Many a grateful space of lawn
From the builder's zeal withdrawn.
Noble are thy public buildings,
If a little thick thy gildings,
Noble is thy Capitol
White and high upon the knoll,
Noble art thou altogether
In the radiant summer weather.
Having duly praised the city
I must mention in my ditty
Charming ladies whom I met,
Courtesy I'll ne'er forget;
Was I on sight-seeing bent
One as guide a morning spent,
One, when sickness laid me low
Strove to mitigate my woe.
One – but time & space would fail
To complete the happy tale
Whereon memory would dwell –
Washington, most kind, farewell!
Philadelphia, all too few
Were the hours I gave to you
All too hasty my attendance
At the Hall of Independence.

This, my Doffal, is the spot –
(Nay, the thought annoys me not)
Where a certain Declaration
Of a newly-fledged nation
Was by chosen leaders signed –
I saw the chairs whereon reclined
These men of Independent mind.
New York! New York! my journey's close
"Last not least" the saying goes.
Babel-like is piled New York
On Manhatten's nervous fork.
Martha Washington Hotel
Is the place at which I dwell,
Women only there reside –
But men may safely step inside
And chat with them in parlors neat
Or in the Restaurant may eat.
Cousin, I would gladly tell
All that further me befel
How delightful friends arise
And with kindnesses surprise
The sojourner within their gate.
Glad would I to you relate
All the things we talked about
All we saw when we went out
For they took me out to see
Methods of philanthropy
Where the immigrants are pent
In the tight-packed tenement,
On the other hand to view
Mansions on Fifth Avenue,
And the weather really tropic
Were an interesting topic –
But my zeal is running low
And the rhymes refuse to flow,
Whatever muse has thus inspired
My doggerel, is growing tired,
And I think I'll write no more
Till I'm safe on England's shore.
Much however do I grieve
From my Doff to take my leave
And I send at least a dozen

Kisses to my furry cousin,
And since fatigue forbids me try
To make a graceful ending, why
I'll say goodbye! goodbye! goodbye!

Macmillan Brown Library. MB 588. L5.

TO SIR JOHN HALL – NOVEMBER 22, 1906

2 The Wilderness. Holly Hill. Hampstead NW.[1]

My dear Sir John

Today's mail brought me your dictated letter of October the 8th just as I was about to post my little Christmas remembrance to you. I am so grieved, so very much grieved to hear of your being ill, but I trust that thorough rest & good care have long before this restored you – yes, to *years* of good health – for we can't spare you yet, Sir John, indeed we cannot. I am so afraid that you are too generous with your strength & felt very anxious when I heard that you had undertaken the responsibility & fatigue of public office at such a busy time.[2]

The news of your intention to found a permanent Boys' Club in Christchurch is of course intensely interesting & most welcome news to me.[3] It is a need which has been very much overlooked, although people seemed to recognise the usefulness of such a thing while it was being attempted. With a suitable building & funds for maintenance thus provided, surely the right man will appear at such a moment to take charge of the enterprise – the right man to fill the right place! This is of the greatest importance as you say, for all the successful Boys Clubs I know have owed at least their first impetus to the devotion of one leader. I believe that with such a leader some of the former members of the old "Gordon Hall" would be found ready to help – and their own experience as club members might perhaps serve usefully. The Gordon Hall of old days was a very modest attempt, but it was a sort of rough sketch of what might be done in a far more complete & efficient way under better conditions. What a help to citizenship – both of the earthly & the heavenly city – such a club might be – a woman's imagination runs

[1] Bethell lived at this address with her mother and sister, and with Effie Pollen, who had recently arrived in London.
[2] Hall wrote that he had been persuaded, in spite of poor health, to take on the duties of Mayor of Christchurch 'for this great Exhibition Year, as I had been the first Mayor, 40 years ago.'
[3] Hall had bought land, and left £10,000 to build and endow such an institution.

away with her in thinking of such things! I can't help feeling restive at being so far away when such a scheme is on foot, and hope that you will tell me more about the plans for the building and so on. Might I suggest *baths* as well as gymnastic apparatus – windows *high up* – and *strong* cupboards? The leader of the admirable club I visited in San Francisco, which has I suppose lost its home in the fire, believed in small classrooms only large enough to hold five at work, and a larger club-room; his gymnasium was below ground. My own small experience tallies with his entirely about the size of the classes – with the numbers restricted to five much *deeper* results could be obtained in any subject, whether e. g. history or handicraft. It is wonderful to think that if as appears not unlikely, I am back in Christchurch within three years' time, the Club may be full swing! I must tell Mrs Packe about this – for she was one of the originators of the Gordon Hall, together with those who were carrying it on before I was invited to help.

[...]

I am looking out on a dense November mist – it is not always *fog* in Hampstead. My sister is learning Nursing at the Metropolitan Hospital in Kingsland Road, so I am not taking up any outside work just now. I see some of the South London lads occasionally, & hear regularly from the two married members of the Gordon Hall in whom I am specially interested. One of them has taken up Sunday School teaching & asks for books on the subject; his boy is my godson.

I will address this letter as you suggest to Mrs. Wilson's care, asking her kindly to send it on to you.

And now, dear Sir John, let me try to thank you for thinking of writing to me when you were in so much pain; this further mark of your unfailing kindness touches me very much & I shall treasure up the letter together with others which have cheered me in times past.[1] I wish you knew how much your affectionate encouragement has helped me, & how thankful I am that the Boys' Club brought me, with other blessings, such a friend as yourself. *Please* get well again quickly![2]

and believe me always gratefully & affectionately yours

Ursula Bethell

Alexander Turnbull Library. MS Papers 1784-263.

---

[1] Hall's letter concludes: 'Goodbye dearest Ursula – the recollection of your friendship is one of the high spots of my memory. Your loving friend John Hall.'

[2] In fact, Hall died in June of the following year.

TO RICHARD BETHELL – [APRIL 12,] 1914

Easter Sunday Kodai Kanal Palni Hills S. India

Darling Richard[1]

I wonder whether you have nearly forgotten Aunt Ursula. If you have I really deserve it because I havn't written or sent a postcard for such a long time – I have been saving this note paper for 3 months to write to you because its rather a nice elephant at the top there.[2]

India is as you know a very hot place, & now that summer is coming it is almost too hot for English people. So my friends[3] have come to a place very high up in the mountains where it is always cool & will stay here until the very hot months are over. I came up with them to stay for a few weeks & then I am going home to England & it won't be too hot there. In order to get here we first had to take the train for a long journey. You can sleep in the train, but you have to take your own sheets & pillows done up in a holdall. Then you ring the electric bell in the train and a black servant comes & spreads them out & makes a nice bed. Very early in the morning – that is, not so very early because the sun isn't up till six! but as soon as it is quite daylight, he brings a tray with a nice breakfast, tea & toast & marmalade & butter & bananas. For other meals there is a diningcar, but he will bring soda water & ice to you at any time. The water is not always clean & wholesome in India, so it is better to drink soda water, or at home one can boil the water & then it is safe. The Indian people carry clean water with them in brass jars or earthenware chatties like this.[4]

The station you get out at for this place is called Kodai Road – its very hot there, so [you] must be careful to put on Topees before getting out of trains. Topees are hats made of a thick pith (I think Daddy had one & gave it to Jack Pochill). From the railway station there is a flat road 32 miles leading to the foot of the hills. Some people travel along this in Indian bullock carts – big ones called transits. They start in the evening & put a mattress & pillow in the cart, so that they can sleep as they go slowly along. I have travelled for a night in a bullock cart, but this time we chose to go in a motor car so as to be quicker. One man drove & another worked the hooter to make the bullock carts get out of the way. Such dozens of them, going slowly along laden with bales of cotton & cases of tea or people's luggage & other things. In the trees beside the road were monkeys playing or sometimes sitting on the road

---

[1] The elder of the two sons of Marmaduke and Thyra Bethell (b. 1905).

[2] The paper bears the letterhead 'Grand Oriental Hotel, Colombo, Ceylon.'

[3] Bethell was staying with members of the Mayhew family.

[4] The letter includes a small line drawing here.

daring us to run over them. Sometimes we saw little boys minding herds of black goats, or tiny donkeys laden with washing being driven along by the Indian washermen.

About two o'clock we got to the end of the road and expected to find twenty three men waiting to carry us & our luggage up the mountain. They had been ordered by telegraph but there was some mistake & the telegram was too late, & we could not get on. We got some poached eggs & tea at the Rest-house & then climbed up into the motor again & went back all the 32 miles to the railway station because there was nowhere else we could get proper beds & food. We went to the "Traveller's Bungalow" (there are no hotels except in big towns) & said to the black butler "We want beds & dinner please" & he said "Very good madam" & ran off to get lanterns & lamps & showed us nice beds ready with white muslin mosquito nets all over them to keep the mosquitoes away. We unpacked our sheets & pillows & towels & soap, while he ran & called the cook to the little kitchen & soon he brought a very good dinner, soup & cutlets & roast pigeon & pudding. When I went to bed there was a big fat frog hopping about my floor catching ants & I was very pleased to see him. In the roof were squirrels running about & bats flying round. Early in the morning we were off again & this time we found our men (coolies they are called) waiting at the foot of the hills. First the baby & his Indian nurse were carried in a dhoolie which is like this[1] & then his mother in a litter & I in another, four men to carry each of us & luggage coolies followed with our boxes on their heads.

We had poached eggs & tinned sausages again before we started & halfway up we stopped & had some tea. Otherwise we went steadily on, tramp, tramp, or jogtrot. Sometimes quite a steep path. The coolies sang curious songs every now & then to keep up their spirits – these songs sent baby Anthony to sleep. There were tree ferns by the road & very large rhodadendrons, quite big trees of them, with red flowers. Once the men stopped & put me down on the path rather suddenly & I looked & saw a bright green snake crossing the path a little further on. They threw stones at him & he wriggled off into the bushes. I don't think he was a poisonous one but some are very dangerous so you must not go out at night without a lantern & the Indian men tap the ground with a stick as they go along to frighten the snakes. The air got cooler & cooler & when we reached the top about six o'clock I was very glad to be wrapped in a coat. We have a nice little house here, & the Indian servants were waiting for us with fire & hot baths & everything ready. No mosquitoes

[1] Another simple sketch appears here.

up here so we don't have to sleep under white nets like down on the plains[1] & very glad to have warm blankets instead of only a sheet.

I went for a long walk yesterday with a friend. We were invited by the Collector of Madura to go & see his Camp – he has come up to the hills to hunt Bison. A collector helps the Government of India by seeing that all the taxes are paid properly & the villages in order & children vaccinated & everything going on all right. He is the most powerful man in the district so all the native people come to him if they want anything or have any complaint to make and he is very busy. We started at half past eight & walked two miles along a mountain road & then the Collector's servant met us & showed us a track over the hills & along a valley, four & a half miles till we came to the camping ground. We did not see any animals as we went along except tame water buffaloes which the Indians keep for milk, but if we had been very quiet we might have seen jungle-sheep, or hyaenas, or porcupines. The camp was on a nice flat green place, one very large tent for the Collector, half of it divided off to sleep in, & half for a sitting room with a carpet on the ground & tables & chairs. Another tent for the servants, five messenger-servants (called peons) one special servant to look after the collector clothes etc & then the cooks & other kitchen servants & the huntsmen – Thirdly a hut for cooking in. So you see its very comfortable.

We were very hungry & enjoyed the luncheon which the Indian cook made in his little hut over a wooden fire. Soup & maccaroni with herring & roast snipe & cauliflowers sweet potato, and milk pudding with stewed rhubarb, and cheese & biscuits, & coffee. After that we went for a little stroll down to a village & saw where they were cultivating coffee, & the Collector showed us where he would go to shoot the bison, & pointed out the forest further on where panthers & tigers roam about sometimes. Then there was a short thunderstorm, & heavy rain but we sat quite dry in the tent, while the rain ran off in the trenches (always remember to dig trenches round a tent) & the servants brought afternoon tea carrying it across under umbrellas. When it was quite fine again we started for home, a village man walked in front shaking the rain off the bushes & grass so that we might get less wet & the collector's peon walked behind carrying our coats & the flowers we picked. There were any amount of wild roses, very big white single flowers, so we brought home a good many because we knew a baby was going to be christened today & its mother wanted to decorate the house with white flowers.

---

[1] A third sketch is included here.

Well I think this must be the longest letter you have ever had & I hope that you are not quite tired of listening to it. I wish you could have been in India with me, there are so many interesting things to see. I could tell you lots more about the towns, & the way the Indian people live, & the hideous idols many of them say prayers to, & the children I have seen in the schools – but I can't go on writing letters all night & as I said before, this is so long you may be tired of it!

I wonder how you are getting on with your lessons this year. I heard from your English granny that you were going to show some sheep at the Waiau Show. Were they black ones?

This letter will get to you just about Christopher Hugh's[1] birthday. If its in time will you please wish him many happy returns from Aunt Ursula? In another six months he will be just the age that you were when I first saw you.

I hope that you are all quite well, Daddy & Mummy & C. H. B & Miss Clark & Hillyer & Lang & everybody. Tell everybody that I asked after them & please write to me when you are not too busy.

With love from
Aunt Ursula

Private collection.

TO EMILY TULL – JANUARY 24, 1915

102 Sandgate Road, Folkestone

My dear Emily

Albert gave me your message yesterday (that you do not wish to hear from me again) – and of course I was obliged to ask for explanations of such strange conduct.[2]

So I hear that you are displeased with Albert & I have asked him to tell me the reason.

Now he begged me to say nothing to you, his one thought being always to be good to you, and I am writing this letter[3] without his knowledge, but I take full responsibility. I know it is my duty as your friend and Albert's, to try & save you from the folly & stupidity of wrecking your own happiness as well as his.

---

[1] The younger of Bethell's two nephews (b. 1910).

[2] Albert Wells, the future husband of the woman Bethell is writing to, had been one of the boys with whom she worked in her days of social work in London. Over 100 letters from Wells are extant, ending suddenly in 1915.

[3] The draft of this letter is somewhat disordered, and includes other pages not printed here, but conveying similar sentiments.

I am going to use plain language because I think you need it. It would be no kindness to slur over matters with a girl who is in danger of making a very serious mistake.

You, Emily, have a devoted lover whose one desire is to make you happy. How are you showing your gratitude to God for giving you this great blessing? How are you show[ing] your thankfulness for all these years of love & kindness? How, but by selfishness – by mistrust – by jealousy. Oh, my dear child how can you be so blind & foolish.

Albert says he would like "to take all the blame" – but where is the blame? He has done nothing wrong. He joined the army because he felt it to be his duty, & how dare you think of coming between him & his duty? No woman worth having would dream of hindering a man from his duty, no woman who fears God would dare to do that. And what do you suppose a man is worth who would go back from what his conscience says is right.

Therefore the only course open to you as his future wife was to make the army life as happy as possible for him by writing him cheering letters, by making him sure of your faith in him, & by loving him all the time he has to be away. That was your plain duty before God.

I now understand that you think that Albert broke a promise by going out to tea one evening this week. If he did make such a promise, *you* had *no* right to exact it. No girl has a right to tyrannise over her sweetheart like that. If Albert is worthy of your love, he has a right to your trust. And he *is* worthy of it. If he were *not,* then such exactions would be the surest way of driving him away from you. In any case they are unfair.

Now Emily, if you trusted him, you might be happy. But are you happy as it is? Oh no you are not. Albert is not making you unhappy you are *yourself* making your misery. Is it your idea of loving him to want him to be alone & dull at the billet? What a curious idea of love. So different from his wishes for you.

Oh no, Emily you are making a sad mistake. You will never be truly happy if you give way to that jealous & exacting spirit, it will poison all your life. Wake up, poor girl, & try to see the truth about yourself.

I think you must have written to Albert in a fit of anger & blindness and you are perhaps already regretting your selfishness. If so, you must quickly ask God to forgive you for your injustice & cruelty to Albert, & then ask Albert's forgiveness & tell him you love him & trust him wherever he goes – and that you want him to be happy, & that you will never have such foolish unkind thoughts again.

But if, as I *can't* believe, you are so stupid as to have persuaded yourself that Albert is not wholly true to you, then, all I can say is that he will be better without you, & that you do not deserve him.

But as I say, I can't believe that you can be so foolish, & so I ask you to be quick & put things right before it is too late & your lover has left England, perhaps for always.

Only a fortnight ago you were kneeling beside me in Church & making I think good resolves. Do ask God's help again to become more worthy of such a faithful & upright lad as Albert is. You have been very fortunate, don't spoil your life by blind selfishness.

I have written severely but not I think too severely. It is for your good & I send it with my love. To Albert I have only said that he must just go on loving you; I could not pretend that I think you have done right. I do not think so.

May God help you dear. Write to tell me about coming next Saturday.[1]

Your friend if you will
U Bethell.

Draft. Macmillan Brown Library. MB 558. C.11.

TO MISS SKRINE – DECEMBER 3, 1916

[No address]

Dear Miss Skrine[2]

[...]

I am sorry that I am not reassured by your explanation (concerning Miss Rolleston's position at the industry) that the hostel committee "have nothing whatever to do with the industry" Miss Hay Cooper founded the whole of her legislation on the religious question on the precedent of your procedure at the industry. She laid great stress on this & you assented – As you had acted at the Industry, so the hostel committee were to act.

---

[1] Bethell's papers include two replies from Emily, both dated the following day (25th) in which she accepts that she was wrong and Albert right, and declares herself unworthy of such a kind and loving friend.

[2] This is preserved in an envelope on which Bethell has written 'The strange episode of H. Rolleston's Weaving Studios.' The full details of the 'strange episode' can no longer be recovered, but it appears that Miss Rolleston, who had been appointed to a position in the studio by Miss Skrine, was subsequently appointed by 'the Committee' to a position in the attached hostel on Miss Skrine's insistence, in place of Miss Gunn, whose Christian Science beliefs made her less acceptable. Bethell and another committee member resigned over the affair.

Nor have you persuaded me that you voted against Miss Gunn on other than religious grounds. It was a question of Miss Gunn's views "about sin". You did not feel sure you said that she thought that what the girls had done was wrong. I suggest that on this important matter Miss Gunn might more fairly have been probed at the outset of negociations.

You certainly gave me to understand when I saw you after the committee meeting which I missed, that you disagreed with those who objected to Miss Gunn's religion. I spoke my mind to you, & you wrote to me "I know that you & I are absolutely agreed about the point at issue." Why then did you remain silent, and indeed consent, when Miss Gunn's religion was condemned at the last meeting?

I do not think that Miss Gunn was unfairly treated only because she was rejected on account of her beliefs, while Miss Rolleston who holds the same beliefs, enjoys yr. confidence at the Industry. I think that the searching questions she was asked about her beliefs should have been put at the first interview Nov. 9th or better by the Chairman or yourself before that interview, certainly before her references were taken up.

Further I do not apologise for having talked to Miss Rolleston about hostel committee affairs. I understood that she was perfectly conversant with the arrangements for the hostel & no secret business was discussed so far as I am unaware. If the "perfect trust in each other" of which you write exists between you it is hard to see how any difficulty could arise in the matter. I should certainly not have accepted a place on the committee even temporarily if I had been told that the proceedings were to be concealed from Miss Rolleston. It is clear that this question of Miss Gunn's appointment concerns her very much indeed. In any case it seems to me that in view of the "perfect trust" above referred to, a warning against discussing committee proceedings if necessary, might have been offered to Miss Rolleston first?

Lastly, I do not quite understand your words about "this religion business, which I loathe as much as you do." I do not follow you here. You have accepted the religious test offered by Miss Hay Cooper as representing your own stand point, so you cannot mean that. I confess that I do not feel in sympathy with the standpoint which imposes this test, but I did not say that I loathed it. To my mind Miss Hay Cooper's questions relating to this test only resulted in a sad misunderstanding of Miss Gunn's beliefs, but I did not hear you suggest that such a misunderstanding had arisen. I dislike a procedure which first suggests to a candidate that "a certain natural religion" (to quote Miss Hay Cooper's words) is desired, hear what her religious denomination is, decides to appoint her (under 2 conditions of course wh. were fulfilled) & at the last moment makes a searching religious examination, in the replies to which the committee votes against the candidate. Least of all, as I have already said, do I understand your own attitude about Miss Rolleston.

I have been frank to the point you may judge of discourtesy. I believe it to be the best way but I am not unmindful at the same time of all that you & your friends are doing for the girls a work which I humbly admire & revere.

Signed Yours sincerely
U B

Draft. Macmillan Brown Library. MB 558. C.8.

II: 1924–1934

TO ARTHUR MAYHEW – [*ante* JULY 15, 1929]

[Rise Cottage, Cashmere Hills, Christchurch, N.Z.]

Very grateful to you. Accept delightedly and waiting publishers first mail giving all particulars.

Draft. Macmillan Brown Library. MB 558. C6.

TO FRANK SIDGWICK – JULY 15, 1929

Rise Cottage, Cashmere Hills, Christchurch, N.Z.

Dear Mr. Sidgwick[1]

– Not "sir" because I infer from Arthur Mayhew's letter that we were introduced upwards of 40 years ago. I have already cabled to him my ready acceptance of what I feel to be your very sporting offer to publish the slight inventions of an unknown dépaysée.[2] He sends me your questions & comments with instructions to reply categorically & finally, which I now proceed to do. There is indeed no time for further reference to me if the book is to be a possible Xmas present in NZ this year. Forgive me if I am somewhat longwinded – you know how anxious one is to think of everything before the dentist puts on the gag.

First. I authorise Arthur Mayhew to settle any points for me if & where you may think necessary to refer them to him and I gratefully avail myself of his kind offer to correct proofs. But generally speaking I am glad to leave the production of the little book entirely in your hands, & what you settle I shall receive in buxomness, meanwhile merely indicating a few small prejudices.[3]

Title. Would "*From* a Garden in the Antipodes" be too long? I think "From" (though not as good as "Aus")[4] helps to describe the nature of the book's content, which in fact began as metrical messages to Ruth Mayhew now Lady Head, and nine of the pieces I've sent are directly

---

[1] Frank Sidgwick, a long-time friend of Arthur Mayhew, founded the publishing firm of Sidgwick & Jackson in 1908, together with Robert Jackson and the well-known Oxford bibliographer, R. B. McKerrow.

[2] Fr. Literally, 'a displaced person.' Bethell perhaps means 'exile,' as she describes herself later in the letter.

[3] The draft originally read 'minor preferences.'

[4] Ger. 'Out of.'

addressed to her and if some are just exclamations many have an absent acquaintance in mind.[1]

[...]

Price. I agree that anyone who wd. pay a florin for this matter would rather pay a crown for it in a comely get-up but we must remember that bookshops here clip out the published prices on the packet & charge 1/6 for a 1/- & 5/6 for a 4/- book & so on (so that one prefers if there's time to write Home & pay 4d postage on a parcel of several volumes) [...]

Blurb. This is the snag! I clearly see that I must agree to anything that will from publishers point of view help the book on but confess to clinging with positive passion desperation nervous persistence positive claustrophobia[2] to private anonymity. In England no matter but in provincial NZ I assure you that publicity is a really painful affair. I suppose it must be "New Zealand" but *must* I be "*a lady*" – couldn't I possibly be taken for a pensive old gentleman? NZ won't understand, if they discover me, this pose of "exile" in the "sister of a prominent sheepfarmer"[3] – there *is* no better place than NZ! (My own friends will understand of course.) I am by birth & choice *English*, but I have lived in NZ a good deal & shouldn't like to be impolite to it. I sent a suggestion to Arthur Mayhew which might serve here perhaps. Something like this

Episodes	
Notes	from a NZ garden
Messages &	introducing (one means "*featuring*")
[4]Meditations	The Gardener, the Housewife, a distant Friend, a large Persian Cat, a small Orange Tree, (? and plants, pests, postmen, passersby etc ...)

Pseudonym. Indispensable. Evelyn Hayes was chosen in haste for the Australian magazine[5] – Sounds rather flabby but there it is – Hayes – Sir Henry of Cork – my great great grandfather deported for life to Botany Bay for attempted abduction of Quaker heiress. Built fine house &

[1] Mayhew must have seen this, for in a later letter he expresses the hope that the 'absent acquaintance' may include more than just Ruth.

[2] Bethell tried out all these variations in her draft.

[3] Marmaduke Bethell was, by this time, prominent in local social and political affairs, having been Chairman of the Amuri County Council for over 10 years. Thyra Bethell was equally prominent in local affairs, leading voluntary work during the war, organising Red Cross nursing during the epidemic of 1918, and helping establish the local Amuri Hospital in 1922.

[4] In the margin between 'Messages' and 'Meditations' she noted 'No that's spiritualism.'

[5] For an identification, see the following letter.

grounds (now public tea gardens) with convict labour. Imported several tons of Irish earth to avert snakes from garden. Evelyn – cowardly vagueness of gender – (perhaps sound association with Evelyn Hope) E. Hayes if you like.[1]

Horticultural. I am a serious but not very experienced gardener. Have read them over carefully from the *English* point of view & think there is no real stumbling block but the Biddybid[2] which I've since learnt to be a Maori word & should be written bidibidi although commonly pronounced as I wrote it.* I suggest that in the first line it be spelt bidibid' with apostrophe for the sake of exactitude and in second instance (where it sounds so) bidibidi. It is a native plant, recognized by Government as a noxious weed. The seed is a burr rather bigger than a large pea & gets among the sheep's wool – (I've seen sheep quite brown with it.) I am told that it is a variety of *acaena*. But I really don't think its worth while putting a note about the *one* New Zealand plant – most people wd. have some way of finding out if interested – the rest are *proper* names, e.g. Omi-Kin-Kan – a japanese variety of orange – "Ruth" a well-known hybrid tea Rose – and so on. I am more afraid of Colonial criticism! One friend already objects that wattles are not everblooming here.[3] I only meant thay they go on a long while in suitable spots in NZ (they are Australian of course). The different varieties carry on from autumn to Spring.

[Added at end of paragraph] *Colonials are wont to slur over the last vowel of maori words.

Acknowledgements. Twelve of the pieces were printed in [Sydney].[4] I have written to relation in Sydney[5] who knows the editor asking her to obtain permission to reprint, whatever is required, & send direct to you. This will save a mail. I did offer a longer version of Roses to the editor of the annual of the NRS (of which I am a member) (National Rose Society) *not for money* & Mr. Courtney Page wrote thanking, but it wasn't printed this year [...].

---

[1] In a note written in a copy of *From a Garden* (now in the Macmillan Brown Library), Bethell identifies the 'fine house' as Vaucluse, and dismisses the name Evelyn as 'just stupidity.'

[2] The word occurs in 'Crisis' (*Collected Poems*, p.23).

[3] The reference is to 'Response' (*Collected Poems*, p.1) which originally read 'everlasting wattle' (see line 11).

[4] In fact, only nine poems were published in Sydney, as Bethell explains in the following letter.

[5] Identified in a later letter of Sidgwick as Mary Dundas Allen.

Number & Sequence of pieces. I really did not suppose that they would be accepted en bloc if at all – and sent 58 tentatively, not knowing how many wd. go to make a book, having cut out some I thought too dull.

Two or three included I thought might be considered too trivial or uninteresting, e.g Nos 6 (Shrubs) & 27 (Oranges). Those you mention as being out of place at the end are some I thought might be out of tune with the rest – having too much of sensibility or sentimentality? or perhaps too much alike? And what about that 58th & last one would it not be better to end with the Easter lines?[1] I have not yet really said goodbye to the garden though I am likely to do so next year, the duty which brought me back to NZ having been fulfilled.[2] Please cut out or include as you see fit. The *order* was arranged to follow the season of the year & to mix the subjects. They were made during two or three years. I have gone over them again carefully and put them as I think they should be if all are retained. Might need rearranging if some are done away with. If one began to explain about seasons & so on however it wd. be difficult because this garden although in the cold South island grows warm north island things, being above the frosts, on the other hand there is risk from cold storms. Altogether I hope people won't take the book too pedantic horticulturally. Also, as to little labels or names of poems please use or not as you think.

People in England who might be notified. I append a short list which I may add to later. Have lost touch with a good many friends during 10 years absence – lost track of their addresses. One's poor friends & relations wd. not be useful & the rich are apt not to be interested in verse. But we shall do our best, & I have begun to prod people out here. I shall hang my head if the work does not pay its way – am not thinking of royalties! The construction of this garden has eaten up many pounds & it would be nice if it brought in a few pence – but, and this brings me to my

Reasons for seeking publication. Not the ghost of a thought of it to begin with. They were slipped into letters. Then when they kept on bubbling up, friends here read them & liked them, & wished that they could be printed in a book. I could not afford to have this done, but finally as one knowledgeable friend said that "*some* publisher *might*" & another even that "some publisher *should*" so I decided to try for it and only then because I knew I could ask for AM's mediation.[3] And am I not

---

[1] Bethell intended to conclude with 'Vale.' See *Collected Poems*, p. 103.

[2] This is one of many occasions on which Bethell indicates a desire to leave New Zealand. The duty she speaks of appears to have involved caring for her ailing mother, who died in 1927.

[3] Arthur Mayhew.

right in thinking that it is because he sent it that you entertained my MS for a moment in the first place?

Decentralisation.[1] Have you never seen a book produced in N.Z.?[2]

Draft. Macmillan Brown Library. MB 558. L1.[3]

TO FRANK SIDGWICK – NOVEMBER 4, 1929

Rise Cottage, Cashmere Hills, Christchurch, N. Z.

Dear Mr. Sidgwick

Thank you for your letter of Sep 10th. I am glad that you have written to me, for I was just preparing to put into a letter to Arthur Mayhew some twisters (I think the Boy Scouts called them) meant for you. Chiefly this, that if the book has no success with the Public, it will be "up to me" (colonial locution) to remember you in my will, so much interest and amusement have you brought into my life, and into the lives of our little circle here, by accepting my poems, & first ennobling them in giving them that name.

E.G. 1 My excited hairdressing lady asked whether I could make a poem about a *Permanent Wave* – thereby creating a fresh moral problem, for I said that, if I couldn't, I supposed I oughtn't to have one!

E.G. 2 It has set me reading any available books about the art & craft of poetry: the Laureate upon Vers Libre[4] – and Abbé Brémond[5] – a little book *Thamyris* which suggests the *Garden* as a subject for verse[6] – and I discovered your own little book about the Ballad[7] (what else of

[1] Sidgwick had written to Mayhew (May 14, 1929): 'There is always trouble in publishing stuff of colonial or provincial interest here in London. I often recommend decentralisation.'

[2] The draft is unsigned. A further page exists containing some notes and corrections, and ending with the comment 'My MS was typed by a girl unused to literary work, think I have noticed & corrected most of her mistakes, but the faults in & absence of punctuation are my own ignorance. Proofreader please supply.' It seems likely that these were intended for Mayhew (the proofreader), rather than Sidgwick.

[3] Later letters from Bethell to Sidgwick have been preserved and are held in the Bodleian Library, Oxford (see below) but there is nothing that corresponds to this draft.

[4] The Poet Laureate in 1929 was Robert Bridges. Bethell is probably referring to his essay, 'Humdrum & Harum-Scarum. A Lecture on Free Verse,' first published in 1922 in *London Mercury*, then included in Volume II of his *Collected Essays Papers &c.*

[5] Abbé Henri Brémond was a favourite author of Bethell. She may be referring here to *Prière et Poésie* or to *La Poésie pure; avec un débat sur la poésie*. Both were published in Paris in 1926.

[6] *Thamyris: or, Is there a future for poetry?* by R. C. Trevelyan (1925).

[7] Sidgwick's booklet, *Ballad* (1914), was published in a series 'The Art and Craft of Letters.'

yours is there for me to discover I wonder?) and *The Death of Cock Robin*[1] – which states (page 10) that "there is at the present moment no publisher who would at his own expense publish a *new* poet. (If there is, let him speak, that we may all look at a brave man)" – *Have* you spoken? or should it be my pleasant daring to write to (would it be "Professor"?) Edward Thompson & reveal you? as in Riverside Nights the curtain was drawn with the proclamation "AND SUCH A MAN WAS MR. PEABODY!"[2]

I now take up the points you mention.

Price. I agree that the NZ market is almost negligible. Sales will be to friends & acquaintances. I have been studying verse published in local papers.

Text. I realize that some of my suggestions & amendments will have come too late. They were of little consequence. It all went much quicker than I anticipated. I thought that publishers argued a good deal preliminarily with their protégés. I am glad you are ending with *Dirge*. *Yahweh.*[3] See Concise Oxford Dictionary under "Jah" where my spelling is confirmed. See also the *New Commentary* (very weighty) just published by S.P.C.K.[4] Pages 68, 648 & 672. Apparently there is *no* correct form but P.672 supports Yahweh & I gather that scholars liked this form at the date when I wrote – '27 or '28. (I like the *sound* of Yahweh.) "Jehovah" was *not* "hallowed" for *me*. On the contrary I misliked Jehovah. Complex due to classic writers & writers such as S. Butler & pietistic childhood instruction. (Dear me, how pleasantly learned all this sounds – I could almost fancy myself back in venerable Oxford!)

Punctuation. I should have been quite unable to take sides in your duels with A.M., having neglected to study this subject, & long ago fell back on the feminine "—" I tried to use commas on the first page of this letter & was speedily "bushed" – Only I am on terms of affection with the colon dividing each verse of the Psalms, & I've often felt the need of a sign something between ? & ! & less emphatic than either.

Acknowledgements. (Yes, much handsomer than without the "e" – I had to give my cable to a friend to send off. I hope she put in the e.) So sorry for this little confusion.[5] I suppose that Psycho-Analysis (still in

---

[1] *Cock Robin's decease: an irregular inquest* by Edward Thompson was published as part of the second series of Hogarth Essays (1928).

[2] *Riverside Nights* was a comic review written by A. P. Herbert and Nigel Playfair, produced at The Lyric in London in 1926, the year Bethell and Effie Pollen made their last visit to England.

[3] The word occurs in 'Appel' (*Collected Poems*, p. 23).

[4] *A New Commentary on Holy Scripture, including the Apocrypha* by Charles Gore, Henry Goudge and Alfred Guillaume (1928).

[5] Sidgwick had written: 'note on the original MS. says *nine* (you specify them by number) appeared in 'The Home': your letter of July 15th says *twelve*.... Meanwhile your Sydney

fashion?) could account for my substitution of twelve for *nine* – correctly stated when sending MS. I might have suspected my Sydney cousin's somewhat impressionistic methods, but it seemed so convenient that she should ring up her friend Mr. Leon Gellert (yes, real name!) editor of the two Sydney periodicals, for it was she who sent some of my verses to him in 1927 & he took (& paid for) matter for 3 *pages* (hence her "three" poems). And he put them in the humbler one The Home, not the highbrow Art in Australia. And she told me that he would *like* acknowledgements tho' not insisting on them.[1]

And apparently she has taken seriously our joking "Chinese Poems". Term arising thus:– I read some lines to my Raven.[2] "Why that's not p(h)oetry" she said scornfully (she's irish) expecting rhyme – "I could do that *misself*" – "Oh," said I "this is like those chinese ones you know" – "Oh *Chinese*" she said, & we let it go at that. Otherwise they were referred to as "Your so called poems" – But since your intervention, Mr. Sidgwick, she's been more disposed to look on verse making as a legitimate occupation for gentlewomen in reduced circumstances.

Agreement. In Re. *Anthologies* ("He's pulling your leg" croaked the Raven. "Oh no, dear, surely not! I *don't* think he would do that – and surely not on *official paper*!") Entirely in your hands please.

And lastly your delightful query about "another book". Here is where *I* should be tempted to doubt your Bona Fides, but will believe it to be further evidence of a Brave Man's Courage.

Yes, one must find expression somehow, and there is, continually, occasion for such expression. The bother is, the terrible practicality of colonial life. So little time to think things out & write them down. The birds fly about in the air but one can't stop to put salt on their tails. *If* the garden book has any success, I could forward samples later on – I've always wanted to do bits from my NZ childhood & so on & call it "Thy Tablets, Memory" (but I daresay someone has taken that name already!)[3] One such, unfinished, actually put tears in my Raven's eyes!

---

cousin Mary Dundas Allen writes an undated letter to say that you have asked her to write to me about 'her Chinese poems, 3 of which were published two years ago in a Sydney monthly, 'Art in Australia'.' (Sept. 10, 1929).

[1] Bethell's contributions to *The Home* were 'Time,' 'Nomenclature' and 'Discipline' published together as 'The garden,' *The Home* 1 August 1927, p. 24; 'Gale SSW,' 'Compensation,' 'Citrus,' and 'Surprise' published together as 'Omi-Kin-Kan,' *The Home* 1 August 1927, p. 26; 'Ruth H. T.' and 'Verdure' published together as 'Ruth,' *The Home* 1 August 1927, p. 32.

[2] One of several pet names Bethell used for Effie Pollen. See 'Grace' (*Collected Poems*, p. 3).

[3] Bethell did use the phrase, in 'Envoy' (*Collected Poems,* p. 41). It originally occurs in Matthew Arnold's love poem, 'A Memory-Picture.'

And early Sunday morning walks to church, some 50 or 60 minutes, noticing. But of course, garden vignettes with a hint of background are one thing, and boundless landscapes with corresponding admiration quite another! A case for rhetoric? (Thamyris, page 74) I daresay too dangerous and difficult ground for me. I have many fragments of these, however.

I wish that I had enough knowledge & skill to do a sheep station all the year round, but I havn't. People don't know what they've *got*. It would be nice to break their perfume-boxes for them.

For my old age, together with a set of lace-caps, I have in hand a book of quotations for every day all on the theme of life on pilgrimage, beginning with Chaucer & Raleigh. For old age, when I shall have time to read plenty of books. No one has truly lived who has not compiled an anthology!

Most days bring something – lately I made a song about willows; to be set to music for a girls' school I think.[1] And lately I was by the death-bed of a lovely girl of 20. (T.B. They – "T.B.s" – come to this hill) The little sister ran to me sobbing with *two pennies*. But all that too poignant to write about, only I did make some verses for them afterwards, which comforted them.

I have no more objections to report; except that my friends can't bear my nom de plume! Nor can I, it was too hastily assumed, but I have no gift of invention.

My sister's request for *six* copies of the notice was characteristically modest. She has, I assure you, been doing some very useful spade-work.

Yours very sincerely
Ursula Bethell

I enclose one "Sunday morning" and the little requiem (tho' it wouldn't be for publication!)[2]

Bodleian Library Oxford. MS Sidgwick & Jackson 142, fols. 75-77v.

---

[1] This may refer to an unpublished poem, 'A Song,' which opens with the lines 'All the willows, all the willows / Have put on green apparel.' The poem is extant in TS in Schroder's papers. A full transcription is found in Charlotte Elder's thesis (p. 127).

[2] Bethell enclosed a draft of 'Rainy Morning' (*Collected Poems,* p. 42) and a copy of a poem 'For Melva's Birthday. Oct 27.' The latter is a memorial poem of five stanzas, each of them working an acrostic on the name Melva. At the top of the poem, Bethell wrote 'You see that I woo them with a very simple first verse for they are simple people & the device of her name was to please them. She said one day 'I should like to get up at lilac time.' She died Oct 16.' Copies of the poem are extant in Bethell's papers in the Macmillan Brown Library.

TO FRANK SIDGWICK – DECEMBER 5, 1929

Rise Cottage, Cashmere Hills, Christchurch, N.Z.

Dear Mr. Sidgwick

Your letter of Oct 31 has come in time to be thanked for together with a package of five copies of The Book, following on the very early first copy. If these six copies are a present it is a generous one, I think, and five more times do I proudly inscribe "From the Gardener". Reactions to Notices are coming along too. My Melbourne University friend reports that she is about to tour the chief bookshops there showing pained surprise if they can't produce The Garden. We are delighted with the look of the book. (The Raven has now wholeheartedly adopted the volume & says "To think that *we* have produced *this*!") & in fact ever since it came I've been in the Glow of Piglet ("The pink went slowly up Piglet's nose to his ears and *settled there*")[1] The paper, the print, the size, the arrangement, the colour – as Raven says Its all so *superior*. (I really think I must post you a copy of a little vol. of local verse recently published to show you what I have escaped – "There but for the grace of God goes" ...) The *only* thing I regret just a little is that the name of the book isn't written on the flat side of the cover so that lying on the table – – but that would no doubt have run to too much expense – And we shall I daresay keep the charming dust-jacket. I think I must tell you, at the risk of being prolix, how the other day an old original Club boy dating back 35 years, a carpenter, not "educated" on being introduced to the book (he hadn't known of it at all) would not put it down & turned over page after page exclaiming "My word I wonder whether anyone else can see you in these things as I do (*like* I do it was really) – I'd have known it was you anyhow".

And I've a feverish message for you from an ex High School girl assuring you that the new generation of N.Z. *loves* poetry – *reads* poetry – and will ultimately *buy* poetry.

Now referring to your letter:–

Agreement. (also to hand)

I will sign as directed & return by next mail. Nothing for dispute!

Acknowledgement & My Cable.

The thing is of no consequence as you say, but it seemed "up to me" to state the facts. Now I post a copy of the book to my cousin in Sydney & she rings up her Leon Gellert & explains that it was her fault & the incident is closed. I think he wouldn't consider my pieces classy enough for his Art in Australia. The Home was their suitable milieu.

---

[1] From the penultimate chapter of *The House at Pooh Corner*.

So "E. Sidgwick" *is* your sister! I was asking A.I.M.[1] about this. We are indeed pleased that she likes the book, being agreed admirers of her work. (Raven counts herself, I think justly, to be a connoisseur of fiction, though she has hitherto overlooked Poetry.) I remember the little Ethel perfectly – long fair hair, composed deportment, & a discreet, demure but very knowing look.[2] When, later on, Ruth Head told me about the Novels, it fitted.

I think after all, I wont send samples of the memory Tablets (sounds like a medicine!) Raven has always said that the garden verses are only acceptable on a string, as a necklace. I think it wd. be the same with these others. I'm a little concerned about the Laureate. Rumours about his latest book lead me to suppose that he has said (and perfectly of course) what I was after trying to say – Beauty meeting one as a child & now in old age again, in the same place, meeting one, in the early morning & evening.[3] Well, well, he has every right to get in first as the boys say.

Of course, *the* thing to do in New Zealand would be Sheep Run – waving tussocks, flocks & herds, dust, rushing rivers, silences. I've lately made friends with a young man of the new generation, who might be able.[4] He has just been appointed to a peripatetic, or more exactly itinerant, sleeping in motorcar, lectureship, University extension in this province – having qualified for it after 5 years of farming & football – an excellent person. He has seen & felt pastoral NZ & can *say* but deplores that he can't *sing*. I told him that if he would attempt a prose Kalendar I would try Choruses. Our problem would be how to bring in the Station Ledger, which looms very large in reality – the problem of all everyday life – the Ledger!

Yours sincerely
M U Bethell

P.S. I will ask Arthur to pay the press cutters – thank you for arranging that. What a dear he has been about the book to be sure, taking all that trouble, with more than enough to do already! I hope & think it has brought him pleasure however. I am telling him that the only

---

[1] Arthur Mayhew.

[2] Ethel Sidgwick (1877-1970) was a popular novelist, well regarded in the early part of her career. She also wrote plays for children, all her work being published by her brother's firm. Sidgwick noted in his reply that his sister had never had fair hair, being much the darkest of the family.

[3] Bridges published his most ambitious work, the philosophical poem *The Testament of Beauty*, in October of 1929.

[4] Geoffrey Alley, formerly Southland farmer and All Black, was employed as a WEA tutor working in rural adult education. He later became head of the Country Library Service, and then of the National Lbrary.

correction I would make is "come" for "came" on page 47.[1] I must have overlooked that mistake on the typed page.

(In future editions perhaps? – just my fun).

I note that there is the same printer's ornament surrounding my paper jacket as on The Love Concealed[2] – most agreeable.

Bodleian Library Oxford. MS Sidgwick & Jackson 142, fols. 84-86.

TO FRANK SIDGWICK – JANUARY 26, 1931

Rise Cottage, Cashmere Hills, Christchurch, N.Z.

Dear Mr. Sidgwick

(You "invite correspondence", and you "think" that I shall answer on a type-writer; painfully aware of the growing disintegration of my pen-writing, the result of haste, I take the latter intimation to be of the nature of a royal command. This is my bought-on-the-instalment-plan and not yet half my own Portable Remington, the darling; I type very well indeed don't you think, and really quite rapidly with the forefinger of each hand; but don't feel yet that my chat flows as freely as from a pen-point, and I have to fight the tendency towards beginning every line with a capital, as with verse, and the formal letters seem to call for precise punctuation, so tiresome – but this parenthesis doesn't look nearly as long as it would written, does it!)

Eh bien! You have added a great deal to the hilarity and general contentment of my – of our Christmastime. I begin with the latter-comer, the broadsheet, which was here by New Year, a very good shot indeed for Xmas in the Antipodes; anything arriving from England during January counts as on the Xmas target. Your Rubber Bottel is delightful![3] I'm so impressed by your knowing that they may finish up as garden-kneelers – I thought that was a bit of sacred lore known only to one of quite the inner circle of the craft of gardeners such as myself. There is only one line which strikes me (though to be sure I'm not very well up in the original) as *not* quite as réussi[4] as the rest - - but I presume!

[1] The error occurs in 'Elect' (*Collected Poems*, p. 18); another is in 'Verdure' (*CP*, p. 21), where 'macrocarpa' is spelt 'microcarpa.'

[2] *The Love Concealed* is the title of a collection of verse by Laurence Housman, published by Sidgwick & Jackson in 1928.

[3] Sidgwick was in the habit of writing 'broadsheets' of humorous and parodic verse, often sending them out to authors and correspondents. I have not seen the one referred to here, but it may well be a parody of a traditional ballad known as 'The Leathern Bottel.' In addition to his book on the ballad, Sidgwick edited collections of traditional ballads.

[4] Fr. 'Accomplished, successful.'

Now I wonder how many people there are in N.Z., or in England even, who have slept as I have in a charcoal warmed bed? Speaking as a rheumatic, the water heating is a very poor substitute though for convenience no doubt much better as you point out - - I imagine that the new-fangled electric dodges one hears of give that dry cosiness to the bones.

Now for the letter (of Oct 28) when it came I cried to myself am I not one with Currer Bell and all the rural authoresses of the past to whom Great Publishers held out their sceptres! And never to such utter rusticity as mine! And now for the Faggot[1] – when *it* came, I said to the Raven, oh do look here dear what a Xmas present has come – a book from Mr. Sidgwick – from THE publisher and she said "*How* exciting." To what you wrote about it in your letter I gave the once-over, as you say, but did not read again, and have forgot so as to come to the team without parti-pris;[2] January has been an unquiet month and brought no chance of giving attention to the reading of it but when and as soon as the opportunity comes, I shall give myself that pleasure, and then the pleasure of addressing you again. These months past I have been wanting to type out and send you some bits of letters and reviews to show you that The Garden is having its little and unprofitable day in N.Z. Unprofitable so far as money is concerned. I am indeed sorry to hear that it is going so slowly in England. One Hopes that your Faggot ladies have a much wider circle of interested friends or stimulated public, otherwise it seems that the publication of verse must represent a libation to the muses!

Here our life goes on much the same, apart from irruptions of the outside world. Michael continues to make sea-beaches of seed-plots, we still have our little jokes. Only that N.Z. is under a financial cloud, like all the rest of the world; but N.Z. has never I think yet felt the pinch of the war. Wool is down, drought is prevalent. Sheep, our mainstay, are perishing of thirst in one place and being driven into the sea in another because they are not worth their keep. I have been warned not to expect my income. Hitherto we've owned to a modest competency, now we fall back on faith, and we have decided to take our adversity as a jest and a work of art. The raven is practising economy foods, and I have in hand a little jeu d'esprit[3] of which I hear her humming the two first lines

[1] *A Faggot of Verse* was an anthology of work by five English women poets, who had all separately been rejected by publishers for economic reasons. In his letter, Sidgwick ranked the five poets, and asked Bethell's opinion of them. Bethell quotes at length from Sidgwick's preface to the volume in a letter to Pat Lawlor (Sept. 2, 1940).

[2] Fr. 'Bias.'

[3] Fr. 'A lively jest.'

"P(h)overty, S. Francis' spouse Welcome to our little house";[1] in fact its a blessing in disguise because it makes us realize how thin our ice has been, and we shall keep accounts, a laudable habit. In short we are happier than before, and after all our wolf has not yet left the backwoods.

Since the prospect of joining our friends and relations has now receded into farther distance, I have been giving some attention to N.Z. scenery (in the intervals of a slight plunge into the Good Works of a retired parish-worker) and some what one might call ecclesiastical occasional verse. This brings me you see to your third prevision, that I should "allude vaguely" to a next M.S. That was a risky thing to say! I shall be definite not vague and say that some of my "stuff" as they call it in N.Z. is in the hands of A. Mayhew, and would be produced on demand: in fact, he wrote more than kindly about it, and asked whether it should be passed on to you; I reply, of course, oh no we wont bother Mr. Sidgwick; for I know there mustn't be an also-ran before the garden has reached the goal (I really should not fall into N.Z. racing parlance I get it mixed-up.)

I asked A.M. to pass on to you an ambitious N.Z. magazine which gave me a useful (but to me rather revolting) review. It represents our highest plane of journalism. The very nice half-australian editor called on me lately – (it emanates from Wellington the capital city whence he on holiday) and invited my contribution, which I now have sent, just as well in these days to set up a local agency for my wares.[2]

You speak of D'Arcy Cresswell.[3] I made the acquaintance of his mother last year, and she read me some of his letters which convinced me of the lad's sincerity, and they are written in precisely the same style as he affects in his book, so that is his natural expression.

But how disappointing is his poetry in the light of his autobiography![4] And when I read (at a bookshop counter meanly) just the same ideas as his expressed in the preface to some much worse verse by a ridiculous person called de Montalk,[5] I infer that after all N.Z. has

---

[1] Bethell enclosed a copy of this unpublished (and unpolished) light-hearted poem about their reduced circumstances. 'Financial Depression, 1931' consists of 14 loosely-rhymed 6-line stanzas.

[2] The ambitious magazine was *Art in New Zealand*, edited by the Melbourne-born Charles Marris. It included a review of *From a Garden* by John Dene, Vol. 3, No. 9 (Sept. 1930), 53-54, and printed Bethell's poem 'Lever de Rideau' in Vol. 3, No. 11 (March, 1931), 190.

[3] D'Arcy Cresswell (1896-1960) was at this time living in England, seeking to establish himself as a poet in London literary circles.

[4] Cresswell's autobiography, *The Poet's Progress*, was published in 1930 (having been serialised in *The Press* in 1928).

[5] Count Geoffrey Potocki de Montalk (1903-1997), a colourfully eccentric character who laid claim to the throne of Poland, had recently left New Zealand to establish himself in

not produced an original thinker in D'A. But I do like The Poet's Progress all the same, and shall always be grateful to D'Arcy for my first and best review.[1] I find that people out here thought him an egotistical mountebank, but *that* by no means = damnation. His mother told me that he was engaged upon an anthology, which I thought rather a senile occupation, but it may turn out to be "significant" as the saying goes.[2]

Enough of typing. We are tired.

To come back to the brittle topic! It occurs to me that some of the bits I sent to A.M. have been retouched here & there so I shall weakmindedly enclose other copies, samples of present season's experiments.[3] The 1st 5 in the bunch, the latest, have not gone to Arthur yet. He has many others!

I had some conversation with school teachers and others about what's going to happen, in the Southern Hemisphere, about the associations of words. Its all topsy turvey. June to a child here suggests frost, December picnics; the northwind is hot, the southerly wild & bitter. How will literature manage? One country schoolmistress told me that she had to change the names of the months in poetry to make it credible to her children![4] Thus spoiling the poetry. This challenged me to put in the names of months deliberately – thus *October* & *April* – in the ones I send. And others in The Turret Hour Glass Set.[5] But someday I shall make a proper book from my N.Z. childhood – "Thy Tablets, Memory." In my next I shall enclose the Garden testimonials & readings of A Faggot.

Yours sincerely
M U Bethell

Bodleian Library Oxford. MS Sidgwick & Jackson 142, fols. 96-98.

London. After being jailed for publishing an obscene poem, he moved to the South of France from where he continued to produce a steady stream of poetry.

[1] He reviewed *From a Garden* for the NZPA on Nov. 11, 1929; a typescript copy of the review is extant in Bethell's papers.

[2] The anthology is identified in *The Oxford Companion* as a commission from the Bodley Head, which was later rejected by the publishers.

[3] Bethell enclosed drafts of the following: 'Levavi Oculos;' 'October Spring' published in *Day & Night* as 'Spring Storm;' 'The Publick Baptism of an Infant;' 'Midnight;' 'Rose-Wreath;' 'Autumn Afternoon;' 'Waves;' 'Weathered Rocks;' 'Summer Daybreak;' and 'Showers of Leaves.'

[4] Sidgwick responded: 'I should very much like to know what your country schoolmistress did.... What a lark! (or does one say what an apteryx in N.Z.?).... it can't be done; you can't speak of 'hoar August' in L'Allegro. No: write your own poems, N.Z.' (April 22, 1931)

[5] I have not been able to identify this reference.

To J H E Schroder – July 21, 1931

Rise Cottage, Cashmere Hills, Christchurch, N.Z.

Dear Mr. Schröder[1]

Geoffrey Alley, who rang up to congratulate me upon your very delightful review in last Saturday's "Press",[2] encouraged me to waive anonymity & thank you for it – may I use his encouragement as introduction & do so? Morning paper & spectacles were handed to me on Saturday with the words "Read *that*. Settle down to it. Its *almost* posthumous!" – But this is divine courtesy keeping the best wine to the last[3] – When my friend Mr. Barker[4] told me that he had sent the book to you I was vexed with him, insisting that it was not to be pushed but make its own way. I thought that it must have become known to the literary editor of the Press in the regular way of trade, so to speak, having been reviewed very well (and characteristically) by D'Arcy Cresswell for the N. Z. Press Assn. & inferred that it was judged to be negligible – But your notice was well worth waiting for. May I say that you are the first reviewer (not 'critic' because friends have sympathised) who, like Mr. Frank Sidgwick himself, appears to hear & see things as I did when writing!

The column goes to Mr. Sidgwick at once; he will enjoy the manner of it, as well as the recognition. Moreover, from another point of view, it should cheer him up. The times are nebulous & publication of verse a risky venture (see note in S & J's "A Faggot of Verse" issued last year). My little book hasn't repaid its expenses yet & I wish it would, & your recommendation will count.

Believe me
Yours very truly
M. U. Bethell

---

1 J. H. E. Schroder (1895-1980) was principally a journalist (although he also wrote some poetry, essays and reviews). He was responsible for the literary page of the Christchurch *Sun* from 1927, then, more significantly, of the *Press* from 1929, where he was in a position to promote a number of writers through the 1930s.

2 Schroder's review of *From a Garden* appeared on July 18, 1931 – 21 months after the book's publication.

3 See John 2: 10.

4 W. E. Barker was an orchardist at Peel Forest, married to Bethell's cousin, Brenda Lillie.

(The Dust jacket, if a bona fide query, Mr. Sidgwick's arrangement of my suggestions.)[1]

Alexander Turnbull Library. fMS-018.

TO FRANK SIDGWICK – JULY 24, 1931

Rise Cottage, Cashmere Hills, Christchurch, N.Z.

Dear Mr. Sidgwick

How ruth-ful I feel when I think of you hastening with the cry "Noblesse oblige!" – to answer my March 23rd by return of post – followed as I fear that was by a Supplement! But now, I have something much better to send – rather late, to be sure, & I wish it had emerged before the Slump – but not too late I hope to affect sales – a really good Review in our local Daily. This man (Schröder by name) carries weight with our small band of literates: he does a column every Saturday under the same heading & does not christen the little book "trivial" – tho' it is that no doubt in a sense.[2] My coadjutor handed me the page & my spectacles saying "There, read *that*. Its *almost* posthumous!" I wonder whether to send the whole paper – mightn't it be cast aside unexamined? Yet it places Culture in our Midst rather well, & the Helen Simpson who writes about Cowper is the friend who described the effect of the Garden upon her ironing afternoon[3] – I decide to enclose cutting as well as post paper – you may not have time to bother with latter.

I've been asking young men & women about the seasons in literature – they say they have a double consciousness, one for N.Z. but feel they know by imagination all about spring in England. However, when one says "January" their first response seems to be "long, hot days".

You offer a reward (= postage of this letter – our postal fees have been *doubled* at one stroke) for author's name of "Truth smashed to Earth" etc. I hazard the guess "Lowell" remembering something about Bigelow Papers in a school prize on American Literature but I "write

---

[1] Schroder's review began by admiring the layout and typography of the jacket: 'Perhaps Evelyn Hayes planned this? Or ... might it not have been Mr. Frank Sidgwick, turning his wit to a note of charming and complimentary resemblance?'

[2] Schroder's column was called 'Trivia.'

[3] On the same page as Schroder's review, *The Press* carried an article, 'The Bicentenary of William Cowper.' The author, Helen Simpson, was a close friend of Bethell's; she completed an English Ph. D. at the University of London in 1923, and taught, for brief periods, at the Christchurch Teachers Training College and at Canterbury University College. The note about ironing refers to a letter from Simpson to Bethell, in which the former speaks of being repeatedly distracted from her ironing by reading *From a Garden*.

away from my books" (stored these dozen years in England). If this is a lucky shot please hand award to a charity.[1]

In re vocabulary – I thought "entelechy" *such* a handy word to have about! – and, please, "Mattamore" alleged to be non-dictionary – see Concise Oxford page 706 (and by no means an all inclusive work!)[2]

No, no, Mr. Sidgwick, you mustn't ask me to be sad about a rich and varied family.[3] They will swim – solitaries sink – And think of my 2 (two only) nephews – so dull – and both taking after the other side – no chance for Mendelian pattern. A.M. is likewise concerned about his 3 – but I say to him what if he'd had to send them to a "Public School" ("public" is 'elementary' in NZ) like so many a parent here, & listen to them speaking English with an uncanny twang.

Our Depression is, if anything, a little better, and the farmer decides on the whole not to kill his store-sheep. And the Public Trustee, imitating your meadow-pipit has built temporary shops on the earthquake-ruined area[4] so that rents will once more flow into my partner's little coffers. And we've lately added gas-oven bread, and cheese soufflé to our répertoire, & spring carrots are coming along, & Michael is if possible handsomer, and the snow mountains most gorgeous at sunrise – Ça va! And from time to time there is a post-box excitement & a letter from some eminent Londoner to quicken the time – And we thank you. [...]

Yours sincerely
Ursula Bethell

Bodleian Library Oxford. MS Sidgwick & Jackson 142, fols. 130-131v.

TO FRANK SIDGWICK – AUGUST 21, 1931

Rise Cottage, Cashmere Hills, Christchurch, N. Z.

Dear Mr. Sidgwick

Having now finished washing up last night's saucepans (cannot leave *that* to the gallant little creature whose contact with household affairs

---

[1] Sidgwick had quoted more fully 'Truth smashed to earth shall riz agin; you can't stop her,' and offered 'Twopence if you know where that comes from. I do *not* mean the Psalms' (April 22, 1931). See Psalm 85: 11. The solution Bethell proposes is the American poet and critic James Russell Lowell, author of *The Bigelow* (or *Biglow*) *Papers* (1848).

[2] Sidgwick had written that 'it is nice to have nice correspondents and authors, even if they *do* write about diastoles and entelechy ... and mattamores which aren't in the Dictionary' (April 22, 1931). See, respectively, *Collected Poems* pp. 40, 62 & 35.

[3] In the same letter, he had complained of the difficulties of 'a bloke trying to wring enough out of books to support a wife and family.'

[4] On Feb. 3 a violent earthquake had struck Napier, in which 256 people lost their lives.

until the 1918 epidemic carried off her father was merely the ordering of two excellent maids & an odd-job man) I take up my pen & your letter (July 1). For a bit of pleasure I answer back promptly, but let's hope that out of pity I shall forbear to post yet awhile!

'Tis dichotomic your letter[1] – I take the brighter half first – (the riro-riro out in the garden harping on his 4 little strings (its a very grey day & these birds really do sing louder in dull weather) contradicts any note of pessimism). Why yes, "cauda sursum." Michael's motto of course (its such a beautiful plume) or to quote the whole of his sentiment

"sursum cauda! cauda sursum! Cat-latin
et cum dignitate otium" (n.b. versus liber)[2]

And yes indeed we are readers of novels by all Sidgwicks & Sedgwicks in ascending scale & even buyers of E.S. (on our shelves is Laura, too clever for local circulation).[3] All we can do at the present juncture is to "enquire" for all these books "at our library" – the "select" library run by our principal bookshop, but affording mostly what its London Buyer thinks (only too justifiably) is appropriate fodder for its clientèle. And yes, I shall read about them in the T. L. Supp. (wonderful 3[d] worth we have not felt obliged to retrench) – by the way I have just lit upon a delightful word, new to me, in that journal – "caudataire"[4] (à propos of cauda!). And yes we do buy poetry also – despite the background crabapple tree – (very poor yield this season what with frosts & blights).[5] I used to make out my little book-lists under headings – practical – political – poetical – theological – historical etc. & boil them down to a permissible residuum. Guided usually in this country by the not always trustworthy reviewer & resisting the powerful suggestion of

---

[1] Sidgwick's letter was in two parts; the first he signed 'disgruntledly yours,' but then wrote a further two pages (signed 'Yours again quite cheerfully'), saying 'I can't let a letter like that go out to our brethren Overseas, and give them the impression that the Old Country is feeling the draught, and that there is spavin in her stables. As the XVth century poet omitted to write: Sursum corda! corda sursum! / Exhilaratio facit versum. (I feel sure your Latin won't boggle over that. Will it allow you to see the slighter deeper jest in the boy's translation of *cau*da sursum, = Tails up!?).' Lat. Lift up your hearts. Lift up your hearts. Gladdening [of the heart] makes verse. 'Cauda sursum' means 'lift up your tail.' Sidgwick's allusion is to Juvenal's Satire VI, 'facit indignatio versum.'

[2] Lat. 'Lift up your tail. Lift up your tail. And idleness with dignity.' [In parenthesis] 'free verse.'

[3] Sidgwick had enquired: 'Did you ever read any of my sister Ethel's novels? She is not the same as either Mrs Alfred Sidgwick or Anne Douglas Sedgwick.' Subtitled *A Cautionary Tale, Laura* was published by Sidgwick & Jackson in 1924.

[4] Fr. 'One who holds up the train of a pope or prelate.'

[5] In the same letter, Sidgwick had complained of the enormous quantity of wretched verse submitted for publication, adding that 'it accounts for there being no market. You don't buy apples if you've got a little tree of crabs in your back yard.'

unblushing publisher's posters – (and how proud & thankful we feel that *my* publishers *do* blush!) And yes, Tennyson is 'doch'[1] one of our poets – I should say my coadjutor's one poet – she recites Locksley Hall to herself over the cooking when she's in High Spirits. And ah yes – Hoover[2] – but oh dear the human race – how *stoopid* as my grandfather (Shelley's housemaster at Eton as I think I told you)[3] would have said – how *can* one "love its silly face"[4] when it goes on registering suspicion & greed & business acumen. The nations remind one of my Walworth Boys Club – one member who had thought a bit explained that everyone beyond the limits of his own family & a friend or two must be considered an enemy – or a possible enemy & even not to be too sure of the friends. For another, sans famille he,[5] I was the only person to be trusted at all. To think of what could be done with Walworth souvenirs, if one had the pen of a short story writer! But I can only put things in my pipe & smoke them – (I will *try* not to enclose any smoke rings!)

And no, my head wasn't turned by the letters of adulation – I know my New Zealand. But one's allowed a glow. They *do* like something from & about their own glebe. Some of them. There are sprouts of sensibility among the tussocks.

And yes, it must be very trying to contend with this mass production of verse – nauseating indeed ("moi, j'aime les bâteaux-à-vapeur" a little French boy said to me with ecstasy "Ça vous fait vomir")[6] I suppose that like teatasters (don't they) you wd. have to intersperse tracts of pungent prose – one perceives that a publisher's rôle is not merely one of breaking bottles of champagne on new ships' bows, or waving flag & blowing whistle as the train starts. Rather the public's idea I fancy.

Sep 19th

A month or thereabouts having elapsed I think this letter's arrival won't be premature!

Meanwhile the new edition of G. M. Hopkins has arrived, long waited for – very exciting indeed.[7] *That's* the way to talk – in a torrent. Why did R. Bridges economise him? but one can't put oneself back to

---

[1] Ger. 'Still.'

[2] Writing of the Depression, Sidgwick described it as 'a ghastly thin-faced time, though the world has just seen a glimpse through Mr. Hoover's action – happy thought!'

[3] George Bethell (1779-1857) had been Bursar and Senior Fellow at Eton.

[4] From 'Wishes of an Elderly Man,' a short comic verse by the Scotsman Walter Alexander Raleigh, c. 1914.

[5] Fr. 'Without a family.'

[6] Fr. 'I love steam-boats. They make you vomit.'

[7] Hopkins's poetry was first published in 1918 (ed. Bridges); the second, enlarged edition was arranged by Charles Williams and published in 1930.

the nineties view – Emily Dickinson (whom I bought because of the Yorkshire Post review & did *not* agree) was a bit like that but then she had no clergy.

Such a cold late spring – patches of snow even on these hills & the mountains all white – yesterday we ran into the country & all the gorse hedges were deep gold against the whiteness – lovely – & shivering young lambs.

Somehow I don't think you will be pestered with any more verse from N.Z. Except for some domestic numbers the stream seems to run underground & soul stirrings spend themselves on verkehr[1] with folk – I'm interesting myself in the son of a back country dairy farm who feels called to be a landscape painter & being penniless has to maintain him[self] at the same time.[2] He has come to the so called School of Art here. (He writes too!) And although, by a series of miracles, we are carrying on much as usual, if in a subdued key so to speak, I am worried about the planet & wondering how one can do anything to improve it. Nevertheless there is that notion about a set of things concerning my NZ childhood which might come to something some day given leisure, & if there were impetus enough left in the decaying brain, & then you might be pestered again, always provided that european civilisation has not in the interim suffered total collapse!

Yours sincerely
Ursula Bethell

Bodleian Library Oxford. MS Sidgwick & Jackson 142, fols. 133-135v.

TO J H E SCHRODER – DECEMBER 19, 1931

Rise Cottage, Cashmere Hills, Christchurch, N.Z.

Dear Mr. Schroder

The little Rise Cottage tune has begun to tinkle again but now you are caught in the Where-are-you-going-for-Christmas? fugue – If not, might the post-Christmas calm be an occasion for mounting our hill once more? We are not, I think, to join the General Post.

Do you know, I thought poetry in the "Press" was for honour & glory – but now, on my return, I find a very charming bit of pink printed

---

[1] Ger. 'Correspondence, communication.'

[2] Mountford Tosswill Woollaston (1910-1998) grew up on a Taranaki dairy farm. After studying art in Nelson, he attended the Canterbury College School of Art in 1931, but found it too conservative. With Bethell's encouragement (for whom he worked as a gardener), he went instead to study with R. N. Field in Dunedin for part of 1932.

matter,[1] on which I meditate with surprise and satisfaction. And what the upshot? intensified diffidence – or shall, slump-wise, hungry shoals of little verse fishes surge around the portals of that fine engraved Office? (I have often wished, lately, that my wares were of a more marketable sort!)

In any case, need I forgo the private pleasure of, perhaps, occasionally, submitting a composition to your kind & critical eye? No, no.

With the season's good wishes

Yours sincerely
M. U. Bethell

Alexander Turnbull Library. fMS-018.

To J H E Schroder – March 3, 1932

Rise Cottage, Cashmere Hills, Christchurch, N.Z.

Dear Mr. Schroder

Back to earth yesterday[2] – "Rolling stones" etc. – walking about all the time, little written – only fragments, out of which I have just tinkered these two, and a triviality.[3] Theme of No. 2 makes me afraid of borrowed plumes, so Press beware. At all events, hoffentlich,[4] no false quantity. ("Antinomy" an old friend from the pulpit which one mixes up sometimes with antimony perhaps!)

Please excuse No. 3! Of course the bellbird, just now, listening to its own note, is beyond words. I'm not sure that you like these néozélanderies.[5]

If you have, I think so, some pieces of mine of which you must say (I do *not* imply, mistakenly,) "These will never do" I should be glad to have them back some day for my dud collection.

That forest & glacier went to my head.

Yours sincerely
M. U. Bethell

---

[1] Bethell had received a cheque for £1/11/6 for the publication of 'Picnic' (Nov. 7) and 'November' (Nov. 21).

[2] Bethell and Effie Pollen had been holidaying in South Westland, including a trip to the Franz Josef Glacier and the Waiho Gorge. The second of the poems enclosed with this letter bears the inscription 'Waiho Gorge. March, 1932'.

[3] Enclosed with the letter were 'Rock Crystal,' 'In the Forest' and 'The Bellbird.' 'In the Forest' appeared in *Time & Place* as 'Forest Sleep;' 'Rock-Crystal' appeared in *Day & Night*; 'The Bellbird' was published in *The Press* June 25, 1932, but did not appear in either collection.

[4] Ger. 'Hopefully.'

[5] A neologism. New Zealand 'things'.

(N. B. No. 2. line 8. botanical truth)

Alexander Turnbull Library. fMS-018.

TO THE PRESS / "V. I. R." – [C. MARCH 26, 1932][1]

Rise Cottage, Cashmere Hills, Christchurch, N.Z.

After reading in last Saturday's paper your kindly critical letter, and the appended apologia (which was hazarded, tentatively, in response to the paper's own misgivings) I prefer to fall back upon my main line of defence – the fact, namely, that before acceptance by the Press, the verses had passed the censorship of a competent scholar in England.[2] Your submission shall be, I venture to hope, to his good reasons when they shall have been procured, and not derisively, albeit courteously, to the hypothetical her

Yours obediently
E. H.

The Plea of "Weathered Rocks"

Arthur passed me for correct,
  Lettered, he, in Greek and Latin;
Virile critic, please respect
  "Diastole" since he left that in;

Say I'm ugly, say I'm bad,
  With your erudition blast me,
Say I'm overbold, but add:
  Arthur passed me.

Draft. Macmillan Brown Library. MB 558. L6.

---

[1] Bethell's poem 'Weathered Rocks' was published in *The Press*, March 12, 1932. Schroder and the editor, Oliver Duff, had anticipated some adverse comments on her diction, and had to hand an 'apologia' by Bethell in which she justified the inclusion of foreign words. As expected, the poem was criticized; a letter by 'V. I. R.' complained that 'to the hurt of my ear, 'E. H.' was bold enough to use 'parabole' and diastole' (two horrible foreigners ...) as if they should rhyme prettily with goal, whole ... whereas the best authors ... are accustomed to make these endings dissyllabic.' Bethell's defence was printed following 'V. I. R's' letter on March 19, but she also penned this draft reply, extant in her papers.

[2] Arthur Mayhew. See following verse.

TO FRANK SIDGWICK – JULY 23, 1932

Rise Cottage, Cashmere Hills, Christchurch, N. Z.

Dear Mr. Sidgwick

Midwinter is *not*, in New Zealand, the right & proper moment to be responding to Christmas Greetings – How can I explain & account for the well-nigh six months gone by since arrival of your very delightful letter & diverting poetry – the latter so much enjoyed by me & the very small circle of appreciate-able people known to me here.[1] My hideous ingratitude resists explanation – yet one thing after another . . . & the fact is, when poverty comes in at the door, leisure flies out of the window – ones clothes must be repaired instead of relegated, one must delve in the earth vice hired labourer, one must keep accounts & cogitate . . . vicissitudes to boot – small ups & downs – minute crises – no verse flows – the back-garden crabapple is frost-bitten – the little craft labours in the contrary winds – one bales – (I throw in this simile as suitable for you of the Dragon crew).[2] What a comfort to reflect that in all probability London does not even notice this failure of Antipodes to cope with passage of time!

Yes, NZ is feeling the pinch & its not doing us any harm. Our scale of living was unbecoming to an agricultural country – we fattened on the war – what a lovely consumption of wool & mutton by fighting Europe! Never shall I forget the *beefy* appearance of the population when I came out in 1919! Now we begin to probe a little deeper. Economists contradict one another in our daily papers just as they do in the English papers. Now we are coming to think that there isn't after all a shortage of goods on the planet, or even a shortage of cash – but somehow or other our arrangements are at fault! Some still think that a self-contained British Empire might float like an ark safe upon the floods of World Depression, but their number is I fancy dwindling. Many confess that they are surprised to find themselves *happier* since the Slump. *Braced*. A rose-nurseryman whom I visited the other day (having got the garden in focus again went out to spend 1/6 on a new plant) said he hadn't done at all so badly this year. People stopping at home more, & working in their gardens . . .

My delightful sheep-farmer nephew (who is in charge of a place belonging to his mother – "managing" is the technical term) was in town

---

[1] The diverting poetry appears to have been another of Sidgwick's Christmas jests, a mock-medieval carol entitled 'Up Taills all: a lytil Consail of Courage in Tyme of Troubil.' The poem is in four quatrains with the refrain 'Sursum cauda, cauda sursum! Exhortacio facit versum.' For these verses, see also the letter to Sidgwick of Aug. 21, 1931.

[2] Sidgwick had attended the Dragon School in Oxford.

for a night last week & came up to spend the evening, bearing gifts – 2 large sacks of pine-cones & 2 ready-handed petrol tins ("bowsers" make these so scarce nowadays) for garden rubbish & food, one. He was brought up softly in the fat years but, temperamentally ascetic, responds gladly to hardship. He works much more severely than the "working man", but of course for a substantial end. His only regret seems to be that, having taken up cattle-breeding, he can't afford a holiday to go around & look at other men's beasts – I find in him all the English ancestors' instincts for the land, & all the squire's concern for his community. The younger nephew is with him now, having left his regiment in the W. Indies. He enjoyed the work, as well as the dash-cutting of a Young Officer, but is settling down cheerfully to the land, & getting on well, Richard said, "with his fencing-lessons" – for a moment I thought of the foils! Richard doesn't think there will be much improvement in Estate affairs for three years or so, whereby my brother cannot redeme his borwe[1] from his sisters. So this year £30 instead of £300 for me from sheep & it will never be 300 again. Pastoral values are down for my lifetime. But everything will be adjusted to match, Michael's meat is already much cheaper, & eggs have been 1/3 instead of 2/3 at the same date last year. I speak as a consumer.

Why all this to a purveyor of intellectual nourishment? well, in some way of course you are knit up with our wool. Not for the moment will N.Z. be thinking of Buying more Books – unless stay at homeness works out that way too. Which reminds that two more people have this month signified their intention of buying The Garden & a third, at present pauper, has discovered it by borrowing from my friend his sister-in-law. He called to thank me – I was suitably employed when he came in throwing up soil from a three foot hole, clad in corduroys – "I don't read a great deal of verse, but that book got me somehow. My wife too – I read it aloud to her afterwards" – But the girl said "I simply loved it" – I like to think that every fresh buyer means another one some day, & when the 400 mark is reached I shall die easily, or else turn happily in my grave.

[...]

I invited Mr. Schroder of The Press to tea & to read your Xmas circular (he is one able to appreciate). Proud to offer such a bait. There are crises going on at the Press too[2] – Liberal minded editor dismissed – another editor coming – will my friend, the literary editor, have to go

---

[1] Bethell quotes the phrase from Sidgwick's 'Up Taills all.'

[2] Oliver Duff's editorial stance concerning the tramways strike in Christchurch displeased the newspaper's board, and his refusal to compromise led to his resignation. He was replaced by Pierce Freeth.

too, also Liberal? The owners are old Junkers. Curious how unsettled times bring Reaction. The Press has been taking some of my bits, even anti-war – but latter must not be submitted hereafter.

And D'Arcy Cresswell "the New Zealand poet" came to tea in the garden & I have taken a *great* fancy to him. He's better than his (so-far) works – No wonder the London lions received him into their dens. If *I* had an upcountry station, how gladly I wd. give him food & let him dream – for NZ Nature is "getting" him – but his parents, he complains, seeing him "idle" send him off to feed the fowls. He has written a very good sonnet sequence lately – much better.[1] I likewise have up-country yearnings & share my nephew's feeling for flocks & herds. D'Arcy thinks I *could* write about the sheep farm round (*not* for him). Mais que faire?[2] I have dates with my quarter-acre which must be cultivated by me.

How I do go on chatting once I begin! But now you have four good months before sending, yes please, your next Xmas quip or carol, & might one venture to hope, letter – and oh, referring again to your last – I *can't* understand the ban upon the expression "darken my doors" – *surely* not "idiotic" but exact![3] Is it because you live in dusky London & not in a sun-bright climate? He does darken my cottage door, the tall man, I can't even see who it is against the dazzle – And did I win the prize with my Lowell guess for those lines about the truth? You don't remember.

Well we have had a marvellous sunshiny winter so far; frosts below, blue skies above, tacsonia manicata[4] still pink-flower'd – yesterday was our first cold storm with snow-showers – *and* the first picture of a spring lamb in the *Press*. We are all quite well thank you, hoping that this finds you the same – and it might be economical in every respect to wish you a Merry Xmas & prosperous New Year!

Yours sincerely
Ursula Bethell

Bodleian Library Oxford. MS Sidgwick & Jackson 142, fols. 142-144v.

---

[1] Cresswell had returned to New Zealand in 1932. He and Bethell met and corresponded frequently, but none of her letters have survived. The sonnet sequence *Lyttelton Harbour* was published in 1936.

[2] Fr. 'But what to do?'

[3] Sidgwick had written of a collection of 18th century letters he was to publish – 'such *cards*, so *English*, ... telling disappointing nephews never to darken their doors again. I always stop in amazement at that ... phrase ... picturesque, universally popular, and idiotic.'

[4] A species of passionflower.

TO J H E SCHRODER – SEPTEMBER 15, 1932

Rise Cottage. Cashmere.

Dear Mr. Schroder

Now *that* is really friendly – *that* is how you write to your Cobbers![1] This I know because the first introduction I had to the venerable doctor J. H. E. S. was the view of just such a missive written to G. T. A.[2] in the watches of the night. So I will use my Economy block en suite. I wd. have replied on the instant but so-called practical things will keep breaking in.

1. In re Boswell query[3] (I hope the "in" redeems) how I wish I could have obliged offhand (as proud as when out of the whole school at Oxford at general knowledge mass viva I alone knew who & why & when said "This will never do" – having happened to have come across it just the day before!)[4] but am not a bit well up in him – my cherished edition has been going to be read aloud by us on winter evenings for many years, but our evenings fizzle out in the drowsiness of the weary Just – women – just. The index gives everything (in itself a divertissement) but Seraglio – but *why* is not the admirable Mrs. Knowles under "woman"! (Birkbeck Hill's learned daughter lived next door to us at Hampstead – what has become of those two prodigies, her boy & girl?)

2. In re Eton – Disraeli – here is the cutting – *and* another. I have tried to get hold of that book Kegan Paul's Memoirs, with its references to my Grandparent, but in vain.[5] Do you perchance possess it? Your sort of book I fancy.

3. Review – yes, I *should* like to, & wish I could, but don't think I can. To review a book one has to know so much about other books & my mind is ill furnished. To be sure I may trail a few wisps of glory from the academic groves – whence I was snatched all too soon to N.Z. – but very sparse. I tried to do a religious work for the S. C. M[6] paper once, but it turned out to be nothing but a précis, & much too long a one at that. All

---

[1] Schroder's undated letter, to which this responds, had been written casually in pencil. It included a number of random queries, which Bethell attempts to address in turn.

[2] Geoffrey Alley. See letter to Sidgwick of Dec. 5, 1929.

[3] Schroder: 'Can you tell me, off-hand, whereabouts in Boswell Johnson makes his delicious remark about imagining himself the lord of a seraglio?'

[4] Bethell quotes (in more detail) the same anecdote to Sidgwick when sending him a copy of *Time & Place*. See the letter of Sept. 1936 for a suggested identification of the allusion.

[5] Schroder had asked for a TLS cutting 'about the Eton mutton (or goose?) custom ... Disraeli ... *Coningsby* ... I am entirely vague'. Charles Kegan Paul's *Memories* was published in 1899.

[6] Student Christian Movement.

the same I should like to see that book on Tea – I have one by a Japanese[1] published in 1916 which is enjoyable – Tea ceremonies etc.

4. When I came to the booklist – to The Spirit of Man – a groan escaped. *Who* has had my beloved copy for just ten years! Irretrievable. I *always* return books *in the long run* – but not *10 years*. Have you read XIX Cent. Childhood? No – & I have not read Modern Symposium (awaiting the right moment) – & he is dead now – what a pity – and herein I require you to answer for a relevant crime. *Where* is War in Heaven – to be given to Mr. Webb? Meeting him casually in the street yesterday he denied receipt of same.[2]

5. In re A. Mayhew's Fist.[3] Yes, it is difficult isn't it (that's why I did not send the whole letter altho' it consisted mostly of a very charming narrative of a present day Jane Austen kind of life at Hartley Court[4] (such a J. A. *name*) with alas, the tragedy of the invalid Dr. Head[5] in the background. And I see what you mean about the Oriental look – but its not India – it dates from his childhood when I used to scratch out the blots in his Latin copybook – & derives from his lexicographical father – a debased form – *that* was beautifully clear on the reference slips – Mayhew & Skeat you know.[6] (I should like to see Joseph Wright's life[7] – just published – is it sent to "Press"?) I sat beside the daughter of N. E. D. Murray[8] at school.

I am delighted with A. I. M.'s attributions in re Chevisaunce[9] – but all I intended was a Spenserian sort of word meaning achievement or victory – Chef, Acend, the head, *the end* says Chambers. Ah, telos, telos – It wd. be fun to have access to the great N. E. D. Words were all our

---

[1] The reference is to *The Book of Tea* by Kakuzo Okakura, first published c. 1906, and often since.

[2] The books referred to are: Robert Bridges, *The Spirit of Man* (1916); Mary MacCarthy, *A Nineteenth-Century Childhood* (1924); G. Lowes Dickinson, *A Modern Symposium* (1908); and Charles Williams, *War in Heaven* (1930). Leicester Webb was a Christchurch journalist.

[3] Schroder: 'My immediate impression was that I was looking at a facsimile of one of those manuscripts – Persian? Sanscrit?'

[4] Hartley Court, near Reading, was the home of Henry and Ruth Head after the former's retirement.

[5] Head suffered from Parkinson's disease for the last twenty years of his life.

[6] A. L. Mayhew, Chaplain of Wadham College, was a prominent lexicographer in his time. He edited a 14th century Latin-English dictionary, and collaborated with Skeat on a dictionary of Middle English and a glossary of Tudor and Stuart words. See also the letter of April 1899.

[7] Mary Wright, *The Life of Joseph Wright* (1932).

[8] James Murray was the editor of the *New English Dictionary* (later the *Oxford English Dictionary*).

[9] The word occurs in 'The Piano-Tuner,' printed in *The Press*, April 30, 1932. Mayhew's letter has not survived.

daily delight in those days. Chevisance – "successful adjustment" – "Chinese historians" says my Teaman, "have always spoken of Taoism as the 'art of being in the world' for it deals with the present – ourselves ... The Present is the moving Infinity, the legitimate sphere of the Relative. Relativity seeks Adjustment; Adjustment is Art. The art of life lies in a constant readjustment to our surroundings. Taoism accepts the mundane as it is, and, unlike the Confucians & the Buddhists, tries to find beauty in our world of woe and worry. The Sung allegory of the Three Vinegar Tasters explains admirably the trend of the three doctrines" etc.[1]

6. Collins – I remarked that ineptitude about the Ode – had forgotten it was MacCarthy. Noticed it because I had just read someone else's enthusiasm about that very picture – (literary doctors do differ!) & didn't he object to "sheety" which seems to me so exactly right.[2]

7. That reminds me to order my mates Cook Books birthday present for November – almost too late.

8. In re Verse for Press. I thought the Press had surrendered to Prof. Sinclaire & was printing only prose.[3] (D'A. C. has sent me his Reply – an admirable piece of writing I think – I am suggesting that it form a chapter in his Progress Part II. Agree not suitable for newspaper – Meanwhile I hope my friend Dr. Helen S. will follow up another suggestion that she should invite D'A. C. to her English Association platform to argue the matter.)

I have now forgotten which pieces I *did* send you – kept no ref. list. In my last note I meant by "Decoration" a little bit about a jar of roses & snow outside, which was in a bundle not meant for Press – The conjunction recurred in July or Aug & I thought oh well, let it be printed if Mr. Schroder likes. But now the season has changed & it no longer applies. I mean to enclose with this a set of corrected pieces (keeping list) among which is probably the Spring one to which you refer. But the one about Spring & hawthorn & snow, which is really about a Tui,

---

[1] The reference is to Okakura's *Book of Tea*. In the allegory, Sakyamuni, Confucius and Lao Tzu each dip a finger into a jar of vinegar and taste it. Confucius finds it sour, the Buddha calls it bitter, and Lao Tzu pronounces it sweet.

[2] Desmond MacCarthy's volume of essays *Criticism* (1932) included a study of William Collins, with particular criticism of the 'Ode to Evening.' Schroder had described MacCarthy as 'dogmatically foolish ... too blind to see, & too confident to look a second time.' The speaker in the Ode implores Eve to 'lead ... where some sheety lake / Cheers the lone heath.'

[3] Frederick Sinclaire, Professor of English at Canterbury University College, had published an article in *The Press* (June 18, 1932) in which he argued that it was in prose rather than in poetry that one found spiritual truths.

applies to October[1] – When I have finished typing my things I hate them, but I dote upon cheques.

[...] At the 1932 Exhibition (a failure I'm afraid financially) I met Mr. Duff – I must take in that Rangiora paper.[2] Perhaps he'd like some Rangiora verses – my childhood spent there – (No cheques of course I know!) and in re Rangiora, where does one read that poem of Phillip Carrington's?[3] (Perhaps I've asked that before.)

Now I must do a bit of spade-work, before tackling typewriter.

There, I've sure outdone you in the matter of garrulity, irrelevance, & parentheses.

Yours sincerely
M U Bethell

Alexander Turnbull Library. fMS-018.

TO J H E SCHRODER – DECEMBER 30, 1932

Rise Cottage. Cashmere.

Dear Mr. Schroder

This is to wish you a Happy New Year – Most of such greetings, I find, include skilful allusions to world economics, but I'll ignore all that (unless one were to adopt an old club boy's happy phrase "wishing you a Reasonable Prosperity"). We are here, making our usual Good Resolutions – more order in the home – system – self denial – daily life a work of art etc. etc. Could not yours include one to send back my scripts? – I realise that I should have "enclosed a stamped addressed envelope" & now remedy that. The fact is I think they must be getting a bit mouldy & should like to review & brush up – would produce anything again on demand. There are some of which I havn't kept copies.

I don't know whether the N. Z. Sun has blinded D'Arcy Cresswell's critical judgement, but he now calls my compositions politely "poems" (I'll do the same!) and thinks so well of the Akaroa one that he asks for it for his anthology, shortened[4] – (The Econome[5] loves a new word –

---

[1] The identifiable poems here are 'Decoration' and 'Spring Snow and Tui;' neither were printed in *The Press*, but both appeared in *Day & Night*.

[2] After his resignation from *The Press*, Duff established the *North Canterbury Gazette* (and subsequently published some of Bethell's poems).

[3] Carrington's poem, 'Rangiora,' was published in *College Rhymes: An Anthology of Verse Written by Members of Canterbury College 1873-1923*.

[4] Cresswell's comments are in a letter of Dec. 1932. He wanted to publish 'The Long Harbour' with stanzas 4 and 5 omitted.

[5] Fr. 'Bursar, steward.' Another name for Effie Pollen.

Seated in the kitchen covering a batch of chutney just now, & surrounded by kind presents of baskets of fruit, & a cauldron of blackcurrant jelly bubbling on the stove, she exclaimed "This is my *anthology*!") I have told him that it belongs to the Press. I am so glad he is happy doing that anthology & find his criticism helpful and stimulating.

It has been a great pleasure to meet "The New Canterbury Pilgrim"[1] – I've heard nothing of you for many a long day & seldom go into town so don't catch a glimpse of you in W & T's[2] – Have enjoyed your reviews – e. g. faithful dealing with James Douglas.[3] I hope now to read the Symposium. Really with my books I'm something like my old Great uncle who got so behind hand with his Times that he came to lunch dangerously excited by the news of a year ago. But that was when there were no events but elections, & plus ça change etc.[4]

The Garden has been very active but is now subsiding. Michael is splendid. I strained my arm rock working & have had to leave the weeds for a bit & rest it. I would have read you some amusing letters from England. The only present I can send my friends is a piece of verse – I should say, poem. So here is the only one lately.[5] I'm sorry its not suitable for the Press & wish it were – I thought A. W.'s came through so very well in that little Art in NZ book – I'd left out a vital line in typing the one they've printed![6] Must write and apologise. I suppose the MS is at the office so address there.

You may be away.

Yours sincerely
M. U. Bethell

Alexander Turnbull Library. fMS-018.

---

[1] A *Press* nom-de-plume of Ngaio Marsh, who had recently returned to New Zealand from England, and subsequently became a friend of Bethell.

[2] Whitcombe & Tombs, a well-known printer, publisher and bookseller.

[3] The 'faithful dealing' included the judgement that 'Mr. Douglas may not be the worst writer in England; he is entitled to the benefit of the doubt ... but ... worse writing would be hard to imagine and harder to achieve.' The work reviewed was *The Bunch Book: For Dog Lovers Only*.

[4] 'Plus ça change, plus c'est la même chose.' Fr. 'The more something changes, the more it stays the same.'

[5] Bethell in fact enclosed two poems, neither of which was published by Schroder. 'In a Hospital' appeared in the *Collected Poems* of 1950; 'Improvements. By a Conservative' has not been published (see Elder, p. 123). It is an unfinished piece attacking a 'Cashmere beautification' scheme which Bethell felt was 'elbowing Beauty out of our borders here, / Not rudely, but artistically, and by degrees.'

[6] *New Zealand Best Poems of 1932* was edited by *Art in NZ* editor Charles Marris. It included two poems by Arnold Wall (Professor of English at Canterbury Univ. College) and Bethell's 'Autumn Roses' – minus line 12.

TO J H E SCHRODER – JUNE 8, 1933

Rise Cottage. Cashmere.

Dear Mr. Schroder

Your letters – allow me to say – are so charming when they do come, that they wd. quite compensate for any gap, if such existed in my consciousness, grievance toned – but having been friends, in the past, with able people in responsible positions, I learnt *not* to expect them to break off & write less than imperative letters. (I feel as if I'd said this before!) Imagine writing such lively letters at 2.a.m. – an hour when its easiest to die – & one associated in my mind with air raid exhaustion, & the pause between serving 1 a.m. suppers & 4 a.m. breakfasts to soldiers in the "great" war – Coffee? I had heard that you were ill & was sorry, & later, that you were better, & was glad.

Well now, that *is* interesting about M. Holcroft![1] I could hardly believe that the articles were by the same one – I had thought, like you, that his mark would be the short story as understood by N. Z. Xmas Number. Did I tell you that he'd announced – he must have been about 11 or 12 – "I intend to be an Author" – There's vocation for you – There was a quaint little younger brother who assured me that I had the best collection of curiosities he'd ever seen – except possibly the show-case of his uncle, a dentist. He liked particularly a Nigerian dagger, which I still have here, & used to brandish it, explaining "When I dag, I dag like *this*" – Pray do bring Monty up, as soon as its arrange-able. The other pleasure that you dangle before me (you once so dangled your *books,* you know!) is most exciting – how could you guess that one of my hungriest unappeased desires was to hear the Schnabel Beethoven – & that since reading what W. J. Turner said in the N. S.[2] Is it possible that you have an E. M. G. Gramophone as well as belonging to the records? (I cure myself of envying friends on the right, who possess these delights – by remembering those on the left, who have never been quite certain about next week's dinner!) And speaking of music, I hope you heard the Trio –

[1] M. H. Holcroft (1902-94) was to become a prominent writer, particularly as essayist and critic, and was best known as long-serving editor of the *NZ Listener* (1949-69, 1973-74). His publications include a monograph on the life and work of Bethell in the OUP series, 'New Zealand Writers and Their Work' (1975). Schroder had deliberately sought Holcroft's opinion of 'The Long Harbour' (published by E.H.), 'and when I identified 'E.H.' for him, his eyes sparkled & his face lit up with pleasure & interest' (June 5, 1933). Bethell had known Holcroft as a small boy whom she taught Sunday School in St Mary's parish, Merivale.

[2] That is, *The New Statesman*, whose music critic was W. J. Turner.

that Cellist is not to be missed, nor the "Ensemble".[1] A friend took me & when they come back I mean to take myself out of my Press cheque. Otherwise I'm moving daily nearer the left hand friends – not but what I've just been called away to eat an apple pasty made with *brown* wholemeal flour – most delicious – very hot & comforting & a meal-in-itself.

I am so glad you like the Autumn Afternoon[2] (others have written too) – It was all true. I can't remember how I got the tune – Once having got that (in the right key or mood) it goes on of itself – or doesn't! I can only do a little gardening. When there is less tune, it goes slower & I do more gardening – for instance, The Long Harbour. One thing I recollect about Autumn Aftn. is having discussed with a friend whose husband is a General Carrier whether one could put a lorry into poetry, & taking this opportunity.

The English autumn pause is so much longer & lovelier "himmlische länge"[3]

D'Arcy pointed out that one line in Burke's Pass was a beat short & I meant to send a correction – I like that story about the breakfast tray. He told me about the tobacco-present. That was beautiful – & so was his manner of telling it. I fancy that either one loves D'Arcy or finds him impossible – Myself, I feel a real affection for him. Did he not send you certain "Quatrains"? Beautiful lines I thought them, but the last verse rather difficult to construe. And are there examples in classical verse of that use of the word "like"? I suppose so.[4]

[...]

Thank you most heartily – [...] for the book & for all that you say.

Yours sincerely
M. U. Bethell

Alexander Turnbull Library. fMS-018.

---

[1] The Spivakovsky-Kurtz Trio, who toured New Zealand in 1933, performed in Christchurch on May 27 and 29.

[2] Schroder had admired 'By Burke's Pass,' and then written at some length of 'Autumn Afternoon,' admiring the 'repetitive, continuating structure wh. to me seems perfectly to express the exquisite sad truth about autumn' (June 5, 1933).

[3] Ger. 'Of heavenly length.' Although Bethell has written länge (long) rather than Länge (length), it is likely that she has the latter in mind. The phrase was used by Schumann to refer to Schubert's Great C Major symphony, and has had an extensive afterlife.

[4] Cresswell has no published poem with this title, but Bethell may be referring to *The Voyage of the Hurunui* (although it was not published until after her death). The first section is written in quatrains, and its final stanza includes the line 'Unless you see deep down like me' – a conjunctive use that was frowned upon in prescriptive grammars.

TO J H E SCHRODER – AUGUST 9, 1933

Rise Cottage. Cashmere.

Dear Mr. Schroder

I've been looking up my commerce with the Press and find that I was right in thinking that there is still a batch in yr. hands to be looked at – they must want weeding and trimming by this time I guess & one in particular I'm uneasy about – I think it was called Limitation – anyhow its about time & I'd like really to consult Archdn Whitehead in case its philosophically bunkum.[1] Not all that the Muse whispers makes sense! ("how one may venture to think not improperly") Several are standing over till the right season "October Spring" & "Spring on the Plain" eg (but I'm doubtful about this one). Herewith the Winter Dawn that you asked for & another on the same theme (liked by D'Arcy). You wished for "Rainy Morning" & its suitable but is it good enough? I have been using metre & have lost my ear for irregular verse. I'll hold it back another day.

"Lighting of the Lamps" you thought too long & it surely is & could not be chopped up (perhaps my best inspiration I think?) Its meant for a choir & I wish I knew someone to compose the music.[2]

It wd. be {a} good wheeze (as my nephews say) to send (*without* indication) the lines rejected by "Press" – long ago, I think before your day!

I really must thank you for bringing Monty. We had a long talk & I heard about it all. I feel that he might do something special – but shall know more about that when I've read the MS of his last which he's promised. At any rate he's fine in himself – "sure" was your right word – I've about given up hoping that "poor" D'Arcy will boil up to the point of communication – but feel easier now that he is in touch with the Governor General who is "anxious but perplexed" about his future.[3] A passage to England wd. be a simple solution for that man of substance & I don't believe that D'Arcy's English friends are tired of him. Monty is truly a great surprise. When I find these boys again I feel like the woman in the psalms you know who was a joyful mother of children,[4] but I must

---

[1] L. G. Whitehead was, at the time, Archdeacon of Dunedin and Warden of Selwyn College. He became a close friend of Bethell, and contributed to the 'personal memories' published in *Landfall* after her death.

[2] Of the poems mentioned, 'Spring on the Plain,' 'Midwinter Dawn,' and 'October Spring' were published in *The Press*, the last as 'Spring Storm.' 'Limitation,' 'Rainy Morning' and 'At the Lighting of the Lamps' were all published in *Day & Night*.

[3] Bethell is quoting from a letter of Cresswell (July 7, 1933).

[4] See Psalm 113: 9.

say they havn't so far run to authorship only truly keeping respectable & *not* oh dear putting inferior fruit at the bottom (and hereunto I *must* append one of my favourite "jokes for a season of woe" wh. may have escaped you in Times Lit Supp. to be carefully preserved please and returned with M.S.)[1]

I daresay that before very long I shall make myself obnoxious by ringing up about Talkies or what not so as to goad you into keeping yr. promise about gramophones. My partner wants to see yr. cook books & talk to you more. That wd. be nice for you I reckon – I hope to leave French papers & yr. book on Friday.

In great haste
Yrs. sincerely
M. U. Bethell

This verse of The Long Harbour I did not finish for Press. D'AC wished to substitute it for 2 others – makes a better sequence.[2]

"White hawthorn hedge from old remembered England,
and orchard white, and whiter bridal clematis
the Bush-bequeathed, conspire to strew the valleys
in tender spring; and blackbird, happy colonist,
and blacker, sweeter-fluted tui echo
either the other's song."

Alexander Turnbull Library. fMS-018.

TO J H E SCHRODER – [AUGUST 11, 1933]

Rise Cottage.

Dear Mr. Schroder

Here's this Rainy Morning. Not very nice.

I've now read M.H. his M.S., a sad disappointment! Its really incredibly dull – oh dear, oh dear. What shall I say about it.[3] Its so immature – not a spark of life in the characters – mere puppets – lifeless conversations – most unconvincing. Impossible to be interested! He hasn't even quite got the English language. Of course there are hundreds

[1] The 'favourite joke' has not survived.

[2] Bethell did include this stanza in the final version of the poem, omitting her original stanza 4 (Cresswell wanted to omit st. 5 as well). For the omitted stanza, see *Collected Poems*, p. 105.

[3] Some indication of what she did say can be found in Holcroft's monograph on Bethell, which recalls 'a stern and crushing verdict, delivered without anaesthetic' (p. 46). Years later, Holcroft wrote to her 'You were right in your estimate of my fiction, and I shall be surprised if I ever write another novel' (Mar. 24, 1941).

of much worse novels in circulation so I hope it will sell. But it surely can't be merely this that he's meant to do! Not a hint of humour but I did not look for that. What is good and real are the passages of philosophy & faith, the fruit of life's experiences, but must they be embedded in so dull a story! I hope its better than I think, & just not my genre. That Manzoni on Saturday was a good piece of work – & I liked the ending.[1]

Yours
M. U. Bethell

I found diastole, just so, in a bit of modern verse the other day.[2]

Alexander Turnbull Library. fMS-018.

TO MONTE HOLCROFT – AUGUST 20, 1933

Rise Cottage, Cashmere Hills, Christchurch, N.Z.

Dear Monte

Miss Pollen has unexpectedly to go to Wellington this week (business not pleasure!) & wants me to go with her, so I'm afraid we must postpone the pleasure of the afternoon we planned. I'll write when we return.

I have been thinking over your work a good deal. I looked out yr. short story in the NZ collection[3] & read again the article "Climate" – which I'd cut out of 'Press'.[4] Both are good to my mind – the magazine story is competent work of its kind, to while away a waiting ten minutes, with the little surprise at the end – & nothing to *jar* – as there is in some of the other tales. The article is *most* excellent – The style hangs together – At least that's what I think – I don't trust my judgement very much! Only I try to make sure myself that I'm saying what I mean, & what sounds good to my ear – & I'm very much concerned with *words* – I listen to them, try them – ring them on the counter so to speak.

You have plenty of ideas – its only an affair of perfecting the implement – unlike others who really have nothing to say. You are young still & will be perfecting your work long after *I* am in my grave!

---

[1] See Holcroft's article on the Italian writer in *The Press* (Aug. 5, 1933).

[2] Bethell's phrase 'just so' may imply that she found the word being used in just the fashion V.I.R. complained of, rhyming with goal, whole – exactly as it does, for example, in Wilde's *Panthea*, or Amy Lowell's 'The End.' It has not been possible to identify the 'bit of modern verse' – the word is less uncommon than her critic presumed.

[3] This must refer to *New Zealand Short Stories,* ed. O. N. Gillespie, which includes Holcroft's story, 'The Ball.'

[4] 'Climate' was published in *The Press*, April 1, 1933.

I find *you* in all that you write – sensibility – & insight learned in a hard school.

I reproached myself for making you so late last Sunday – you were tired – I must have mistaken the hour the first time I looked at the watch – I hope you caught the tram – but couldn't hear.

[...]

Its been such a pleasure to know you grown-up – You have my deep respect, & very best wishes for your work.

Yours sincerely
M. U. Bethell

Alexander Turnbull Library. MS-Papers-1186-03.

TO J H E SCHRODER – SEPTEMBER 23, 1933

Rise Cottage. Cashmere.

Dear Mr. Schroder

Herewith the fruit of phrenzy[1] – a drive out on the plain yesterday helped – I hope you will like it now – a bit of a mix-up perhaps – at any rate I must be quit of it. Verse 2, line 6, I had "*b*loom-bright", the machine wrote "*g*loom-bright" – rather a good idea for gorse (clair-obscure, chaud-froid)[2] but dare one?

Item a ditty – which by the way has already been set to music, making quite a pleasant part song (for the time of the year).[3]

Please note, I wd. like the October one to be called "Spring Storm" – and the usual refrain, please return if not required!

Do pray cast your eye on the middle page of Monday's Press – or was it on Tuesday? and see why my newspaper-addict partner ran to me with the cry "Look, the fat's in the fire now!" Which is good irish for "The cat's out of the bag" – And please sympathise with the feeling of mixed anger, amusement, and gratification which took me – Ye gods & wilhemina Stitches! I was almost moved to make you my congee – but then the all-too-useful cheques – and then, the Lookforwarders! So here

---

[1] A week earlier Bethell had described 'Spring on the Plain' as 'quite hateful' and was 'rewriting it in a fury.' The poem was printed, as 'Spring Day on the Plain,' in *The Press* on October 28, 1933.

[2] Fr. Literally, 'Light-dark, warm-cold.' The first is a term used in art (the equivalent of chiaroscuro), the second in cooking.

[3] Probably refers to the willow song that Bethell mentioned to Sidgwick (Nov. 4, 1929).

you are. But does the lewd fellow suppose that one shelters behind a silly pseudonym for no reason?[1]

I havn't quite finished The Unrealists, but must not hold it up any longer.[2]

Yours
"E. H. of the Press"!

I now wish please to read 'The Street' (& others?) and 'Rangiora' and the works of Mr. Fairburn – Can you assist? Yes, certainly you can.[3]

Alexander Turnbull Library. fMS-018.

TO J H E SCHRODER – SEPTEMBER 27, 1933

Rise Cottage. Cashmere.

Dear Mr. Schroder

Business first. I've had another shot at Spring Day (*so* tired of it!) There were 2 very bad spots & you put yr. finger on one of them.[4] The other, two last lines of verse 2. Its better, but still rather an awkward way of conveying that to look into a gorse fence in bloom is eye-dazzling & the scent intoxicating! A few other amendments & back to capitals at line beginnings. As I said, if rejected by the Press, Mr. Duff wd. likely approve of the sentiments.

I am glad that you will not print Rainy Morning – its not really fit for the public – perhaps if I dig it about & dung it[5] it may improve. But a wearisome job –

The little flutter in the Press coincided with a fit of disgust for my own writings – a tinny little lyre, mine! I'd better stop. And I am thinking too much of what this one & that will think – Impure – Oh, vexation bids fair to be drowned in amusement – I have had several condolences from friends who know & sympathise with my Victorian dislike of publicity. But my nephews, whom I saw on Sunday, are really impressed! Anything in the nature of an *ad* – appeals to their idea of concrete value – & my brother writes to congratulate! I do hope they

---

[1] An address to the English Association by L. F. de Berry, in which he identified Bethell as Evelyn Hayes, was reported in *The Press,* Tuesday Sept. 19, 1933.

[2] *The Unrealists*, by Harvey Wickham (1931), was a philosophy of science loaned to Bethell by Archdeacon Whitehead.

[3] 'The Street' was Schroder's own poem; 'Rangiora' was the poem by Carrington about which she had enquired earlier (Sept. 15, 1932).

[4] Schroder's criticism of this and 'Rainy Morning' has not survived.

[5] See Luke 13: 6-9.

won't take to *reading* my productions! especially now that they are so depressed with drought & bad times.

Then pleasure – Thank you! – & we *do* prefer afternoon – tho' we can better emerge in the evening as summer approaches.[1] Unfortunately in the afternoon one can't hope to provoke a coruscation of cocktail! Cocktails are rather since my day, but I have found one helpful on occasion. How very Wodehousey to be able to invent one.

And, if it be possible, Bach please – There is a threatening of a hope of being asked to hear Schnabel Beethoven – and I have just read Schweitzer's My life (another Whitehead book) & what he says about Bach and Organs.[2] He – Archdn Whitehead I mean – did not give instructions about returning books – but that he wd. be in ChCh soon & able to collect those I have here. I wd. like to know what Geoff Alley wd. say to The Unrealists.

[...]

Yours sincerely
M. U. Bethell

Alexander Turnbull Library. fMS-018.

TO MONTE HOLCROFT – JANUARY 8, 1934

Rise Cottage. Cashmere.

Dear Monte

I was getting ready yr. packet of books to send & now here is your letter. The Books' loss is my gain – yr. letter is delightful & brings your surroundings with it. Quite good, I think to lie fallow for a bit – good for Brother Ass to have a turn. I had been thinking that the broken weather wd. make it difficult for you to find quiet to work in, but as it turns out, that has not mattered. I feel *very* envious about the birds – we can't get *them*, out on our picnics. – I've always heard how they abound at Wainui, more than at Akaroa.

By this time you know that the Press has not given you up. I was interested in that Contention & wondered whether it was argumentative enough for their scheme – it is meditative.[3] I sent it to my friend in London – (who godfathered my Garden book) & asked whether he

---

[1] Schroder had invited Bethell and Effie Pollen to his home to listen to recordings of classical music on his recently acquired gramophone.

[2] Schweitzer's *My Life and Thought: an Autobiography* had been published the previous year.

[3] On Nov. 18, 1933, *The Press* began a new, thought-provoking column, called 'Contentions' (to which Bethell had been invited to contribute). Holcroft contended (Jan. 6, 1934) 'That the Novel is Dying.'

thought there wd. be an opening for your essays in English journals – but I don't know whether he will remember to answer the question!

Having retrieved my wonderful G. M. Hopkins at last, it cost me a pang to part with him again, but I know how much he will enrich your holiday. I'm almost sorry that the book makers have got him into focus, & are expounding & annotating him – he was something special & rare – but one must admit that he calls for explanation at times.

Seeing that Traherne suits, I have put in another English mystic – much earlier – in this little book he is connected up with India. (I have his own writings) Sorry its so pencil scored I marked it for reference when I got it & have not rubbed out marks. Traherne wrote a lot of poetry too – you know, but it is quite a failure.[1] Do you find the passage you quote pantheistic – I don't think I do.[2] The 'you' is so distinct. Pantheism seems to end up in muddle, not mystery. There is a lovely sentence somewhere in T. about angels & acorns.[3] Also I have put in another book for the pocket which was on the shelf with Rolle & there must be some connection! You will think that I am much addicted to Oliver Quick.[4]

The Riro came back with the rain to this garden on Tuesday morning before Xmas, & has stayed, off & on. It struck me that his little song was like an old carol – (do you know "the rising of the sun, the running of the deer" one?) & the NZ carol[5] took shape & was done in an hour. If a rhyme like that begins it easily ends!

---

[1] Bethell's opinion may be coloured by the editions of Traherne available to her, which reflect the (detrimental) alterations made by the poet's brother, Philip.

[2] Holcroft had quoted from Traherne's *Centuries of Meditations*, i, 29: 'You never enjoy the world aright, till the Sea itself floweth in your veins, till you are clothed in the heavens, and crowned with the stars' (Jan. 5, 1934).

[3] 'Pigs eat acorns, but neither consider the sun that gave them life, nor the influences of the heavens by which they were nourished, nor the very root of the tree from whence they came. This being the work of Angels, who in a wide and clear light see even the sea that gave them moisture: And feed upon that acorn spiritually while they know the ends for which it was created, and feast upon all these as upon a World of Joys within it: while to ignorant swine that eat the shell, it is an empty husk of no taste nor delightful savour.' *Centuries of Meditations*, i, 26.

[4] Richard Rolle was a 14th century English mystic, 'the hermit of Hampole,' whose exuberant spirituality had something of the flavour of 20th century pentecostalism. Oliver Chase Quick (1885-1944) was Canon of Newcastle, Chaplain to the Archbishop of Canterbury, and later Regius Professor of Divinity at Oxford University.

[5] A cutting of this poem is held in Bethell's papers. The cutting has been taken from a publication called 'Mothers in Australia' and is dated December 1, 1934. It includes an attribution to the *North Canterbury Gazette*, where it was presumably published around Christmas 1933. Unfortunately, no copy of the *NCG* appears to have survived. The poem

Evening. I lent Santayana because he is surely a master of style.[1] He's very sad.

[...]

My holiday has taken the form of ignoring the outside world & gardening steadily, if weather permitted, from morning to night. Very restful, physical labour, – if freely undertaken! And after a good deal of social contact about Christmas-time, a nice change. Many thought journeyings, but nothing, so far of crystallisation on paper. Of course there is much letter writing demanded just now.

I look forward to a good talk on your return – if, in the meantime you feel moved to write about Hopkins or Rolle it will give much pleasure to

Yr. friend
M. U. Bethell

Alexander Turnbull Library. MS-Papers-1186-03.

TO MONTE HOLCROFT – FEBRUARY 1, 1934

Rise Cottage. Cashmere. ChCh.

My dear Monty

Now I have thought over yr. last letter, & it is time to answer it. I am still surprised – I agreed that, for the reasons you gave, yr. visits had better cease – at any rate for the present – but was not prepared for this solemn farewell, not only to me, but to the *books*![2] Is this really necessary? I can easily leave them in town for you, if you don't want to come here. You wd. soon come to the end of my library, no doubt, but what about all these people I have been stirring up to obtain the sort of books you said you could not come by, yourself? I have not heard from the Archdeacon, & think he must have gone through but can send him a list – his library is well furnished with philosophy & ancient history I am sure. There is already the Plotinus & others to follow if desired. And then I am to meet Professor Sinclaire shortly & was going to obtain (if you wish) an invitation for you to visit him. I am sure that he, too, has the kind of book you require – (They say that he is very deaf – & shy – not at all academic – I think you wd. find him accessible – couldn't say

is headed 'A Carol from Maori-Land,' but this is likely to be an editorial headline; the title is 'Rainbird (Riro-Riro) at Christmas-tide.'

[1] George Santayana was an eminent philosopher and minor poet in the early years of the 20th century, with a particular interest in the philosophy of religion.

[2] Holcroft's letter has not survived, and the reason for his 'solemn farewell' can only be guessed at.

this of all professors!) Of course there is such a thing as over-reading & you may feel that you want to chew the cud now for awhile. But I'm certain that you will have to study far more before you are ready to produce the work you had in contemplation.

There are other perplexities. Do you know that I am supposed to be coming to see Ray & the son?[1] She invited me to do so & I asked her to let me know as soon as she was settled again. Our converse has been quite friendly – indeed both she & her mother rang me up & spoke warmly of their gladness about your visits to me, & the advantage, they thought, of these visits to you and yr. work. It was in accordance with what they said, & Ray wrote, that I came to make them a weekly institution. I know of nothing, unless I have been too *churchy,* that could have changed their outlook. Only that it is quite usual for wives, especially young wives, to "mind" their husbands going out without them, & I have thought that perhaps Ray in her care for you, was trying, by urging the visits, to *make* herself like, for your sake, what she did not really like at all! Which is touching.

Also she may have disliked a rather long letter I wrote her just before the holiday, about those 'clairvoyance' faculties of which she spoke & wrote to me. I had disliked very much something she wrote to me about my poetry & at last came to feel that I must explain to her what I conceive to be the christian point of view about these phenomena. Perhaps she showed you the letter. Was it too much of a preachment I wonder?[2]

Both she and her mother spoke to me about having the baby baptised, and the Church, and I thought that if it were her mind to lead her son along the Christian path, I might be of some use in that way, out of my experience.

But, *of course*, if the little wife doesn't want to be friendly, I have no wish to press the acquaintanceship. In fact I have so little time, I very much wish NOT to add to my obligations! But we both liked her & hoped to see her again, & you too, but I can explain to Miss Pollen that you now want a period of unbroken work, & what D'A. Cresswell calls "to be withdrawn".

There are other loose ends – my sister is posting out my Wm. Law volumes, in a beautiful edition, for you to read. Will you not have them? – you could keep them some time. And am I not to send on the bits I put on one side likely to be of interest, and e. g. The Criterion this time, just arrived, has good matter. And I have two others of Santayana! And I

[1] Ray (Aralia Dale) was the second of Holcroft's three wives.

[2] Nor has this letter survived.

have never shown you the Day book I am making of passages looking on life as a journey "The Pilgrims Book". There are some noble pages, but I shall not finish it in my lifetime at the rate I go & am asking my friends to copy any pieces or passages to contribute & hoped you would remember. But never mind! And those O.T. volumes were for a present, if you wd. like them, I can easily make use of them if you would not. You ought to inspect them first, & think you wd. prefer the Authorised version.

There's another present I should like to give you some day, the same as I had made for another friend, the collects epistles & gospels & the psalter bound up together,[1] without the rest, to give you the rhythm of our year. Don't forget, by the way, that every day at 5.15 *in term-time* (but not after all on Fri & Sat & Sun!) there is a good sung evensong at the Cathedral & only about 10 people so you wouldn't feel over crowded – and, if you want quiet for prayer, at 7.30 *every* morning (not Sunday) there is the communion or Mass in the side chapel & an even smaller congregation (but this time one really *bent* on religion) & anyone at the back is not noticed.

Some day I believe you will explore the riches of Christian theology, the tremendous doctrines of the Triune God, & the Word made Flesh, and the Spirit – but this may not be for a long while yet. There was a deep passage in your first letter from Wainui – "contact – a sort of warmth, sometimes denied & sometimes given ... a grace from without –" That is profoundly Christian. As Traherne said (*I think*) "He seeks our love with infinite esteem"[2] (in one of his bad poems) and withdraws to allure. It is tremendous. I feel that I have very little time left in which to work out what this life is meant to mean for me. For us all I say the noble hymn "Veni Creator Spiritus"[3] –

Come, Holy Ghost, our souls inspire,
And lighten with celestial fire.
Thou the anointing Spirit art,
Who dost thy sevenfold gifts impart,
Thy blessed unction from above
Is comfort, life, & fire of love.
Enable with perpetual light

[1] These are the two largest sections of *The Book of Common Prayer*.

[2] 'He courts our Love with infinite Esteem' occurs in a poem simply entitled 'Another,' which takes its title from the preceding 'The Recovery.'

[3] This Latin hymn has been attributed to various authors, including Charlemagne and Gregory the Great, but the best claim to authorship is probably that of Rabanus Maurus (d. 856). Bethell quotes from the translation of John Cosin, found in the 1662 Prayerbook.

The dulness of our blinded sight.

Am I, too, being solemn? But it isn't necessary, surely, to make a goodbye of it, while we inhabit the same town (which indeed I hope ***not*** to inhabit for too long!) and our "paths" might quite easily "converge" in Cathedral Square or Whitcombe & Tombs'! Isn't it a little fantastic? However you will do just as your Inner Light directs, & I'm quite sure that if for whatever reason (there seems to be something to which I havn't the clue) you decide to forego the books as well, you will lose nothing. There are the great sayings about seeking the Kingdom first, & losing life to save it.[1] Your "daimon" has led you on. Its a commonplace that one of the compensations of growing old is to watch the younger ones advance – but how true. And when its a case of not blind Destiny, but the workings of Life Light & Love, then how wonderful!

I've read great things this morning – the week's epistle "I therefore so run not as uncertainly; so fight I, not as one that beateth the air" ... and the day's psalm about the man whose "delight is in the Law of the Lord" who "shall be like a tree planted by the water-side: that will bring forth his fruit in due season"[2] – our lovely English, what a perpetual joy! How awful if religion were clothed in ugly, halting language!

I meant to "answer" yr. Wainui letters, but am not sure now that you wd. like it. I sent too many books, but that was because in yr. first letter you said you could not work, & I thought you might need them on wet days. I agree about Hopkins, but what *I* find foreign in his work is not his Catholicism, of course, but the Roman strain in it. I think it was a pity his hymns were included. (I expect you feel like that about my little Xmas carol) Bridges was right there. That couplet you quote from the Margt Clitheroe fragment does not remind me of Hood, but of one of R. Browning's grotesque bits.[3] There is grotesque in Hopkins, but his noble pages will carry it. I like the sonnets best.

[...]

The driven clouds from the east are making such a lovely lattice-work on the plain, of grey & green & russet. We have had further losses to offset the rise in wool. But it doesn't matter at all. We are very happy – & so please God will you & yours be ... tho' creative work must mean much pain as well as joy. Life must be "integration thro' purification" in oneself, & in relationships & in work.

---

[1] See Matthew 6: 33 and 10: 39.

[2] The quotations come, in turn, from 1 Cor. 9: 26 and Psalm 1: 2-3.

[3] Margaret Clitheroe was a convert to Catholicism, arrested in 1506 for harbouring priests. She refused to plead and was pressed to death. The couplet Holcroft and Bethell found grotesque may have been 'Her will was bent at God. For that / Word went she should be crushed out flat.'

Now for a "parting shot"? If & when you write again please, *please* don't adopt the Australian-American signature "sincerely" without the "yours"! Only once before have I had that, & from an Australian journalist! As for me I will sign

Your old friend
M. U. Bethell

The French quotation I gave you was I think, correctly, this: "Ce sont les vies dépourvues qui ont enrichi le monde". Who said it, I can't remember.[1]

[...]

Alexander Turnbull Library. MS-Papers-1186-03.

TO J H E SCHRODER – AUGUST 22, 1934

Eastbourne Hotel, Wellington.

Dear Mr. Schroder

We went on having more Influenza after that lunch hour music day & at last escaped yesterday to a milder clime, without, I regret to say, returning your overdue books, to wit, C. Carswell's account of D. H. Lawrence,[2] which fills up gaps in the letter, & the preposterous "Life" of Katherine Mansfield,[3] of which one wd. like to say "Let it be deleted" but thank you for letting us be shocked. And M E Coleridge – (you know Bridges about her?) but it is The Seven Sleepers of Ephesus I want to read.[4] All these are ready to come on our return in perhaps two weeks.

Meanwhile I want to ask your advice. D'Arcy invites me to have a dozen or so of my poems printed in a booklet by his man in Auckland. His lecture was the first proper looking pamphlet I've seen produced in N.Z.[5] Do you think it would be acceptable by the public? In other words do you think that if I took £10 of my slender capital & had it done ("in time for Xmas) I could expect to – putting it bluntly – "get my money back"? I should have to see about it immediately.

---

[1] Fr. 'It is the destitute lives that have enriched the world.' I have not been able to identify this quotation. It was obviously one Bethell valued; she also quotes it to Eileen Duggan (June 23, 1937).

[2] Catherine Carswell's *The Savage Pilgrimage: a Narrative of D. H. Lawrence*.

[3] This almost certainly refers to the poorly-received biography by Ruth Mantz (with J. Middleton Murry), *The Life of Katherine Mansfield*.

[4] *The Seven Sleepers of Ephesus* (1893) was Mary Coleridge's first novel.

[5] Cresswell's 'man in Auckland' was the young typographer, Robert Lowry, who had printed the lecture, *Modern Poetry and the Ideal*, earlier that year.

Has D'Arcy written to you about his "Stream"?[1] His letters certainly are a rich entertainment. He really seems to be 'getting something done' & sounds happy. We now seem to be involved in a controversy The Pagan Gods v. Christianity. He says that I don't understand his Polytheism & I say that he doesn't understand my Christianity.

I simply can't bear that Nigel Playfair has died.[2] Too many people are dying. I have stayed too long in the antipodes!

I hope that you will pluck up courage to face our isolation & countrified-ness again, when the spring sets in.

Yours sincerely
Ursula Bethell

It is time I made another effort to turn my wares to account – would the enclosed trifle do for The Press?[3] Please return if not. Have you seen Mr. Sidgwick's book on versification?[4] There are some delightfully Sidgwickian bits in it.

Alexander Turnbull Library. fMS-018.

TO J H E SCHRODER – SEPTEMBER 17, 1934

As from Rise Cottage. Cashmere.

Dear Mr. Schroder

I have just left at The Press office, addressed to you – the D. H. L. and K. M. books (already thanked for in letter 3 weeks ago – we came home on Thursday) – respecting the latter Miss Pollen apologises for delayed return of dust-jacket, which she removed to preserve its integrity & forgot to replace – but has in safety (Rather Irish to preserve *dust-cover*!)

[...]

I am trembling on the brink of this Christmas poem-booklet – won't you put out a hand to restrain – or to egg me on? – One pictures you with finger on Public's pulse – would it be a little tired of E. H. – or wd. there still be some appetite. Could you suggest a good, catchpenny title. Anyhow I daresay that D'Arcy's man would not get it done in time – his

---

[1] Cresswell proposed this publication to be printed by Lowry. Although it is mentioned in Helen Shaw's edition of Cresswell's letters, there is no evidence that it was ever printed.

[2] Sir Nigel Playfair was a prominent English actor who became manager of the Lyric Theatre from 1919 to 1932 (where Bethell saw *Riverside Nights* in 1926).

[3] Bethell enclosed 'Short Story,' which was published Sept. 1, 1934.

[4] *The Making of Verse: a guide to English metres* by Robert Swann and Frank Sidgwick (1934).

own work has not appeared yet. Its for private circulation only he says, so there would be no hurry about that.

This month coming round reminds me of that mis-rhyme I was going to correct. Here is the amendment enclosed. Would you allow me to print it, if it fitted in?

Yours sincerely
M. U. Bethell

Correction (to Anniversary 1933)[1]

Beyond those trees, the morning's opened gateway
And the great ocean's sharp, responsive blue
I saw, & new snow-silvered ranges,
And snowy Tapuaenuku –

Alexander Turnbull Library. fMS-018.

TO J H E SCHRODER – SEPTEMBER 23, 1934

Rise Cottage. Cashmere.

Dear Mr. Schroder

Your words are always worth waiting for – the painful stage notwithstanding when one begins to ask one's self – is he 'most – *too* bored?

My hearty thanks, please, for the really thoughtful advice about proposed publishing venture – just what I needed.[2] In the light of what you say we think – better give it up, or at any rate postpone. D'Arcy first made the suggestion some months ago, when I was feeling rich with my wool cheque in hand, & it seemed quite an amusing gamble, incidentally solving "my Xmas present problem" – But now the money's gone & it wd. be a case of risking capital – less & less a sensible proceeding. D'Arcy said that £10 would produce a booklet of about 12 pieces. Yes, *I* was to pay. Did he not send you his broadcast lecture on poetry? It was very nicely got up, better than anything I have seen in N.Z. (I don't altogether like the Art in N.Z. Productions – a little too Arty?–)[3] The

---

[1] In the TS in Schroder's papers, this stanza reads: Beyond those trees, the morning's open portals / And the great ocean's sharp, responsive blue / I saw, and the snow-beautiful Kaikouras, / And snowy Tapuaenuku ...

[2] Schroder had argued against it, pointing out that books paid for by their authors seldom succeed, but offering to help should she go ahead.

[3] Schroder had confessed himself ignorant of the Griffin Press, and suggested either Harry Tombs, who published *Art in New Zealand*, or the relatively new Caxton Club, whose work he admired.

Griffin Press is his friend in Auckland. Bob Lowry I think was the name.[1] He is printing something for D'A. which should have been out before now, but was involved in 'free speech' disturbances & was, I gathered, in prison for a time.

I thought of having for the 12.

1. Three Poems in Spring ("Willows in the Valley," "October Storm" & "Anniversary")

2. Three poems in Autumn ("Autumn Roses" "Showers of Leaves" & "Autumn Afternoon" or "Nursery Rhyme")

3. Three Places – ("The Long Harbour," "Levavi Oculos" & "Burke's Pass")

4. Three Songs – ("Ditty" "Parakeets" & "Christmas Carol")

nearly all from "The Press" – (I loved your arithmetic about Press payments – just the sort of imaginative finance I like to indulge in!) perhaps this scheme would serve for next year, when I may know more about getting things printed.

Miss Pollen asks "*Do* people want little pamphlets of poetry lying about?" Her answer is No & she would like to spend more in getting a more numerous collection done in book-form, and preferably in England. I thought people in NZ might be inclined to lay out 1/- or 1/6, or even 2/- purely from the Xmas present point of view. You gave me another idea by citing the Caxton "New Poems"[2] I saw that in Wellington – very neat, as you say, outside – even superior – a bit flimsy inside – the paper I mean. Supposing I got them to do the Riro Carol in a red cover to be sold for 6[d] as a Xmas card – I'm not terrible set on it myself – but it pleases people. It was in the North Cant Gazette. (I can't imagine anything less likely to appeal to the personnel of the Caxton Club!) or the "Lighting of the Lamps" which you said was too long for The Press – I do set some store by that – but its not christmassy. I don't suppose I shall do anything. This itch to have things salvaged must be the corollary of sterility – old age partly & partly sheer fatigue from too much doing ("la détresse de l'animal").[3] The fact is this place is too much for us without supplementary labour & I foresee that Rise Cottage will be To Let next year.

[...]

The notes on your reading put me into respectful despair. This situation is familiar, hopelessly pledged as I am to trivialities. Dante – I can get the lilt of the verse, having listened to the intonation of the

---

[1] The Griffin Press is usually associated with Ron Holloway rather than Lowry (who ran the Unicorn Press), although the two were friends and shared premises.

[2] *New Poems*, ed. Ian Milner and Denis Glover (1934).

[3] Fr. literally, 'the distress of the animal.' Perhaps 'bodily anguish.'

language in Italy. Its said that translations of Dante always throw the reader back upon the original. Virgil – I "did" Latin in my girlhood – enough to delight in the sound – & Latin *is* the aqueduct at Nimes – but can only read translations. I have Blackmore's Georgics in a very expensive centenary edition – which I ought really to sell. Thinking that, yesterday, I thought, what *can* one do with such possessions in N.Z.? Useless to leave them to be entombed in a Turnbull Library. If I were rich, I went on to dream, I could found a *lively* home for books & works of art. A noble house of many rooms, surrounded by a spacious garden – Something like the Millbrook Garden,[1] but bigger. People would belong by election, & poor scholars wd. be excused from subscription. A room for books on music – a room for art – Natural history – & so on – for science no, science looks after herself in these days. Works of art would adorn but not be set out museum-like. When I wished that I could buy Robert Field's marble "River and Ocean" I realised that there is nowhere in N. Z. where it could go![2] Refreshments I would allow in this Library Club, but strictly limited to Sherry, Madeira, Lager beer, Perfect Coffee & Huntly & Palmer's biscuits. Radio strictly prohibited. An E.M.G. gramophone wd. be established in a distant room – But Silence would be the prevailing note. In the garden in summer I wd. appoint weekly country dancing & pastoral plays. I wd. allow archery in a further field, but no games where one person works evil upon another. I wd. put the whole in the charge of a sort of Lady Abbess, really awe-inspiring – with a staff either of nuns, I think, or Chinese scholars. The top floor of all shall be a chapel, the fittings copied from the English church at Venice – renaissance – & quakerish-plain. A mass shall be said other weekly by the Chinese christian chaplain, who's in charge of the Theological & Philosophical libraries. He wears Chinese dress & is allowed to play his reed-flute in the garden in the morning. If he can't do all the work, he shall have a Japanese assistant. And there shall be from time to time demonstrations of how not to read poetry aloud – (Have you ever heard it really well-read? cf. Appassionata) So I ran on – And this morning (You have read Dunne's "Experiments with Time")[3] I take up a book in which

---

[1] A small area of parkland adjacent to Christchurch's Hagley Park.

[2] On Bethell's efforts to acquire this sculpture, see Vicki Hearnshaw's article in *Bulletin of New Zealand Art History*. The piece is mentioned several times in the letters to Brasch following. Field was born in England and trained at the Royal College of Art in London before taking up a post at the Dunedin School of Art. With Bethell's encouragement, Toss Woollaston studied under him in 1932. Later, Field's commitment to the Oxford Group also influenced Woollaston.

[3] J. W. Dunne's *An Experiment with Time* (1927) included the notion that it was possible to 'recall' events before having been exposed to them.

I find an account of Abraham Cowley's "Proposition for the Advancement of Experimental Philosophers" his college of 20 philosophers & cooks & four old women & a Chaplain is clearly a relation of my library – A "young" country could do with many converted Millionaires or Conservative communists.

I was pleased that the Press printed "Short Story". Absence in other parts with other papers brings out the excellence of The Press – I arise from reading Professor Wall's & Monty Holcroft's confessions – Delighted that Monty should be in touch with such a body as the English Association (Thank you for handing on books – he wrote.) I had thought that religious issues were banned from the Contentions, but if so, the ban has been lifted.[1] This at any rate will stir up controversy & the habitués[2] of the correspondence columns will rush to the fray with all their notions as usual – I should like some competent person to contend for the Jewish & Christian doctrine, ignored by the Professor – Or even to quote Emily Brontë[3] – Yet I don't know – these things are too big to be picked up in a newspaper article.

[...]

With reiterated thanks
yours sincerely
Ursula Bethell

PS Monday. So Arch Whitehead is to take up the running.

Alexander Turnbull Library. fMS-018.

TO THE EDITOR OF THE PRESS – OCTOBER 1, 1934

[Rise Cottage, Cashmere Hills, Christchurch, N.Z.]

Sir

Among the correspondence printed this morning on Professor Wall's and Archdeacon Whitehead's articles are some verses signed "E.H." Since these initials are the same as those which have appeared

[1] Arnold Wall's 'Contention', Sept. 22, 1934, proposed 'That We Ought Not to Believe in a Future Life.' It did indeed stir up controversy as Bethell anticipated; in addition to various letters, it drew an opposing Contention from Archdeacon Whitehead, published the following week.

[2] Fr. 'The regular' (contributors).

[3] The notion of a future life occurs in a number of Brontë's poems, but Bethell may be thinking of 'No Coward Soul is Mine,' which criticizes those who 'waken doubt in one / Holding so fast by thine infinity; / So surely anchored on / The steadfast rock of immortality.'

under my own occasional contributions to "The Press," may I disclaim the use of them this time?[1]

Yours, etc.,
E.H.

No MS extant.

TO MONTE HOLCROFT – DECEMBER 29, 1934

Rise Cottage, Cashmere Hills, Christchurch, N.Z.

My dear Monte

I am going through, and destroying where expedient, many boxes of letters & papers, preparatory work to selling this house. I have come across one of yours, written rather more than a year ago, which makes me resolve to write to you, it may [be] a kind of farewell.

I think that you cannot have seen the Press or the Sun on Nov 9th, where the notice appeared of the death of my dear friend Miss Pollen, the day before – for surely you would have had the heart to send me a few lines. It was very sudden; she had severe head pain, heroically borne, for about 3 weeks before, but until an hour before the end – the doctor assured me that there was nothing seriously wrong. In spite of that I had been very anxious for a week, & was alone when the last seizures began, so it has been a great strain & nerve-shock to me, & I am only just beginning to be a little better physically.

It means a complete shattering of my life; from her I have had love, tenderness, & understanding for 30 years, & close & happy companionship (in spite of the inevitable superficial differences) in this home for 10 years. I shall not want another home on this planet.

Not long before this happened, I had arranged to transfer my house in town to the Church, to be "St Faith's House of Sacred Learning" – which so far has been carried on in very cramped quarters.[2] As soon as I was left alone, my friend the Head Deaconess[3] came & took charge here, & at once offered me a flat in the house, to be at least a temporary refuge. The college will not move there till May, but we have to make some alterations beforehand, & as one or more of the flats will be

---

[1] One of the letters in support of Professor Wall consisted of 4 stanzas of verse by an unknown 'E.H.' Bethell was quick to deny authorship.

[2] In 1929 a diocesan commission in Christchurch had initiated arrangements to provide for training for Anglican women who wished to undertake work for the church. Initially, St Faith's House of Sacred Learning was based in the deanery, and then at the Bishop Julius Hostel, until May 1935, when it moved into the house gifted by Bethell.

[3] Joan Spencer-Smith (1891-1965) had been educated in theology in London, where she had also taught divinity and theology, before her appointment to St Faith's.

vacated earlier I may leave here in March. It is of course the house where you came to tea as a little boy. The Post Office will be notified when I change my address to 47 Webb St. St Albans.

I think however that I shall get away to England in about six months' time, when my affairs are settled, to see my sister & her sister.

Before I sail I hope to have printed a choice of the poems which have appeared in the Press & shall have pleasure in sending you a copy, if you wd. care for one. And I have written to my publisher, asking that the rest of the edition of the Garden in the Antipodes (which is no longer selling) shall not be remaindered for I wish to pay for what has not been recovered of the cost of production, from the proceeds of the sale of this house (owing to a mortgage there cannot be very much [left], but I trust there will be *some*.) I shall therefore be able to give you a copy, if you still wish for one. The book has now become to me a kind of sacred thing, & I want the remaining copies to be where they will be valued.

My books will be housed at St Faith's for their use. The Deaconess will be very pleased to lend you (as I shall ask her to do) any book that you might find useful. Perhaps I may venture to say that I have never quite understood your attitude about the books Archdeacon Whitehead offered to lend, & the Plotinus offered by another friend. You did not even say thank you for the offer – it seemed to me ungracious. I expect, I have no doubt that there is an explanation, but it troubled me on your behalf.

I may tell you that we had decided to let this house furnished for a term in 1935, in order to have a change of scene, so that I had had, in these latter months, a sense of finality, but I did not think the ending would come in this way. You will remember still, I think, the birthday outing in 1933, which was "for the Holcrofts". This year we drove again, on a lovely afternoon, round by Loburn, taking one to whom we had promised an outing. It was our last drive. I wonder indeed that, that week, I had not an inkling, so much importance did my dear friend give to my "diamond jubilee" week, & so much kindness did she spend on it. My heart was so full of thankfulness on the second Sunday of that October! that with an energetic impulse I offered to God all I had, friend, home, life itself. How swift, how apparently ruthless was the answer! I have always felt the pressure of the "Either-Or" of life – deliberate cruelty or deliberate love. Just now I am conscious of nothing but darkness, nothing but heartache – but these purging views, my reason says, *do* purge. At once, in a flash, I saw unrolled the many occasions on which I had shown hardness of heart & selfishness, & made *stupid* mistakes arising from selfishness, and such a showing *is* purgatory. So let us take heed, Monte, to cherish the opportunities of kindness to the fellow-travellers given to us, while we are yet in the way with them. Many things become important, & others trivial, when the opportunity is gone. Death is indeed, to the desolate, a transvaluer of values – & yet what was real before, is real still.

[...]

And "E. H." has ceased to be. Already another "E. H." had been signing letters & "poems" in "Press" & "Sun", & I had decided not to use the signature again. There will now be no occasion to do so.

Herewith I send my usual good wishes for the progress of your work, & general good wishes for 1935. There is one discovery in life worth making, is there not, the discovery of God ... or one should say rather that He discovers Himself. When this present darkness passes, I shall surely find that I know more of Him. Whether or not it is His design to make of you "a great author" one can't tell, but I shall pray that there may be discovered by you what must be His 'perfect will' & do you, Monte, please make that prayer for

Your old friend
M. U. Bethell

Alexander Turnbull Library. MS-Papers-1186-03.

TO FRANK SIDGWICK – DECEMBER 30, 1934

Rise Cottage, Cashmere Hills, Christchurch, N. Z.

Dear Mr. Sidgwick

I now write to tell you that my "little Raven" (Garden in the Antipodes page 13) flew away suddenly on November the 8th. I was alone when the last seizure came, & saw Death pounce upon her with dreadful mastery. She had had severe head pain for some 3 weeks, & bore it heroically, but up to the last hour the doctor assured me that there was nothing seriously amiss. So neither of us knew that she was going away. But she had celebrated my 60th birthday (on Oct 6th) with such particular enthusiasm & loving kindness that I might almost have felt *fear*. From her I've had tender love & understanding & dependence for 30 years & 10 years of happiness in this home, & now must begin again alone.

The reason I write now is to explain that the book has, by the stroke of death, become something "tapu" to me, & to beg of you not to "remainder" the unsold copies, or whatever sad thing is done to dead books.[1] From the proceeds of the sale of this house, I wish to indemnify

[1] Sidgwick replied (Feb. 12, 1935), 'We are out of pocket some £25, and never thought of remaindering because there is practically no remainder market.... There *is* an euthanasia

you for the loss your firm has incurred, if you will kindly let me know what that loss is, and in the meantime I ask you to be good enough to send me 12 copies & charge them to my account – I know of people in N.Z. who would value a copy, but have not been able to afford one. At the moment I have no money in hand, but shall have – the Slump is by no means over in N.Z. but it is better, & it is again possible to sell property upon terms – & I hope to sell this house quite soon, & even if, as the agent says, I shall lose £1000 upon it, such considerations do not affect me now.

My address will now be *47 Webb St, St Albans, Christchurch*. A little while before the blow fell, I had arranged to transfer our old home in town (which I had let in flats) to the Church for a house of training & instruction. (To be called St Faith's House of Sacred Learning.) The Deaconess in charge is a friend of mine & she offers me a flat there, to be at any rate a temporary refuge. (Make to yourself friends of the mammon etc!)[1] Now I shall take back the furniture to them – I shall not want another home on this planet. All this has shaken me very much – I've had my share of earthly chastisement, but this is the most severe. I go on winding up Rise Cottage, & soon it will be a dream. It is a kind of dying.

I am very restless, too – & as soon as it seems possible, think of going to England – & so may yet hope to "clasp your friendly 'and" as the Salvation Army sings.[2] Before I leave NZ I hope to have printed in a paper pamphlet, by a young man who turns out a good job, some at any rate of the pieces which have appeared in our "Press" – If this is done, I shall send you a copy. And that will be goodbye to another phase, for I can't think of being anything but dumb till the Lord gives me a new song,[3] which I cannot sing now.

I can't refrain from adding – my head & heart are so full of little Effie (her parents, at a loss for a name for a *girl*, opened Lord Tennyson!)[4] two little bits of her. Like most of the Irish she never grew up (we were always laughing) & like many not-Irish never learnt to spell – I found a little fragment among her papers as follows: "The Cronacle of the blessings of U.B. & E.P. caught in Gods own country* In the winter of 1931

"by Slump & Earthquake for their sisters D. & R.

---

for books: the unbound pages are reduced to pulp again, the ink dispersed through the fibres, and all becomes papier maché – or poetrie manqué.'

[1] See Luke 16: 9.

[2] From 'Will you meet me at the fountain,' by Philip Paul Bliss.

[3] A recurrent image in the Psalms: see 33: 3; 40: 3; 96: 1; 98: 1; 149: 1.

[4] The name occurs in Tennyson's early poem 'The May Queen'.

"Economy having to be the order of the day by necessity
"U.B & E.P. decide they will enjoy it. So they begin
"by counting their assets, which are:
"First – themselves. Each is lucky to have each
"other. They fully recognize that – in spite of
"the many annoying ways of the other.
"Next comes the Home – –

And then some notes "Cat" "Car" & on the "Climate". I don't know whether she ever finished or sent it, but it was nice to find it now.

[Added in margin:] *(patriotic New Zealanders call it so of course)

The other scrap is a dream (a *real* dream) which I copied out myself when she told it to me & wrote it down on St Patrick's Day 1929 – I thought it had a good deal of charm – (and hope that I have not sent it to you before!)[1]

We'd sometimes thought of writing about the *interior* of "the home". It was *so* nice – lovely old things we have with their patina of associations, on both sides. But the meaning has gone, & the associations are with the dead.

Yours sincerely
Ursula Bethell

Bodleian Library Oxford. MS Sidgwick & Jackson 142, fols. 145-146v.

---

[1] Bethell enclosed with the letter the narrative (about 350 words) of Effie Pollen's dream, which is still extant in the Sidgwick & Jackson papers in the Bodleian Library.

III: 1935–1937

TO MONTE HOLCROFT – JANUARY 3, 1935

Rise Cottage. Cashmere. Christchurch.

My dear Monte

I don't want to side-track you into a correspondence with me, but your letter has been so curiously helpful that I feel I must thank you for it before the week is out.[1] Not only the human sympathy, which always brings some little alleviation, but chiefly what you say about God & prayer. I have always known that life is totally meaningless without God - - God is the beginning and the end, and the ground, & the meaning & the will.[2] '*This* is eternal life, to know God, and'[3]... Now I am in darkness. But if, as you say, you gained that much, then God must have been at work somehow in me, without my knowing or feeling it. It is a very sustaining thought, in my tears.

Its so true what you say also about seeing all things from one's own consciousness. In this case the relationship was prevailingly maternal – (tho' she was very protective & supporting to me too) & that is why every fibre of my being calls out for her now. (They are mistaken who think that such relationships are only known when physically based) – That would be my private grief. (But I suppose there must be perfect paternal relationships too.) It is a strange experience! Being happy, offering for safe-keeping to the God of love, my loved friend, and home, and life itself – not only for safe keeping but that I might know this God better – behold it all gone – three fearful weeks & then the blow. I seem even to have lost God. No, He exists – & my reason & my whole experience tell me that He exists & that *nothing* is lost, but I am in the dark & in pain. You say that this sorrow will bring gifts, & I believe that to be perfectly true – or else everything is madness. I never could slur over things, or take anodynes, I want to know it all – and this death & *destruction* that I *saw*, must be lived through & known.

But I must tell you this: – The *consciousness* of God came to me, as to so many, chiefly in the solitudes of Nature. Face to face with horrors in east London, in the war, that wasn't enough – I looked at my crucifix & tried to understand. I took Christianity for my life pattern, finding no

---

[1] Holcroft's letter has not survived.

[2] Although the notion of God as beginning and end is ultimately Biblical, the language here is reminiscent of the writing of Julian of Norwich; in particular, the notion of God as 'ground' occurs throughout her *Revelations of Divine Love*. Cf. Chapter 62.

[3] See John 17: 3. The text continues 'and Jesus Christ, whom Thou hast sent.'

other better one, or nearly as good, & it has been my road. But (how shall I express it?) a blind following – a dim road. And now that everything is broken up & I am starting out again alone, I begin to wonder, am I now to learn what that "and" really implies. "This is eternal life to know God *and*" –

That one 'acquainted with grief'.[1] There was evidently a perfect relationship of Love – could one not say a perfect human relationship – and then 'Why hast Thou forsaken me?'[2] It is very deep.

I was talking with one yesterday who has been thrown with Spiritualists. That's not the way. One is tempted to say "Oh, if she could only come back for ten minutes & I would tell her how sorry," but no, one must accept this destruction, & get to know the real life. One flash of *knowledge* that the life has gone on, & the love is still there, & the rest of the way wd. be joyful. No mere guesses will do. There must be a complete *reversal* of mortality. That end of the creed, one says so glibly in church – "the communion of saints – the forgiveness of sins – the resurrection of the body – and the life everlasting" – am I perhaps to get to *know* what it really means – but I will anticipate nothing.

Thou hast forsaken me. Into thy hands.[3]

Dear Monte, I recognised in you a true faith, a willingness to risk all, & go out into the dark. I told you that I saw you were further on than I was about this willingness to *lose all* & plunge into the unknown. Now I am dwelling on your thought that life is *preparation* (I've held that as a *theory*!) Perhaps those ten years in our cottage were too happy – too *earthly* – true – & I must change over to 'eternal in the heavens'.[4]

But first there is this desolation, & stepping off into the dark. Prophesying without knowing, she made my birthday a reminder of my own pilgrim-emblem.[5] The cake surmounted by its "60 years" milestone, was adorned with my pilgrim-shells. She made me read the Bunyan hymn "who would true valour see" etc.[6] – So now I start.

Thank you, Monte. I shall be glad to feel that you are pressing on.

M. U. B.

Alexander Turnbull Library. MS-Papers-1186-03.

---

[1] See Isaiah 53: 3.

[2] See Psalm 22: 1; Matt. 27: 46.

[3] See Luke 23: 46.

[4] See 2 Cor. 5: 1.

[5] Bethell had adopted as a private emblem the scallop-shaped shell worn by English pilgrims to the shrine of St James at Compostela.

[6] The hymn is found almost at the end of Part II of *The Pilgrim's Progress*, just as Mr. Valiant-for-truth reaches the Enchanted Ground. It also appears in *Hymns Ancient and Modern*.

TO J H E SCHRODER – DECEMBER 9, 1935

St Faith's House, 47 Webb St.

Dear Mr. Schroder

I should have answered about the flat before now, but there has been a jostle of things these last days. I wd. gladly have minded your goods, but am afraid its too soon.

I want to get away from ChCh, for the winter months & *not* to pay rent then. You do not say what rent & how many rooms? I still have a good deal of furniture but can leave it here. My room here will be wanted by the institution before long, but I *think* I can stave it off.

Won't you come & see me? I should be so glad. I am accessible quite apart from the institution. Come to tea – or why not lunch & *cook* it. I am doing that very awkwardly & unwillingly, but am learning.

Some books of mine have come from England which I should like to [show] you. You will easily hit on some albatross or ostrich reason, if you don't want to come & I shall not take it amiss!

Yours sincerely
M. U. Bethell

Alexander Turnbull Library. fMS-018.

TO MONTE HOLCROFT – DECEMBER 20, 1935

St Faith's. Webb St. ChCh.

Dear Monte

I am so glad to hear from you – & must tell you that I was going to post a note to you this very evening (having got away greetings to distant places this aftn) to say that I was back & should be so glad to see you. I stayed away longer than was planned & it did me good. Now I am here for some months I think. [...]

ChCh is certainly a place one needs a change from – it tends to be depressing. I asked the Deaconess to keep anything with your signature in the Press for me, so have read your contributions, & congratulate you.

I am glad to hear that things have been better for you materially – but *must* it be at that price?[1] I am reminded of the litany "In all time of

[1] Holcroft had written a note in which he referred to 'our most prosperous Christmas so far,' but noting that 'this indescribable sweetness of Communion does not survive the days of prosperity. The world rolls back its tide; you stand upon your own foundations, and even though you strive hard to keep that subtlest beauty of contact, it somehow fades.' (Dec. 20, 1935) However, the context does not make clear whether the

our tribulation, in all time of our wealth, in the hour of death, & in the day of judgement"[1]... I, on the contrary, seem to have lost something that I had in the days of our wealth – almost I wd. say the presence of God, but my intelligence tells me that God *is* still, & that I must be patient. These times are remedial I believe. Some day it will be said "Its all over now. You can go." I have been shocked & numbed, but this Xmas-time brings a very keen pain of loss. It was like a sudden fuse of all the lights in the house of the soul. But one must make the effort of prayer, in the dark.

With all good wishes
M. U. Bethell

Alexander Turnbull Library. MS-Papers-1186-03.

TO JOHANNES ANDERSEN – JANUARY 4, 1936

47 Webb St. N.1. Christchurch.

Dear Sir[2]

My friend Mr. D'Arcy Cresswell advised me to get into touch with the N. Z. Book Week.[3] I do not know what, or where, or when the Book Week is, but since you are, I am told, in charge of it, I am posting to you a copy of my little book "From a Garden in the Antipodes." This was written during the ten years I spent on the Cashmere Hills – I don't know whether that constitutes a claim to be called a N. Z. author. If this be a way of making it better known, I should be glad to take it, if only for the sake of the publishers, who did not advertise it in N. Z.

Yours faithfully
(Miss) M. U. Bethell

(The book you see was signed "Evelyn Hayes")

Alexander Turnbull Library. MS-Papers-0148-029B.

'Communion' refers to a religious experience, to human contact or to communion with nature.

[1] The concluding petition that Bethell omits is 'Good Lord, deliver us.'

[2] Johannes Andersen (1873-1962) was at this time Librarian of the Alexander Turnbull Library. Danish by birth, he had a particular interest in Maori culture, having published collections of Maori myths and legends, and accompanied Elsdon Best on ethnographic expeditions.

[3] Bethell is referring to the 1936 Authors' Week, organised by PEN, and held in several main centres in April and May to celebrate and promote New Zealand writing.

TO JOHANNES ANDERSEN – JANUARY 24, 1936

47 Webb St. N.1.

Dear Mr. Andersen

Your very kind letter leaves me still in the dark about the "Book Week" of which Mr. Cresswell spoke! This was the reason for sending you mine – I hoped you wd. say what one has to do – to what one is committed? My names are:- Mary & Ursula, but I do not wish to give up the dull pseudonym, & did not think they would be required. I have, since the book, gone further afield for the subjects of my verses, & a good many about the N. Z. scene have appeared in the Press & North Canty Gazette (mostly rhymed).[1] I am hoping to have a selection from these printed in N. Z. in the course of the year, if I find I can afford it, & shall have pleasure in sending you a copy when & if it is done. Sidgwick & Jackson took all risks about the Garden Book. I have not much acquaintance with N. Z. Flora, but noticed in the upper Rangitata Valley, whence I am just returned, what looked like a pretty rose-coloured acaena. The Teddy Bear made of burrs is a delightful idea – thank you for telling me about that.[2]

I am no longer a gardener, nor a householder. The friend who shared my Cashmere home died suddenly a year ago, & the house is sold & everything changed. I am not quite as old as your friend at Wanganui,[3] but am "getting on" & do not suppose that much writing will go on after this break up in one's life.

With many thanks for your kind words.

Yours sincerely
M. U. Bethell

P. S. *January 27*

I was vexed to find, yesterday, this letter overlooked upon my writing-table & must beg pardon for the unintentional discourtesy. Meanwhile I have been prompted, by references to landscape in your

---

[1] Andersen replied at some length to Bethell's first letter, assuring her that her volume did 'constitute a claim to be considered a New Zealand author – though you give your love altogether to exotics' and describing himself as 'charmed with the verses ... even if you only occasionally succumb to the lure of rime' (Jan. 21, 1936).

[2] Andersen had commented on the native piripiri (*acaena*), found in Bethell's 'Crisis,' and related an anecdote of his son constructing a teddy bear entirely from the burrs for a horticultural show.

[3] Andersen had mentioned 'a Suffolk lady, over 90,' author of *My New Zealand Garden*. The work was published anonymously in Wanganui in 1902, and subsequently in London in 1905.

letter, to send the enclosed 3 pieces,[1] which may be of some interest – and envelope for their return when you have had time to look at them.

M. U. B.

Alexander Turnbull Library. MS-Papers-0148-029B.

TO RODNEY KENNEDY – JUNE 28, [1936]

Mt. Harper Hostel. Peel Forest
(really 22 miles beyond & up!)

My dear Rodney[2]

[...]

This certainly is a wonderful spot – the view is magnificent! The hubbub of skating crowd last weekend wasn't altogether my choice – but the hot thaw today suits my purpose very well (tho' no skaters means no gain to the enterprising ice-area & hostel folk) & I am getting on with letters.

So far with the booklet. The MS is complete & in D. Glover's hands[3] – but I couldn't think of a title – I went back to arrangement by seasons – on D'Arcy Cresswell's advice – & am wondering whether "Time and Place" or "Seasons & Places" would do. I think it will look very nice, handset, and dressed in grey & green. We think 2/–. Fifteen pieces of verse.

I posted Lyttleton Harbour – but the Poets Progress (a copy to replace mine was given to me!) is left behind in Webb St. Toss might collect it. I look forward to hearing from you about the Fields & everything. How kind you were, planting those trees, & bringing apples – which are so valuable & refreshing here.

I brought a lot of solid books, but fear they won't be read amid all this stir. The lorry journey was enjoyable, & all my gear came so easily. I am rather yearning for water colours which I couldn't find at Webb St – but of course I couldn't really convey it. [...] I wander about looking at the mountains as of yore, but private human pain sweeps over me now –

---

[1] Two of the three can be identified from Andersen's reply as 'By Burke's Pass,' and 'Levavi Oculos.'

[2] Rodney Kennedy (1909-1989) was at this time an artist, and passionate supporter of modernist developments in the arts. He studied with Robert Field, and was a very close friend and sometime lover of Toss Woollaston. Later, he became an influential art critic and collector.

[3] Although he later became known as a significant poet, Denis Glover (1912-1980) had at this stage just begun his career as printer and publisher under the Caxton imprint. Bethell's book was one of the first significant publications from the press.

& the world of nature has gone dumb. Never never must one capitulate to a negative view, however, whatever one's *feelings* may be. You are sad sometimes I know one must include pain in the universe – & at all costs as Paul said *Stand* – "Having done all – stand."[1]

This air is helpful – one feels so *well.* I really think Toss must come up, before or after Dunedin. At meals I am reading that little book about Chinese art called The flight of the Dragon[2] – It is quite interesting.

How did the poor little cyclamens get on? It was rather cruel to upheave them just as they had leaved.

Well, I suppose I must go out for exercise though it is [a] waste of a good quiet hour – Tell me what you think of the names, or suggest something else.[3]

M. U. B.

Hocken Library. MS-0741-002.

To Toss Woollaston – July 10, 1936

Mt Harper Hostel. Peel Forest. Sth Canty

My dear Toss,

It seems to be *your* turn. I did *not* write to ChCh, knowing that with our slow & infrequent mails it couldn't possibly get to you.

[...]

Your all-night journeys in this wintry weather sound rather too severe & I am glad there is to be a lull before the Exhibition.[4] I wish I *could* be there! (tho' no good at speech-making) but you know I am tied to spots always by lack of money nowadays – paid 5 wks in advance here, so feel I have a roof over my head. How one *could* move around if one were wealthy! One of my oldest friends[5] writes from Honolulu that he inspects schools in Fiji before going back to London & it would be such a chance to meet! And I'm not very courageous about winter travel.

I find myself wishing for cobalt, ultramarine, yellow ochre & something to make grey shingle & purple shadow, & a sketching-block – all of these are buried at Webb St. This longing to reproduce is curious –

---

[1] See Ephesians 6: 13.

[2] Originally published in 1911, Laurence Binyon's essay on 'the theory and practice of art in China and Japan' had just been republished by J. Murray (London).

[3] Kennedy approved of the first title, describing it as having 'a universal savour about it,' and also of the return to the seasonal arrangement (July, 1936).

[4] Woollaston's first solo exhibition, largely conceived and organised by Kennedy, was held in Dunedin at the end of July.

[5] Arthur Mayhew.

it wd. only end in disappointment – but the lines & colours are extraordinarily beautiful. I suppose the wish to draw comes from the fact that I can't write now. Not that the landscape *excites* me as it used to do – I seem to be paralysed in mind. But I look at the scene with a kind of wistful amazement.

[...]

Yesterday evening I went for a walk towards sundown & it was so still that the snow peaks were reflected in the bright blue stagnant reaches of the river & a succession of shadows from the nearer rocky hills lay across the scene, shapes sharply outlined. It was a wonderful pattern.

[...]

I won't write to Rodney this time, but thank him for his letter. I always enjoy his incisive remarks & have a real respect for his judgements. So glad he approves of "Time & Place" for the booklet – Denis Glover was all against it,[1] but Dr. Helen Simpson (Ph.D. you know not medical) calls it "inspired, nothing less" "the exactly right title". So I shall insist. Does Rodney perceive an implicit answer to Browning's "Never the time" etc?[2] I was pleased when I thought of it. I am not sure that there's *room* now for "Time, tacit wardress"[3] – Yes I do feel more self reliant now!

[...]

Well, I must get more mail ready. Have had such a spate of letters here – but very advantageous for dealing with them. 31 pages of theology from Arthur Prior. I ought to become quite educated at last, with all of you young progressives assisting me!

Yours affectly with good luck to the show
M. U. B.

Hocken Library. MS-0996-3/225.

TO TOSS WOOLLASTON AND RODNEY KENNEDY – JULY 22, 1936

Mt Harper Hostel. Peel Forest.

My dear Toss & Rodney

What exciting letters – I don't often feel, these days, that I should really like to do this or that – but I certainly *should* like to see that Exhibition. It is quite *noble* of you, Toss, to send those materials, to

[1] Glover's reservations are quoted by O'Sullivan, *Collected Poems*, p. 105.

[2] Browning's poem (with this title) begins with the lines 'Never the time and the place / And the loved one all together.'

[3] The poem in question, 'Limitation,' appeared in *Day & Night*.

think of it in the first place, & take the trouble, & then I fear you have *bought* them! – You certainly shall have them back – & with *interest* from my supplies in ChCh! It seems to be up to me to have a shot at it – anyhow I can't anymore say "I wish I had etc" & *imagine* results.

[...]

This Groupism is really a tiresome phase – or seems so to me – for a person like R.N.F! but we must wait & see how he emerges.[1] I can't stand the *jargon* – American tags & slogans. R.N.F. when there were no others there, came out like a moon from the clouds, fitfully. He is a great dear – He was trying to help me & do me good. No doubt he did.

Thank you for hint about vice-ultramarine, but I wonder whether cobalt & rosemadder will make this *steely* grey? Must experiment. The shingle I mean. The children's lino cuts in this book make me want to draw.

But the one thing that has given me a little quiver of *happiness* here is a lone stray riro-riro – who began to sing (to me – it seemed) in the matagouries a few yards away – He seems to know some secret – Always was a special bird of ours.

[...]

Rodney – so glad you like Lyttleton Harbour. It has bored many & I thought might bore you – Of *course* keep it – I was only prepared to relieve you of a redundancy.[2] D'Arcy wd. be pleased with what you say. Do you still want to borrow the Poets Progress. Its in ChCh. safely. How could you hurt your knee at the Fields' flat? (Now if it had been planting trees at Webb St!) Can't you get him to come & see you & Toss, unmixed with Groupers?

You both complain of being tired – will it be better after the show? I wish you were both here to paint my scenery – but the show seems to forbid it. I think I have another 4 weeks, about, here. The air here is so marvellous – it feels as if it belonged to a different planet – higher & more sparkling far than even Cashmere in winter & I'm afraid no cobalt wd. convey this scintillant blue – & the noise of the rushing water adds to the sparkle – But I can't respond as I used – so dulled. "Shell-shocked".

---

[1] The Oxford Group, a nondenominational evangelical movement, was founded in 1908 by a Lutheran preacher, Frank Buchman. It stressed honesty, unselfishness and a pure lifestyle, together with daily prayer. It changed its name to Moral Re-armament in 1938 when Oxford University protested the use of its name. (Another 'Group' appears in these letters: an independent exhibiting body of artists.)

[2] Bethell had offered to send the book (Cresswell's *Lyttelton Harbour* had been published earlier that year) to a friend in England if Kennedy had not wanted to keep it.

Caxton Press lecturing me about giving away booklet! & has put price up to 2/6. Only 250 he says, *can't* be given away – Well, I shall give one to Toss, not Rodney – because latter has been recipient of D'Arcy!

[...]

Best of good wishes to both.
M. U. B.

Hocken Library. MS-0741-002.

TO RODNEY KENNEDY – SEPTEMBER 14, 1936

St Faith's. Webb St. ChCh.

My dear Rodney

I'm so used to green letters from you that red-brown seemed quite uncanny – but I hadn't thought it gory till you pointed it out. That *was* a kind thought to write a welcome back letter – & I take the will for the deed. I found my quarters chimney swept & spring-cleaned & have since been making a real effort to bring order into my chaos – now that I am to stay here for another year for sure, it must be done. My parlour is already vastly improved, as I am sure you wd. agree – Its very sad work settling my things alone, but I must not go on in this muddle – I don't know where my books are – One has to remember that the lost friend would rather have me found in pleasing surroundings so I shall go on with it to please her.

I should not have guessed that such a job as your present one existed in N.Z.[1] – I thought that everything even tic*k*s (no, not "tics" that has another meaning) would already be illustrated in books. That was really funny about the legs – stupid scientist not to unbend to your wit![2]

Toss has sent me his review & I think it is very good.[3] I mean a good piece of writing. As I have said to him people might consider it too indulgent, but no one could call it anything but intelligent. I feel very grateful for it (thanks to you too – this is like the birth notices! for the trouble you took as intermediary–) because the one in the Press is distressingly feminine.[4] Don't you think Toss has been clever in his

---

[1] Kennedy was working as an illustrator at the University of Otago Medical School.

[2] Kennedy related having to enlarge a drawing 'as test of ability.... the drawing ... had no representation of that variety of tic's legs so another was substituted. ... I archly asked whether I should label it Amblyomina Hebraeum legs courtesy of Amblyomina Tholloni – this levity was coldly received.' (Undated letter.)

[3] 'Verse: a poet's second book' by M.T.W. *Otago Daily Times,* Sept. 12, 1936.

[4] 'Songs from a Quiet Place,' a review of *Time & Place* by M. A. Innes, was published in *The Press*, Sept. 12, 1936.

conveyance of rather subtle ideas? Yes, he has insight. It may be too kind, but it does please me! I have told him how glad I am that you both like the Envoy, which was specially for the book. Denis Glover thought it was the best one of the collection. I think its the end.

"Tacit wardress" enclosed as requested. It was in the M.S. I sent to D'Arcy Cresswell beforehand & he thought well of it – but it had to give way to the Envoy, because of the paging.[1] D'A.C. wishes to do a review.

In re "personal". I am sure that any paragraph composed by you would be reticent & in good taste![2] The "NZ Mirror" kind of thing is so very dreadful. Being a Victorian I can never understand how people part with their privacy so readily. That is, private people. The great, who are in the public eye, *have* to do so – but why rush before the curtain! They wrote to me once for photograph etc – I rather think it was that Innes again – She *is* silly. "E.H. knows no school mistress but her garden"![3] – the garden being a brief episode in a life otherwise spent – far otherwise.

But you *can't* live on £1 a week! Surely you mean that is pocket-money. I think this Govt. won't allow such a wage – they are all for the wage-earner – But they are killing out the Rentier (myself e.g.) with their taxation. I've been warned not to expect interest from the Estate next year – I see that its time to hasten to the P.O.

M. U. B.

Hocken Library. MS-0741-002.

To Rodney Kennedy – September 26, 1936

St Faiths.

My dear Rodney

I must send you a few lines today, because T. & E.[4] were here yestery. [...] It was queer to think that it is actually *years* ago that I saw him last. He certainly has been a sticker. Afterwards they took me back to see his work – I admire the landscapes & presume to think that I can

[1] Kennedy had remarked on its absence, but approved the substitution of 'Envoy,' despite finding it 'cold and sad and final.'

[2] Kennedy had arranged with John Moffet (literary editor of the *ODT*) for Woollaston to review *Time & Place* and suggested sending 'a little potted biography as he likes to publish a little about the author.'

[3] The phrase is quoted from her *Press* review.

[4] Woollaston had married Edith Alexander (herself an artist) on Aug. 20, 1936, after a whirlwind romance that coincided with Woollaston's exhibition (and that rather distressed Rodney Kennedy). Bethell had hoped the marriage would take place at St. Faith's, but it was not to be.

understand them a little – especially one which is coming to live with me presently. But the people are utterly beyond me – And so is RNF's symbolic drawing. Tiresome to be blocked in this way – same way as *my* things utterly baffle – say the St. F's students. I heard the parent of one of them remark to her daughter en passant, looking at my lovely brasses & coppers assembled on a shelf "What are those fearful & wonderful things up there?" The *common* voice & the withering contempt of tone made me feel *sick* with anger for a moment – Well, there's no disrespect in my attitude to modern work, but I can't pretend I'm not at sea.

Edith – she is not a girl, she is a *woman*; a developed person. I think she will be a friend. She will need all the character she's got in the life that's coming. Well, you must be feeling a pretty nasty blank, both of them at a distance – "Life feels like a sore hole, like a tooth out" said a girl when the man she wanted didn't want her after all – and I often have felt like that after departures. All the same when its two happy people who go, one *can* give them to each other. There they are tangible, concrete, alive – Not like this gone awayness of death. In spite of all one's faith & hope, in spite of the giving back to God impulse, the darkness that rises up & quenches everything is terrible sometimes.

[...]

D'Arcy C. is going to review Time & Place for Tomorrow.[1] Have you seen his 'Eena Deena Dynamo'? He is always vigorous & amusing – but I fear talks out of pure ignorance of his subjects! He is engaged on a Poetic Drama.[2] (I believe Caxton Press, that is D. Glover did that E.E.D. for D'Arcy as a spec & out of friendliness without charge – but this is confidential. D.G. has the same feeling for D'A. that I have.) It gave me just a little "frisson" of life when D.G. said that he wd. be genuinely sorry if I didn't write any more! I wonder. It doesn't seem very likely. Yet the landscapes of Toss made me feel that art *is* something to go on with if there's the faintest urge.

I must go to the post.

M. U. B.

Hocken Library. MS-0741-002.

---

[1] 'Whence cometh our strength,' by W. D'A. Cresswell, *Tomorrow*, Oct. 1936, pp. 19-21.

[2] *Eena Deena Dynamo or The Downfall of Modern Science* (1936) argued that in the modern world the faculties of reason and sense were no longer in harmony, and that modern culture needed to be reformed by poetry. Bethell's amusement would no doubt have been occasioned by Cresswell's beginning, which notes with dismay the presence of both sexes in the audience, observing that 'The Christian Almighty Himself made a notorious blunder about this. He tried a mixed Paradise, and you know what happened.' The verse drama was *The Forest* (1952), a polemical play on similar lines: the role of the poet and the primacy of homosexual love.

TO FRANK SIDGWICK – [C. SEPTEMBER 1936]

St Faith's. Webb St N.1.

Dear Mr. Sidgwick

I am sending you a little present by which you will perceive that you are no longer "My publisher"! That privilege now belongs to a young N.Z. anti-God communist (who's really mistaken his label). His enterprise "the Caxton Press" housed in an abandoned stable, & consisting of himself & another youngster,[1] is probably carried on at a loss – he earns bread & butter by lecturing on English at the university. Hitherto he has printed "modern stuff" in bold and startling type & colours & it must have been rather difficult for him to see it the way I wanted it. In this benighted country we could not get the paper I meant & the margins are narrow to save money, but I think it is quite good all the same, don't you?[2] I have been glad to assist this local industry. It may interest you to know, being in the trade, that it cost £17 to produce 250 copies, advertising included. He doesn't think I shall get very much back, so I am afraid there will be a lull in my dozens of The Garden. If I had 7/6 to spare, & I havn't, I wd. send you as well D'Arcy Cresswell's "Lyttelton Harbour" done by a rival press in Auckland. He thinks highly enough of his work to clothe it in boards & endpapers & cellophane etc. I'd send the copy he presented me with, but then you wd. have the trouble of posting it back – It is quite a relief to have got this collection done, a tribute to the past, and – but the booklet speaks for itself. The 'envoy' is the only thing but one I've written since – The Caxton is all agog to do another book but I'm dumb now – everything is changed – no cottage, no garden, no car, no cat, no view of mountains – or any view – no temptation as it were to sing in the bath. But its not any of those things – its *no friend* – I was away all the winter upon and among the mountains, not face to face with them, & I was just as dumb. If anything starts me again it will be these very young people who are now busy painting, writing, reading, arguing – just a few of them, but nice. The Caxton helps to run a revolutionary fortnightly, with bomb-shell verse &

---

[1] Glover was indeed working out of a disused stable, with his partner, John Drew. They had published 'modern stuff' by Curnow, Mason, Fairburn and Glover before taking on Bethell's second volume.

[2] Sidgwick's reply described it as 'very like the sort of book that earnest young printers always print ... composition better than the press-work (tho' this press-work is quite good).' The poetry he described as 'very *you* ... perspicacious, imaginative, slightly exotic.' (Nov. 11, 1936.)

politics.[1] We encourage each other, & sort of take in each other's washing. (I enclose a review done by one of them for the Dunedin daily paper.)[2] I have deliberately refrained from replying, sooner than this, to your very delightful & welcome letter – letter*s* in fact – you could not remember whether you *had* written the former one, but happily it is before me – It must be so tiresome for publishers to have the planet littered with extinct authors so I have kindly held my peace. In one of them you set me a conundrum which I happened to be able to answer, & now do – "Personal relations – telegrams – anger" – it was somewhere in Howard's End I think.[3] He is a favourite author. Long ago when 'The Room with a View' appeared the Raven & I were in lodgings together – before the time she came to share my home – just lodgings, nasty boarding-house, and we were so refreshed by it – we read bits aloud to each other. I am just about to read Abinger Harvest. I felt as proud about that quotation as I did when at the Oxford Girls High School we had a General Knowledge viva, all the school in Hall, & no one knew but me "Who said 'this will never do' & on what occasion"?[4] I knew because I'd just been given the Golden Treasury Wordsworth Selections, with that told in the preface – it was G.T. wasn't it? Yes, that must have quite turned my head. Your sister wd. have known *all* the questions – I rather think that was my only flash – and Oxford reminds me of another bit in your letter – the Shakespeare play. I believe I have a photograph of the Merchant of Venice group stowed away somewhere – but I remember best Arthur as Ophelia. I wonder whether you were in that one.[5]

Arthur is now on his way back from Fiji to London. He was only 4 days away from N.Z. & it was really a desperate affair that he had not the time to come round by N.Z. & I had not the money to go to Suva! However he is a marvellous letter-writer, (almost miraculous when one

---

[1] A radical, left-wing political journal that began publication in July 1934 until it was closed down during the war, *Tomorrow* also provided a forum for poetry, short fiction and literary criticism.

[2] This was Woollaston's review, about which Sidgwick was less than complimentary. He singled out expressions such as 'cosmic nonchalance to things temporal' and 'synthesis of immediacy' and asked 'do they really know what they mean by such phrases?'

[3] Writing in response to the news of Effie Pollen's death, Sidgwick had quoted 'It is only personal relations that matter, and not all this world of telegrams and anger', and challenged Bethell to identify the source – which she does, correctly, as E. M. Forster.

[4] The expression occurs frequently – in Congreve's *Way of the World*; in *Hard Times* and *Bleak House*; in *Mansfield Park, Villette* and more. But the reference to Wordsworth here makes clear that Bethell is thinking of the famous negative criticism of *The Excursion* by Francis Jeffrey in the *Edinburgh Review*, which began 'This will never do.'

[5] Sidgwick had written of returning to Oxford for a Shakespeare festival, drawn by memories of having played Lorenzo in a school production of *The Merchant*, with Arthur Mayhew as Jessica (Jan. 22, 1936).

remembers all the other kind of writing he has to do) & sent a true & full account with comment of his travels & conferences & "contacts". There is an Educational Conference in N.Z. next year at which he wd. be so valuable – but that wd. be too miraculous.

[...]

I lit on your Making of Verse – & enjoyed it so much. Not as a serious study, but the jokes.

[...]

A typical spring southerly storm is going on – & as there is a lull I'd better hurry off to the post.

Yours very sincerely
Ursula Bethell

I have found four misprints besides the ones he owns up to, & I daresay there are others – I've lost one I meant to correct. I fear they were mis-spellings of which he is not aware![1]

Bodleian Library Oxford. MS Sidgwick & Jackson 142, fols. 151-153.

TO RODNEY KENNEDY – OCTOBER 8, [1936]

As from St Faith's House.
At Cashmere.

My dear Rodney

I wished to use this bit of time for writing a few lines to you but brought no materials & there is no paper in my friends' visitor's blotter. This birthday telegram will serve. It was for Tues. (S. Faith's Day) when after our early mass I escaped from the anniversary meeting etc, wh. still have too painful memories for me, leaving Edith in possession of the flat for *her* birthday yesterday & Toss to spend it with her. [...] This morng I descend to join her for the lunch which she will assemble, & this afternoon she is to be confirmed in our chapel. I found that for some years she had been thinking of coming in to the Ch. of E. & felt sure that the Bishop, who is fortunately in ChCh, would arrange this. It will all be carried out thoughtfully & quietly for her. She will need all the help & cheer that the Faith can bring, in her courageous life – I am glad that there is this further bond between her & Toss & 47 Webb St. She has been a wonderful gift to me at a difficult time. I need not say more about what she is, since you know her so well.

I remember Sir Lindo,[1] & see the situation – and reading of your rage feel inclined to say to you what I said to a small nephew years ago

---

[1] For the identified errors, see the letter to Schroder, May 27, 1937.

who was raging because he'd [been] made to come indoors from the fascination of the farm & put on a clean rig-out – "Its not worth it, old chap" says I, "its not worth it" "It *is* worth it, Aunt Ursula, it *is*" he shouted, and howled & wept afresh. But this rage at the unjust slaveries of life is fundamental – and joins [us] up as you say with the torment of that marvellous picture, which I had never seen. Its not the serpents, its the Fate. [...] Connects too with the crucifixion – I was thinking of El Greco's contemporary, San Juan de la Cruz whose life I have been reading.[2] Persecution & physical torture & injustice from his inferior rulers in the Carmelite order & his complete inner freedom of mind. He left the immortal poetry of "The Dark Night" & his tormentors are forgotten. I have not (should not wish to imply it) fully that inner freedom of the will wh. is sacrificial but I see that therein lies the emancipation from the sense of being trapped –

[...]

D'Arcy's review is sure to be amusing. I saw the one he did – of the Garden in the little London NZ paper – before I had heard of him, or knew who had written it. It was hoity-toity & condescending but worth having. I liked it very much. I love the English tongue & when those of the younger generation such as yourself & the critical Denis Glover (who said quite quite sincerely & apart from his trade that he for his part wd. be really sorry if I wrote no more) encourage me to begin again, I feel that it might be an aim. But I do think one must have an impulse, or at least a subject – not necessarily a fine phrenzy.[3] I suppose that the true artist has the general sense "this is my vocation" & that I am not really an artist! At any rate you can't write without feeling, & mine has been paralysed, certainly in the face of nature. A perpetual aching pain, which allows me to live in the experiences of others, but dims my own life, is now my portion. I think I have to do some more dying, before I can live again. And life's a gift from God. Edith understands. [...]

You are a helpful friend Rodney – I don't wonder that E. said she had depended on you a good deal.

M.U.B.

Hocken Library. MS-0741-002.

---

[1] Sir Lindo Ferguson, Dean of the Medical School. Kennedy appears to have had a number of disagreements with the Dean, whom he described to Bethell as a 'silly footling ... old man with one foot in the grave [who] has left me cursing and furious, self-distrustful and disgusted.'

[2] Several accounts of the life of St John of the Cross have been published in English; the most accessible for Bethell would have been the then recent translation by Benedict Zimmerman of the text by Bruno de Jésus-Marie, introduced by Jacques Maritain (1932).

[3] 'The poet's eye, in a fine frenzy rolling ...' *MND*, V. i.

TO RODNEY KENNEDY – OCTOBER 16, 1936

St Faiths. Webb St. ChCh.

My dear Rodney

[...]

There is so much I could say but it seems almost an impertinence to write about Edith whom you know so well. Elect soul! – Should one say like a deep cool pond – like a cool tree – no, too lifeless for her love – She is a *healing* person – & has helped me greatly. It was so delightful having those two happy ones, I thought I should feel lonelier than ever now – But it has left a kind of peace I had not before. It was their pure joy, but also her deep understanding, & feeling & thoughtfulness. I found myself looking at the bright spring green, this afternoon, for what it is, not only for what it was. She has unfrozen something. Yes, it was true, your post-script. Nothing can be said to allay another's pain.[1] How dreadful is the way untried people have of offering platitudes – Its one of the good things in our Deaconess that she has never handed me good advice or cheering up. "Faith & patience" have been her only words. But I had been hurt so often – this time it seemed too hard to begin again. Yet, if one were offered the choice between suffering and no suffering, human life being such as it is, I know what one would choose. And perhaps its a little help when there is some one else there – as in the air raids & you could say "Its getting louder" "Its further off" – "It will soon be over now" – Or perhaps as when they crossed Jordan in Pilgrims Progress, someone to say "Courage, my brother, I feel the bottom, & it is good."[2]

[...]

Have been lent G. M. Hopkins' letters to Bridges & Dixon wh. will be a treat.[3] That reminds me – it always bothers me when my critics say influence of Hopkins having always wished particularly *not* to copy him. So many *have* aped him & its such a mistake. You see Tomorrow don't you? I wrote of course to D'A.C. I told him he had "done me proud" – Whether one agrees or not its splendid d'Arcy.[4] [...]

---

[1] Kennedy's postscript read: 'I understand what you feel but I can't help you: and you can't help me. I am alone and so are you, terribly isolated.'

[2] The lines are spoken by Hopeful to Christian as they cross the River of Death at the end of the first part of *Pilgrim's Progress*. Bethell also quotes this to Brasch on several occasions.

[3] Hopkins's letters to Bridges, and his correspondence with Dixon, had both been edited by C. C. Abbott and published the preceding year.

[4] Cresswell's review appeared in *Tomorrow*, Vol. 2, 33 (Oct. 1936), 19-21. Cresswell had suggested that 'these verse aren't for a wide public ... They are a difficult and sometime harsh and unpleasant grammar of a nearly lost art' but he concluded by describing Bethell as 'the most original, and the most significant' of our poets.

Your gorse scene reminded me of one of our picnics – I don't think they are good verses – stiff & awkward but what a day it was![1] If I can find them, I will send. *Doesn't* one learn to select in N.Z.! To leave out the houses. I seldom saw those on each side of Rise C., but in photographs they cannot *not* be seen.

Have you heard about the L.C. Webbs buying that Mapua drawing for 5gs. less frame, which T. painted the right red on the spot. Having unintentionally been the instrument in bringing this about I was all the more pleased – But their genuine appreciation was better than the money.

Yrs affectly
M. U. B.

Hocken Library. MS-0741-002.

TO RODNEY KENNEDY – OCTOBER [28], 1936

St Faiths. Christchurch.

My dear Rodney

I am recumbent on my balcony & disinclined to get up & verify the date. I had a tooth out yesterday with very powerful new "local" & am rather under the weather – not sure, in fact, how many lines this will run to – but didn't want the week to end without at any rate a few lines to you –

I told T & E. not to write till they were settled – but by this time am beginning to wonder how they are getting on – & hoping that there have been no contretemps.

So it was you who 'put Edith wise' about her neighbours up there – I had noticed her guarded attitude. Her dignity & reticence will stand her in good stead.

"And how the silence surged softly backward
when the plunging hoofs were gone"[2]

nothing of "plunging hoofs" about my travellers (her quietude indeed was all the more refreshing in contrast with the roughness of these students!) but the lines rang in my head after their departure. The loneliness closed round me again to which I am growing accustomed & only sometimes

[1] The poem referred to here may be 'A Day Out,' a comic piece in 4 quatrains that includes the lines 'By alleys of golden gorse, / Towards mountains of dazzling snow / On our hale four-cylindered horse / Over the plain we go!' It has not been published, but copies are extant in Bethell's papers, and in Schroder's.

[2] Concluding lines from Walter de la Mare's 'The Listeners,' from *The Listeners and Other Poems* (1912).

dare to think of the years when everything was shared. But these two spring months – or is it spring & summer months (Oct. & Nov.) are poignant – & the very leaves on the trees speak of pain – we were at Waimate these days & had found out that the country was doing no good – rather she was worse. Curious little things come back to mind. A boy with a very charming voice was there – he had brought in a family of baby rabbits from the hillside & was watching them with eyes of love. We said we thought they were unhappy & wanted to get back to their wildness – "Oh no" he said after a thoughtful pause, "They're happy. They're happy" – There was a quality in the child's voice which made it sound like a revelation – it made me think of a choir singing "Blest are the departed"[1] – It made the same impression on both of us – And the sweetness of his shy voice came through again on the Sunday Evening when he & his sisters were singing a negro spiritual with the refrain "Grace & dying Love – Grace and dying Love"[2] – Such memories as these, trivial, small things, but with their small peculiar beauty, become lost as there is no longer any one to share them. I shall try to slip away to the country for Show Week – She died in the middle of it. The date is much earlier this year, but I don't feel like being in ChCh for the "Carnival". I am not proud, Rodney, of all this sadness & looking back; I think it is limiting God, because it is as good as saying that His resources have run out, that He can't do as much again, that something uniquely beautiful has perished – I don't really hold with that – but in the meantime it does seem as if this darkness were something I have to endure & go on with – till sorrow is turned into joy.[3]

I have called at W & Tombs & prodded them to send more copies of T & P to Dunedin – They swear that they sent 6 to begin with. They seem to have sold 60 copies or so – £5 odd. With this money I should like to send for R. N. F's River & Sea – It was made in N.Z. & should come back. I have just had a very appreciative letter from my chief critic – the book just caught him on his way back from Fiji to England – I value his praise because he is a true scholar & very critical – steeped in the English classics. *He* says that the "form of the wheat poem" (North Canterbury) – which a Knox College critic complained of as being tiresome is "most graceful" – and specially likes "Autumn Afternoon" which D. Glover could hardly bear to have in the book, so jog-trot! I may hear from England by next mail.

I am reading Hopkins' letters to Bridges. (So curious how useless his proposed emendations of Bridges' lines were, & vice versa. Bridges quite

---

[1] From an oratorio by the German composer Ludwig Spohr.

[2] 'Free grace, and dying love' is the refrain to the spiritual, 'Mary and Martha.'

[3] See John 16: 20.

rightly didn't adopt them, & H. was obstinate in refusing B's blame !) And a book on The Sacred Dance,[1] which I will lend you if you like. It is not ponderous, but a scholarly work. And I have galloped thro' a delightful sixpenny sent to me for my birthday a story by H Belloc, illustrated by G.K. Chesterton. Most entertaining.[2]

Toss pinned one of his drawings (Taranaki) to my screen – I look at it a good deal & am getting to understand it much better.

I enclose the Gorse poem – as I may have said before it was a vivid experience, but awkward metre I think. It doesn't *sing* easily. There are still enough in MS to make another book, but I don't know whether they are good enough. Enclosed too is a very personal one. I wrote it last year – this year have written nothing.[3]

[...]

My head has held out quite well after all. The next effort is to get myself to the post.

M. U. B.

This friend says that this series are "not so 'original' in conception as the Garden series but there is a depth of feeling & what one can only call a cosmic note which puts them on a higher level – They are, I think, a fine example of emotion recollected in tranquillity" –

Hocken Library. MS-0741-002.

To Rodney Kennedy – November 11, 1936

As from St Faiths. Webb St. ChCh.
At Peel Forest

Dear Rodney

I don't know whether I told you that I meant to get away from ChCh for this Show & Race "Carnival" week – It was this very Thursday Show & Race Day, with every house around me deserted, that I found my dear unconscious. Its all *branded* on my memory & seems like yesterday. Came on Monday, having begun neuralgia on Sunday where I

---

[1] The reference is to *The Sacred Dance: a Study in Comparative Folklore*, by W.O.E. Oesterley (1923).

[2] This may refer either to *The Haunted House* or to *The Hedge and the Horse*, both written by Belloc, illustrated by Chesterton, and published in 1936. The word 'galloped' may suggest the latter is meant.

[3] The 'personal' poem is the first of the six annual memorial poems Bethell wrote (*Collected Poems*, p. 79). The second was not written until the following month. Kennedy replied, describing it as 'very beautiful – a direct cry of pain and love – so simple – so intimate.'

lately had tooth extracted – Pain got worse but is now beginning to subside & I don't think I need go back before the week is out. Don't want to because I had invited my most valuable & faithful Charwoman & friend to come down for weekend. So I've hugged fire instead of going for walks, but hear bellbirds in the distance – A quiet farm house. Quite disinclined for effort of letter writing but want to thank you warmly for sending me that one of Edith's. I was so disappointed to find when she wrote that she did not get herself on to paper, to me, at all. I don't say it wasn't a good letter, but it wasn't Edith, it was a composition. Now of course you will not betray me by telling her this, because she then wd. become less spontaneous still. (The note from Toss was just as usual – he does get on to paper with immediacy & so do you.) This letter to you brings it all before me – garden etc & all the little details – such as lav. wh. I warned them wd. be insuperable bar to visiting them (so very unlikely a happening anyhow!) As an exscout I say decent latrines *first* consideration in arranging camp.

[...]

I *am* amused about "Robin Hyde"[1] – She wrote to me, I think when D'Arcy C. had lent her some things of mine, & I felt that it wasn't my sort of thing. Their letters are so extraordinarily *uneducated*, these "literary" folk, & so full of indiscriminate enthusiasm – about her eccentricities one must remember that, as I have been told, she is a little odd – "nervous breakdown" it is called. D'Arcy said she was living in a Nursing Home for nervous cases. He called her "very distinguished" & she must be a brave woman if she goes on writing big books such as I suppose that Hell one to be,[2] if she is feeling ill & shaken. Oh dear, if she comes to ChCh I realise that she may call on me & I rather dread that. "Too much talk" as a little boy said when first taken to church. Of course D'A. is "a little odd" too, but not in that amorphous way – You are right about his grievances – he once said he would stop that when he had let off enough ire. I once read in a novel "a woman of the world may have a grief. She should never have a grievance" – One might say the same of an artist.

I was disappointed in that gorse poem – it was such a *brilliant* day – I suppose one shouldn't try to gather all the impressions of one day under one head. The first lines unrolled themselves as we drove along, but when I was established under the great gorse hedge the rest didn't follow

---

[1] Iris Wilkinson (1906-1939) adopted the pen-name Robin Hyde in 1927. She wrote 5 novels and 3 books of poetry, and was also a journalist of some note. In an undated letter, Kennedy had written 'Robin Hyde is in Dunedin making a nuisance of herself.... She sounds pretty bloody.'

[2] *Passport to Hell* was published in 1936.

in a nice *tune* – Can you see those willow trees at all – they were just like green thistledown balls along the creeks – but if one didn't know Canterbury it wouldn't be a picture – "Are you getting poetry?" she wd. say as we drove along "I won't talk" – Yes, those last October lines *are* "intimate" – I couldn't show them to more than one or two – & not to anyone who hasn't been hurt.

[...]

I must now get up. This is the first fine day here & very radiant – dazzling green pasture – dark blue Bush – If I were not so limp I wd. climb the hill & get nearer those birds.

How I dislike the stationery they sell in NZ – have almost run out of my English & saving it up. That last of yours is nice & tough.

Such nice people at this farm – real country – & *Happy*. Did I tell you that I was reading G.M. Hopkins' letters to R Bridges & Canon Dixon? Delightful prose – (& reminding me in places of D'Arcy's best moments.)

Yrs
M. U. B.

Hocken Library. MS-0741-002.

TO W. F. ALEXANDER – DECEMBER 3, 1936

S. Faith's House. Webb St. N.1.

Dear Sir[1]

Mr. Ramsay Howie has sent on to me your letter respecting my little book "From a Garden in the Antipodes" – & I have told him that I would write to you direct in reply. Whitcombe & Tombs here promised to stock the book, but order only a few copies at a time. I have ascertained by telephone that they have only two left at present, so when I am in town tomorrow will see that one of these is sent to you, & in the meantime am posting one of the copies I keep by me – thus there will be at least one in the shop to show to possible enquirers.

It vexes me that NZ booksellers should charge 8/- for a 5/- book (& for which *they* pay much less than 5/-) & cannot think it unfair to them for me to sell one occasionally for *6/6 postage paid.* If it would save you time & trouble to send one cheque or P. O. I can easily pay W. & T. for you.

---

[1] A journalist and newspaper editor, W. F. Alexander had, with A. E. Currie, edited the first anthology of New Zealand poetry (1906). He was a keen supporter of local writers, and had organised the Dunedin portion of the Authors' Week mentioned in the letter to Andersen (Jan. 4, 1936).

May I say how pleasant it is to hear that "The Garden" is still giving pleasure to fresh people – especially when it is to discriminating ones, & more especially now that it is all a thing of the past – the friend who shared the garden gone, Michael gone, cottage sold.

I wonder whether your friend near Blenheim has a spare MS of his work to lend? One would like to see it. A difficult & fascinating subject! To judge from my own experience it *is* possible – or was, up till "The Depression" – to have a book published at Home, even one that is not likely to pay its expenses – as Mr. F. Sidgwick (of Sidgwick & Jackson) foresaw, when he took the risk, without much hesitation, of bringing out The Garden!

Believe me

Yours faithfully
(Miss) Ursula Bethell
(= "Evelyn Hayes")

Alexander Turnbull Library. MS-Papers-0423-1.

TO RODNEY KENNEDY – DECEMBER 3, 1936

St Faith's. Webb St. N.1. ChCh.

My dear Rodney

I agree that its much pleasantest to answer a letter at once – if one puts off, other things, including other letters, intervene. I can't read the date on yours but a week or two must have gone by – & my silence may be put down to dentist (toothache gone now) – Sunday duties – & last but not least darkness of mind. Perhaps its flat ChCh, or flat me, I don't know – but I get tired & sad & so oppressed by the sense of the *futility* of my life here & now. (All the while holding on by *intelligence* to the fact that no part of the pattern can really be futile).

[...]

What does give me a real thrill of joy, (I have discovered,) again,* is putting flowers about my rooms. I wasn't the one to do that at Rise Cottage. I wish I could paint *quickly*, the bunches in my room now – *Spiry* pale blue delphiniums & just as spiry snapdragons (the tall sort) & a very pale pink lupin – and again "bleeding-heart" (have you that delightful cottage-garden plant?) with pinks & jasmine. I made some notes on the preceding arrangement – iris & lupin – *wonderful* colours – for a possible piece of needlework – but my stodgy drawing is nothing like the reality "springing in their fugacity" if I may quote my own words.[1]

[Added in margin] *This "again" refers to "feeling joy" which I thought was gone altogether – not to arranging flowers.

[...]

The Glovers tell me that "Robin Hyde" has gone back to Auckland – a relief, because I thought I might be called upon to meet her & didn't much want to – Nothing *real* could have come of it, surely – Denis G. said she was 'rather ghastly' – She *does* seem to be very vain & schoolgirlish about her writing! The best plan is to remember that it is one of these "nervous breakdowns".

Ramsay Howie has sent on a letter from a Mr. Alexander of The Dunedin Evening Star (no relation I suppose of Edith's family?) a very pleasant letter about "From a Garden etc" & wanting to know where to get 2 copies. He wrote that review of T. & P.[2] & Ramsay forthwith sent him his copy of The Garden – very sporting! I have now written to Mr. A. with copies.

Do you care for these lines? ("Short Story") I am rather fond of them. Not *Christian* philosophy of body & soul of course – but they came into my head when I was afraid I was collecting too many possessions – that was in the winter of 1934 when we were contemplating a move in 1935. (And the move happened sure enough, but not as we planned it). [...] The Christmas one *is* Christian – I have ascertained that verse 3 is quite orthodox[3] – I have never been able to respond to the "midnight bell" – but this year am free to do so & think of accompanying the Deaconess to midnight mass at our anglican convent – They say that the procession of nuns round the cloister with candles, & then the blazing chapel & the Crib is most impressive – & can well believe it. Last year the Deaconess made such a good Crib with cut out figures mounted on cardboard for a country church. [...] That wd. be a thing to do – make Cribs & sell them for funds! St F's is very hard up. Sometimes I think of collecting up my religious verses & selling them for St Faiths! How bad G.M. Hopkins' ones were! So different from the rest. I have been reading those last sonnets of his again – nothing like them for black times.

I broke off The Sacred Dance to read two new Sheed & Ward publications – both translations from the French. One a curious "Art of

---

[1] The phrase is from 'Kakemono' (*Collected Poems*, p. 13).

[2] *The Evening Star* carried a brief, unsigned review on Sept. 26, 1936.

[3] 'Short Story,' *The Press*, Sept. 1, 1934, p. 15. 'The Christmas one' is 'In a Hospital' (*Collected Poems*, p. 73). When Bethell submitted it to Schroder, she had crossed out the 3rd stanza, having 'noticed possibly unorthodox expression.'

Suffering" & the other studies of a list of interesting men I wanted to know more about – Bloy, Péguy, GK Chesterton, Solovieff etc[1] – At meals I have read the letters of "Anne Douglas Sedgwick"[2] – author of several by no means to be despised novels – *very* readable – and "Totem" – a fierce attack on TocH. Y.M.C.A. Groups & the like.[3] Its exaggerated & I do not agree with his reasons & its all *negative* – but I *feel* very much as he does about their way of talking.[4]

Dear me, it seems quite as difficult to leave off a letter, once begun, as to begin it! I am now hungry (*2:30*!) & must descend & get some lunch –

Yrs Affectly.
M. U. B.

Hocken Library. MS-0741-002.

TO MONTE HOLCROFT – DECEMBER 23, 1936

St. Faith's House. Webb St. N.1 ChCh.

Dear Monte

I read with pleasure a little story of yours in the Children's part of the Press the other day,[5] (not cheaply done – well written – interesting) & thought I would send you a few lines of goodwill for Xmas. Although I think my last to you remained unanswered. I also heard of you from the Glovers as taking an active part in the English Association, & was glad. I confess to being a little disappointed that you said nothing about the little book which Denis Glover printed for me ("Time & Place") but perhaps you have not seen it.

---

[1] The first is a translation of Louis Bertrand's *Le livre de consolation*; the second of Karl Pfleger's *Geister die um Christus ringen*, which appeared as *Wrestlers with Christ*. In addition to the names mentioned, it provides studies of Gide, Dostoyevsky and Berdiaev.

[2] *Anne Douglas Sedgwick: a portrait in letters*. Chosen and edited by Basil de Selincourt (1936).

[3] Harold Stovin, *Totem: the exploitation of youth* (1935). TocH began in Belgium during WW1 as a rest centre for soldiers, and continued after the war with community-based programmes aimed at 'renewal, regeneration, and rebuilding' of society through friendship, service, fairmindedness, and spirituality.

[4] Stovin's book is a trenchant survey of the 'social and verbal behaviour of a number of organizations which ... represent the Youth Movement in England.' He argues that the movements and their language prevent the emergence of individuality and spontaneity of action, and entice youth into mediocrity through 'groupism,' and mass cultural activity.

[5] 'The Boundary Hut,' a boys' adventure story, was published in *The Press Junior*, Dec. 17, 1936.

I hope that all goes well with you in every respect & that you feel you are getting on towards attainment in your writing.

I am stronger in health now, getting over the nervous shock, & always busy; but life is a sad affair, & times & seasons such as the present bring back the happy past too vividly. Well, one can't always *feel* the mighty truths that one *knows*.

Your friend & well wisher
M. U. Bethell

Alexander Turnbull Library. MS-Papers-1186-03.

TO RODNEY KENNEDY – DECEMBER 28, 1936

As from St Faith's. Webb St. N.1. ChCh.

Dear Rodney

My hostess has gone into town & this is my chance to thank you for your Christmas letter. I generally write my letters before getting up in the morning when I am "staying with" but – reaction from pre-Xmas scramble no doubt – I've been much too sleepy so far. We seem to have settled down to a wintry summer – it is pouring from the south today – rather a pity here, because there's a big garden to sit out in with a westerly view over the plain – However there is also a spacious drawing room with enormous log fire, lovely old furniture, Persian rugs, Spode china, lots of books – perhaps a rarer attraction in N.Z. than a garden bench.

[...]

Thank you for wishing to send me a picture that you like – this impulse in itself gives pleasure, whatever the impact of the picture may be [...] Yes, I will tell you what I really think. Its much best, if one is not afraid of hurting the person – a friend of mine used to point out that one had to discover how "fragile" a person is, before being perfectly honest. Have you noticed the different degrees of fragility? It isn't always a fault – My lost friend used to be amused with what she called my "cold honesty" & yet I used to measure it with her. If one has an ardent wish, in a childlike & sensitive heart, to give another an immense pleasure – it can't help being a hurt if the pleasure doesn't come off. I loved to watch her joy when she was quite sure that it *had*. I determined, long ago, to try & not be "fragile" myself! My difficulty with "things" nowadays is, of course, where to put them in my circumscribed quarters. I have put some away in boxes, against a shadowy & unlikely future. But already I have been glad not to have parted with certain objects, which for a time I thought had better go. Do you know Jeremy Taylor's definition of friendship? Here it is, from a little MS book I found the other day in a box I hadn't opened for 2 years – (where I found my painting things too). "By friendship I mean the greatest love, & the greatest usefulness, & the most open communication, & the noblest sufferings, & the most exemplary faithfulness, & the severest truth, & the heartiest counsel, & the greatest union of mind of which brave men & women are capable"[1]

[…]

I must end after glancing at yr. letter to see whether anything else calls for comments. Yes, the verses were both spares – you must not let such sendings be a burden, necessitating critique – but only if anything comes into your head. I have some lines written about the time of the anniversary, still in the rough. Otherwise I can't write. A very nice note from Hawkes Bay about Time & Place – begging me to go on interpreting "the land I love". I wonder what you find "victorian" in the "Short Story" – I should have thought the Mode its done in dated before then.[2] Its not meant to be taken very seriously of course.

I am glad that Christmas is over – I got through by making my mind a blank to all but the next practical thing to do. Too many associations. The letters that came were the best things. One of my friends gave a wonderful present for St Faith's – the painting of the whole house! I shall try to get more to the core of things during 1937 – thank you for the good wish. If I could only feel that there were some sense & object in being alive, beyond winding up the past.

So glad to hear that there is a prospect of seeing you in Febry.

M. U. B.

Hocken Library. MS-0741-002.

TO RODNEY KENNEDY – JANUARY 14, 1937

St Faith's. Webb St. N.1. ChCh.

Dear Rodney

I came back yesterday – but have been endlessly busy about things which have to be seen to here – I wanted to write at once about your poet. A very interesting & beautifully painted picture.[3] I have been

[1] The passage is from the opening paragraphs of Taylor's *A Discourse of the Nature and Offices of Friendship*, first published in 1657.

[2] Kennedy had described the poem as having Victorian traces, but added 'not that I use Victorian with the obliterating contempt of the young Georgians,' and described it finally as 'a very fine achievement.'

[3] Kennedy had sent her a copy of the portrait of the Tuscan nobleman Leonello d'Este by Pisanello, painted in 1441. Bethell's description of the subject as a poet reflects an

pondering over my walls & the upshot is that (faithful to our contract) I think I can only have him to stay with me – Already I have some of our Rise Cottage pictures packed away & had decided that in the "parlour" I wd. only have perhaps temporary works produced by my friends – to replace old favourites. Upstairs there is *no* place – I shall get to know him well by the time you go south again & he must go with you & you won't have to give him up for good. Thank you very much for your thought, which has borne its fruit. How many beautiful things there are in the world & of what great variety! (now that I think of it there was a R.L.S. quotation to that effect!) if only I could feel *moved* by them again! That sick pain does interfere so.

[...]

Its curious to be back down here – feels cramped & rather shabby – & yet nice to be in one's *own* corner – The air has no life in it. Very quiet with everyone away – my charlady is coming to sleep. Dear Rodney I ought to be [a] good one to sympathise if you are in a phase of depression! Its a daily fight with me – I preach to myself courage & remind myself of the Pilgrim birthday. "To go on living instead of dying" with no reason for it but the will of God ... Sometimes my little wireless fades out in the middle of a piece & I can't hear anything, then there is sometimes a sort of bang & it suddenly comes through loud & clear again. I think to myself that perhaps there will be a bang in my mind, & I shall hear & know. Meanwhile one plods on & the odd jobs are a great help. Have you ever read Julian of Norwich?

[...]

Now, dare I dash to post & back? I'll risk it. Don't know where to address to you.

M. U. B.

Hocken Library. MS-0741-002.

TO RODNEY KENNEDY – FEBRUARY 3, 1937

St Faith's House. N.1. ChCh.

Dear Rodney

I think I do owe you a letter. This one from you has no date – the hieroglyphic on the left can't be a date – it includes 1936 – & the letter before has 1936 on the left & 1937 on the right. Do you live outside of

---

anecdote related by Kennedy: 'I once told somebody that d'Este was a poet in the Medici court. A pure romantic lie or a wish forfillment [sic]. He had been superciliously polite about the painting so I told him this tale. He went one better as he said he had read some of the poems.'

time? You must condescend to those who don't. I can't think whether I have written since Cashmere – of course I have, about the Pisanello. It was such beautiful peace here without the inmates – but I filled it up with much busyness. Now the peace is over & I shrink into my corner. I don't think I can live for ever (if I do live) mixed up like this on the staircase with all & sundry & hearing their strange noises. For the present it is cheap & suitable. Throughout all, peace & unpeace, I have felt since Xmas such a profound sadness & weariness of life* that I think sometimes it must be nearing its term – Anyhow I pull myself together & remind myself that my object just now is to get affairs so set in order that I may die tidily & without giving anyone any trouble.

[Added in margin] *This was called *Accidie* in convents & counts as a bad sin!

The flowers are still a solace – Today it is such a beautiful arrangement of shell pinks & rose pinks & lilac michaelmas daisies – & in another place sharper pinks tending to vermilion. It is like music. But always the sense that once these beauties were shared, & now they are not.

[...]

I've got Abinger Harvest, but haven't started it. Too busy. I ought I suppose to tackle more of T. S. Eliot – who has had such an influence. But when I read 'Ash Wednesday' I kept on asking myself "*Is* this really good?" Good enough to *tussle* with? I never ask myself this about Hopkins. Wish I had more uninterrupted time for reading – the days are chopped. In the evenings eyes & head too tired. This is the result of keeping up life to the small hours – (*not* in dissipation such as parties!) in my younger years.

[...]

I am rather in despair about my lost books. Yes, someone still has Death of a Poor Man & worse still, The Whistlers Room. I didn't lend you "War in Heaven" did I?[1] Its one of my favourite books, & missing for [so] long. Since you like Athanasius I must lend you Helen Waddell's Fathers of the Desert[2] – beautifully done. I have bought a lot of theological books lately with one eye on St Faith's – not that the present run of students can use them – but a sort of vanity for the house. I had a wool cheque it really has to pay off a mortgage & is capital, but I can't resist depriving my heirs of a few pounds – & the prospect of going Home is so remote it doesn't seem worth while saving up for *that*. So

---

[1] *The Death of a Poor Man* (1927) and *The Whistlers' Room* (1929) are both translations of German novels, by Franz Werfel and Paul Alverdes respectively. Bethell mentions Charles Williams' *War in Heaven* often.

[2] *The Desert Fathers* (c. 1936) is a translation of extracts from the *Vitae patrum*.

please take this for your Wellgn-Nelson flight – I'd like you to have that experience.

[...]

There, I've had a really peaceful 2 hours on my balcony & no sound but the wind in the trees, and the sparrows, – household quiescent. At such times the torn nerves are soothed, & one begins to think that the past is now, & what has been is, & what shall be, is. One remembers majestic sentences, such as – Sorrow enduring for a night, & joy coming in the morning.[1] And "all manner of things shall be well"[2] ...

I am writing out the lines for you. They're personal, remember – I do not want you to bother about criticism. I don't send the verse as literary product, but part of what one is thinking.[3] You will do me a service if when looking up Sappho you will copy out some bits for me.[4] I have never read her – & have only a notion from school days that she was lamentable! & perhaps not quite respectable? or is that a mistake! – I confess that I wondered whether D'Arcy had ever read her! No doubt I did him wrong. I suppose the connecting link was the sadness – otherwise an extravagant comparison of his I thought. In my youth my notion was Greek – Classic – Dignity – Restraint – but later learnt how very *un*restrained they really must have been! Screaming & crying out & torn with passion – There can be no doubt I suppose that Christianity (drawing from Hebraism) brought in a new quality of love & tenderness. Agapé – not Eros – You've read that book?[5]

[...]

Au reviour then
M. U. B.

Hocken Library. MS-0741-002.

TO RODNEY KENNEDY – APRIL 23, [1937]

S. George's Day. St Faith's. N.1. ChCh.

Shakespeare's birthday & a red rose from the garden patch on my writing table – we used to go to S. George's café Trafalgar Square on this day because of red roses on the table.

---

[1] Psalm 30: 5.

[2] From Chapter 27 of Julian of Norwich's *The Revelations of Divine Love*.

[3] This refers to the second of the memorial poems (*Collected Poems,* p. 79).

[4] The request was prompted by Cresswell's comparison (in his *Tomorrow* review) between Bethell's verse and some classical work, especially that of Sappho.

[5] Bethell is probably thinking of *Agape and Eros. A Study of the Christian Idea of Love* by Anders Nygren (1932).

I wished to put down a few things about the last evening of Ballet[1] for Rodney before they faded yesterday, & because Dr Helen Simpson came to tea & there was a good fire, I thought I ought to see the fire out down below so dismounted [with] pen & paper. No good – the parlour is for company & chat, & when I am alone I must be up here. Now this morning, ensconced (to revive an old fashioned word) at my desk, with the sun coming in (not very warm!) at the east windows & neglecting all household duties & all the other correspondents, I try again.

[...] You were surprised when I quoted the London paper about the audience at the Alhambra being perhaps as distinguished as the performers – not so *our* audience! I took the inner seat to begin with, next to (a correctly enough dressed) nitwit who kept up a running commentary not too sotto voce in a contented N.Z. dialect, with his equally half witted (by strong family likeness inferred) sister. "Now she's doing so & so" "now they've shut him out" "Now he's coming back" "that's good" – So exasperating with other more distant mutterers, that I felt murder on the left to be imminent & told my companion so in the second interval when she changed places. Thus the 100 Kisses & the School were a little spoiled for me (They changed Nos 2 & 3 about) but both charming – only complaint being that Kanevska was not so much an awkward pupil as a contortionist – She's the only one of the company I could do without.

Well then the Rose – impossible really to write about, as you will agree [...] a hush fell on the house, even on our moron, who was, Helen said, quiescent till towards the end when he observed cheerfully "That's a good waltz".

Exquisite – the moonlit scene – the grace – the dreamlike quality. In this more than any of the others I was at length carried out of myself into the art – The unbrokenness, the absence of applause was such a relief – The perfection of motion & repose – Even such is found in God, they say, pure act & pure rest. [...] It was very, very beautiful, and peace-giving, and a pain that it must come to an end. I supposed that the members of the Ballet were no more conscious of the gracious influence of their work than the beneficent red rose by one's bedside – & only thinking of how it is done! Then there was the Beau Danube, which we liked immensely, (but what a misleading name!) to bring us back to earth.

I was rather glad that, because of enthusiasm & bouquets (but such dull looking ones – sheaves of hard gladiolus – bad time of year) we missed our trams & so walked to the north belt [...] Such a lovely, *balmy*

---

[1] Colonel de Basil's Monte Carlo Russian Ballet Company toured New Zealand in March/April of 1937, playing to packed houses. It opened in Christchurch at the Theatre Royal on April 12.

night – great white moon-lit clouds & black chasms between – (It turned to the south before morning & last night was bitter – on our hills starry and sparkling no doubt, but all *misty* here – I suppose the poor Ballet has met this at that godforsaken little place Timaru – but today is bright.)

[...] My impressions somewhat subjective no doubt! The truth is I know more about literature (& theology!) & life in general – than art or music – forsook *them* for East London 40 yrs ago. So only a smattering. This ballet week has meant however a little milestone in my private life & needed courage. It *has* been possible to enjoy something (a word I've hardly used all this time) without an ache for a little while – without the little creature beside me sharing, "all agog" as she used to say, & her little hand tucked into mine in moments of greatest joy. It isn't that I'm forgetting, but perhaps a glimmer of the truth that universal joy *will* prevail – Its so hard, so hard, to give up the limited human, mortal, tangible part. It seems for a while that there's nothing else. I was thinking about the gospels last night & how the son of God knew all about it, & saw through it, this life – "I take it up – I lay it down"[1] – so *free*. And so those events afterwards, whatever they really were ("veridical visions")[2] couldn't be spared – everything just the same for those friends, nothing lost.

[...]

H.S. & I agreed that we were decidedly the better for our Ballet going & should like to be able to attend once a week, say, always. [...] She is delightful & I must arrange that you meet her when you come next to ChCh. I suppose my oldest friend in this country – tho' very much my junior of course. She knew & appreciated & loved my Effie but we hadn't seen much of her since her marriage, & they have been away in England. The bother is she has taken on (with her husband I suppose!) a strong anti-clerical bias – rather tiresome, living where I live, & thinking as I do! – However we avoid thin ice & get back to cats & poetry & education & the Past. [...]

I must now write to my nephew for his birthday & acknowledge a very pleasant note from Mr. Alan Mulgan enclosing a sensible review of T&P. (in Auckland paper & by himself I infer)[3] wh. I must send you some day when you have returned to everyday life [...] this afternoon reading aloud get my teeth into "The Ring & the Book" & be careful to

---

[1] See John 10: 17, 18.

[2] This phrase is used in Biblical scholarship, especially in connection with resurrection appearances of Christ, to distinguish subjective hallucinations, objective (veridical) visions caused by God, and genuine physical appearances.

[3] Auckland journalist and 'man of letters,' Mulgan reviewed *Time & Place* under the heading 'Notable N.Z. Verse' in the magazine section of the *Auckland Star*, April 17, 1937.

touch very little on the Ballet to Miss Allen[1] – Oh, to lose the sight of one's eyes! what would one do *then*? She is so plucky.

Tomorrow the waiting list of correspondents – the lonely bachelor in California – The broken-hearted widow of club-boy in Canada – the oldest friend of all at the Colonial office, whom I have not even thanked for his amazingly appreciative critique of my booklet – the artist cousin driven from life-long residence in Italy by fascism & from her art by failing eyes & since her widowhood to spiritualism – the parson friend & the spiritual, *not* spiritist! events in his Sussex village parish – the east end ex-factory hand & her window boxes got ready for the coronation! – the sad one in the south of France – the backblock schoolmaster in N.S. Wales (to come back to the antipodes) & how much *dare* I tell him of the badness of his Australian literature sample[2] & his own English – its ill work criticising on paper – Only one of that list is not lonely, or two perhaps. So no more Rodney, for a long while, & if the Ballet *has* got to Dunedin, you won't be reading this yet awhile either!

Yrs affectly
M. U. B.

Hocken Library. MS-0741-002.

TO ALAN MULGAN – [APRIL 23, 1937]

[47 Webb St.]

Dear Mr. Mulgan

I am much obliged to you for sending the cheering review of "T & P" & for your very kind note enclosing it. Its so agreeable when competent critics say what one wd. like to have said! & I am particularly glad that what I have written pleases you personally. Not a New Zealander born I have now for many years mused upon this landscape, & wished to express its influences truthfully.[3]

With many thanks

Yours sincerely[4]

Draft. Macmillan Brown Library. MB 558. L2.

---

[1] Sister of the Dunedin novelist, C. R. Allen (who was also blind). Bethell regularly read aloud to Miss Allen.

[2] See the postscript to her letter to Holcroft, May 9, 1937.

[3] Mulgan's review had praised Bethell's fidelity to the local, and admired her accounts of Canterbury landscape.

[4] The letter is in draft form, unsigned.

TO MONTE HOLCROFT – MAY 9, 1937

St Faith's House. N.1. Christchurch.

My dear Monte

I have meant so often to thank you for your letter at the New Year & for what you said about 'Time & Place' – I became involved, here, in all sorts of odd jobs (altho' I am really merely a tenant of the institution) which make time go by excellently well, but correspondence is put off again & again. I wish indeed, that you had reviewed the little book in the Press, & suppose that I might have put in a request to that end – don't know really – what the etiquette is. I should have valued a few sensible remarks! Mr. Schroder spoke to me apologetically about it, when I met him on his return from England.[1] There was a good notice in the Auckland Star last month, done by Mr. Mulgan. He sent it to me. I am glad you like "Picnic" – others besides yourself have enquired for it. I don't know whether there are enough stray pieces to make another little book some day – its all so much a thing of the past to me now, I can't feel that it matters very much.

It is writers like yourself, who still feel the urge, who count! I am always so struck, when I read you in the Press, by the way you have gone on steadily pursuing the best things. I hope that you have meanwhile taken up the post of which you spoke, which wd. give you more time for this pursuit[2] – I heard a rumour that it might take you away from Christchurch, but I expect the same address will find you.

I should be much interested in seeing the N.Z. novel – would there be a chance of reading it in typescript?[3] Another friend has lately sent one to take its chance with London publishers – I read a bit of the MS & thought it quite promising. Otherwise I've had more to do of late with young friends who are engaged in the other arts – painting – music. Perhaps its more useful to help them, than to be trying for expression oneself. Anyhow, I have probably said all I had to say, & life is getting on.

Yours sincerely
M. U. Bethell

---

[1] Schroder had been on an extended trip (including a honeymoon) to England when *Time & Place* was published, and so was unable to ensure that the work received a competent review.

[2] At the end of 1936 Holcroft had been invited to become leader writer for the *Southland Times*.

[3] Holcroft had had three novels published in the 1920s, but the one referred to here was not published.

Have you seen "People in Prison"?[1] It is really Miss Baughan's I think, I have always thought her "Brown Bread" about the best thing done in N.Z.[2]

I am told now that N.Z. is ahead of Australia in culture. Certainly someone sent me a magazine – called Sydney Mercury I think – which was perfectly *dreadful.*

Alexander Turnbull Library. MS-Papers-1186-03.

To Rodney Kennedy – [May 23, 1937]

Trinity Sunday St Faith's 47 Webb St.

("Il reviendra à Pâques, il reviendra à Pâques, ou à la Trinité" – I think you'll find that quoted in Peter Ibbetson – which I must have read about 40 years ago.)[3]

I have refrained deliberately from writing to you, dear Rodney, because of so many pressing calls on my time, altho' wishing to thank you for yr letter. Now there is every reason to write – 1. the case of apples has arrived. [...] It is indeed a noble present [...]

Otherwise I wanted to write to you about China – the Ballet has faded and the art & civilisation of the Chinese Empire supervened.[4] I am told that this Loan Exhibition is going to Dunedin – I forget whether the first one did. Anyhow don't fail to see it. Its housed in the new Gally & costs a pilgrimage to see it – but it's a much better setting & its arranged in a quite sophisticated manner with chrysanthemums growing in pots, dotted about among the Show Cases. [...] Gazing at those beautiful objects a great calm invades the soul & for a little while one forgets one's private griefs, one forgets the turmoil of the world, & that a barbarous West is destroying that exquisite civilisation – (Founded on a slave class like all the rest!)

[...]

And I have been battling & battling with black desolation – its partly the coronation I think – & how eager that little creature wd. have been

---

[1] Blanche Baughan was committed to prison reform, and at one time was official visitor at Addington Reformatory for Women. The small, and at the time controversial volume, *People in Prison* (1936), reflected some of her experiences with prison inmates and authorities.

[2] The work's full title reveals its content: *Brown Bread from a Colonial Oven: being sketches of up-country life in New Zealand* (1912).

[3] Fr. 'He will return at Easter, he will return at Easter, or on Trinity Sunday.' *Peter Ibbetson* is a novel (1891) by George du Maurier.

[4] An exhibition of Chinese art had recently opened at the Robert McDougall Art Gallery.

at the wireless & off to see all the doings. I could hear her excited voice. I really think the pain gets worse, & the loneliness more terrible – And yet I have so much to be thankful for, & *am* thankful. And at the end the only thing that would matter would be to have *given up*: "persevere to the end"[1] – One of my thankfulnesses is to *feel* the flash of beauty, even if its only for a moment – as before those chinese ceramics – or the epistle this morning[2] – those majestic & scintillating sentences – I'll probably not be writing again till the mountain. I'd better keep lectures – there was one standing over I think – till your next visit!

Your affect. friend
M. U. B.

Hocken Library. MS-0741-002.

TO J H E SCHRODER – MAY 27, 1937

St. Faith's N.1 Christchurch.

Dear Mr. Schroder

I am leaving the books at your office, as I am afraid there may not be time to call at S Elmo[3] before my flight.[4]

I have only found one of the mistakes in the "Garden" – Page 47 – & have now forgotten what the others were[5] – I havn't looked into the book for many months & confess that its hard to do so – in fact, tho' I suppose its really too sentimental to say so, I found I couldn't sometimes see the print for tears. It seems to me, now, pretty good, as far as it goes, & I am glad that the person who then was put it down while there was time, & the people who read it won't know how dreadful it is to the writer that its all past & gone – I have ventured to do what you have not asked, signed under the title, which I find is the custom, but if you, who are particular about books, regard it as a blemish, I can give you another copy in exchange.

The mistakes I have found in Time & Place are P.11 Elixir. P.26. accomplished. p.27. Mien. p.33 lights (not?) there may be others.[6] They

---

[1] See Mark 13: 13.

[2] The epistle for Trinity Sunday is Revelation 4: 1, a vision of heaven, of the twenty-four elders, and the four beasts worshipping at the throne of God.

[3] Schroder's home address, in St. Elmo Courts.

[4] To a 'competent dentist' in Wellington.

[5] See the letter to Sidgwick, Dec. 5, 1929.

[6] Glover had printed 'elexir,' 'ascomplished,' 'mein,' and 'light's;' there are others, as Bethell surmised – 'dissolved' for 'dissolve' in 'Forest Sleep,' and an instance of dittography in stanza 10 of 'Autumn Afternoon.'

are misprints, I could not see proofs, being away at Mt Harper at the time – so D. Glover deserves much praise for turning it out so well.

I'd better return Religious Verse now because of going away. It is more comprehensive than the Golden Treasury one, but the format is not pleasing is it.

With kind regards to you both

Yours sincerely
Ursula Bethell

No hurry about returning D'Arcy's book, & the nice review in Tomorrow. I *think* I have another copy of the latter somewhere – Its very amusing. But I feel quite impersonal about reviews now.

Alexander Turnbull Library. fMS-018

TO EILEEN DUGGAN – [JUNE 23,] 1937

Mt. Harper Hostel. Peel Forest. South Canty
Vigil of S. John Bap. & Midsummer Eve![1]

Dear Miss Duggan[2]

Many thanks for your letter. I was about to write & enclose this article which I meant to bring to you in Wellgn. Written by the Deaconess in charge of S. Faith's House for an English periodical. I thought it might interest you to see yourself quoted. We have another copy so don't need it back.[3]

It is exceedingly cold here this year, & rather congealing but the bracing change does good afterwards. Its always a satisfaction to turn over the shortest day.

I am glad that you like The Garden, as I hoped you would. My most respected English critic, deeply versed in English literature & the classics (& the brother of my English correspondent "Ruth" who really exists – in fact everything in the book is "from life" –) could not at first do with the irregular form – but became converted & now thinks it more interestingly original than Time & Place – tho' he's said some very supporting things about that too. His opinion sustained me in having the verses printed. I must explain that T&P, tho' it appeared so much later, is made up of things written about the same time as the Garden pieces – in the same burst of excitement – of joy. (Except the dedication) Now I

[1] Bethell is referring, of course, to the English midsummer.

[2] Eileen Duggan (1894-1972), author of 5 volumes of poetry, had at one time a considerable international reputation, but her popularity declined at the end of the 30s. Like Bethell, she wrote from a noticeably religious standpoint in much of her verse.

[3] No copy of the article has survived in Duggan's papers.

am a tree struck by lightning – dead. I can think things, but not feel them – One must feel to write – All joy is lost.

> "Shee, shee is dead; shee's dead; when thou knowst this
> Thou knowst how dry a cinder this world is."[1]

> "What can I do in Poetry,
> Now the good spirit's gone from me?
> Why nothing now, but lonely sit,
> And over read what I have writ."
>
> (The Departure of the good Daemon. Herrick)

I found these in the New Book of English Verse edited by Charles Williams,[2] which I brought with me – a magnificent collection. I must try to read poetry again.

If one could write, one might have some sensation of being alive. But it is not given to me – No impulse. I might take up some unfinished pieces & see whether they finish themselves. Thank you for your encouragement.

I liked the two by Denis Glover in the Miscellany[3] – I'm not sure that he isn't the best of the N.Z. bunch – speaking of the younger ones. What do you think? He seems to me to have not only feeling but the sense of words.

As I wander about these mountain roads I try to pray, and try to know that prayers *are* heard when they seem not to be. It is all pain . . & sense of failure – I am told that purgatory begins in this world – S. Teresa wouldn't count me nearly poor enough, even now – I've always liked that saying – but do not know who said it "Ce sont les vies les plus dépourvues qui ont enrichi le monde"[4] – Yet rather frightened, really, by the thought of greater poverty, materially! Quite probable. Yet nothing frightens truly for oneself – anxiety was for another & that's over. I used to be full of fear, instinctively, fought by conscious mind; now wake up not to fear, but to pain, again to be fought by conscious mind. Forgive all these "I's" – but you have more faith.

Yours sincerely
Ursula Bethell

---

[1] From 'The First Anniversary' in Donne's *Anatomie of the World.*

[2] Williams's selection was published by Victor Gollancz in 1935.

[3] *A Caxton Miscellany of Poems, Verse, Etc.* Glover's two poems (there are only seven in all) are 'Root, and Crop, and Stone,' and 'Landing Field.'

[4] Bethell here gives a slightly different version of the passage quoted in a letter to Holcroft, Feb. 1, 1934. 'It is the most destitute lives that have enriched the world.'

I am enclosing further, & troubling you to return, the only two pieces of verse (other than the Envoy) I have been moved to write since the shock – It does show perhaps that the small talent wd. be found not withdrawn, if one were recalled to feeling.

Catholic Archdiocesan Archives, Wellington. Eileen Duggan Papers.

To Rodney Kennedy – June 24, 1937

Mt Harper Hostel. Peel Forest. Sth. Cant.

S. John Baptist. Midsummer Day.

Dear Rodney

A fine snow has been falling all night which may cut us off from the world – a lorry got through with difficulty this morning bringing supplies, & if ready this will go back by that. I have been here a week & a half & so far it has not been as agreeable to me physically as last year – too cold – But very good for the skating trade – The hostel has been more frequented during the week as well as weekend, & the new telephone across to the ice, which my cousins like me to answer as go-between, does not make for peace. However the real reason I havn't yet answered your very nice letter is not interruption but heaviness of spirit. I get into a sort of routine now in my Webb St rut which carries me along – & after a change of place I have to face life from a fresh angle & fight those drowning waves of misery again. And not so very fit – tired I was & tooth troubles continue.

Enough of myself! Yr. letter – 2 letters – have much of interest – but I am discouraged by that loss of mine. I daresay there was quite a lot in it – in fact I think there *was*. I still feel afterglow from Chinese Art & think you will – one needs hours & hours to spend in contemplation of those ceramics – a day for each kind. Emerging into ChCh streets the barbarity struck more acutely than ever.

[...]

In Wellgn I went to see the film "Green Pastures" & was quite fascinated[1] – Don't miss it on any account. Its the only film perhaps I've ever seen (I havn't seen many) in which there's nothing to grate from end to end. In fact I think it has converted me to the art of the Film. [...]

[...] And rushed about seeing many people, besides dentist, hostess kindly driving me often. No wonder I was tired. The first drive was to

---

[1] *Green Pastures* was made in the United States in 1936 with an all black cast. It presented various Old Testament stories in the manner of folk tales from the Deep South, with a popular actor, Rex Ingram, as 'De Lawd.'

my darling's grave with her favourite pink carnations & the white narcissus she used to bring me as soon as they appeared in the shops. Curious how a grave, meaningless really, is in one way all there is. Just her little name on it – "Effie" – & soon there will be no one left there who knows; who will stand beside it. Its mine as well as hers I think – Life as we knew it, has ended. This queer hurtful lovely life – the other must be *brewing* underneath all the time & one has to learn to live in it consciously.

[...]

Oh, I called on Eileen Duggan in Wellgn & liked her very much. Simple & sincere. She is R.C. you know – a serious one. She told me about [a] lecture she attended on GM Hopkins by a priest with literary tastes[1] who said he wd. read some lines by a NZ writer in the same rhythm & she recognised a quotation from Time & Place – which had been given to her as Xmas present by two different friends – 2 copies I mean. Such is fame! Miss D. struck me as very sound in her judgements of people.

I picked up in Wellgn a 1/2 price (NZ 1/2 price) copy of The New Book of English Verse edited by my favourite Charles Williams & am quite delighted with it. It will I believe start me on reading poetry again. I have it beside me here. Good print – important for me nowadays – And in Wellgn I retrieved my copy of his "War in Heaven" wh. a friend had forgotten to return & I rather suspected she might have it but wasn't sure. You must read it, but there wasn't time to send it before I left – indeed I don't want to do any more lending *in haste* – its too disastrous, when one can't remember where books are – Also I must lend you the latest Caxton production with 2 good poems by D. Glover. [...]

I want you to borrow T.E. Hulme's 'Speculations'[2] from A. Prior[3] if you have not read it, & tell me what you think. I have bought it & find it a great acquisition. How satisfactory it is when a book turns out to be all that one hoped! The new anthology for instance – it has passages I have wanted to know as well as many known but scattered about in different books which I am grateful to have assembled. The last one in the vol. is that great sonnet of Hopkins which has so often spoken for me these

---

[1] This probably refers to Fr. Francis Walsh, a friend of Duggan's, and later an acquaintance of Bethell's. He wrote a lengthy and generous appreciation of the latter's work after her death, published in the *New Zealand Tablet*, Feb. 7, 1945.

[2] The full title indicates the scope of Hulme's work: *Speculations: Essays on Humanism and the Philosophy of Art*.

[3] At this time, Arthur Prior (1914-1969) was an assistant lecturer in philosophy at Otago. He later became an internationally prominent logician, holding chairs at Manchester and then Oxford.

years "Not, I'll not, carrion comfort, despair, not feast on thee – Not ... cry 'I can no more' – I can, Can something hope, wish day come, not choose not to be" etc

Well I think I have come to the end of what there was to say – I have an unfinished letter to Arthur P. yours seemed to be the more pressing.

Yours affectly
M. U. B.

Hocken Library. MS-0741-001.

TO RODNEY KENNEDY – AUGUST 14, 1937

St Faith's House. Webb St. N.1. ChCh.

My dear Rodney,

I posted 'War in Heaven' to you – because your letter sounded as if you could do with a Chas Williams novel. Does depression make your handwriting shrink? I did not recognise the address & was pleased to find who the writer was. Your word "nostalgia" made me smile a little – so very mild in relation to the agony of loss that flowed over me again on returning to my loneliness – But I have known that too, & know how crippling it is, how it destroys the life in things. To each age its own sorrow! Yes, I've gone that way. This is more desolate. Yet all the joys one has known, all the loves that have been taken away, have been worth while – "But in the midst of all this a great peace reigned in the deepest depths of my soul, founded on the solid basis of my will"[1] – Yes – deep down under the frozen surface of the heart there is a little spark of hope, & prayer somehow, I don't know how – keeps it alive. "Frozen surface" – that is what we have in nature here – for there is no spring "about" here – not to notice – such as you speak of – ChCh is its usual dismal winter self, bare trees, water logged ground, choking, foggy evenings & nights. I have always detested this town! Some one said that there were signs of spring in the public gardens – I must go & see – but when? I am very busy – one is soon caught in the web of local circumstance – & its a good thing to be busy. I should not be writing this letter at the moment! Certainly the mornings are lighter & one's eyes not so tired –

Yes – I hope you'll go on with drama – You certainly should be busy with some art-form – Would you say that all human life is art & only trees grow like trees – Yet the Gospel brings one back to the seed

[1] Bethell is quoting from Kennedy's letter.

growing secretly – without effort or striving. I suppose we are everything – nature & art & Supernature –

[...]

Should I come to Dunedin in the spring & see the new Art School & the new Babies? I expect not – my nephew came in this week to announce his engagement & I must save up & behave a little handsomely to him.

I am now counting the last of your apples. They get sweeter & sweeter & more & more rosy – I've never relished raw apples to this degree before – I see the *name* wine-sap in the shops – but they look so different – Thank you again.

I always feel rather hopeless about posting to Dunedin at the weekend. Such a long gap.

Yrs affectly
M. U. B.

Hocken Library. MS-0741-002.

TO RODNEY KENNEDY – AUGUST 29, 1937

St Faith's. Webb St. ChCh.

My dear Rodney

Just before I read yr. letter I had been saying to a visitor (Rae Miller) how curiously vague & indeterminate life seemed to have become for me as it draws on to its end. In youth there were landmarks – one passed examinations & that was that – one saw new places & they were there – one discovered new ideas & they were registered – one took up new jobs – but now the days & months slip by like a river – no meaning – nothing definite to show for it. You seem to have been experiencing something of the same mood, adjustment to the infinite? Contentment not to see the other side? I don't think I ask for a pattern now – so much of the design must be out of sight. The "answer" – oh, that must surely be beyond these limitations – except in parts. Just enough answer to keep one going. And curious that you in your letter were asking for something "tangible", "concrete", "round & hard as an apple" – And Toss in his letter had been wanting something "as real & obvious as a brick"! & thinks he has found it in Wellington with the Groupers! R.N.F. will approve – but how will it strike you? Toss is very impressionable; I fear a reaction – I've always felt that simplicity of the saint in him – but sanctity means a long & painful discipline. He's so delighted with the exchange of confidences with his groupist uncle[1] – the same release that you felt in your heart to heart avowals west coast wards with your Fred Simpson. That's all very well & "merely usual" – but the experience seems to have gone to T's head a bit – & *so* silly of him to write all about it to V.M.[2] who was revolted by his letter – & finds emphasis upon Sex-experience morbid & disgusting – even used the word salacious. I've known Toss a good many years now, but with V.M. he wd. have done well to preserve more reticence. I fear I have written unsympathetically to him. If I had seen him, I should probably have felt more kindly. But somehow I can't feel that the Groupist movement – I was just going to say Stunt – is truly a flowering of the christian spirit. Its a hybrid one would think an American hybrid. Contrast the lives of the Saints. Take for instance John Woolman the Quaker, who prayed to be "baptised into a sense of the needs & conditions of all men"[3] – At the group meeting I went to they were taken up with *themselves*. The Ego enjoying itself thoroughly. Dear Toss – I do hope my letter isn't horrid. I suppose the uncle made him feel more virile. [...]

[...] I always try to get away for November Show & Race week – the memory of those days when my little dear lay dying in such pain still too vivid – I feel the pain myself. People remind me that all pain is over for her, but I can't grasp it, the pain seems to be in my heart & in my physical frame – There are places more accessible than Dunedin. I think I shall go to Akaroa for my birthday – have never seen it in the early part of October, when it is said to be at its most charming.

[...]

Can you tell me whether you have sent back Maritain?[4] If I move from here, I shall try to have quarters where I can have all my books round me in one room – This is so confusing.

I am so sorry Rodney that I failed to send you a birthday greeting – there it is down in my book – same day as MTW's wedding – but I only succeeded in remembering that it was also the 6th birthday of a godson &

---

[1] Frank Tosswill was the older brother of Woollaston's mother, Charlotte. He had a considerable influence on Woollaston in matters of religion, and to a more limited degree on Kennedy too.

[2] Valmai Moffet, noted cellist and wife of John Moffet of the *ODT* (see letter of Sept. 14, 1936).

[3] 'We took the meetings in our way through Virginia; were in some degree baptized into a feeling sense of the conditions of the people' – from Chapter II of Woolman's *Journal*. Woolman was one of the most celebrated of 18th century Quakers; his spiritual autobiography was published in 1774, two years after he died.

[4] Probably a reference to his *Art and Scholasticism* (1930) – a favourite book both for reading and for lending. Jacques Maritain was a French philosopher / theologian whose aesthetic theory was influential with Bethell, and with Kennedy and Woollaston.

managed to send a present. The Deaconess has something characteristic about birthdays – about its being a "day's march nearer home" as well as something else I forget – in any case a day for rejoicing. She is rather good at innocent festivals.

[...]

Yours affectly
M. U. B.

Hocken Library. MS-0741-002.

TO RODNEY KENNEDY – OCTOBER 10, 1937

As from St Faith's. Webb St. N.1. ChCh.
Akaroa

My dear Rodney

I have wanted to write to you, since you said you had been out of health. So have I – terribly tired & ending up with a cold. That is partly why I came away here – & partly to be quiet during this week – one of those difficult anniversary weeks. I could wish that you were beside me now taking in the lovely scene – but of course Dunedin is more like this than ChCh is – I am out of doors all day, so long as weather permits – and it *has* permitted most of the time. This early morning was exquisite, enchanted colours in the perfect stillness when I went to "early service" – and only the faintest lapping of waves. As the day has gone on the wind has risen, but it is still beautiful, with sparkling, hurrying little waves across the bay, & tree music drowning the notes of the birds which sang in them this morning. So many different trees. What adorable shapes the manukas take when they have made their full growth. There's one group I wish to carry away & am sorry I did not bring the camera – G.M. Hopkins could have drawn them with his pencil – I was so much struck by the drawing in the new vol. of his diary etc which has been lent to me.[1] In this Domain there are little glades just like Robert Field's picture in my parlour. I am too late for the daffodils, but it wd. be churlish to regret any phase of spring – it is so green & lovely now. What a mercy that "Progress" still passes Akaroa by, its wonderfully "unspoilt." Of course it hurt dreadfully coming back here alone, but I think one learns to accept & include, (very slowly, indeed) the pain which is the other side of love – so that, being reminded, here, all the time of what has been taken away, I am yet beginning so to mix up the pain with the loveliness

[1] Hopkins's *Notebooks and Papers* (ed. Humphrey House), which included some of his sketches and drawings, had been published earlier that year.

that in the end it will be part of it, & not wring & exhaust the heart as it has done till now! Sometimes I think I like birds better that anything else in the world. It is the same nonchalance & gaiety & simplicity & withal pathos that charmed me in that little one.

Monday. I started off with my lunch today up a road labelled hopefully "To the waterfall 1 1/4 miles" – Two at least I should say & "uphill all the way" & I have not seen the waterfall – but have heard a loud noise which no doubt was it. I did not want to scramble down through the bordering bush to the stream which makes the valley voiceful – one has to bear twisted ankles in mind when one is far from other human beings – I did not want, anyway, to see a waterfall (they are usually disappointing) but to get away from the boarding house human beings to a quiet spot among the trees & birds. I burdened myself with writing tackle & a packet of letters which will probably *not*, after all, be answered – but I am carrying on with yours, after lunch under one of the French walnut trees. I have been in the depths again, & glad that no one could see my tears – it must have been starting off on one of our walks by myself, & this season of the years brings back all that happened 3 years ago. [...] I have been wondering this morning whether a life of solitude & contemplation would be the way to battle through the dark illusions to reality – the advice has been to throw oneself into the lives of other people – perhaps now the other path might help. Being alone with nature like this is a wonderful experience – always has been with me – the absence of trivialities – The riro is singing his heart out & sometimes a tui pipes – what must it have been before the colonists broke in & destroyed the forest. So many birds that have since been exterminated, & no noxious animals – Man is the noxious animal! Yet one is dependent on one's fellow-humans – food & shelter are provided for me.

[...]

Apparently you are still sheltering under an umbrella from the Group deluge – Toss seemed to think you were to be drenched. I wish you might have the joy & confidence of those people, without the tags & the weaker features which are marked enough. It is so hard to understand why American salesmanship methods should capture fine natures & "put across" the very truths which have been handed on through the ages by the masters of the spiritual life. For instance this "surrender" is in all the books in other words. In Maritain's little "Prayer & Intelligence" he quotes from a classic that the first step must be abandonment of oneself to God *without reserve*.[1] And there is something

[1] Originally published as *La vie d'oraison* by Jacques and Raïssa Maritain (English translation, 1928). The 'classic' Maritain quotes is the *Doctrine spirituelle* of the 17th century French Jesuit Louis Lallemant.

rather "get rich quick" about the group methods – the mystics say that the process of sanctification is a long & difficult road, & often in the dark. A road winding "uphill all the way" like this one. And in that little meeting I went to it sounded as if the girls were much more taken up with themselves & their silly little sins than with God. Everything hinges on God's existence & nature, to my view. If one should despair, that is to deny Him – & to make nonsense of creation. But as to His nature, as Gore said – people think "God is Love" such a simple little text – whereas its really the most difficult & profound doctrine of theology – Got at through Christianity.[1]

[...]

Yours affectionately
M. U. B.

Hocken Library. MS-0741-002.

TO RODNEY KENNEDY – OCTOBER 26, 1937

St Faith's House. N.1. Christchurch.

Rodney my dear

Its late & I have just been downstairs to wake myself up with a cup of strong coffee, because I want to answer your letter tonight, there wont be time tomorrow, or the next day, or the next.

There may have been a spot of telepathy, for I too have been thinking lately that I should like to have a chat with you – Good to think of you with the Friends.[2] I have been in touch with them from time to time; there was a beautiful bare Meeting House at Hampstead where I lived for 3 years – and when I was in U.S.A. I stayed at a Quaker ladies (run *by* not *for* such I mean) Boarding House at Washington D.C. – & again at the "Young Friends Association" at Philadelphia – where even the negro porter was called "thou" – (& you know what *that* amounts to) – & there I made a pilgrimage to 'Mount Holly in Virginia' where Saint John Woolman lived. Do you know his lovely Journal? ('Get the journal of John Woolman by heart' said Elia)[3] I found that Friends in N.Z. don't know it, their own classic! – "Baptised into a sense of the needs &

---

[1] The quotation (from I John 4: 8) occurs so commonly that it is difficult to be sure of Bethell's reference, but she may be thinking of Charles Gore's *The Religion of the Church. A Manual of Membership* (1916).

[2] Kennedy had written 3 days earlier that he had been going to meetings of the Quakers 'and have found my special niche or as St Augustine would have it my resting place.'

[3] The sentiment can be found in the essay 'A Quakers' Meeting.' Charles Lamb first published the *Essays of Elia* in *The London Magazine* in 1832.

conditions of all men" – how often I've thought of that – "I felt a stop in my mind"[1] – (I could have wished that the girls at the ineffably silly womens Group meeting I went to had felt it!) and all their other expressions. (That's a dialect I *do* like!) I've often said 'Either Catholicism or Quakerism' but Catholicism had it.

It *is* strange, this impact of "Groupey" (as Arthur Prior calls it) upon Toss & you – I must rail no more against the methods, for I recognise that you are being very much helped – The train was laid in you Rodney – the fire & was set & the sparks smouldering – & now the flame leaps up – & I shall not question, for "the Spirit bloweth where it listeth"[2] – or I might say like the old woman in a story my sister used to tell "The Almighty knows His own queer ways best!" – I was afraid after that 1st letter from Toss of excitement, superficiality reaction – but now I recognise that a deep work is going on in you, an experience in line with the mystical tradition. I think I wrote to you from Akaroa, but forget what I said. That week did a bit of healing in my soul I think – the quiet, the 'détente', & talks with 2 friends – There again one must accept "queer ways" – for the younger friend who was very unhappy & aimless after a sorrow was "converted" or "changed" by the "Church Army" mission[3] & now lives her life in joy, by *their* slogan "Conversion – consecration – churchmanship"! Horrible to me these slogans & the two C.A. meetings I attended *revolted* me but its a very gracious work in her (& her rock-garden wd. enchant you.) The older friend has followed a more Hindu path, but I understand her language.[4] It is always the same thing; "Surrender" "abandonment" "obedience" "renunciation" "offering". Its in the Old Testament 'the *daily* sacrifice' & 'Are you able to drink of My cup?'[5]

Wonderful even for a few moments to be conscious of an alleviation of the pain that wrings my heart – like when toothache stops. Then you know it *can* stop. But its not for me to say whether it is to be allayed – only I have had a few such moments since Akaroa.

[...]

---

[1] Bethell quoted the first extract in her letter of Aug. 29, 1937. The second comes from the first chapter of the *Journal*, and reflects Woolman's anxiety about the growth of his tailoring and retail business.

[2] See John 3: 8.

[3] The Church Army was a voluntary social work organisation within the Anglican Church, founded in London in 1882, and in New Zealand in 1935.

[4] The 'older friend' is Blanche Baughan, a convert to the Indian Vedanta philosophy. I have not yet identified the younger friend.

[5] The first phrase occurs several times in the book of Daniel; the second is in Matthew 20: 22.

Thank you for your closing words, which I have been pondering.[1] Thank you for remembering me with love at the anniversary time. The summons to "squander love on the world" fits in with my time at Akaroa – Yes. But it makes me think how the utter devotion & love of an Exquisite person was *squandered*, daily, hourly on me – and by one who needed me – For these three years I have been waiting to know what to do with this desolation. The first task was to go on living without tenderness, without joy, without *fun*, without sharing, *needed* by no one – because it was the Will. And going deep into the bitter knowledge of how much more I might have given. Now I have come to this, that I can thank God daily for life, even stripped of what used to make it rich, because I know there must be a raison d'être (I felt this strongly when my charlady announced one day that as for her she couldn't see *anything* in life, which consists [in] doing what you don't want to do, & going without what you require, and she just didn't agree with Creation!) But I tell you this, Rodney, & you may remember it some day when I'm not here – you may offer everything to God, & not know what you are doing, till He takes it, & you are left in great darkness & dread. Yet not in despair, knowing that the offering must have had a meaning, & to reject God makes nonsense of everything. Some people don't understand this.

Its surprising how many good things there are to thank for when one comes to reckon them up! even thru' one's tears!

[...]

People tell me that I have had rich experiences in many ways – & should be able to hand things on to people in N.Z., but I am always being pulled up sharp by the different mental background & wonder whether I should do better back in the other environment. In other words am I needed out here? Time will show – we always meant to go back, & the thought of going back without the companion renews the desolation. I have no superstitious feelings about cemeteries, but it will be something to do on that 8th of November, when she was caught away, to go out & put a bunch of flowers beside her name – (However much one may tell oneself that time shall be no more).[2]

Looking over your letter, there are still things I've left out – those note-books – *why* do you find one indispensable? It is customary among Catholic Christians to have notebooks for meditation & self examinations – but I have always shirked them, being an unmethodical person – and by the way I didn't imply an *antithesis* between Quakers &

[1] Kennedy had written: 'My love went forth to you on your birthday and during your exile. Be of brave heart. Come back and squander as much love on the world as you can. We need it and the world needs it.'

[2] See Revelations 10: 6.

Catholics – The Catholic Church wd. ideally be the "Society of Friends", & would, & often does, afford periods of silence. I think its wider, more in touch with many sides of life, more comprehensive – in short more catholic! But the Catholic Church never seems to be quite there, one is always thinking of what it *might* be – the Bride from heaven never quite come. [...] Yes, I will come with you to the Quaker meeting – but I wish it were in the large white empty chamber on Hampstead Hill with the London Sunday silence outside.

What you say about peace in the world is what I was trying to say after that meeting at Professor Sinclaire's – He said that international warfare had nothing to do with peace in the heart (or words to that effect) & I thought it had everything to do with it! The Sinclaires came to tea & he was so surprised to find my collection of "mystics" (his private study) & he borrowed some – and wanted Maritain.

The Groupist "surrender" is in them all – For daily reference I have a little book of extracts from them – Last week there, from one: "The way of inward peace is in all things to be conformed to the pleasure & disposition of the Divine will. This conformity is the sweet yoke that introduces us into the regions of internal peace & serenity"[1] [...] & again "Thus I saw that God is our very peace, & He is our sure Keeper when we are ourselves in unpeace, & He continuously worketh to bring us into endless peace – And thus when we be made meek we are fully safe: suddenly is the soul oned to God, when it is true peaced in itself; for in Him is found no wrath." (Thats Julian of Norwich – do you know her?)[2] [...] and "The soul perfected by humility – sheds the fragrance of patience around the Creator & its fellow creature & itself. It has grace & quiet in its mind & it has found peace in warfare, because it has driven far from itself will founded in pride" – (that's S. Catherine of Siena do you know her? She was the one who was with the young man at his execution sustaining him till his severed head fell into her lap.)[3] And again

"A quiet silent person may possess
All that is great or high in blessedness.
The inward work is the supreme .....

---

[1] The extract comes originally from *A Spiritual Guide* by Miguel de Molinos (1685), a Spanish priest whose Quietist spirituality was eventually condemned by authorities in Rome.

[2] This comes from Chapter 49 of *The Revelations of Divine Love.*

[3] This from the 'Letter to Monna Agnese Malavolti,' a letter whose pervading theme is 'Sanctissima Pazienza.' Catherine's biographer and friend, Raymond of Capua, records the incident of the beheading in 1375 of a young political prisoner, Nicolo di Toldo, attended by Catherine.

A man that seemeth idle to the view
Of others, may the greatest business do.[1]

That's Thomas Traherne – didn't I lend him to you some time ago? (no, he's not missing!) I have not been able to read him these last years – delightful as he was. He's on my tear off Kalendar today too. "Never was anything in this world loved too much, but many things have been loved in a false way; & all in too short a measure."[2]

We were talking at Akaroa, Miss Baughan & I, about those "reserves" – kept back from the offering, which remain to be brought daily to the altar – And I said it was like falling down through floors, one after the other – Yes, she said once you've known there is a mattress at the bottom!

Heavens, what a long letter. The difficulty is when one conducts a letter on the lines of a conversation, to bring it to an end! Well, you may get nothing more from me this side Xmas – [...]

Yours affectionately
M. U. B.
(*Ugly* initials!)

Hocken Library. MS-0741-001.

TO RODNEY KENNEDY – NOVEMBER 2, 1937

All Souls Day St Faith's. Webb St. N.1. ChCh.

My dear Rodney

Yr second wire just come – a disappointment.[3]

[...]

My first question was going to be "No set back yet?" You see I've lived through so many revivals, & missions, & seen them flare up and flicker down – but always some remain perservering & after all you are more mature than some I have in mind. I am thinking of all my imperfect self-dedications, from confirmation – let me see – it must be 47 years ago, onwards. I said to myself coming back from 7:30 am Mass at S. Matthews yesterday (All Saints Day) "You wouldn't be sobbing & crying like *this*, if you knew God as well as you thought you were going to, *then*!" However there are two considerations 1. The Creator seems to allow persistent pain for chastening purposes – 2. nerve-shock – the spirit

[1] These are the opening lines of Traherne's 'Silence.'

[2] The passage comes from Traherne's *Centuries of Meditations*, ii, 66.

[3] The 'wire' was cancelling an expected visit from Kennedy.

may be (more or less) willing & the flesh continue to be wracked[1] – Remember this when you are as old as I am, & have had many griefs.

I'm writing this while I take the well-earned & so valuable, but so seldom achieved after luncheon rest. How I wish you could see those pale pink & tender green not quite in flower lupins & their green, pointing upwards in lovely curves & the drooping "bleeding heart" in the corner above – and in the parlour blue lupins at the same stage with white viburnum, & canary yellow tulips & scarlet geums & the clear green young lime-leaves – a few branches I pruned & put them on top of the cupboard.

I must go out now – Shall hear in due course why you were coming & why you did not come –

I hope you are well –

Yours affectionately
M. U. B.

Dear Rodney – "Bethell. Webb St" is *not* enough address – I am not so famous! There are *nests* of flats in Webb St. It gives so much trouble. And talking of fame – did I tell you that Dr. Helen Simpson will broadcast for 10 mins from 3YA tomorrow (Wedy) morning about 11 – about gardening with readings of my garden verses. She should do it nicely as she loves the book. This will be too late I think to make you listen.

Hocken Library. MS-0741-002.

TO RODNEY KENNEDY – [DECEMBER 26, 1937]

The Feast of Stephen 47 Webb St. ChCh.

Dear Rodney

I am now embarked on Christmas *thanks*. Your letter was very nice. I liked hearing about those roses. I have a bush of Shot Silk here, (brought down from Rise) but the summer flowering is over – I missed the roses by being away in Wgn – I think she does give some blooms again in the autumn, but am not sure. Not all roses do. Such a willing & brilliant rose.

I turned your good wishes into a prayer – that I mightn't put limits to God's goodness in my mind by refusing to believe that "deep joy" and "lovely experiences" are still possible in my life. But the will of God still seems to be sadness for me, so I must go on being patient. At times I do

[1] See Matthew 26: 41.

feel little shivers of what used to be joy, looking for instance at the grace & beauty of flowers – but its all too different still –

[...]

I shall reciprocate your wish for me, dear Rodney – "deep joy" – and "lovely experiences" – adding, "courage" if these are not vouchsafed – courage, & faith, & patience, & hope –

M. U. B.

Hocken Library. MS-0741-002.

IV: 1938–1939

TO EILEEN DUGGAN – [JANUARY 30], 1938

4th Sun. after Epiphany 47 Webb St. Christchurch.

My dear Miss Duggan

At last I have your book – and trying, do you know, not to be envious of its lovely get-up, & the preface by such a poet![1] (You did not tell me about *that.*) I tried several times, as I told you – & then they'd sold out! Not that *that* means so very much, I am afraid, they that is W. & T. are chary of stocking more than a few copies of a volume of poetry! They are more stationers than booksellers. [...] I *have* your book – have had it beside me for some days indeed – but I can't *quite* say that I have read it – poetry takes a deal of reading – & at the moment I like for that reason the simplest ones. I read the introduction after I had dipped into the book, & was so pleased to find W de la M noting a line that had arrested me, about "tussocks *brittling* from dew into frost"[2] – (I shouldn't bring myself into this, but I think that is just here, at that kind of word inspiration, that I come short) – (and by the way I thought it was the mother not the foal "dying & defiant" & so it was![3] Did you notice that in the preface?) "The Oxen" "Twilight" (especially), "The Bushfeller", "The Blacksmith's Wife" "The Bankrupt" – these are the simple ones I have taken in first, & like *very* much. One wonders what are the pieces you would have put into this collection, & the publishers would not! Wont you print those in N. Z? I read somewhere, & must hunt it up, a poem of yours, long ago – which struck me – a city scene – evening – the sky stooping – I forget how it went – but the last line (I think it was) had the same thrill, the something peculiar, as the tussocks "brittling into frost".[4]

[...]

And now to thank you very much for your Christmas greeting & encouraging words thereon. No, no more writing here! I have been too busy with everyday life, & too sad. Christmas is a very upsetting time! Your card says "enough joy to share" – the trouble is that if a little twinge of joy comes – the colour of flowers, or what not – there is no one to share it with! I havn't given up *all* hope (age notwithstanding) &

---

[1] Eileen Duggan's *Poems* (1937) had an introduction by Walter de la Mare.

[2] The line comes from 'Twilight' (*Poems*, p. 30).

[3] The allusion is to 'Endurance' (*Poems*, p. 18).

[4] Duggan wrote few city scenes; Bethell may be thinking of 'Sunset,' which was first published in *N. Z. Tablet*, Aug. 10, 1922 (p. 24).

perhaps if I were in a less busy & interrupted situation something might be done. [...]

I am going to see whether there are enough pieces out of the past still left over to make another little collection – perhaps that would be like pouring water into the pump! (You must have done that often if you lived, as I infer from the poems, in the country formerly.)

[...]

I wish you would take a holiday & come & stay in our little "Wayfarer's Room", which I had built for tired people. You should stay in bed all day, with the porch windows open on to the balcony. You wd. not find the atmosphere unsympathetic I think. (This tiny room was my little *practical* memorial to the one that's gone – the other was "Time & Place")

Now I must write some questions about that Akaroa Cottage.

With hearty & sympathetic congratulations
from Ursula Bethell

You know I think one has to write – about anything – out of *faith* – great poets may write out of great grief – but faith must impel the little ones. If I could find *that* again – or even a *lively* hope instead of a faint one!

Catholic Archdiocesan Archives, Wellington. Eileen Duggan Papers.

TO CHARLES BRASCH – APRIL 16, 1938

47 Webb St. N. 1

Dear Mr. Brasch[1]

I am glad that I forgot to say, as I meant, not to trouble to return that catalogue, since my forgetfulness has brought your charming note. You have no idea how it cheers me up to hear that the things belonging to happier days still give pleasure to a new reader.[2] [...]

I value your judgment of course – in part because it is that of the writer of the poem in Tomorrow.[3] I told Mr. Page[4] that I was arrested by

---

[1] Charles Brasch (1909-1973) is best known as founding editor of *Landfall* (1947-66), poet, and patron of the arts. He met Bethell when visiting New Zealand during a break from teaching at the Abbey School at Little Missenden.

[2] Brasch's note, with his comment on Bethell's verse, has not survived.

[3] The poem is 'Waianakarua,' first published in *Tomorrow*, and included in Brasch's first collection, *The Land and the People*. It speaks of the eloquence of 'the thorn ... inhuman matakauri ... [and] gum-trees.'

[4] Later to become known as one of the most influential music teachers in New Zealand, Fred Page had just married the painter Eve Polson. Their rented cottage at Waitahuna was a gathering-place for artists and musicians.

the juxtaposition of gums & matagouri (as I've been used to call it). I have never seen that. Perhaps your landscapes are imaginative – whereas mine have the meticulous exactness of a pre-Raphaelite! (You recall, e.g. the accommodation-house & the cemetery at Burke's Pass!)

I thanked Mr. Page for bringing you to call – & should be glad to see you if you ever had time to come again, but hesitate to invite people here, there is so little to ask them *to* – it was very different at Cashmere.

I did write a line to Robert Field, but in the meantime I think my friend Rodney Kennedy has been hoping to effect the introduction.

Yours sincerely
Ursula Bethell.

Hocken Library. MS-0996-3/19.

TO RODNEY KENNEDY – [May 10, 1938]

Caulfield House. Wellington.

Dear Rodney

Your letter reached me here – & so has Toss in person! I was so surprised when he rang up [...] "Providence has been about" as we used to say at Rise Cottage. I have had a quite breathless time so many people I know seem to be collected in Wellington & I find myself able to say that I am *enjoying* it.

[...]

I am glad you had a candid talk with R.N.F. *but* you should not have passed on what I told you & T. about their visit to me. This is where you fail me, and it makes me feel that I can't chat freely with you, sure that you know which parts of a conversation are in confidence between friends. In the second place it was unkind because it puts me wrong with the Fields. I told it you as a joke completed by the humour of my next supper invitation when I was too ill to share it with my guest. Now it has become mixed up with serious matters & the Fields will take it heavily & perhaps write to me about it. I am vexed about this.[1]

[...]

Love to you from
M. U. B.

Hocken Library. MS-0741-002.

[1] From a letter of Kennedy (May 3), it appears that the 'candid talk' involved Kennedy's rejection of the Group. He writes: 'In the course of this catharsis I told him [Field] that his behaviour to you was typical of his general behaviour and that I thought it rude and unfeeling.' However, the incident giving rise to Kennedy's remark is not mentioned.

TO RODNEY KENNEDY – MAY 20, 1938

As from 47 Webb St. Christchurch.
At Wgn.

Rodney my dear friend don't be hurt like that[1] – I am sorry. I put it harshly & yet not sorry for even blunders & misunderstandings can be turned to good account – I am going down tonight in the teeth of a southerly. Very tired after packing & with 20 mins in which to try & say something to you – On board tonight will be imposs. I fear as its so rough – I want to say at once that I have often – perhaps not so much now – been guilty of blunders & betrayals – speaking when I should have been silent – After all this wasn't a very grave matter & I should perhaps have trusted your judgement in using the incident when confronting Robert Field – But I don't quite trust you yet evidently – & I daresay I'm wrong. Its so comfortable to talk freely with perfect confidence in the discretion of one's hearer. That will come – Give me a little more time yet to know you better. In the matter of the seriousness or amusingness of those 2 supper parties both rather a failure – The Fields were of course most discourteous & stupid & it left me tired & disappointed – but I *could* find explanations to some degree – their bemused Groupist state & their very different conception from mine of what Sunday tea wd. amount to – & then I was amused – To be amused –

Saty

Time ran out & too rough on boat. Will post this so far & continue tomorrow.

With my love
M. U. B.

Hocken Library. MS-0741-002.

TO RODNEY KENNEDY – MAY 22, [1938]

47 Webb St. ChCh.

I had to break off just as I was going to expound something about the qualities of different sorts of amusingness – but in case I can't finish I want to put that aside & first tell about some Wellgn things, after Toss had gone – he will tell about when he was there. First – the evening at G.G's[2] room

[1] Kennedy's intervening letter has not survived.

[2] George Gabites, at that time working in the Parliamentary General Assembly Library. He and his brother Paul became close friends of Bethell.

when his friend Mr. McCormick[1] said 'no' to the wonderful records G.G. had ready & with him for 2 hours went slowly & deliberately, with long spaces of silence between their comment & discussion, over & over the parcel of M.T.W's work, while I listened. It was most illuminating. If only Edith could have been there in the spirit. Now he *is* being taken seriously. They are going to be shown to more circles of people up there – so that at any rate his name will become known.

Then there was me going to see the other McCormack's pictures on Thursday (at last I know which is *Mick* & which is *Mack*!)[2] [...] It was a heavenly time! That large airy studio (I remember it as Miss Richmond's) & that quiet withdrawn man with the gleaming eyes – (a head that should be painted? by?) Peace & a very slow pace I saw it would be, & sat quietly letting the pictures soak in – They *did*. There was no difficulty at all – (am I becoming enlightened?)

[...]

You know Rodney you have changed a good deal since I first knew you, especially latterly – I told you you had things to learn – so you have – Don't mind my saying this. So have I! & I have lived twice as long & had a pretty rich experience. You'll realise that later on, & that I'm not being "superior" – And so much of it has been suffering, as Father Kelly says. But now there is intermission from that agony & that bit of Purgatory nearly done – There will have to be more – but I think not so dreadful once there has been a break – and this is what I am so anxious to tell you about Wellington – I was free to enjoy it. Everything seemed to have prepared for it & it fitted in at the right time. G.G. arranged it all for me, & took endless trouble. He is what you call "a lovely person" & is now one of my special friends. Tho' shan't see much of him, as is the way in this N.Z. I shall now own up, not too Groupily, to what may have been a breach of confidence on *my* part. I couldn't resist showing to George your Xmas note which I had with me because of the wishes at the end – for "deep joy" & "many lovely experiences" [...] When I read those words I smiled rather supernally at God! & thought I knew better. How wrong I was – I did *not* hope "to see the goodness of the Lord in the land of the living"[3] – You were prophetic – I *can* feel joy again. I

---

[1] Eric McCormick (1906-1995), recently returned from post-graduate study at Cambridge, was assistant to the Dominion Archivist, and soon to be secretary of the National Centennial Historical Committee. He became a firm friend of Bethell, and an influential reader of her work. Few of her letters have survived, although their correspondence must have been extensive.

[2] T. A. McCormack (1883-1973) was by this time becoming recognised as a painter of some importance, especially as a watercolourist. The studio Bethell visited was rented from another artist, D. K. Richmond.

[3] See Psalm 27: 13.

suppose partly the dreadful nerve-shock took all that time to be mended. A little while ago I could not have met all those people in Wgn without exhaustion. Do you remember saying to me when you left last time that you wouldn't worry about me any more because I was getting back my courage? That helped me. You have understanding.

[...]

Please write & say that all is well.[1] Faithful words of a friend you know – And I believe the divines say that if we are too upset – its self love! I have often reminded myself of that. I must try & write to Miss Allen – it wd. be cruel to write to her about seeing pictures – it must be about music & people – And so, leaving a great deal unrelated for the present

with my love
M. U. B.

Hocken Library. MS-0741-002.

TO CHARLES BRASCH – JUNE 24, 1938

47 Webb St. N. 1.

Dear Charles Brasch

When I woke up this morning I felt I must write & tell you how happy the success of your Mapua visit has made me! (But I didn't ask about your address so must enclose to Rodney K.) And now comes a note from Toss to tell about the magnificence of your purchases.[2] [...] T. says he is "too tired & inarticulate from the shock" to write more than a few lines – that "it was a great shock to get so much money from a person who loves pictures" – It *is* wonderful for him to have this encouragement – quite apart from the material aid – when one thinks of all his struggle & trials & discouragements. He has been brave & single-minded. His faithful Rodney will be delighted. I'm going to see the Leicester Webbs, to tell *them*. How enjoyable for you to be able to make such a gesture – and what a nice person you are! (hope that doesn't sound impertinent.)

Yours sincerely
Ursula Bethell

Hocken Library. MS-0996-3/19.

---

[1] Kennedy wrote 'your tender and very beautiful letter today brought such a rush of warmth to my heart. It felt as if all the birds had flown back having journeyed in dark strange lands' (May 24, 1938).

[2] Brasch had bought a landscape for £20 and three drawings for £2. 2. each.

TO RODNEY KENNEDY – JULY 6, 1938

47 Webb St. ChCh.

My dear Rodney

[...]

This room feels better since it has been more inhabited & I am getting it better arranged – And I must tell you that in the place of honour hangs – *not* the Little Faun[1] – but MTW's charcoal drawing,[2] & *in your frame* – which suits it exactly! When the drawing came back from Wellgn the other day I thought it SO good & hit on this idea – fully justified – I am evidently being converted to modern art! I am looking forward v. much to showing it to C. Brasch who is coming to see me on his way north – I want him to see the Webbs' one too. Has he I wonder said anything to you about my plan for Toss which has been hovering in my mind for some time, & now brewing up.[3] You know I was wondering about European travelling scholarship & made enquiries in Wgn. but nothing doing. And Mr. MacCormack so little in favour of artists leaving N.Z. So I came to envisage an untrammelled painting holiday for Toss this summer – a sort of orgy – & wrote to him about it yesterday, to get his view. After all this stimulus of sympathy & recognition he ought to have a chance to work freely & I am sure I can gather up enough from interested people to give him some months of moving round. Toss & Edith not to know who the contributors are; & the latter not to know either – who the others are I mean – I am sure that would be pleasantest & easiest for Toss. [...] Do you think its a good idea? Toss has often spoken of wanting to go to Central Otago, to paint.

[...]

With my love
M. U. B.

Hocken Library. MS-0741-002.

TO CHARLES BRASCH – JULY 27, 1938

47 Webb St. Christchurch. N.Z.

Dear Charles

---

[1] Perhaps a reproduction of the painting by Charles Sims (c.1905-07).

[2] In 1938, at Brasch's suggestion, Woollaston executed a portrait of Bethell in charcoal (now in the Christchurch Art gallery). This may be the work referred to here.

[3] The plan, largely financed anonymously by Charles Brasch, provided funding for a scholarship so Woollaston could study for a term at the Canterbury College School of Art, and later spend time painting in Taranaki. See Jill Trevelyan's note in *Kotare* 4, 1.

You havn't sanctioned that address – but could you try to put up with it? For I am bound to call you so "behind your back" to Toss & Edith & that's how I think of you. I was minded to put down some things for you while the sweet peas are still here – as they are today but may not be tomorrow – lending brightness to the little parlour, dark in relentless rain [...] Now this morning comes your letter, one of the most interesting I've ever had – & how I wish that other correspondents had a like natty, shapely & legible handwriting – wish I had it myself – should get more on the page for this new-fangled air-mail.

Its now *Aug. 8th* & mail day! Other calls of the pen intervened & paralysingly cold weather ("the severest winter since 1901") – much correspondence with & about the Woollastons & I think I had better begin with that matter – so very much in hand. In the first place I want to explain to you the red herring I've drawn across your track – when my friend Mrs. Wilson, widow of Dr. Edward Wilson of Scott's South Pole Expedition, was last in N.Z. she told me to apply to her for help for artists – she had a fund for such a purpose.[1] I think it is the proceeds of sales of Dr. Wilson's drawings – reproductions I mean. So far I havn't felt there was anything definite enough to occasion such a request to her – but since this recognition of Toss's work, (in which you have had so large a share) – I feel the moment has come – I don't know what the fund amounts to, & I daresay it won't bring more than a pound or two, but you see what a useful function it performs, don't you, in our present plot? As it is I have to repudiate suspicions about my own share – (I really think it must be worse than being unjustly accused of a crime!) Mrs. Wilson has been rather gravely ill, but as soon as I heard from her that she was really better, I wrote to her about this. [...]

Toss will probably have written to you about his varying plans – so many of them, & mutually exclusive as he says. I think the present plan is for him to come to School of Art here next for Life Class & painting Lyttelton harbour at weekends – & Edith perhaps to go to a friend of mine near Kaikoura – but its not quite decided. E. wd. have liked to cling to her home while T. roams – but Mapua is too far away for her to be left there if he comes to ChCh. I should like to have her here in January when the house is empty & they could go on sorties together – Central Otago for the autumn is my idea. Toss has told me how you wonderfully sent them another cheque from Auckland. That tides them over & I think pays the journey till "scheme" begins – I said I thought it wd. be a

[1] English born Oriana Wilson visited New Zealand on two or three occasions, but it is unclear whether she and Bethell met here or in England. She was in New Zealand in 1912 to greet her husband on his return from the Pole, only to learn of his death on the return journey.

good plan to supply £10 a month & contracted to do so (how safely I could they didn't know!)[1] for six months at least beginning Sep. or Oct. (I have now another £10, about, in hand.) Toss has written so very sensibly about it all, with some interesting self-criticism on his work. [...]

Now I shall go through your letter. I thought it so wonderful of you to give me that prompt account of your travels, when they had been almost breathlessly rapid – things are always better hot out of the oven! – I was of course delighted with your appreciation of George G. who is indeed very dear to me – I have always myself felt that about his Englishness. When I saw him first in that Library – I thought rather stiff & pedantic surrounded by all those books but soon got to know him better. Yes, I know the "wearied" air,[2] but its quite personal to him – I wonder whether devotion to, responsibility for, an invalid mother has something to do with the grownupness. I attributed his very great kindness to & thoughtfulness for myself to the same cause. I loved that little garret of his with the harbour view – it reminded me of our lifted-up situation at Cashmere – there wasn't much wind when I was in Wgn. There *is* today – a real, oldfashioned Norwester – the first, & a definite crack in weather, tho' no doubt to be followed by a Southerly. (Anything is better than frost & fog in this place, which is often as smokily foggy as London.) "Der wind, der wind, das himmlische Kind" was my first bit of by heart German.[3]

Relating to your remarks about G. G's "standards" there's a parenthesis about your own "facets" which I so well understand. And I certainly shouldn't regret your way of setting about relationships. What you say there connects up with a book I am reading (rather in snatches) just now – Martin Buber's "I & Thou" – a philosophical work.[4] If you don't know it I think I'm safe in recommending it to you. And wd. suggest that it gives the clue to the shiftingness of C + X, C + Y, & so on – the other factor, the inclusive Thou – you'll see what I mean.[5]

---

[1] Bethell could make the promise because Brasch had already committed to send £50, and in fact sent £60 for the scheme, with additional funds later.

[2] Brasch had described it as 'the weariness of a Triton with the minnows' (July 21, 1938).

[3] Ger. 'The wind, the wind, the heavenly child.' Bethell probably first learnt these lines from Grimm's 'Hansel and Gretel;' this is the reply the children chant when the unseen witch asks who is nibbling at her house.

[4] Buber was an influential philosopher/theologian, whose *I and Thou* was originally published (as *Ich und Du*) in 1923.

[5] Brasch had written that 'having no standards' he offers 'a new facet to every person' with the result that 'I feel myself not a centralised person at all, but merely an agglomeration of facets, not C., but C. in relation to X + C in relation to Y & so on' (July 21, 1938).

And about D'Arcy. I am glad that you saw him. It must be five or six years since he used to come up to Rise Cottage & I saw him last, & I daresay he has changed a good deal. He must be well over 40, as to age, but I am sure my friend who's gone was right when she used to say "he's never grown up" – I am glad that you felt there was "something very nice about him" – so did I. George seems to have found otherwise. Denis Glover's account of the present day D'Arcy – really from Auckland friends – disturbed me – Denis said roundly "worthless fellow." I don't know whether he gave the same account of D'A. to you. I havn't the least idea what friends D'Arcy still has in London; I may be quite wrong, but it seems unlikely that he should have the same reception as when he went Home young & untried. He himself has high hopes. I don't know – but if these fail, & if you were friendly to him, I should expect him to turn to you – I think you should be prepared for that – penniless. I may be wrong, but there's the possibility. I wish to call myself D'Arcy's friend – I saw enough of him in those days to wish for that. And I sometimes wonder whether I could have been more useful to him. But there's an unreliable streak in him – I don't know I'm sure how far he "kids himself" – how far he really believes in himself. I have some sympathy for his being drunk & disorderly in Auckland, when he was feeling as lonely as he said. But I find I can't, in his case, sympathise about the homosexual goings on which Denis reported. I thought the references in D'Arcy's writings were just a pose, but Denis says not at all. I feel its a dip down for D'A. & a thing he's deceiving himself about. [...] Miss Baughan by the way knows a good deal about D'Arcy, & had the same feeling for him as I had. Respect for some of his quixotic actions, & generous ideas. We both wondered whether, at some time, he'd suffered some head-injury. All this I write, because he may turn up – and you may feel moved to take some trouble about him – I don't know of course – but there it is. In his letters are some *very* good things. Sometimes I feel that he should have died young! But that's *not* for *me* to say!

[...]

I think all this must seem very remote to you now, & N.Z. faded into the background. I've had letters from two lately gone Home friends – it all sounds so vivid – so actual. And you will have had the journey across that tremendous U.S.A. with your clever friends. I hope you *will* come back – but *not* literary for you I say – but human beings – I wish you could be drawn into plans for an independent school, which are in some people's minds – if only you'd had a little more time in Wellington!

Letters from England always make me wonder why I linger here – just cowardice perhaps – fear of what is now the unknown, once the taken-for-granted familiar. My nephews think I'm too old & not strong

Above left: 'Ursie,' aged 6 years, Jan. 1881.
Above right: Ursula with her father, Richard, c. 1881–82.
Right: Ursula (in front), with Rhoda and Marmaduke, c. 1883.

Above: In the garden at Rise Cottage, with Michael, c. 1930.
Above right: The parlour at Rise Cottage, c. 1930.
Below right: The passageway at Rise Cottage, c. 1930.

S. P. Andrew Photo.

MISS EFFIE POLLEN, *a well-known social worker, who died at Christchurch on Thursday. She was the eldest daughter of the late Dr. Henry Pollen, of Wellington.*

Above left: Ursula, about 1942.
Above right: The only known photograph of Effie Pollen, *Evening Post*, Nov. 10, 1934.
Left: The wedding of Merlin and Kathleen Davies, Dec. 31, 1941.

enough to take money risks. [...] A sale of my effects, a bit of Capital out of the Savings Bank, & the thing wd. be done! But here I hide, the impulse lacking. Perhaps I'm meant to finish up here. Perhaps a little grave is the tie. I don't know. But I have made a number of new friends lately, belonging to the country, & they do certainly weigh down the N.Z. balance-side.

But I havn't nearly finished with your letter! Shall I tell you next about this severe Critic of G.G's? – the verdict came last week, & it is so good it can't be true! Far from thinking that one or two of the unpublished pieces might be rescued, he thinks that *all* should go into a book, and soon. However there's no need to decide about that for I have no fund at present for publishing, & Sidgwick & Jackson couldn't take the risk of another for me, since The Garden didn't pay its way. [...] E. H. McCormick included in his critique The Garden & Time & Place & I have been a good deal roused & moved by his words – he assures me that it is not a hasty, but a well-considered opinion. I wanted to tell you that everything in The Garden (wh. goes with your books) is true to fact – no fancy. "Ruth," an old friend, is Lady Head, wife of the wellknown neurologist, Sir Henry Head. Such a brilliant man he was; he has been an invalid for many years now.

My critic thinks I should include in the book even the unfinished fragments[1] – I should like, as he wishes, to finish them but I seem so old & tired now, & always grubbing about at housework! It would make a much bigger book than Time & Place & I should like to call it "Residuum" – But its all nebulous.

Thank you very much for giving me a copy of your own book,[2] soon to appear – I am looking forward to it, though I think it may be a little difficult for me – (That's what I tell G.G. & his friend – my verse is far too *simple*, in comparison with the subtle expression of the present day.) I havn't seen Denis quite lately, except en passant. I must "have them round."

I see that I must get ready to go to the five o'clock post – The rest of this letter must follow afterwards – that will give you a breathing space! But I want to say 'right here' that whatever your N.Z. visit was or wasn't to you, it has been very enriching & stimulating to N.Z! And all so quick & direct. It was a great accomplishment.

Anon!
Yours ever

---

[1] This may refer to the 'By the River Ashley' sequence, which Bethell worked on from time to time in these later years; but there are numerous other unfinished fragments in her papers too.

[2] *The Land and the People and other poems* (Caxton) did not appear until the following year.

Ursula Bethell

Continuation – Tuesday evening

(If I leave these till next mail I shall have forgotten what I have already written!) Your letter came back to subject of Toss. Yes, suffering & struggle.[1] But then the difference since Edith – she sees & shares. Your question about pain must (at my age) be answered from my own experience. But looking back over my knowledge of Toss, I think I may say that one can see what he has gained. Whether he wd. have been a better *painter* by this time, if things hadn't been so hard is what I can't tell.[2] Is anyone in the position to make that judgement? Can pain be taken away from this planet? Can any of the political schemes do it? In my own case, looking back, I should say that life has been mostly suffering. A fair share of physical pain, – illnesses, & witnessing the agony of others, which is far worse, especially when they are dear to one – but nothing compared with what some have to endure. What has been my lot is another kind of pain – & its only by inference & faith that I could say that it has been useful & necessary. When, forty years ago, I left my music & painting & freedom, with a rather morbid conscience perhaps, to live in "the East End", I knew the fatal defect in myself – uncharitableness, want of sympathy, a narrow heart. Before my crucifix I prayed that this might be cured, even if it hurt a great deal. I was "asking for it" you see. It wd. be obstinate for me to say that the prayer wasn't heard. One after another the people for whom I have greatly cared have been taken away from me, by illness, by death, by insanity – finally, the perfect relationship of the latter years, the one who was to me, one might say, all the children I might have had, sudden stricken down, no goodbye, and all that happiness gone with her. And now I am very lonely. Your question is, is it useful? Is it necessary? I only know that it is the way it has happened. Now I do care for people pretty much – but it is still a matter of faith & interpretation what one says about the pain. In my younger years I said to myself 'This is either deliberate cruelty, or there is a good purpose in it – it can't be just random.' It all comes back to what God is & does. For me life would not have any sense without belief in God. I daresay this all sounds very crude to you but it is the best I can do by way of answer & you will respect the confidence. I don't think the answer can be made within the limits of this present life. (By

---

[1] 'I must tell you now how shocked & hurt I was to see in Toss's face what suffering he has had ... & ... a look ... as though he expected cruelty & humiliation .... But what he has brought out of suffering!'

[2] Brasch's question, essentially about the meaning of suffering, is couched in terms of whether Beethoven 'would have written more & greater music if he had been in easier circumstances.'

the way, in connection with your question you write yourself down non-Christian – I should have thought – there are so many ways of being – but it is not for me to attach labels –) I am a coward, but I must say that the worst, so far, has not been so bad as looking forward to it would have been, if one had known beforehand. You say that you have not suffered, but I notice that you suffer by sympathy.

I like what you say about the inner & the outer.[1] I shall look out for it in your poems.

[...]

Thank you for what you say at the end of your letter – but my Cook's Tourist contribution was very small,[2] & it was a great pleasure to know you. I was the gainer – Goodbye again – & au revoir some day. Where?

M.U.B.

I & Thou by Martin Buber translated by R. G. Smith is published by T & T Clark – 2/6 in papercovers – not a book*let*.

Hocken Library. MS-0996-3/19.

TO RODNEY KENNEDY – AUGUST 10, 1938

47 Webb St. Christchurch.

Dear Rodney

I should have liked to thank you for your quick sympathy even more immediately than now[3] – but the days have been impossibly full – & an English mail to get off. [...] But this is not the Race Week during which she died – that was the November one, called also the "Carnival Week" when the Agricultural Show goes on as well as the Races – She took an immense interest in the Races, of both kinds, but we did not go to them, tho' we often meant to, but we used to drive ourselves to the Show Grounds & make a picnic of it. All that week she was in agony, & the doctor telling me there was nothing serious the matter – & on Show Day, Judging Day, when the Terrace was deserted & I all alone, I found her unconscious. In heavenly summer weather, & the garden never so lovely as just after she'd gone. Each year I've run away from it – but I thought I wd. try to face it this year. Tonight the same heart-ache – for another

---

[1] 'I've moved about on the surface, absorbing little, & achieving nothing of my now constant underlying aim, which is to collect myself in some stillness so as to hear, as it were, simultaneously both the inner & the outer world.'

[2] Bethell had offered suggestions (with her own sketch-map) about places Brasch might visit, including Mt. Harper, Mesopotomia, and Akaroa.

[3] Kennedy had written (Aug. 7) a note of sympathy for what he mistakenly called 'your week of sad memories.'

kind friend has taken me to the matinée, & it was so very good. Don't think I am rebellious – no, I am very thankful for what I had. We are told that our 'sorrow shall be turned into joy'[1] & we must wait. And then we shall understand why. – *Why* I've never been allowed to keep the special ones I've loved. And all the other folks' "whys" – for every one has their own. I think its wonderful for you to feel for me – with me – like that. I take your hand & thank you.

[...]

Oh, I am tired! How wonderful to wake up & not be tired anymore – and oh, my wireless, (wh. *rests* me) has been getting Dunedin since it was mended & so more chance of music & on Sunday evening I happened to turn on Dunedin Cathedral just as the first lesson was being read (*well*) out of "Wisdom" the seventh chapter & about the 24th verse – (You have the apocrypha) so beautiful – it smote me with its beauty, coming over the air like that unexpectedly. I did not much care for the service – do not like sung matins & evensong, but I like sung mass. [...]

Now, really goodbye. I have a feeling that I have forgotten something I wanted to say. Oh yes, the apples. They are *wonderful*. But I am sure the case is twice the size it ought to be! We must go into that matter one day.

My love to you, and thanks.
M. U. B.

Hocken Library. MS-0741-002.

TO CHARLES BRASCH – AUGUST 18, 1938.

47 Webb St. Christchurch. N. Z.

Another post-script to say that I have now actually dispatched the books – I packed them with care & hope that they will travel well. I am sorry that Sidgwick & Jn. seem to have run out of the Garden dust-jackets – they were rather charming (– of Mr. S's devising, not mine).

[...]

I felt afterwards that my first postcard must have been rather incoherent – written late at night, tired, with the fiercest gale of the season raging without. It was one of those questions to answer which seemed to mean the whole of life! And I didn't think you asked it like a 'jesting Pilate' not waiting for an answer.[2] I had the same thoughts about G. M. Hopkins as yr. friend had about Beethoven – it seemed such a *crippled* life – Yet, as his friend pointed out, he'd not have written so

[1] See John 16: 20.
[2] The phrase is drawn from Francis Bacon's essay 'Of Truth' (1601).

powerfully out of an easy one. How his Despair sonnet has often "propped my mind"![1] Yet to help somebody else only pushes on the problem further & is no answer – the least little bit of pain is the stone in the pool of the universe – And to "get over things" as people try to do is an evasion. One soon sees that its bound up with life on this planet, & paradoxically the other side of joy – and the Utopians wd. only abolish both. Acceptance? No, there must be something more dynamic. Useful? Then an instrument only one beyond this [life] could use. And paradoxically one must fight the causes – I'm one who was struck by the war most hard (tho' already, then, hurt with the rest) twenty years after it began – For the seeds of my friend's fatal [illness] were sown, the doctor thought, by the epidemic of '18. In one respect I've changed my attitude. When I was young I was tempted to cry out "Is this Thy Justice?"[2] – now I wd. admit without reserve that its truly "my Desert." Well I know that these faltering remarks are in no way original! But its what I have been living with. At first I was too much numbed & hurt by the shock to think – then one begins to ponder & finally there are words. If I have said too much to you, please take it as a tribute to your own candour & sincerity! [...]

(I have lately liked this passage from Julian of Norwich – "It is God's will that we take His behests & His comfortings as largely & as mightily as we may take them, & also He willeth that we take our abiding & our troubles as lightly as we may take them, & set them at naught. For the more lightly we take them, & the less price we set on them, for love, the less pain we shall have in the feeling of them, & the more thanks & meed we shall have of them."[3] – The clue is there I think, a personal relationship.)

[...]

M. U. B.

Hocken Library. MS-0996-3/19.

TO EDITH WOOLLASTON – OCTOBER 20, 1938

47 Webb St. Christchurch.

Such a long silence on my part Edith my dear! – I've been distracted by holiday plans – & getting ready – & seeing people – & rather tired by everything. Thank you so much for your very nice letter from Stratford

---

[1] The phrase is from Sonnet XIX in Sydney's *Astrophel and Stella*.

[2] This phrase occurs in W. E. Dubois' 'Litany of Atlanta' (1906), an impassioned protest against widespread killing of black men and women.

[3] The passage occurs in Chapter 64 of *The Revelations of Divine Love*.

St. I've heard of you since from Toss of course – He's been so companionable & thoughtful that I suspect you of lecturing him a little on getting me into focus! Anyhow I feel I'm getting to know him much better as the *grown-up* Toss – & I am sure that your companionship has done a very great [deal] for him – altho' I've always thought of him as a quite out of the common person as you know. And now I'm to have the chance of knowing him even better. You will have heard about the cottage at Scarborough.[1] My Akaroa plan fell through, providentially I now feel, because of holiday – "no accommodation." I felt that it was extravagant to go there as well as to Wgn – but wished so much for a quiet rest before that sure-to-be-busy visit – Toss's cottage will be just the thing – I look upon it as a sort of Retreat! We go on Saturday. He first with his own goods. He stayed at Rise Cottage last night so as to paint on the Hills – that won't be called for again as he can do hills from Sumner. Unluckily the weather has turned cold today & I think he will have had to beat a Retreat into shelter. I planned a picnic luncheon in the Gardens tomorrow & am now wondering whether that will be possible.

[...]

I must go now or I shan't find the milk-shop open – I hope Joe[2] has *quite* settled down. I still think of coming in Nov-Dec, & look forward to seeing you.

Very affectly,
M. U. B.

Hocken Library. MS-0996-3/225.

TO EDITH WOOLLASTON – OCTOBER 28, [1938]

47 Webb St. ChCh N.1.

Came up from Scarboro' yesterday & going on tomorrow to Wellgn. Wish I had time to write more than a few lines. That cottage plan won't do, I saw for many reasons, but the few days were well worth while. It wasn't Toss "getting me into focus" it was meant for, but my getting *him* into focus! – Either I havn't had a chance or was stupid but now I have seen him at work I am fully convinced of his genius, whether its allowed to find expression on this planet or not. Hitherto I have not really understood his work – I don't now as connoisseurs do of course – but I

[1] One of several unsatisfactory short-term homes Woollaston occupied during his months in Christchurch.

[2] The Woollaston's first son was named Graham, but Bethell found the combination of first and last names unpronounceable, and called him Joe.

think I see what he "is after". Also I am aware of his needs, in order to work – & I see that solitary backing, at the mercy of meaningless people too constantly dropping in, won't do – & Scarboro' tho' peaceful is too far off I think & not the right time of year there (east wind & mist) & the owner of cottage too stupid to be of any use – quite the contrary. So I am glad he is turning to our old friend Mr. Thomson – He needs also a studio & I wish to goodness I were not going to Wellgn at this moment. But Leicester Webb has just called in to hear my account and he says studio essential & may suggest how to find one – & I am writing to a friend about it. I see now that I should have done more about finding quarters before T came down. I did not think Hereford St wholesome. No proper ventilation.

We had only one fine day at Scarboro' but that was lovely. We had a nice picnic lunch & a rest & then I watched T. coming to grips with his landscape. What a very great dear he is! he was so good to me & did all the washups & so thoughtful. I realise better how brave you are in sending him away to paint even for 3 or 4 months. I do hope it will repay you I think so. I am much impressed by the last thing he did at the Sch. of A. T. has helped me spiritually – that was sent to me at this specially sad & difficult season of the year – I feel rested, & ready for the Wgn Excursion – was too tired before.

And now I hope that all is going well with you & Joe in the meantime & time not seeming too long.

Very much love
M U B

Toss means to paint Mt Grey from Rise Cottage garden.

Hocken Library. MS-0996-3/225.

TO CHARLES BRASCH – [OCTOBER 31,] 1938

As from 47 Webb St Christchurch.
Wellington

Eve of All Saints

Dear Charles Brasch

Here am I spending the evening in G. G's new room. It is large & stately – but to my mind not nearly as snug[1] & gemütlich[2] as the little attic. He is reading for his M.A. Exam next week & I maintaining strict silence. There seems to be so much to tell you that I don't know where to begin. First to thank you for the letter written on ship-board – most

---

[1] Bethell actually wrote 'smug.'

[2] Ger. 'Comfortable.'

interesting & welcome. At the moment its inaccessibly locked up in my despatch case & the key lost! I must have the lock forced tomorrow. I've made several attempts to begin upon an answer, but new events always intervened. [...]

Nov. 15. Still in Wellington – and this morning your letter of Oct 22, so welcome, & yet adding so much to my debt – for the little reports about Toss don't of course count as letters. I see its just as I thought – N.Z. has dwindled & dwindled to a point for you. (It wd. dwindle for me, I expect, tho' I have lived here for so long now.) During "the crisis" I had a dazed feeling of looking on helplessly *at* it – not being helplessly *in* it, as one was in 1914.[1] The newspapers gave one no notion at all – only English letters coming in have brought it home. [...]

You will understand how trivial & remote our N.Z. doings appear to me also in the light of all this. And yet what else can one do but go on with the life one knows. To try to build here faithfully [may][2] count in the future – however little, its something. About yourself I feel cut to the heart and profoundly ashamed when I think of the position of my own community –

Yes, you must be there.[3]

Hocken Library. MS-0996-3/19.

TO RODNEY KENNEDY – NOVEMBER 5, 1938

Caulfield House. Sydney St. Wellington.

My dear Rodney

So much has cropped up that it has been less than ever possible to write letters, except those connected with matters in hand – & so far just as difficult here as in ChCh. I have had quite a lot of writing to do about Toss's affairs. But I have thought of you very often, & hope that you have been conscious of it. [...] The pacifism of several of my friends has been severely strained lately. Charles Brasch writes about it – I was struck by what Toss said he had written to him – "that pacifism at this time was watching with our Lord in Gethsemane". [...] I thought that he wd. easily find something suitable. I cannot regret the cottage fiasco,

---

[1] The 'crisis' arose from German demands for the independence of the Sudetenland Germans and the subsequent negotiations between the German, Czech, French and British governments in the middle of 1938.

[2] Bethell wrote 'make' and Brasch has pencilled a correction on her letter.

[3] This letter was left unfinished. Bethell included it with another she posted from Christchurch on Nov. 20.

since it gave me a wonderful three days "Retreat" with Toss in charge – I was very tired before I went down. I seem to have discovered Toss! & now understand more about his genius. Whether or no it will find expression on this earth remains to be seen, but I do think the S. of Art has been useful – if only for the set hours. Toss has helped me very much – it is wonderful how succour is provided at this season of the year. You can imagine how delighted I am that he should be sheltering now at Rise Cottage & intent on painting our view. I do hope & trust that the picture will come into being – Thinking of it I am reminded of a line at the end of a poem which will be in the possibly "forth coming book" –

"loved, & long-known, and beautiful, and new."[1]

[...] Its so much easier to get into open air in Wgn than in ChCh. On this first really fine day I sallied forth with my writing things directly after breakfast & only across the road find the grassy eminence of Parlm Buildings with benches. And here I bask looking up to green hills & trees – no long tram ride. The roar of the traffic reminds me of London – But I could do better without the Guy Fawkes crackers. But no, these bring the last Nov 5th at Rise Cottage, & a frame of mind for which I have not yet ceased repentance, nor ever shall – Next Tuesday is the anniversary of the falling asleep of my darling. I shall keep it as a quiet day & take cut flowers to her grave & try to see whether I have now accepted the Destruction & begun to find the Resurrection. I havn't brought your last letter out with me – I wonder whether there was anything specially for comment.

Later I had to come in for meal & now must post – I'm sure many things standing over – will write again, but do you please answer this.

And my love
M. U. B.

Hocken Library. MS-0741-002.

TO CHARLES BRASCH – NOVEMBER 20, 1938

47 Webb St. Christchurch. New Zealand

My dear Charles

I must really make a fresh beginning & try to write a consecutive letter this evening. I am met on return by such sad news about the Pages – you are almost sure to have heard already of his motorcar accident on the Hills – I knew that he'd gone home after being in Hospital for shock

[1] The line is from 'Summer Daybreak' (*Collected Poems*, p. 69), first published in *The Press*, Feb. 14, 1934.

– In case you have not heard, he went over a bank in a fog – But it wasn't merely shock – evidently there was another hydatid cyst after all, & it must have burst. [...] It means I'm afraid, judging from other cases, that he will never be out of the wood of this hydatid trouble. How hard it is to accept suffering for others, easier for oneself.

I find it hard to turn to other news, but there must be my Toss report. (This in answer to yours of Oct 22.) I [hope] you won't feel, in spite of your friend's judgement that the effort to help Toss has been wasted.[1] I have felt so strongly since I have seen more of him that it is right that he should have his chance – I don't know myself even now whether he will be able to objectify what's in him in a picture – But in some way what is in him *will* count. He grows slowly, but there is spiritual depth & reality.

[...]

I find that he interests me enormously! Of course he was merely a boy when I saw him frequently before. It seems that he can't work at painting *only* – he feels the need of an alternating rhythm – gardening & so on. He works steadily at the S. of Art – but its an effort to go on next day. Physique perhaps. Seems to need the pressure of an alternative occupation to provoke the painting. And yet he's *seeing* all the time – and constructing – He makes me feel that I want to stay alive to see what happens next! He is with the Quakers here – I don't think myself that he's being "pious" when he uses those religious expressions you spoke of – its just his natural idiom. I have taken it upon myself to tell him that I think he should stop writing verses! The last ones were to me more than ever incoherent & un-rhythmic – & I've said flatly that its a waste of time & his thoughts & emotions should be canalised in painting.

I had a really interesting stay in Wellington. Saw more people – went through my MS with the extremely sensitive critic – quite a wonderful experience for me. We are winnowing some out. He's writing a history of – is it literature or "culture" in N.Z. for the Centennial & George is doing furniture – There are some half dozen able young men at work at the Centennial Publications department[2] – Caustic remarks might be made about "culture in N.Z." – but I am finding the prospect of making a life in this backwater increasingly tolerable & even attractive. A

---

[1] Brasch had shown some of Woollaston's work to friends in London ('I respect their judgments') but reported that 'they did not care for his drawings, thought them quite amateurish & none positively interesting.'

[2] Then Secretary of Internal Affairs, Joseph Heenan, initiated a series of historical publications to mark the 1940 centennial of European settlement. At this time, McCormick had just replaced Oliver Duff as series editor.

spiritual colonisation but am not [sure] whether the phrase means what I think.

I will borrow The Trial. My critic has sent me "The Castle" to read – the form of the parable doesn't appeal to me very much – but it remains in one's memory. How very unsatisfactory translations are – especially those of Rilke – surely they could be better done – they drive one to the original.[1]

Yes, I think the Labour régime *will* make me poorer,[2] but if their schemes succeed one should not resent that. I am rather "cynical" about party government – This party will make experiments & get us into a pickle & then there will be a revulsion, & the other party will get us into another sort of pickle – But all is overshadowed by world affairs. There's no hope looking round, only faith – & I suppose that the outlook has been as hopeless more than once before. But N. Z. is spared the most stress – only imaginatively does one experience it. I was *in* the last war. Your letter is so sad, it saddens me. When prayer was bidden in church for Jewish sufferers, I thought very vividly of you, who suffer through sympathy. Toss came in for some supper just now & spoke with such deep affection of you – NZ may count little for you for the time being, but you count a great deal to N.Z. Toss will post this – its a very wet night – so I must not go on longer. There will be another mail. I know there was more I meant to say.

We send our love to you
Ursula Bethell

Hocken Library. MS-0996-3/19.

TO CHARLES BRASCH – DECEMBER 11, 1938

47 Webb St. Christchurch. N.Z.

Dear Charles

My letters to you have such a tendency to run to inordinate length that I am quite afraid of beginning one! However there are things to be said – In the first place, all good wishes for 1939 – I had intended this to be a Christmas greeting, but failed to catch the mail.

---

[1] Brasch had recommended Kafka's two works to her. He was also an advocate of Rilke, and some of his own translations from Rilke's *Letters to a Young Poet* had appeared in *Phoenix* (1. 2) in 1932.

[2] Given Bethell's earlier description of herself as a 'Rentier' (Sept. 14, 1936), the allusion here may be to the Labour Government's State housing scheme, which had begun about twelve months earlier.

This is Sunday. I got back from a fortnight in Dunedin on Friday evening. [...] Staying with the Whiteheads. Dull, cold, overcast, tempestuous weather all the time, but I saw the people I wanted to see. Including your sister – who came to a tea party, kindly arranged for me by Rodney K. at his room at Medical School. She was leaving for England the next morning! I was sorry to hear from R.K. that it is for health's sake she is travelling. I had hoped that Archdeacon Whitehead would do something about introducing me to your grandfather (of whom he spoke so warmly) but he was so end-of-term rushed that nothing came of it. However on Wednesday afternoon I was walking up to a park with R.K. when the rain cleared up & we fell in with Mr. Fels on his way to his office & were given permission to walk thru' his garden – How delightful he is! I was quite captivated. The garden was very green – I thought there was something truly European about it.

The country around Dunedin is beautiful I think – more colour than in mid-Canterbury – Thursday morning was wild & wet, but it cleared up for long enough to allow of our planned drive into the country in the Archdeacon's ever busy car – the stormy lights made it very fine.

[...]

I hope it isn't altogether too illegible – I am writing against Time. That reminds me, what interesting new philosophical books abounded at Selwyn College! There was one on Time – I must give you the name of another highly recommended by the Archdn wh. I am finding very absorbing. "The Ethics of Power, or the Problem of Evil" by Phillip Léon (Allen & Unwin, 10/6) – Its *assimilated* psychology – If you don't know it, do get hold of it. It seems to me to join up with Buber.

[...]

I have just remembered an important matter I want to consult you about. Do you know anyone at or near Thaxted? (Essex – very fine old church – Communist rector Conrad Noel.) The Fields stayed there for some time while they were in England. They took Home a stone carving "The River & the Sea" & could not afford to bring it out again.[1] They said it might be mine, if I could pay expenses & freight. I admired it very much when it was exhibited in ChCh about six years ago – & think it ought to come back to N.Z. where it was inspired & made. It was left at Thaxted, to be taken to Father Noel's house, but when Robert Field wrote about it, he found it had never gone there – Father N. is blind & old & R.F. doesn't like to bother him. *Miss Pattenden*, who has a dame-school at Thaxted, let a shed in her garden to R.F for a studio, & another

[1] Bethell made strenuous efforts to have this work returned to New Zealand. See the article by Vickie Hearnshaw in *Bulletin of New Zealand Art History* 18 (1997), 87-88.

to a weaver named Cayton who is probably there still, R.F. says. He thinks the carving is still in her garden, perhaps turned out as rubbish! (*She* might think it ugly!) This is deplorable – we valued it as £40 in the exhibition. He says there is a builder in the village, Mr. Ratcliff, who is reliable & wd. give assistance about removal. Some shipping agent wd. have to pack it. These are clues, in case you are able & willing to do something about it. The enclosed snapshot may give you an idea of the work – its symbolical of Life & Death. I hope that I shall like it still if it comes out! I wish you could see it & say whether you think it *is* worth the freight, which will run into £5 or more. I can't think of anyone to ask. My sister is far too busy & so easily tired. Well, I know you are very busy too! But you have more vitality. I hope that if your school[1] goes to Hindhead you *will* see her – its so near. She is witty & wise – & would like to know you – I feel pretty sure that you would take to her.

I must enquire of Denis now about your book – We have eliminated the worst of my unpublished pieces – & G. G. is to look them over during his vacation & perhaps eliminate more. I think he is probably severer than E McCormick, tho' he doesn't think himself such a good judge. He esteems the Garden highly, & that pleases me – it treats of things so near my heart. One evening at Wgn when I was very sad GG did not attempt wordy consolation, but took down The Garden from his shelf & read it aloud to me – until the Past seemed to be the Present, which it must be really & I was comforted.

There seems to be a lull about war-threats, but not in the European terror – I daresay it overshadows us too little here – but yet, do not let us fret & do not be ashamed of your safety – you are making it fruitful! If there is no guiding Power in charge nothing has any meaning, & if there is, we may look forward without terror to the End, may we not? Evening church bells warn me that I must begin upon another letter.

With all good wishes
Ursula Bethell

[...]

Another book I read in Dunedin was Maritain's new one "True Humanism".[2] Its all philosophy & theology at Selwyn – no belles lettres!

Hocken Library. MS-0996-3/19.

[1] Brasch had been involved in an experimental school for 'problem children, originally run from The Abbey at Little Missenden.

[2] This translation of Maritain's *Humanisme intégral* was published by G. Bles, 1938.

TO JOHN SUMMERS – JANUARY 29, [1939]

St. Faiths. Webb St. Christchurch.

My dear John,[1]

I wrote a hasty note today to go with the copy of "Time & Place" I promised – & should like to add a few lines tonight. There will be no chance at all of writing tomorrow, & very little on the succeeding days, if I go to Nelson. I shall have to think a little before sending off books – no use sending confusing variety, & I find I want to look into them to refresh my memory about them. I consulted a friend who thinks general philosophy rather a wide field & unrewarding – & suggests sending an account I have of Thomistic Philosophy, which presents a complete system, which one may or may not accept, but is a clear pattern. I think I shall send first the "Psychology of Study" which is interesting in itself.[2] *Don't* force yourself to study when you are very tired physically – it only means overstrain. Brain depends on body, fatigue affects both. Another thing taking exercise to keep brain clear. I am following a line of enquiry which might lead to making systematic study possible *before* deciding what your ultimate vocation is to be – in the meantime, if you can do a bit of reading & thinking, & save up money, all to the good. I am so glad that we got to know each other very well so quickly – otherwise I might have lent books which wd. look as if I were trying to influence you towards Anglicanism – but you know now that is not the case. This idea of going to Nelson is altering my plans somewhat, but I expect I had better take the chance. I will try to see Connie first.

I would not have let you be so late on Thursday if you had not been going away, & am sorry you were wakefully tired. I was looking through your M.S. book for an hour and more after you left – so as to get a better idea of it before other concerns intervened. I find an improvement in expression from the place where you say that henceforth you are going to express only yourself. Its more concentrated. I don't think one should look for or expect literary excellence – you are not equipped. I cannot say that I find it. But this way of expressing yourself I find good & to be encouraged. And on those pages where you speak to your Maker in the manner of Augustine there *is* a "gleam". I must thank you for allowing

---

[1] John Summers (1916-1993), born in England, became, from the 1950s, a poet and fiction writer and, together with his wife Connie, a well-known supporter of arts and letters in Canterbury. Summers' second-hand bookshop was a Christchurch landmark. He also published two volumes of memoirs, *Dreamscape 1* and *2*, in the first of which Bethell is mentioned.

[2] *Psychology of Study* by C. A. Mace (1937).

me to see such intimate records. That is very real experience – I do thank you, John, for allowing me to share it.

Feb 1. Wedy.

[...] I am quite happy about you, John – God *will* use you – & if I am allowed to help a little, that will make me very happy too. I think you have the right attitude now – just go on trustfully as you are. [...] Will you think this idea over – would you like to work for a *degree*, here in N.Z.? before you decide what vocation is yours. A degree is a help to other things. It would be a grind – but you certainly have the brains. My feeling is that you are meant to deal with human beings, to help them – I don't yet know how. But I do know that your affection has helped *me*. That is very nice what you say about my Darling who left me so suddenly – it describes her.[1] I daresay I could tell you more, some day. You belong to the same climate, I think. I hope to write again before long in less of a scramble. [...]

Try learning a short psalm by heart – the rhythm is very beautiful. When I was very ill 35 years ago – (the Dr. thought I was dying, so what I felt wasn't mistaken) I couldn't think of anything but the "Out of the Deep" one – it said itself over & over in my mind.[2] You probably know the 23rd. There are some short ones after the 119th.

[...]

Dear John Summers, you know that I have you in my heart, & in my prayer. *Perseverance* is the thing, for us all.

Your affectionate friend
M U Bethell

Private collection.

TO JOHN SUMMERS – FEBRUARY 18, 1939

As from 47 Webb St. N1. Christchurch
At my brother's station near Culverden

My dear John,

Your letter of Monday was awaiting me here on arrival yesterday. I said goodbye to Archdeacon Whitehead at Culverden on Monday & went a bit northwards again to stay with some other relations before visiting my brother – I meant to write to you from there, to add some things there wasn't time for 'viva voce', but had no opportunity, & now you have forestalled me. I wish that there had been a little more time to

---

[1] Summers made numerous comments about Effie Pollen; it is not possible to determine what is referred to here. The earliest extant letter from him postdates this.

[2] Psalm 130; Psalm 23 is 'The Lord is my shepherd'.

spare, but what there was we made good use of I think – we were lucky to find you so quickly. I thought the meeting went off very well, & did not find you inadequate, but I shall pass on your nice thanks to the Archdeacon. [...] I must explain that I purposely refrained from telling you who was driving me, because I thought it better for the meeting to be spontaneous & unprepared, & I had not told him so very much about you.[1] I thought that your natural self would make its own impression on him, & left him to propound his scheme, or not, as he felt inclined. [...] My chief object in making you known to the Archdeacon was to get help & advice about your further education – that's why I laid stress on "brains" – to assure him that for my part I believed your abilities to be well worth further training. He is one in whose judgement I have great confidence, & if he recommends working for a degree as the best next step, I think you would do well to take his advice as a 'pointer'. Of course dear John its not only or mainly for the intellectual possibilities that I hold you in regard & affection, as well you know (and the Archdn. understands that this is so) but for the purposes of that 'contact' my shirt was on the brains!

And of course its always God's John Summers I shall work & hope for, & all in prayer for you & under His will. It is so good & so secure that you see this must be so, & have said it first. I don't want to be fanciful, but remembering the prayers, I can't but think that Monday's meeting, which came about so unexpectedly & so easily, may be an essential part of the pattern of your life – & of mine. Your intelligence is the weapon which must be tempered & sharpened for use in the working out of God's will for & in you – the talent which ought not to be buried.[2] I am glad that you had not 'turned down' the idea of working for a degree; no doubt there will be a great deal of laborious drudgery involved, & much in College life you wouldn't like, but it is a definite object, and a useful key to locks, & at the end of a year or two you would know better where you stand, whether you passed the examinations or not. You have done a good deal of exploratory reading, presently it should be canalised, & more intensive study undertaken. I don't think the drudgery will dull your mind – it won't if its done in the spirit of love & prayer. I do love your sense of humour, it would never do for *that* to be damped!

Back in ChCh. Thurs 23rd.

I had to leave off there & had no more chance of continuing. We had a terrible gale on Saty night – many of the trees in my brother's

---

[1] Summers wrote: 'I was a little abashed when I found your friend was the Archdeacon.'

[2] See Matthew 25: 14-30.

plantations were uprooted. I set to work to help clear up the débris in the large garden they have. Now I have a sheaf of letters to deal with, but you must be attended to first, & if I manage to post this tonight I think you should get it before Sunday. I quite understand that you havn't much time or energy for letterwriting in the summer season – don't let that worry you – I shall wait. But I am very pleased with what you have written already.

[...]

Yes, I *did* feel "happy & fresh" on that journey (I am touched, my dear, by your noticing it!) it was very stimulating & new. Its always a hard time for me when I get back to ChCh – I feel the *not-thereness* of my darling (& every corner of the roads 50 miles round reminds me of our picnics) and I have always disliked the town, & found the climate very depressing, & never meant to live here – So I fight my way along just now, under the clouds. So I beg you, 'of your charity', to remember me in your prayer – we are allowed to help one another like that, aren't we? Sometimes it is easier to pray for another, than for oneself. Perhaps I should look on this sadness as a part of "Lenten discipline" – for I know how needful chastening has been.

[...]

I have been down to get some supper, & returning, reflect that you are probably quite familiar with all the foregoing![1] However I thought I would rehearse it. I think my church makes rather a poor showing out here – shorn of much of her richness.

As soon as I have time I must look into your M.S. book again. There are some faults of grammar I must bring to your notice. I was interested in your plea for your christened name! What is it that people try to turn you into? Toss called you "Johnny" to distinguish you from the other John,[2] & I thought it suited some of the aspects! When I think of you gravely its "John" – but "darling Johnny" sometimes when I think of you with affection & amusement.

[...]

That is a very famous passage you have hit on in S. Augustine.[3] It has consoled many a mother.

---

[1] The 'foregoing' was a long account of the liturgical year, given that Summers might become 'conversant with [the] Christian Seasons.'

[2] Perhaps referring to their mutual friend, John Moffett.

[3] Summers had quoted: 'But she would not be persuaded but pressed him the more with entreaties & tears to see & reason with me, till at last he took umbrage & cried, Go, & God be with you; it cannot be that the son of these tears should be lost.' The passage occurs at the end of Bk. III of Augustine's *Confessions*.

When I began Boys Clubs I used to be sadly disappointed if a boy did not turn out as I expected he would! Most promising-seeming ones would suddenly disappear from the scene! and I found it most upsetting! But that was long ago. It was part of the 'possessiveness', which you have recognized as an evil & a danger. I think too my present sense of loss must have some of that possessiveness about it. It is so hard to do without the tenderness that belonged to everyday life. But what is required of us is to go on *giving* love – & that can only be done by the grace of God. After all, if one has asked for love, one has asked for pain – Just as to him who asks to be a saint is said: "Can you drink of the cup?"[1]

About "Time & Place" – I am glad you like 'Envoy' – I think it is good. It seemed almost inevitable. My chief N. Z. critic agrees with you in thinking that my rhymed & regular metred pieces are the least good ones, all the same "Autumn Afternoon" was commended by my chief critic in England, for reasons which perhaps would not weigh with you. (There is more in the rhythm perhaps than appears at first reading?) I will type you a copy of "Waves", which you ask for. [...]

Dear me, what a long letter this has grown to, & even now I havn't got on to books – Next time! I must post. [...]

Goodnight dear John – Thank you for the kiss! Thank you for your letter. You are very dear to me.

M.U.Bethell

Private collection.

TO RODNEY KENNEDY – MARCH 2, 1939

47 Webb St. Christchurch.

My dear Rodney

I have had a very severe letter from Toss,[2] (which touches me deeply, because it must have cost him so much to write) & feel that you ought to have a few words from me before Sunday, though I hardly know what to say. I was "stupidly cruel" you have said, about our conversation that Sunday morning. (I do appreciate the 'tu quoque'!)[3] It seems hardly necessary for me to say that I am sorry because I believe that you forgave me at once for any stupidity in my attempt to handle those matters & for

---

[1] See Matthew 20: 22.

[2] The 'severe letter' has not survived. It would seem, though, that Bethell made some unwelcome comments about the relationship between Kennedy and the Woollastons, complicated as it was by the sexual relationship that had once existed between him and Toss, and further by his declared attraction to Edith.

[3] Lat. 'You also.'

any unwitting cruelty. I did not *want* to talk about those things & my feeling for you at the time was entirely kind – you know that. If I said anything wh. seemed to you to be unforgivable, and you are angry – well, then, the best way is not to write to me anymore, because evidently you are better without my friendship. I have often been hurt, but have found that one can make use of even that. Please make use of anything that was true in what I said, and forget the rest. I have explained to Toss that I approached our conversation seriously & in fear, & with prayer – & for the last reason I venture to trust that in the long run no harm may come of it. I cannot at the moment remember anything I ought to withdraw, except perhaps some impertinent criticism of your friends. I rejoice to think that you have had a clarifying conversation with Edith & Toss – I probably did wrong to intervene about a relationship where I do not belong – but did so with good intentions, & in the hope of helping you not to make mistakes. I have made many mistakes, & this appears to be another. I need forgiveness for them all.

I must now hurry to the post – & wish you happiness & healing. Of course I knew you would be hurt, but risked it. God bless you.

Still your friend if you wish it[1]
M.U. Bethell

Hocken Library. MS-0741-001.

TO JOHN SUMMERS – [MARCH 12], 1939

3rd Sunday in Lent 47 Webb St. Christchurch.

My dear John,

Your letter was just what I needed to cheer me up yesterday – I wasn't expecting one from you yet awhile, knowing how hard at work you are. I rather think it crossed with the second half of mine to you, relating to book parcel. I want to answer you at once – (though really I should be writing to England today!) because I think from something you say about Selwyn Coll. that you are taking it to be a place for Anglicans. Its not that – the majority of the residents are in fact I believe materialistic, unbelieving medical students! But it is run by the Anglican Church – & the Archdeacon generally has three or four theological students in hand. I suppose they wd. be working for their B. A. as a preliminary. There are services for *them* to attend which are not obligatory for the others.

---

[1] Kennedy replied on March 5 – a Sunday, which he described as 'a good day to make the peace and to remember that we all have wasted a lot of content in anger. A devastating emotion. Pax.'

[...]

To return to your letter. I think you can't do better than carry on at the farm steadily, & go on banking your money, till next summer. But may I say something about one sentence in your letter? this: "I am not sure of myself, nor even that God means to help one [who] is so undeserving of help" – darling Johnny, doesn't the whole of the Christian religion say that *everyone* is undeserving? "I came not [to call] the righteous but sinners to repentance"[1] – we are all bankrupt & dependent on God's mercy. Isn't it true that if we flatter ourselves that we *are* deserving, then we are making ourselves independent of God's help. (If that were possible!) It is because you are insecure that you are safe, if you offer yourself to God's will. WHAT He will do with you we don't know. That will be shown – I can't help thinking that you are meant to minister to people spiritually, but I don't know how. And you have intellectual gifts, which as I said, look like talents to be traded with. But it wd. be fatal if you felt that you were "deserving"!

(I write as if I were a very enlightened person. I'm not – but I think I see that much.)

[...]

I do like your letters Johnny – (no, I don't think you are five years old! far from it – but that's how I think of you). They make me *laugh* – which must be awfully good for me – we used to laugh all the time at Rise Cottage, but I never do here.

[...]

And now I must tell you how very much touched I am by your writing about my Darling as you do[2] – I think most people are too afraid of saying anything, & so do not mention her. Few knew her here – the few who did always have said that she was unique. She really *was* quite unlike anyone else – so young in her ways, so funny, and so wise. Sometimes you have reminded me of her just a little, the way you are "out with things" – I think it was quite a rare relationship & there wasn't a scrap of 'possessiveness' on either side – maternal on my part no doubt, but not just that. It was such a wonderful companionship – it filled up life for me – & I do think it made up for what I might have had in marriage. As a matter of biography she did come to me just when I lost my sweetheart, & her tender sympathy was amazing. She was a shy, frightened little thing at first – not really frightened, for she was as

---

[1] See Matthew 9: 13.

[2] 'You & your darling have been in the back of my mind because I have often thought of your wonderful friendship. It reminds me of E. A. Poe's Annabelle Lee.' Summers compares Poe's poem with 'Envoy': 'they both carry the *beauty* which was the essence of the friendship.'

courageous as anyone I have ever met, but retired within herself. After her father died, my home gave her just the shelter she needed I think. And there she was merry & at ease – when we were not overshadowed by my selfishness & ill temper. That's what I cannot forget, though I know she always forgave me. The very thought of her makes me cry now. I do my marketing at the same shops in Papanui Road where we used to pull up the car & buy food going to, or coming from our happy picnics. I little thought then that one day I should be walking there with my basket, sadly & alone. That's why coming back to ChCh "gets me down" not only the oppressive climate, but the reminders. You may well ask whether I don't *know* that she is sometimes with me – I never have been given that consciousness, which other people so strongly have. I believe that she must be, but that is not quite the same thing; it is a faith, not a joy – yet. Matthew [illegible] says that "faith is a desolate thing"[1] – It seems as if the earthly time together had been so vivid that the mortal can't be effaced – I see her, I hear her, but as she *was*, alive on this earth. About the house, about the garden, about the town. And now she is gone. She was pottering about in the kitchen seeing to my supper (and I *was* tired) in her rose-pink dressing-gown, with much *too* bright eyes, in terrible pain – the very evening before she died. And then I saw her dead – I cannot forget it – Do not think that I brood upon this, or mope, but it is, as you say "at the back of my mind" – I know with my intelligence that love cannot die, but I have not *experienced* the Resurrection. I don't know whether this sense of loss has been allotted to me as discipline, a purgatory, or whether it is that I have not been diligent about religion. I should have been more diligent *when she was there*. I have failed very badly, John. In some sense the past must become the present, and the future. Perhaps when I die myself (& that won't be so very long now) I shall *know* suddenly – or perhaps, with the disciples, I shall at last know, here on this earth, the Resurrection. Those disciples witnessed *destruction* – but afterwards rejoiced in the knowledge of the resurrection & other christians have had the same experience – I have never ventured to ask God to make an end of this darkness – should I perhaps ask more? I don't know. The comfort that has come to me has been through the affection of other people – and once or twice a sudden relaxing of the tension & a faint sense of joy – not related to the concrete situation – but a sense, like faint music, that everything is well, & nothing is lost. It seems as if I'm not to know her, individually, alive still – But first the knowledge of life & immortality, which came by Christ. Perhaps I have

---

[1] Bethell quotes the same expression to Brasch (July 31, 1941). The surname is difficult to read – it appears to be Weyer – but I have been unable to identify the source.

not opened my mind enough yet, perhaps I do allow grief to prevail – but there it is. I am waiting. One of my friends, who has had what I feel to be trustworthy "mystical" experiences, lost a great friend, & said she felt her so much *more* real, after her death.[1] She wrote to me "Do not expect to feel 'presence' – only their *influence* & reality & vitality". *She* knew my Darling, & always called her "The robin". I have been very much struck, darling Johnny, by the way you have accepted her with me, as it were. You are the first person, who did not know her on earth, to speak of her as if she were a real person to you – It is a great help. Should I say perhaps that she has a part in this? Anyhow it is something new God has given me. (Toss, last year, had his own way of sharing & helping, too.) Perhaps you are not the only one to have felt that (her reality, I mean) but you have told me about it. Another of my "new" friends did say this much "You know you never come alone".

I have written all that because it will be useful for you some day to remember peoples experiences in sorrow. You have an intuition which will stand you in good stead if you have to deal with "souls" in your vocation.

I cannot say that I think E. A. Poe's lines very good poetry, but they are very touching & simple, & carry conviction. I should like to *give*, not lend, you an anthology of poetry to have by you. What is the date of your birthday? There are so many books I could lend. I am always thinking of another. Julian of Norwich is one of the mystics you certainly should know – Have you seen her "The Revelations of Divine Love"? Yes, I think send Traherne to Toss. You will wrap it up well, won't you? It is a nice book.

What you say about the early morning reminds me of those dawns at Cashmere – I used to get up & lean out of my porch window – it was unearthly. I like your description. I *must* get that book printed! there are some pieces about daybreak you would like. No use getting up early here; no view, no air, no scents, no mystery. The nights were altogether wonderful up there – such stars, such silence.

You say that you always wake up happy, but often go to bed miserable, & that too much of your thinking has been "negative & self-pitying". Let us analyse that – *what* do you pity yourself for just now? Is it that you are lonely? or don't like your work? or that not-sore, sore throat? Or just the don't quite know why of youth & immaturity? Accidie. Now, its just the opposite with me, by evening my conscious mind is in control, & I have many things to think of, & glad to have finished another day, & go to bed – But *I* wake up miserable! I can't always say

---

[1] Another reference to Blanche Baughan; see also the letter of Oct. 26, 1937.

why – because I am lonely – because I don't like Christchurch – because my eyesight is failing – because there doesn't really seem much object in my going on – & so forth. Its *facing the day*. Only yesterday morning I caught myself dwelling on such thoughts as I dressed & suddenly thought "*Coward*"! Its so absurd when I reason it out – here we are for such a little while & how sorry I should be afterwards if I tried to scamp the lessons. "The sacrament of the present moment"[1] is given by God. (I am lecturing myself, not you.)

Yes, I agree that "Miss Bethell" is a little absurd![2] The question has arisen at times, when the club boys grew up, & became friends. I have often wished there were some name the younger friends could use. Christian name doesn't seem quite suitable either – & I am not very fond of being called "Aunt". [...]

I am trying to cut out merely *pleasurable* letters, until Easter at any rate, because I have so much else that ought to be done. But to you I will write when there seems to be something to write about, because you are rather isolated, & I venture to think that my letters may help to bring a little mental nourishment! But you are not to think that *you* must write to *me* – I shall not expect it. You will often be tired, & you must get on with your reading, & you must attend to the other twelve![3] I am sure we are often together in spirit. So now, with as much affection as space allows! I say goodbye – & am your friend

M U Bethell.

Private collection.

TO JOHN SUMMERS – APRIL 18, 1939

47 Webb St. Christchurch

My dear John,

[...]

Now for the discussion in today's letter on different kinds of art[4] – *That* you should discuss with Toss, I think. Is there really any room for the second best? no, everything as good as it can be of its kind. The trouble in this country is that people are so contented with second best.

---

[1] The phrase is particularly associated with the 18th century French Jesuit Jean-Pierre de Caussade, author of the spiritual treatise, *L'Abandon à la Providence Divine*.

[2] Summers felt that continuing to address her as Miss Bethell prevented any intimacy in their relationship, and asked what other name he might use.

[3] i. e., other correspondents.

[4] Summers had written comparing Toss's art with the very different work of his own father, and proposing 'that there must be more than one standard of aesthetics.'

I must send you, as soon as you return any of the volumes you have done with – "Art & Scholasticism" by Maritain, which Toss & Rodney both like so much. I wonder sometimes whether in your conversations with yourself – thinking things out – you are too eager to come to a *conclusion*? I used to have to leave so many things in suspension – I still do – but perhaps it *is* better to think it out to a provisional conclusion. The great thing is that you *should* be thinking, and about such vital matters.

[...]

Well now, darling Johnny. I told you that I agreed that "Miss" was stiff (Toss tells me that some Quakers think that any use of titles is positively wrong! but I couldn't go as far as *that*.) & if you feel that Felicity describes me, well & good – (I've been called many things in my day).[1] It means "happiness" doesn't it!

[...]

I don't agree with Arthur about the Mystics – the best, the true Mystics.[2] He and I would differ about many things you know! I can't get on with his Barth at all. But of the depth & reality of his religion I do not doubt, & there are many things on which we *do* agree. He *has* limitations. Not one word in his letters of the *beauty* & fascination of England, of the charm of London! He is a student, & always will be, & lives in books. He hasn't the poetic streak that you have, John – I don't say that you write good poetry! but you have a poetic response to the world.

Then more warnings about there being a bad side to you – but, of *course*! We *all* have very bad possibilities, & we are all egotists more or less. And the lively ones are in some dangers that the more stodgy are not. What you must think is "God's sure hold of you" – (there are some oft quoted lines about that – I *think* Newman's.) Try to think of the perils of your nature rather as talents, if God uses them. Didn't our Lord choose hot tempered disciples? You know very well that what you need is discipline, and stability – so now is your chance to learn to be a "*sticker*". Discipline is unpleasant. Humiliation is unpleasant. Don't miss by impatience the chances your present occupation is bringing to you. Your position is isolated, but it is not for ever. At the end of the year you will be so glad if you have submitted to the discipline, & feel the stronger for it. I know it isn't easy, away from your family, away from your friends & leading a somewhat monastic existence – not easy to one of your type. But you wouldn't *really* rather be let off the difficult endowments, would you? They are forces. They can be used. I remember one of those

---

[1] From this time on, his letters were addressed to 'Dear Felicity.'

[2] Summers had reported Arthur Prior as believing mysticism to be 'egocentric & individualistic & a thing to be sacrificed.' Prior had left New Zealand in 1937, and was working at odd jobs in London.

Londoners saying how glad he was, for all the difficulty, that he'd been entrusted with a spirited team of horses. He hadn't always been glad, but he got to be glad, having persevered. So *dedicate* the passion, it will be used.

It *is* horrifying to look down into the depths of one's badness, it is most horrifying: but we must look up & say "with Thee is plenteous redemption".[1] Prayer is the thing. There comes help suddenly – one can't tell from where. You must often have had that experience.

[...] I don't think your calling is to painting or writing, I think its to living & helpful contact with human beings, to "help souls" – but for that you need discipline & preparation, to purify & fortify the love. Of course I may be wrong, but that is my impression. And believe me dear John I *don't* see you in a glamour – you have been candid about your faults. Let us be thankful that you are not blind to them. The upward path will be painful – But when I was your age & prayed to be made better I did not ask to be spared pain. Nor I think do you.

Then you ask me whether when I write poetry I "like" it. When I used to write – it was a sort of compulsion – when the piece was done there certainly was satisfaction in recognising that it was well done according to my ability. But I never feel that it is quite mine – I don't know how the words come. I suppose vanity does come in, when people praise them, but that is not your question. Occasionally I read over my own things, & think, Yes that *was* how I felt, that *is* an exact description, that is a good piece of work etc, but when I read great poetry, I feel very humble about my own. I have been able to finish (for the next book) a poem of 1934 that was left unfinished, & enclose it for you to read.[2] There is a good deal of work in it. I really must send you an anthology of poetry – you ought to have one beside you.

And now my dear I must get to bed, I am tired – And I wish this had been a better letter – you are in my heart & in my prayer.

M.U.B.

Private collection.

TO JOHN SUMMERS – APRIL 26, 1939

47 Webb St. Christchurch

My dear John,

---

[1] See Psalm 130: 7.

[2] The poem is not extant, and not identified in any subsequent letters.

The books came this morning. Thank you. I will now send another packet of small ones for you to look through, to vary the fare. (Sometimes I think it should be varied with something really frivolous such as a detective story!)

1. "Pan, Caesar & God" – This book you may keep for good if it interests you. I have others which cover much the same ground.[1]

2. The Anthology of Verse is until I buy you one for your own. I have put a marker in page 191 – "The New Ghost" is a modern poem I like very much.[2]

The other four arose from thinking of St Felicitas (the Latin form) & looking round my shelves. Three of them are Roman Catholic, but nothing in them you would dislike I think. Perpetua & Felicity is to look at & return.[3] Going round continental picture galleries one becomes familiar with the saints in art & their emblems (Lucy & her eyes – Catherine & her wheel – Lawrence & his gridiron & so on) but so much is legendary. The martyrdom of P. & F. is historical – Something in that brought to my mind the little book "Early Christians in Rome" which is a rather out of the way little book.[4] To be looked through & returned fairly soon with the martyr book – You may have read Father Martindale's "What are Saints" – but if not you will find it *very* readable & informative.[5] You will find an account of the Curé d'Ars – He is a past master at boiling things down. If you like this you may keep it – I can get another copy. And lastly a small book, also by Father Martindale, which I thought of partly because I like his way of putting things & partly because of something you said in your last letter.[6] You may easily imagine how I used to search for useful books in the London Boys' Club days – they were very ignorant of biology. Later on as they grew up & gave me more of their confidence I was appalled by the type of book they'd had recourse to themselves. The *nice* girls were ignorant as well as innocent & the young men wd. come to me for books for *them*. It was quite difficult to find the right book – *science* one could get – but science set in a religious, spiritual (*not* sentimental) light was more difficult. This

---

[1] By Renée Haynes (1937), part of a series entitled 'I Believe.'

[2] 'The New Ghost' is by the Georgian poet, Fredegond Shove, first published in *Dreams and Journeys* (1919). Although it appeared in several anthologies, I have not found it on p.191 in any of them.

[3] Perhaps the recently-published translation of the Passion of Ss. Perpetua and Felicity by W. H. Shewring (1931).

[4] By H. D. M. Spence-Jones (1911).

[5] C. C. Martindale's book, subtitled 'Fifteen chapters on sanctity,' was originally a series of broadcast talks.

[6] Fr. Martindale wrote a very large number of books, but the likeliest title to be meant here is *The Difficult Commandment: notes on self-control especially for young men*.

book of Father Martindale's pleased me by the way it is put, & I should like to know what you think of it. I am not expecting you to learn anything from it, it would be meant for rather a younger age. Of course a good deal of it assumes the institution of confession.

Your remark was that you are 'primitive lustful' – but my dear John – aren't *all* fully equipped human beings like that, among other things? We are indeed a mixture. That is the theme of the drama. Von Hügel I remember speaks of the *tension* there must be in the art of living.[1] And if you think you've been given unfairly strong instincts – is it not (*if* you have) just through this experience that you will be the more able to help people? There is a vocation for every temperament – certainly the very childlike & innocent do help to keep the world sweet by just being what they are – but the world needs also the sort who have overcome, & can sympathise. If you could look on it as an enrichment, not as a degradation!

It is something like what you were saying about better to have 'loved & lost' – having known love, one would rather have had it than not, & pay the price of sorrow. One wouldn't say "spare me love".

You are not being spared the tug of war, & I daresay that the more earnestly you desire to prepare for life the more conscious you will [be] of your defects – that is quite in order. Now you must accept the discipline of patience & submission & self-control – you can't win freedom in any other way. Take one day at a time, & let your prayer be for one day at a time – sometimes I've had to take one *hour* at a time.

I was dissatisfied with the letter I wrote you – my head was not too good. I am now much better. (There is a real epidemic of Flu.) You mustn't think that I was not interested in what you wrote about art – far from it, but I always find aesthetics very difficult – I know more about literature than art – the art of painting, I mean. All the arts are of enormous importance – Beauty – religion has been too much separated from these. [...]

I think I must have a quarrel with one of your words in that letter! – why "egocentric" – why not just self-centred which is plain English. And do you know the exact meaning of the word Sophist?

Also I want to say that I did appreciate what you wrote about my Darling – & have kept your words in mind. Very slowly I'm getting on – she's not separated from the truth of *everything*. I must learn to know more of God & the meaning of 'Thy Will be done'. To use your own words "a gradual *bending* of the will until it is in harmony with that of

---

[1] See, for example, Von Hügel's letter of Jan. 20, 1922 in his *Letters to a Niece*.

God, till its very joy is in being one with God." Then He will give perhaps that 'awareness of her' which I long for, but dare not ask.

Now I must go to the post. I have been awake since 4 this morning – I like waking early, it gives one time to think. There were such lovely colours at dawn (new rust colouring)[1] & I tried *not* to feel sad & pent up that one sees so little of the sky here! But those dawns at Cashmere were so marvellous – in fact all night long it was lovely – the moon over the sea – the stars over the mountains – the lights on the plain – the keen, light air.

[...]

Goodbye darling Johnny. How much I look forward to seeing you, when your dairy farm discipline is accomplished, & you go south with a satisfactory P O Savings Bank Book!

M.U.B.

Private collection.

TO JOHN SUMMERS – [APRIL 30, 1939]

Sunday – 3rd after Easter 47 Webb St. Christchurch

My dear young, very young John

[...]

Did you read the Epistle & Gospel today, I wonder. I always think that is such a wonderful passage from the Gospel – "your sorrow shall be turned into joy"[2] – And the Epistle filled in what you wrote about the young man's problem.[3] The fleshy lusts do war against the soul if they are allowed to. There are laws for the Christian & 'free love' for the Christian is freedom to love under obedience – "whose service is perfect freedom"[4] – when [he] wants to be "free" what is it he wants to be free from – laws he doesn't believe to be just? Or *does* he know them to be the truth for human nature & therefore denies his conscience when he argues for 'free love' – If he thinks the rules are irksome & unfair & impossible, imposed by a society he doesn't agree with, or a religion he only half believes, there might be something useful for him in Fr. Martindale's little book. Because chastity *is* worthwhile, even for the

[1] The first word is difficult to distinguish; it may read 'near rust.'

[2] See John 16: 20.

[3] This refers to a young co-worker about whom Summers had written on several occasions. For the Epistle, see 1 Peter 2: 11.

[4] This phrase comes from the Collect for Morning Prayer (2nd Collect for Peace) in *The Book of Common Prayer*.

person who isn't the "slave of Christ",[1] and isn't in love with purity. The price to be paid varies, from mere irksomeness for some, to sheer anguish – "heroic virtue" – for others. How does he figure out his solution I wonder. A series of furtive indulgences with any woman he discovers to be willing – nothing very beautiful or free about *that* – he couldn't feel happy about *that* – if he is at all conscious of himself as a human being – he couldn't call that "love" – free or unfree. [...]

One is thankful that the dreadful "conspiracy of silence" which reigned in *my* young days has come to an end. Perhaps there is too little reticence nowadays, but better that than the bewildering & shameful silence under which we grew up. I imagine that no young person of either sex today is ignorant of the physical facts, as we were, however vague they may be about rules & ideals. The parents I know nowadays rightly never leave children's questions unanswered. And I am glad to find on the whole an awareness of the beauty of passion, *and* of the fact that passion's satisfaction doesn't satisfy as an *end* – But unpossessive love *does* satisfy. That *is* "freedom" & peace.

[...]

So *you* have Art & Scholasticism! I had quite forgotten. I want you to get your teeth into that soon (don't skip it out) & let me have it back – I want to read it again myself. And will you try that book of Evelyn Underhill's on worship.[2] It *may* be a little too "Catholic" for you – but how glad I was this morning to have that material & symbolical altar at which to offer my tears & my prayers – my tears for myself – my prayers for so many – for darling Johnny & so many others.

I have other small books to send when you've got on with these – pending the Big Book era. No hurry whatever about sending back "The Good Life".[3] I am so glad you like it. It was said to be a very remarkable work to come from an old man – his mind was vigorous to the last. In his earlier years he was thought to be daring & dangerous, but thought moved on, & latterly he was considered to be conservative! I heard him when I was a school girl give one of his Bampton Lectures on the Incarnation,[4] in the great University church of St. Mary's, Oxford. I shall never forget the hush, the rapt attention, & the impression of those

---

[1] Bethell may be thinking of Romans 1: 1. The Gk 'doulos' is usually translated as servant, but it may also be read as slave.

[2] Underhill wrote extensively on mysticism and prayer; this is a small pamphlet (1929) on the nature of worship.

[3] Charles Gore, *The Philosophy of the Good Life*, being the 1929-30 Gifford Lectures delivered at St Andrew's.

[4] Gore's 1891 Bampton Lectures were published as *The Incarnation of the Son of God* (1892). The lectures had sparked some controversy because of Gore's exposition of the doctrine of kenosis, which his critics felt underplayed the divinity of Christ.

words when he paused & said: – "Blessed are the pure in heart, then, for they shall *see God*."[1]

[...]

I am so pleased, & indeed relieved, to read what you say about being in the country – that you are still responsive, & that the beauty is still there for you – I was afraid you were lonely. How I long for the country myself, sometimes with an aching longing. And I am glad about getting on with the young people.

[...]

Ah yes, yes, *yes*, one does long to share – you have to look forward & be patient – but I have to do without. Having known what it is, – but I would rather have known than not.

Now about the "piece" you enclose.[2] I think you must put a little more grammar & coherence into it before I hand it to the Deaconess. I like it, but I am sure you could make it more comprehensible – I want to type it out & put some comments & send it to you, but havn't time today – so that will follow. I was reading a poem of T. S. Eliot's to my blind friend last week & neither of us could make out the meaning so you are obscure in good company, but I think for different reasons – I think he had said, or expressed, what he intended to – but I don't think you have achieved that.

[...]

Much love from your Felicity.

My critic-in-chief puts Autumn on the Plain[3] into my top class – so it will go into the book – I'll [send] something of Eckhart[4] later. Please note "intrigues" which is a *French* word means "*puzzles*," *not* "attracts my interest" as the newspapers think it does.

Private collection.

To Charles Brasch – July 31, 1939

As from 47 Webb St. Christchurch. New Zealand

My dear Charles

I must account for my silence by beginning with my recent history & present situation. The latter – a convalescent hospital (quite well now)

[1] See Matthew 5: 8.

[2] It has not been possible to identify the enclosure.

[3] See *Collected Poems*, p. 52. Originally published in *The Press*, June 17, 1939.

[4] The Dominican Meister Eckhart was an influential figure in late medieval spirituality, but the vivid imagery he employed led to misunderstandings and later to condemnation of some of his work.

– very warm & comfortable in the severest weather known, I think they say, for 30 years. (30 is a favourite number.) I came to Wellington early in June to stay with George Gabites, meaning while there to look about for quiet winter quarters – but before a week was out succumbed to the prevailing form of influenza – a worse type than I'd already had a dose of in ChCh. When I tried to get out & about again I found that I wasn't responding to my usual tonic, but struggled on for some weeks, kindly sheltered by G.G. in his very nice little flat, & having taken on the housekeeping I was just making up my mind to go to a doctor when I had such a "nasty turn" that I had to send for one instead, & after a hypodermic was packed off in an ambulance to rest my heart in this Institution. Its at Seatoun in good fresh air & finding that what has up till now been one of the heavy new taxation grievances – "Social Security" – deducts no less than two guineas a week from by bill![1] I am staying on for a bit to complete the rest-cure, which will be all to the good I think. But as I said I am really quite well.

It worried me that I couldn't achieve an answer to your letter about the knight errantry of the Thaxted search – but it happens that two of my oldest & nearest friends in England have died this year[2] & I had a good many letters to write after that & had to postpone the rest. I really was feeling pretty ill – the question is, however, did I or did I not write a note or a lettercard to congratulate you on the appearance of your poems? I think & hope that I did. We all agreed that it is much the best piece of work Denis Glover has yet produced – More of that presently.

It was exceedingly good – but not, in the light of what I know about you already, surprising – of you to take all that trouble about *my* River & the Sea. I am glad that the church & country side were rewarding – I'd planned to see Thaxted in 1926 (my last sight of England) but could not manage it. [...] It vexes me that the carving should not be in N.Z. Thank you very much indeed for all you did, and for writing so fully about it. In the same letter are passages about English country which made me feel uncommonly homesick – Most people write that "England is quite spoilt" & "I wouldn't know it" – It amazes me to reflect how I've settled down in this kind of desert, remembering with what *horror* I contemplated, twenty years ago, the thought of living in N.Z! I think you shouldn't come out if you feel that it would be stifling & sterile – it

---

[1] The then Prime Minister, Michael Joseph Savage, had introduced his Social Security bill in April, and the legislation was officially passed in August. It provided, among other things, for a universal free health system.

[2] Ruth Head died in 1939; the other friend is identified in a letter to John Summers (Feb. 16, 1940) as the man Bethell had intended to marry. (See Introduction for a suggested identification.) Frank Sidgwick also died in 1939, but not until the following month.

might easily prove to be depressing if you had no aim in living here, and no duty calling you. I *had* to come – & though I could have extricated myself with an effort after my mother's death I don't think I could now – at any rate I don't seem able to make the effort, or take the (financial) risk. So I turn it the other way round & see what can be made of the actual situation – & that turns out to be enough. I confess, that since the deaths I spoke of, which recalled past times & places so vividly, I've had a revived wish to see it all again. England *was* my country without any doubt. But as an inhabitant of N.Z. one naturally wishes that it wd. attract kindred spirits – I mean people who are alive to art & literature & the spiritual values. They *are* springing up however – witness Toss & my latest friend the theologically minded cowboy, who has lately been staying at Mapua – a happy visit for all of them. Toss I expect has written. He has been painting vigorously & in a new manner & sent over a head of Edith & a landscape – George thought the former an advance, but could not esteem the latter. However Toss said that he expected criticism, because he hasn't worked out the new approach yet. The feeling seems to be growing that he won't get very far without, at any rate a short time in Europe – but he's against that – would rather battle on in N.Z. and the European proposition certainly seems to present insuperable difficulties. They are so happy working out their life there – perhaps its better than painting very well! He has been *most* grateful for the money – I have sent £15 to date & promised the other £5 for next month – I think it was wiser to produce it in instalments. I hope that you *will* agree to letting me off the vow of silence about its provenance. So far they havn't the least idea – but I really think they would like to know who's been helping them this year – I won't ask to be allowed to dig up the past – it might prove to be rather overwhelming – tho' I'm afraid its given them rather a false impression of *numbers* of possible patrons in this country & I *had* to leave that notion of numbers undisturbed.

[...]

Akaroa has been entirely cut off. I think I am glad I didn't go there – it would not be the summery Akaroa I know and without bedroom warmth (which I couldn't hear of) nothing could have been done about the book. In spite of disadvantages I did a bit of sorting in G.G's quiet & pleasant sitting room & have gone over them here & am now allowed to use type-writer to make fair copies, but *only* while the next-door patient is having her bath! the tapping noise is supposed to be trying as no doubt it is (coughing, that tries *me,* is of course involuntary!). So its slow work – Denis wants the "stuff" about now he said, to get it out in the spring. I have just written to let him off doing it, if he wishes. It bothers him to carry on by correspondence, & I do not expect to get back to ChCh. till some time in September. However I hope he will do it – I am tired of having it talked about & want to get it off my hands. The effect of going over the verses to correct spelling etc, on me, is to induce great weariness of them, & the feeling that its all rubbish. However I trust to the judgment of my critic who eggs me on. I wish he were not so overdone with his Centennial work – I should like to ask his advice more than I dare. He's a person who will always give a firm opinion. How I wish I were competent to do that! That is why I tremble when you ask me for a calm critique of your book! I am *not* competent. I think I *might* have been, if I had gone on from where my education left off, instead of plunging into the slums. Where modern work is concerned I am quite at sea – I have been trying to get something from 6 numbers of "Twentieth Century Verse"[1] lent to me, *not* recommended to me, by A W Stockwell, G.G's friend, who is just leaving for Oxford on his postgraduate scholarship, having taken his MA in English with honours[2] – I simply can't make head or tail of most of it, as to meaning, nor hear that it is poetry. And I have been turning back to the "Golden Treasury" of my youth – so old fashioned & limited, & finding so much of the Wordsworth & Shelley boring! But my old favourites still give the same feeling of restful delight & the feeling is that the further back one goes the better they are. Among (comparatively) moderns I can read Hopkins, Hardy, Edward Thomas, with understanding & what I might call restfulness. When Denis, for instance, asks for my opinion about his poets, I wish that I'd never handed him anything of my own, because there's the implication "that's how I did it" – whereas that consideration shouldn't come in. I don't know why I did it *like that* – & I don't expect his young poets, being very modern, to care at all for my sentiments or my mode. However I do think that I know better where I am with work in the more traditional forms – and that is why I am obliged to say that the two typed poems[3] you sent me confirm in me the impression I had that your vocation must be rather to deal with human beings than to write – (you *asked* me to be candid!) I do not find them very good. I should say that the Land & People ones were better, but there, as I said, I feel that I'm at sea. *Not* competent to give an opinion – The one I like best so far, & can understand is the third "Land & People"[4] – I once

---

[1] The literary magazine begun by Julian Symons in 1937.

[2] As Bethell reports later, Archibald Stockwell was forced to return from Oxford when the war broke out. He later became a reader in English at Canterbury University College.

[3] These are no longer in Bethell's papers.

[4] Brasch has four with this title in the collection; this one begins 'There are no dead in this land, / No personal sweetness in its earth' (p. 23).

began some lines on this same subject – *they* would not have been so good!

It interests me that you now say in your note giving the Honolulu address, that you are writing much better, & have come to look on the "Land & People" poems as Juvenilia – Because that is very much what my critic (I don't think you met him – name is E. McCormick) said after examining the book. I pass on that verdict – rather gratuitously! Time will no doubt show that I was wrong about your vocation. But what is this about "middle age" in July? Do you mean that you have turned 30? I felt *very young* at 30! & even at 40! Its 50 I think that gives one the middleaged feeling, & my 50th birthday began the ten happiest years of my life. I ought to say that Toss was *very* enthusiastic about your book – so its evidently what the newer generation look for & are able to appreciate. I should have begun these feeble remarks with thanking you very warmly for the present of the book – (it is after all *you* –) as I do now. Denis too admires the work. [...]

Your later note sounds less like coming on to N.Z. Oh no, you couldn't stand ChCh! Wellington wd. be the place – and its so much more in the traffic, as my little dear used to say. I often wish I could live here myself, but over at the Bays. My people seem to tie me to Canterbury however. [...]

The end of your long letter was from St John's, Oxford – How well, oh how well, I know that garden! I can smell it almost! And yet I don't remember that fig-tree. [...] I had a fig – you would find it twice in the garden book![1] one of the things I specially wanted to have – for the *look* – but it made leaves only, mostly.

[...]

At that point my "Tea" arrived & I discovered that I was thoroughly tired! And so will you be perhaps. I was admonished "not to write too much" – it would not do for the Sister to see this letter. I enjoy your natty handwriting which packs so much in. I must stop "right now". Good wishes for all your journeys.

Yours affectly
Ursula Bethell

Forgive the bluntness of my remarks about the book – of course I need to read them more times. And what is the use of criticism which can't give its reasons? [...]

Hocken Library. MS-0996-3/19.

[1] It appears in 'Detail' (*Collected Poems*, p. 5) and 'Ficus' (p. 15).

TO JOHN SUMMERS – OCTOBER 8, 1939

47 Webb St. Christchurch

My dear John,

I have been back a week, but am not very strong – the effort of writing a long letter has so far been beyond me, on top of other things. But today I am keeping [to] my bed, & hope to get one written to you in the course of the day. So now to begin, at 8.30 am.

Your letter was not a surprise to me. That is the effect a war has on too many – unsettlement. For my part I had been wondering whether the funds for scholarships would under these conditions still be available, & was going to write to Archdeacon Whitehead on the matter. You must please understand that in giving you my opinion about your change of mind I am not trying to influence or direct you – you must work out your own problem – and you must do away with the idea of personal disappointment on my part, for, as I have explained before, my wish has been to help you if the way opened – I have not built anything upon these plans. [...]

The scheme for getting you to college was that you might go on with your education. You are afraid that it was for you the wish to be "in the limelight" to have "power" or "security" – I'm sorry for that. I hoped that it would reveal to you your own ignorance & need of mental *drudgery*! You are one of those of whom there are so many in N.Z. who try to run before they can walk. (You cannot use the English language – you do not understand the meaning of words!) But you have quite enough mental ability to learn. The question was whether you should use those abilities in the service of your Creator & your fellow man. It is possible that in choosing to be a simple farm-hand, as you say, you are 'wrapping up a talent in a napkin.' This is not to despise farm life, far from it, but to decide how you can best help & be useful in this distressed world. I have written quite enough in the past about that, & need not repeat myself. You say that to take up a bursary at college in order to improve your education is to find reasons for carrying out your own selfish desires (There is no need to drag in the tag "rationalisation" – its the sign of being half educated to indulge in the use of these clichés, you know.) Isn't it possible that to find reasons for staying on the farm is really shirking the thought of mental drudgery & going among strangers?

You say that you have not grown in prayer-life, & are no more disciplined – would you not be more likely to improve the former if you accepted a routine of worship & help from others – and would not college life in itself be discipline? You have far too much opportunity for introspection & are too much taken up with yourself. (No need to fall back on the word 'ego'.) It would be a good thing, I fancy, if your busy brain were so much occupied with objective studies that you forgot 'John Summers' for a bit. Its the *foundation* of study that you lack.

[...]

I have written baldly & positively to save time, but shall qualify what I have said by disclaiming any special insight or knowledge. I may have been wrong. The Archdeacon may have been mistaken. You have no doubt committed your way to the direction of God's Holy Spirit (but we must use our own common sense under that direction) and if you are sure that you are meant to work with your hands mostly, that is very good. But you can't have it both ways. I am in doubt about sending you more books, or what kind to send. I have some good ones, but the question is whether what time & mental energy the farm-work leaves to you, should not be given to some simpler & more definite study. Something to build on. The history of the Bible perhaps? Could you join a correspondence class & answer questions? I don't know whether you could study the English language in that way. (I like your letters because I know you & love you, but I should not like them if I did not!)

[...]

You are happy to have the quiet of nature round you, the beasts and birds – now that you have made up your mind to that work I hope you will feel peaceful. (One thing I have forgotten to remind you of, though, that with every year that passes brain-work becomes more difficult to resume. One of my old club boys who wished to improve his education (as a pastor of souls) later in life described study to me as "an agony".) I have been all the winter in or near a town, & mostly indoors. If I can afford I may go away again perhaps to Akaroa, to hear the birds – & have *meals* provided for me. I'm really not up to housework – could do with a hench-man like Johnny! But first I must see my book through the press – it should be out by the end of the month. "Day & Night" its to be called. I suppose it is my last. I was pretty near death for a few minutes in Wellington & it seems to be taking longer than I supposed to rest the heart. But it looks as if I were meant to go on living, so I must rest patiently in order to be able-bodied again presently.

Now, darling Johnny, I must write to my sister who is near London. I have not had a letter from her since war was declared. She is one of those, christian and *saint*, who think that this war is *right*, & to be pursued with every energy. I notice a great difference in the spirit of the community on entering this war from what we saw in 1914. Very little war fever & so far no abuse of the Germans. But one fears that the spirit of hate will flare up as the fighting goes on. We must pray to be saved from any kind of hatred or fear "let us love one another with a pure heart fervently."[1]

I know that you forgive anything that I may have said misunderstanding, or too sharply.

Always with love
Felicity.

Private collection.

TO J H E SCHRODER – OCTOBER 19, 1939

St Faith's Webb St. ChCh.

Dear Mr. Schroder

And what happened next I wonder – did Akaora prove to be what I know of it & complete the cure? – What happened to me was, that I went to Wellington early in June (where your note found me) and in a few days' time caught a bad form of influenza, went about too soon & too much & was sent to hospital with a "dilated" heart for six weeks. The poison's worked out now, but I am not strong & find it rather much to cope with my jobs here – so *my* thoughts are turning to Akaroa for further rest – can you recommend your hostelry, whichever it was? Those places change so often.

In hospital I was warm & thankful, & was able to go over the collection of verse I had planned. The Caxton Press is doing it & it should be ready next week – "Day & Night" its called – I am obliged to feel rather commercial about it & hope to catch the Christmas market! – but overshadowed by the war I am afraid there won't be much sending to England. I suppose that you have a list of Regulars (is that word a war influence?) to do reviewing, but if not – I should like to ask A. W. Stockwell to do it – & if he would, would it be acceptable for the "Press"? He is just back, having given up his post-graduate Oxford, under the distracting circumstances. I've been impressed by his literary judgments – & as I said would prefer sensible severity to easy praise (I'm assuming that you *will* accord me a notice!) I hope you will like the book, when your copy comes – some think that it is "as good as the Garden" – but they all belong to more than five years ago.

You are concerned with the sad courageous Iris Wilkinson[2] (I wished when I was reading your study that she had used her own name –

---

[1] See 1 Peter 1: 22.

[2] Robin Hyde had arrived in England from China, ill and without money. She spent some time in hospital, convalescing on one occasion with Brasch. Increasingly desperate, she

but I suppose she had good reasons.) Why did her courage fail her, when she had achieved success in her career? Some on-set of ill-health depression no doubt – I've learnt to understand & sympathise with even that, these last years – and *that* must need courage. I heard of her last from Charles Brasch who said that she was wretchedly ill. I missed the Press for 4 months (and *did* "miss" it) so may have failed to see something of his. I wonder do you ever have a little paragraph, like the T. L. S. saying that the Caxton Press has in hand a further collection of verse etc many of which first appeared in these columns? No, I don't think I should *really* enjoy that. I am so shy of the things themselves! (The Editor said last time it wasn't necessary to *ask* permission – so we have just put acknowledgements –)

You heard of course of Mr. Frank Sidgwick's death in July – after Influenza? I feel very sad about it – he was quite a friend. I cherish his letters. My friend Arthur Mayhew, who was his schoolfellow, wrote to tell me.

My kind regards please to Mrs. Schroder & I hope that she is well.

Yours sincerely
Ursula Bethell

Alexander Turnbull Library. fMS-018.

TO J H E SCHRODER – OCTOBER 27, 1939

St Faith's. Webb St.

Dear Mr. Schroder

Here is now the little book.[1] Thank you for making me feel happy & comfortable about a Press review. I think you may not like it very much – it does not resemble "The Garden" tho' written in the same place and time.

I agree that it would not be easy to review one's friends – privately as man to man I wouldn't mind pronouncing a failure & risk hurting feelings – but to exhibit it in public would be different!

I was anxious to make my bow before the more important Centennial publications appear! – they are going to be very good.

[...] Akaroa is the one place in N.Z. for which I feel an *affection* as one does for English places – everywhere else it is another sort of response – I was sure you would like it.

---

took her life by benzedrin poisoning on August 23rd. Schroder published a three-part tribute to her, under the title 'Struggle and Dream,' in *The Press* on 14, 21, and 28 October.

[1] This letter accompanied a presentation copy of *Day & Night*.

If you fall back upon A. W. Stockwell,[1] his address is 12 White Street, Timaru.

Yours sincerely
Ursula Bethell

Alexander Turnbull Library. fMS-018.

TO JOHN SUMMERS – NOVEMBER 12, 1939

As from 47 Webb St. Ch.Ch.
At Akaora

At last my dear John I take up your letter!

Even here I have not managed to catch up with my correspondence – In fact I was so tired that I have spent a good deal of time doing nothing – luckily out of doors, listening to the trees. Today after a southerly its too cold, & I am in my sunny room, which is really better for letter-writing. I was out to Church before breakfast with a friend.

But first about books – Before leaving ChCh. I did up & left to be posted to you – a small packet – which contained 2 more nos. of 'Theology' (which you need not return) a little book which has in it all of Eckhart I could find – & which I think you will like for the rest of it as well. A small book on Prayer of which I have another copy & you may keep it if you like it – its not a recent book, but has some sensible things in it if I remember rightly – & my Garden, which I am so glad to give you, having some copies by me, already paid for. I find however that I mustn't give away copies of the new book ('Day & Night') *yet* except in a few cases where there is an obligation. It has been very expensive to produce – (£50 – I have paid half of this) and we must first see how many copies we can sell, to recover some of this outlay. Later on there will be some left over.

When I go back I can send 'The Dark Night of the Soul'[2] (tho' I don't think myself its the most useful reading for you) & some others.

I should like to type out some of G M Hopkins for you, as he will be so long in coming. He is in some anthologies, of course. I am afraid that Francis Thompson isn't considered to be a very good *poet* – his religion of course is good (he was one of those wastrels you write so truly about) but I suppose it is a good thing to read him in his turn & for his thoughts.

And now for your letter – or letter*s* rather – I liked very much all that about your afternoon among the poplars – I know that kind of stone

[1] There is no indication that Schroder did. The review is unsigned.

[2] The spiritual classic of St. John of the Cross. Bethell may have considered it too advanced in its spirituality.

& grass place with its spaces of soft turf. It made me wish very much to be there too. The aromatic poplar scent always brings back England to me – Oxford especially, where I was at school – & there too, later, the lime-flowers – the scent of willow-wood & of burning blue gum takes me back to childhood in N.Z. – at Rangiora to be precise. I wonder whether you know Akaroa? It is very lovely just now – the different greens are most vivid – and the blue of the harbour is always changing. It makes me sad too – I have been here so often with my lost dear – especially one November when "The Long Harbour" was written – She left me here for 2 days longer to finish it & went back alone to Rise Cottage – (oh, there was a housekeeper there, of course) & I am so glad that it turned out to be a good poem! – Sometimes I can almost imagine that she will come round a corner of some hill. She died on Nov. 7th, at dusk of the evening.[1]

[...]

And now for the letter of indignation![2] I don't want to argue about it, tho' there are one or two points I could take up. I think perhaps you have keyed up the matter rather too high – I wasn't by way of luring you to dizzy intellectual heights, little Johnny, but of strengthening the foundations, so as to make you a better teacher – (you were planning to be a teacher of some kind). To speak of playing Judas is an exaggeration. You say that if you went to college you would not work, but would only browse & dream. Well if that is all the seriousness you could bring to it, I agree that you do better to milk cows to the glory of God! Browsing & dreaming is good too, & I think its very true that modern life suffers from forgetfulness of the place of *contemplation* – but practical equipment *is* necessary. You may be perfectly right in choosing the rural life – it is for you to judge – none of us can follow up all our possibilities. One of your gifts is a keen intuition – & I hope & have faith that it will be very much blessed. Oh yes *please*, I would *much* rather you wrote freely to me & without much deliberation. That is why I have refrained from offering any correction of grammatical mistakes – I don't mean that they are numerous! Anyhow I thought they wd. be dealt with at college! (You might look out for a tendency to use nominative when accusative is correct – after a transitive verb. e.g. – (I can't find an example of that in this letter from you tho' I think there is one) & prepositions – "for you and *me*" not "I" – "between you and *me*" not I – & so on. I'm not wanting you to be pedantic. And I should like to see what you said about pacifist behaviour in war & the essay deriving from 'Ends & Means'[3] & the other

---

[1] In fact, Effie Pollen died on Nov. 8th (see the letters of Dec. 29 & 30, 1934).

[2] I have not traced this letter, but clearly Summers was upset by some of Bethell's remarks when he declined the offer of a scholarship to university.

[3] This may be Aldous Huxley's work, so titled, an enquiry into the nature of ideals.

books – but I suppose you won't allow me that after all my criticisms! You say "there are more disciplines than intellectual discipline & more sources of wisdom than books" – Of course! Of course! Of course! That's a commonplace – Nevertheless there *is* such a thing as intellectual discipline, and there *is* wisdom conveyed through books! With all you say about moral & spiritual training (not your words but that is the gist of them) to be had on the farm I thoroughly agree – Its what such people as S. Theresa of Spain insist on – I wish that *I* had submitted myself more truly to such discipline in the past. I have not lost faith in you, dear – not at all – or faith in God's work in you.

[...]

Afternoon. I am out of doors after all – The sun has come out in strength & I have found a dry & sheltered spot & the quality of the air after a southerly is so refreshing. There has been a tui near, but he has flitted away. I think there are fewer native birds here than there used to be. I do wish the human race wd. be content with what a new country gives them – instead of clearing it away & imposing the alien. It seems so *insolent* – this destruction of the forest & of the forest denizens – & the birds are the best things in NZ – surely!

So far my letter has been mostly a commentary on yours – and I don't know that I have anything of my own to give you. My heart is all right again, but I was too easily exhausted at the flat & I hope that more rest of this sort may set me going again. I have been feeling depressed about the future – my brother urges me to move to somewhere where I can be looked after – but I have no inspiration. I have always disliked Christchurch & its climate, but I don't know where else to go. This illness has brought home to me what an infirm old age would be, lonely & dependent on others – However I need not think of what may never come!

[...]

Now, Johnny darling – write again when you feel the impulse to do so & forgive me for what seems a carping attitude. It may be useful really. As for your staying at Murchison, its probably your wisest plan, instead of another change of scene & so I shall take it – & say no more about any other plan. God be with you & with me your sad friend.

Much love from
Felicity.

Private collection.

TO J H E SCHRODER – NOVEMBER 19, 1939

As from 47 Webb St. Christchurch
In the Domain at Akaroa

Dear Mr. Schroder

Mr. Duff has most kindly sent me a copy of your broadcast review,[1] & I feel that I must ply you with another note, (or even letter,) to thank you for the "few sensible remarks" (more than "few" to be sure) I craved for! Mr. Duff praises the broadcast very highly as a broadcast – may I second him? Its so well arranged, so succinct, says so much to the point in a given time. I am so glad that you took the landscape line of approach – just right for the purpose I think, and that you seized the occasion to preach the gospel of true patriotism – what you say makes me feel almost sorry that I wasn't born in N. Z.! tho' it has been no affectation in me to be wont to call England "Home". Childhood however was spent in Canterbury & that must count. It is a happiness to be told that it has been allowed me to give back a little of the excitement & happiness that the landscape has brought to me on coming back to it. I wish I'd had a suitable unpublished one to offer to the centennial, but I hadn't.

You justify the title & the arrangement – both of which cost me some pains – And you find more in the book than I saw was there! – *that* is criticism to "prop one's mind".[2] And thank you for making time to read a *whole* long poem – two even and, *three short* ones as well! – that gives a much better notion I think than bits. It interests me that one was the spring morning which I added diffidently as an after-thought, feeling that it was perhaps too crudely ecstatic.[3]

And what a splendid advertisement the exordium was for my wares! As a matter of fact I hate offering them for sale, but its the only way –

Thank you for it all.

Akaroa is most green & peaceful – "very quiet" the hoteliers say in wistful accents, in another sense. It has changed somewhat – one hears the native birds less – I suppose more bush has been destroyed. (I am afraid that New Zealanders have not respected as much as they should what the country held for them – some more powerful writer than I should cry this reproach aloud) or perhaps its rather late in the season to hear them at their most vocal. But birds or no birds, it is health-giving here.

---

[1] Schroder had broadcast a review of *Day & Night* on his 3YA radio programme on October 31 (since published by Charlotte Elder).

[2] See Sonnet XIX in Sydney's *Astrophel and Stella*.

[3] 'Out on a Spring Morning,' *Collected Poems*, p. 44.

I am reading The Prelude, 1805 version, & Swifts letters to Stella – whereby I feel inclined to sign myself

Your obliged servant
M. U. Bethell

Alexander Turnbull Library. fMS-018.

TO CHARLES BRASCH – NOVEMBER 20, 1939

As from 47 Webb St. Christchurch.
At Akaroa.

Dear Charles

At last! Actually, I have with me quite a long unfinished letter to you dated Oct 29 – but looking at it I think its out of date & stupid – so it shall be scrapped. It was, this is, in answer to yours from Honolulu, dated Sep 17. I'll return to that directly – but first to explain that I got back to ChCh at Michaelmas – I had to be there for the final stage of the book 'Day & Night' – but found "home-life" too tiring still – Cooking *or* visitors I could have coped with, but not both, so I escaped from both by coming here for further rest early this month. D.G. has made *such* a good job of the book – I want to send you a copy of course, but had better wait till I know for certain that you are settled in N.Y. for a while. Not that I expect you to like the contents! my works can't be but vieux jeu[1] to the younger generation. G.G. & his circle are the exception I fancy. Mr. Schroder gave the whole of his broadcast (on books) one week to a very favourable review & I am sure sincere review – but I do not think he is a severe critic. He said some interesting things about N.Z. local colour – Mr. Duff sent me a copy of the script (I did not know about the broadcast & missed it) – I might type you a copy one of these days. Anyway I want you to see the get up of the book – I was rather in despair about the binding, there was so little choice – & the best paper had been used for you! But with G.G. to advise something satisfactory was in the end achieved. I don't think its better than 'The Land & People' but its different. I wanted it to look as like The Garden as possible & insisted on the old style of type etc. The book would not have appeared at all without the help & encouragement of friends, especially the editor of the Centennial books – As soon as it was out Denis went into hospital – for a minor op. (hernia) which I understand had been postponed for some time because of his being so busy. His devoted little wife was very worried, but all went well. I said that it sounded ("gone to

[1] Fr. 'old-fashioned.'

hospital") as if my work had been too much for him! How irrelevant all this sounds in time of war – but my critics insisted – just the time to go on with better things – The public is more likely to buy the Centennials than poetry – which I truly dislike offering for sale & would rather give but that's foolish I know. The Centennial pictorials are wonderful value for 1/- each.

I am sitting by the sea on the loveliest morning – very blue & very green hills (totally unlike the Canterbury plain atmosphere – or rather absence of atmosphere, which there *is,* here) & the looking-glass harbour all colour – but now the wind is getting up to ruffle it. The incoming tide is making the beautiful lapping noise I always remember here & the vociferous, sealing-wax legged terns have withdrawn to a distance – Its such a restful place – & does me good – though at first very saddening, because my dear was so often here with me in happier times. For the last five days or so I have felt really better – in fact quite back to usual health – I go back to town next week & shall begin again with more courage – I have had good fortune about weather & have spent most of the day out of doors so far – one or two showers at night. In Wellgn weather never fit to "sit out". But I havn't felt inclined to walk any distance. Its all very green this year here. Season quite 3 weeks late, so manuka not in flower yet.

You see how I have put off speaking of the war! Your letter brings me to it. That letter touched me – how you enter the lives & concerns of individuals! Do you remember how John Woolman the Quaker desired to be "baptised into a sense of the needs & conditions of all men."[1] And you are such an *adequate* letter-writer, I feel that my dull ones can't be at all repaying. The happiest thing in it was this, that the actual outbreak of war clarified the issue for you & made you see, as you say, the *necessity* of pacifism. I think I should have been glad, even, if you had decided the other way – a state of doubt is the worst. I hear opinions from every point of view, & while I listen can see things as the speakers see them. There are those who are sure that this is a kind of Holy War & that we are the instruments of justice to put down the tyrant & rescue the oppressed; there are the Quakers – Toss, Rodney & the others – equally happy – There are those who say they wd. refuse to fight in this capitalists' war but do believe in the use of violence. There is my farmer nephew, not at all military minded, who thought it right to enlist at once, punish aggression – & *he* says join up with the germans to "wipe out" communism! – If the country is "organised for war" – which has been foreshadowed – I suppose he might be sent back to the land. So far

---

[1] Bethell has quoted this before; see the letter to Kennedy, Aug. 29, 1937.

authority promises "NO conscription". In any case I am assured that the really conscientious objector will not be interfered with. The ones I am sorry for are those who do not believe in the use of force, but under conscription would go, hopelessly & perhaps cynically. In 1915 I came to feel that conscription wd. be fair & a relief to troubled consciences – "ought I to go?" Some went who shouldn't & then there were unprincipled shirkers. But reading about it lately, it begins to look like a violation of "civil liberty". I meant not to stray into the subject of the war – for me the nightmare has come & must be lived through – (I did not think to live through another). I am sometimes fearful – but now is the time to abide by choices made long ago – the faith that good is stronger than evil, that redemptive love *is* at work – that the victory of good over evil is potentially won, & will in the end be manifest. I think my part is to go on doing ordinary things (last time I was *in* it) & to be more assiduous in prayer than in the past.

You know best about not coming to N.Z. but it is a disappointment – you would have been a help to these others. But I can understand that you would feel isolated. I hope that you have found the work you can throw yourself into. When I was in Wgn – before my illness & before the war – G.G.'s imagination was active making plans for you! You were to find a "job" in Wgn & buy or build a cottage in the Bays opposite & let it to me for the coldest months – or allow me to be yr. winter housekeeper (That was a good testimonial to my efforts on *his* behalf!). My winters indeed have become a problem since this illness – it seems inadvisable that I should have to go away for them. My brother is urging me to move from Webb St – my quarters there are certainly not very convenient for an infirm person, but they are *cheap*. Anywhere else in the city would be as cold, and I do not think I could go back to sunny Cashmere alone – sometimes I contemplate a migration to Wellington, but it is far from my relations. I loved being with G.G. but was only a hindrance to him in my invalidy state, so I was glad when I was well enough to return to ChCh. It has frightened me a little, thinking of old age dependent on strangers. But that may not come, & meanwhile I am quite well again. I asked myself whether I could live as a recluse *here*, like Miss Baughan (she is well & happy) but I doubt it. I love the place, but think I'd feel the need of people. The passer-by often looks me up at Webb St, & that couldn't be, here. I rather yearn for a cottage again – but my brother says I can't be alone & I can't afford a servant. Its always puzzling when there is no special "call" & no reason for being anywhere in particular – The Recluse says that I shall know when the time comes!

[...]

Its quite hard *here* to realise that violence is going on – except when the wireless is turned on in the boarding house – But nowhere is there much *appearance* of war. Petrol restrictions have been lifted & cars on the road again. Hotel keepers lament that 'Trade is so quiet' – but of course *that* suits me very well. I notice a great difference between 1914 & now – no war fever. I suppose the atmosphere [may] worsen & a spirit of hatred grow up, but so far the people I've heard are sober in their speech. It was a shock to me yesterday to read in the paper that our letters – overseas I suppose – are being censored – I hadn't thought of that – apparently at this end. Pieces cut out of letters received in England. It naturally affects one's freedom of speech! I remember how the ranks in the last war hated having their letters censored by their own officers – later there were the special envelopes. That is terrible – the *hopelessness* of your friends – there are so many who do trust each other. Cannot this solidarity be built on? The thought comes that there has been a collapse of humanism – that we cannot build apart from the Divine "Except the Lord build the house".[1]

[...]

Yes, Iris Wilkinson's end – as you will have heard no doubt – was suicide. I was puzzled, because she seemed to have achieved success in her career, & had just done what surely must have been a successful book about China – but I suppose it was her nerve illness – We all know moods when nothing, however successful, seems worthwhile – & in her case such states of mind must have been extreme. Its so sad – because she seems to have attracted friends everywhere – I never met her. [...] Mr. Schroder has had 3 long articles about her in the Press. I wonder whether you would like to have them? I can't but think that they do more credit to his heart than his head. I believe she was a great friend. However I shall keep them, so ask for them if you would like them. I expect you have been sent the enclosed Press review of your book. I don't know who wrote it – It shows that you *are* appreciated in N.Z.[2]

I am going back to the past for my reading & have with me Swift to Stella & 2 Hardy novels & The Prelude 1805 version. Before that it [was] Matthew Arnold & I shall return to him. (Swift's "little language" seems to have anticipated J. Joyce!) I believe that of the moderns I ought to tackle T. S. Eliot in real earnest – he has had a great influence on style.

[...]

How I have run on! I seem to have taken your words (that my letter couldn't be too long) au pied de la lettre![3] My circumstances favour running on – I must have written more letters from here than in all the

---

[1] See Psalm 127: 1.

[2] Brasch's verse was reviewed on Oct. 14, 1939.

[3] Fr. 'to the letter, literally.'

rest of the year. [...] My sister sends me a postcard weekly, to keep me reassured. [...]

Driven in by N.W. shower – winding this up & looking for your review to enclose – nowhere to be found! Maddening! I had it with your letter – It must have blown out to sea! [...]

Goodbye – forgive my ramblingness. I may even have repeated myself. I think of you often & send you my very best wishes – if you have found constructive occupation it will make it all better for you I am sure.

Yours affectionately
Ursula Bethell

Hocken Library. MS-0996-3/19.

TO RODNEY KENNEDY – NOVEMBER 22, 1939

As from St Faith's. Webb St. Christchurch.
At Akaroa

My dear Rodney

I am touched & grateful to you for remembering me (again) in this sad November month. I came here on Tues. 7th, the very day of the month my dear left me, but it was the Thursday Show & Race Day that year[1] – There are many reminders in Akaroa, where we used to come, together, but it is so quiet & beautiful, it is healing. Particularly quiet this year, there being so few "tourists" – I thought of spending a fortnight here, but have decided to stay on for a 3rd week – it is only for the last 4 or 5 days that I have felt really better – but now I am quite well, & can walk up hill with ease. The weather – which has been too dry for the Canterbury Plains – has been kind to me. I have been able to sit out of doors every day until this morning, when rain began – If it were not norwest rain I should imagine that it was the wet weather you speak of coming north.

[...]

Now I come back again to your letter of the 9th – It is very nice what you say about The Garden – (Johnny happens to write about it too, in his letter today!) I wonder what was the line you were searching for – I suppose that was really my *freshest* writing. I have seen no review of "Day & Night" yet – I daresay you wd. have noticed it, had there been one in the Dunedin papers. [...] Everyone says how well the Caxton Press has done it. I quite see, altho' I promised not to give it away, that I must send you a copy for Christmas! that is – if you would like it –

---

[1] In fact, in 1934 that Thursday was the 8th not the 7th. Bethell is again confused about the date of Effie Pollen's death.

I love lily of the valley & I did have a beautiful bunch in my room the week before I came away brought to me by friends – the plants I brought down from Cashmere havn't taken hold yet. I expect to see some growth in the border when I go back next week – it was pretty bare when I left.

[...]

A trawler has just come in – shipping is fascinating – When the harbour is calm like this it reminds me of the Swiss lakes I've lived on. Sometimes I wonder whether I could live here, like Miss Baughan in her "Ashram" – one would have to decide to be a Recluse.

You won't have had much time for reading among the cows – I hope you have had some good thoughts. Any prospect of a holiday for you at Christmas? Thank you again dear Rodney for your sympathy & thought for me.

With my love
M.U. Bethell

Hocken Library. MS-0741-001

TO RODNEY KENNEDY – DECEMBER 5, 1939

St Faith's. Webb St. ChCh.

My dear Rodney

How good of you to send the review so promptly – I must thank you at once – It *was* bad luck to fall into the hands of C.R.A![1] Poor fellow, I don't like saying such things because of his infirmity – but literature is *not* his forte, really & truly. Its a *stupid* notice – I am not thinking of praise or blame, it wd. be as stupid either way – That G. M. Hopkins influence obsession! Most of my verse was written before I knew G.M.H. except for bits in anthologies, & he does *not* influence me – One often notices his influence – but it does not have that effect – he is unique & *not* to be imitated. And I do not read E. Underhill very much – & certainly do not admire her *style* (I daresay E.U. is the writer *he* happens to have read!) The Evening Star is stupid too – I enclose the Press wh. you may not have seen (please return) I don't know who did it, but it sounds more like an educated person.[2] I wish for the sake of D.G. that it had said something in praise of the get up wh. is really very good –

[1] C. R. Allen's review appeared in the *Otago Daily Times*, Dec. 2, 1939 – and more than deserved Bethell's adverse comments.

[2] *Day & Night* was reviewed anonymously in the *Evening Star* under the heading 'Poetry for the Elect' (Nov. 25, 1939), with the general thrust being that the poetry was 'not for the multitude.' *The Press* carried a brief, but more balanced, note on the same day.

Denis was right when he said that it is a waste of money sending review copies to papers. We only sent to 4.

[...] I hate "Evelyn Hayes" & wish people wd. now break through the anonymity – tho' I don't want to lie about on bookshop counters.

[...]

I can't cope with Christmas this year – neither mind nor money for it. (I am well now, but soon get tired.) I am sending you D&N however.

Yours affectly
M. U. B.

Hocken Library. MS-0741-001.

TO MONTE HOLCROFT – DECEMBER 17, 1939

St Faith's House. Webb St. Christchurch.

My dear Monte

Thank you so much for sending me the thoughtful review. I should have liked to write at once, but you know what these pre-Christmas days are, even in war-time. It is interesting that you and my Roman Catholic reviewer are the ones to choose The Lamps for special notice.[1] I did not think of it myself as satisfactory without the music.

The R.C. review likewise brings in G. M. Hopkins – but it can't be an influence from his work because I did not know it (except bits seen in anthologies) when those things were written! The same applies to Rilke, who is a writer I feel one *ought* to know & hope to tackle presently. So far I have only seen enough of him to recognise that he is very badly translated & I fear my German is too rusty to appreciate him in the original. Translation of poetry is a difficult problem isn't it.

I always own up to being influenced by the psalms. I am not proud (I agree with you) of that line about "Diurnal subsistence"[2] – but it came into my head & often I find I can't substitute anything for first thoughts, though sometimes able to improve (as I think). I am glad you prefer "Time & Place". I tried to choose the best ones for that. To my mind the best one in Day & Night is one called 'Waves.'

---

[1] Holcroft reviewed *Day & Night* very favourably in the *Southland Times*, Dec. 2, 1939. He described 'At the Lighting of the Lamps' as 'the most impressive work,' and concluded by describing Bethell's poetry as 'the work of a mind in which thought and discipline have found their alliance with an integrity of imagination and spirit.' I have not traced the 'R. C. review.' The book was reviewed in two Catholic weeklies, *The New Zealand Tablet* and *The Zealandia*, but neither of those contain these comments.

[2] The line occurs in 'Morning Walk' (*Collected Poems,* p. 43).

I *had* intended to put my name to this collection, but in the end reverted to previous custom. I don't mind its being used. The R.C. reviewer aforesaid does so.

I have been ill this winter & it was during the 6 weeks in hospital that I was able to sort out & arrange a third sequence – but I don't think I should have persevered but for the encouragement & help of friends. It all belongs to the past. I like to think that the verses have given you some pleasure.

I hope that you are well & send you good wishes for Christmas & as much happiness in the New Year as may be hoped for in these troublous times.

Your friend
M.U.Bethell

Alexander Turnbull Library. MS-Papers-1186-03.

V: 1940–1941

TO JOHN SUMMERS – FEBRUARY 4, 1940

47 Webb St. Ch.Ch.

And now John dear I will try to *finish* a letter to you – it was impossible yesterday – a friend came to lunch and that with domestic chores exhausted my strength. I really need someone to work for me if I'm to get other things done. I smile to think that in 1910-11-12 I lived here with a whole time servant to wait on me & the whole house for my occupation!

[...]

I like you better when you are putting down your thoughts as it were for God, or heart to heart to a person in conversation, than when you are didactic. I doubt whether the time has come for you to be a preacher. A helper of individuals you can & must be –

Now I come to some pages wh. I thought at first were addressed to the general Public, but reading on saw that they were meant for me! I don't always succeed in recognising myself from your diagnosis – E.g. I think I'm pretty "personal" – otherwise should I not establish myself for this Old Age in some retired spot such as Akaroa, in contact with Nature? (In youth I could do that). *Too* personal perhaps – like all selfish people I find it hard to put up with persons who bore me. (P. Leon I think points out that only egotists are "bored").[1] I'm not *sociable*. But do we know what we mean by the word "personal"? You say that you think I believe in "a personal God." But of course! A member of the church *has* to – "Three Persons in One God" – But there is a great deal of argument over that word "personal". When will you start on a series of books on the great Christian Doctrines? e. g. The Trinity – The Incarnation – & the rest.

You say that now I have lost my Darling "I turn to God desiringly" – but I always did turn to God – what I asked was to know His will & to be made better. I think I have never known Him truly as "Love". It has been "Maker of all things – Judge of all men" – in the august words of the prayer book – in the service which commemorates & carries on His love in Redemption.[2] I accept that as an article of belief – but I havn't had a

---

[1] There is little to identify this reference, but it may be to Philip Leon, who had published a study of the Oxford Group the previous year, under the title *The Philosophy of Courage*.

[2] The phrases are taken from the general Confession that precedes reception of Communion in *The Book of Common Prayer*.

"personal" love of God – if that is a right expression (doubtful). I've had & have a strong sense of guilt – you know there is repentance, & penance. These five years past have been a chastisement.

I'm certainly not refusing more human love if its sent, (& it has been) but I feel (faithlessly I daresay) that there can't be that fulness of affection again. I proved to be unworthy of it. [...]

I like what you say about hers being "active, living love" & that "it is one in being with the love that is here now." *That* is exactly what my sister wrote when my darling died "Its all the same love" but I could not take it in then. All I knew was that love had gone. I am beginning to take it in now.

I have been thinking much about the war since you were here. It comes as a challenge I think to one's whole outlook. I have a big library of pacifist books & have debated the question since 1918 – but now that it has come, it calls for a decision. The vision I have is that it *is* wrong – but, the world being what it is, & the Church having failed as it has, it was apparently inevitable. It is a great responsibility to differ from the best & holiest people one knows, who think that the war is very dreadful, certainly, but the only way to put the world right.

Later.

It was after nine P.M. when I was writing those words & I heard steps below – my soldier nephew on his way back from the farm to camp. (Its now 10.15 so this letter probably won't be finished tonight after all.) He is the most conscientious & unselfish person I know after my sister & those very virtues have taken him into the army. He has no military ardour. One sees that for him this step represents God's will – it is costing him much anxiety on behalf of my brother left to farm work. He would not understand my thoughts about the war. It is thinking of such as he that I most deplore any unnecessary criticism, any bitterness – & I am glad that the open air meetings have been stopped. They were provocative.[1] This may seem a policy of cowardice – but I do feel most deeply that a pacifist Christian must be humble & chastened about their christianity. If my own faith in God is imperfect how can I have faith for others in danger. If my love for my neighbour is imperfect how can I stand for love of the enemy. The crisis is one for my own spiritual life,

[1] Throughout the later months of 1938 and much of 1939, pacifist organisations had held open-air meetings to promote their beliefs. In September 1939 and January 1940, the Wellington and Christchurch City Councils respectively withdrew the permits for such meetings, effectively banning them. The meetings continued to be held in Wellington, in defiance of the ban. Among those arrested there (and imprisoned) was Connie Jones, later to become Summers' wife.

not a call for argument. (I feel that Toss should qualify for pacifism by complete heroism in his own life!)

Monday

It was too late to go on. [...] I wanted to say that since you were here my prayer has grown better – not so much "a cry" as you said but a resting on that "stillness" of which you speak. It has to do with my thoughts about the war and I owe something to you.

[...]

Would you let me have Lady Julian as soon as you can. I will try to get her for you to keep. Its a book you should have I think. For myself, I'm trying to get T. S. Eliot's new book "The Idea of a Christian Society". Goodbye Johnny dear – I wish your old friend could get more done in a day – the northeasters last week were exhausting – since the southerly I have more life in me.

Your loving F.

It isn't so much that I "live in the past" as that the past so often seizes hold of me suddenly – I think only mothers understand the pain that I have – I don't think it can stop – but I accept it as part of the Pattern.

Private collection.

TO JOHN SUMMERS – FEBRUARY 15, [1940]

Wainui House. Nelson.

John dear

We got here for lunch yesterday & the above is my address. The drive up from ChCh was lovely [...] but so far Nelson has disappointed me for its very chill & windy & my rheumatism won't go. And this boarding house so crowded that there wasn't a nice room available – mine is on the cold side & noisy.

[...]

I return the lines by Toss – I don't think they are well-expressed & I do not follow the thoughts. I get his thought better in prose. Toss is an interesting person & I have a great affection for him as you know – he is uneven. He has great enthusiasms & then they cool down – (perhaps that's "the artistic temperament"). Sometimes I think him really silly. At other times a good deal of a saint. He had a very bad start in life, & when one thinks of that one sees how he has progressed, & made good use of defeat. Somehow his foundations are not solid – & he has not achieved "wholeness" – there is an emancipation or a confirmation needed, I feel, which surely would affect his painting. I am sorry to be cold about his "verses" – but for myself I should always wish my writing to be judged by absolute standards. I have tried to help him in his painting work-life. I can't help him in himself. I admired the way he chose the whole of life & its risks – instead of being a painter only. Edith was a great gift to him. I needn't say, dear, that if I write to you about Toss, or any other, its in confidence & because I trust you. He himself knows his weakness – He surprised me a year ago by saying that he hadn't learnt to pray – Not to pray seems to be living by impulse – I think he felt that painting was his prayer – but painting would not be the whole of him. Prayer is not contemplation only – it is obedience, it is dependence, it is penitence.[1]

I will now read again the pages headed Aloneness.[2] I am glad to know that you are working that out, as I am working it out in a different way, you in your youth – I in my old age. In youth "loneliness" is certainly the word for sex-hunger – especially with women. When I was in my "twenties" I was at a settlement in London with thirty women, & looking back now I realise that most of them must have been suffering in that way. That matter of masturbation was badly handled in the books of instruction available in my early days of boys' club work; (I still have a parcel of those out-of-date books waiting to be bon-fired) and there were books current of a terrifying nature which were merely intended to drive lads to buy nostrums. I think things have improved, & boys should have a better chance in their growing years. (I have tended to think of self-abuse as a boys' habit because, although one knows that sex-stimulation is common among girls too, I have never in my experience come across it, either at school or later.) [...]

I shall think a good deal about your words "the gift of loneliness". "I have always rejected my loneliness & this year I hope to take it as the gift it really is." – Those words entered into my prayer & I became more obedient to the Will & more fortified for life. But in the very same hour the pain of my loss, and the heart-ache, became more acute & I accepted that too as a 'sending'.

I am so glad, darling Johnny, that you feel you've "got to write" to me – the pages are never too many. I watch your growth, & you do help me.

---

[1] The four preceding lines from 'Not to pray' are all underlined, but it appears to be a later addition, not Bethell's emphasis.

[2] The following remarks relate to material in which Summers appears to have been trying out ideas relating to sexuality. Some of what he writes is reflective, some almost prayerful, while some retains the style of a letter. Bethell refers to this again when writing to Kathleen and Merlin Davies, describing it as a 'magnum opus' giving 'a Christian philosophy of sex.'

I must take my letters to the postbox now. I wish it wd. turn warmer. I have a good deal of rheumatism & neuralgic pain. This may presage a severe winter like the English one. Are you well in health now? And the work not too taxing? Take care of those beautiful teeth – they are a most valuable possession – the *evening* is the important time to brush them.

Very much love from
F.

Private collection.

TO JOHN SUMMERS – [FEBRUARY 16, 1940]

As from 47 Webb St. Christchurch
Wainui. Nelson.

John my dear

[...]

Your letter answering mine came yesterday evening. I am much struck by the growth in you since last year – & even since the holidays – & I do "*feel*" as you say the inward stability increasing with experience – as I notice the increasing ability to express in words. You have answered some of my misgivings. (I may have told you that the man I was going to marry decided that he couldn't meet me, & later that even writing wd. be a mistake, when his health broke down. He acted according to his strength (he was a sick man – but did not die till last year) & though it cost me suffering I am able to say 35 years later that I think it wd. not have been a successful marriage. Also he wished to leave me free, & I have been free, & could not marry anyone else).

[...]

I wish I had time to say more about yr. letters. They have brought you much nearer. Thank you Johnny dear for your affection, & for being yourself.

F.

I have seen that arrogance (Toss). He has balancing qualities. I think you won't have done any harm by dealing with him faithfully. You know whether its done in love.

Private collection.

TO JOHN SUMMERS – FEBRUARY 19, [1940]

As from 47 Webb St. Christchurch
At Wainui House. Nelson.

Dearest John

I have both your letters. I am glad & touched that you care to "share" these experiences with me. At first I thought it might be enough to express my sympathy & make no comment. But I think perhaps that to say a few things wd. be more helpful. I did not hear you call to me but I have had you in mind & in my prayer pretty constantly these days. Passion is running high with you just now – I must borrow a military tag – "steadiness under fire". I do think that you are working out your sexual life consciously & with an end in view – the consciousness of the aim seems to grow clearer, letter by letter. That is, freedom & mastery. Happy those who have grown up straight & freely, without your tangles – there is nothing like *that* wholeness – & yet you win a different treasure in the struggle "With *a price* I obtained this freedom"[1] – as St Paul did not have to for the Roman citizenship. Don't listen to Strauss, Johnny, that's bad, that's weakening. Listen to Bach, Mozart, or even stormy Beethoven – always choose what is bracing – for there *is* a technique you know. As for Marie *I accept her with you*. As for her figure! no doubt that will grow slenderer presently – & a woman of that build should make a good mother. That's what you've got to think of "Would she be a good mother to my children?" It does not sound to me as if she would be your companion intellectually – but there have been many successful matings without that. Only the wife must not be jealous – must be so sure of her true mate as not to mind his enjoying intellectual companionship – very likely with another woman. (I am looking forward to a time when I shall be gone from this world.) I think your criterion of "beauty" is pretty sound. Only I wonder whether what wd. be beautiful for pagan Greeks would be beautiful for young Christians? *Did* I do well to lend you Daphnis & Chloe?[2] It is a responsibility, because you act so promptly on what you read. Christianity has gone further – *Sanctity*. We are involved in a spiritual war. There seemed to be many messages for you in Church yesterday, beginning with the epistle at "early service" – "everyone should know how to possess his vessel in sanctification & honour ... for God hath called us into holiness"[3] – & the psalm "I will walk at *liberty*; for I

---

[1] See Acts 22: 28.

[2] A pastoral romance, written late 2nd or early 3rd century A.D. by Longus, which tells of the passion between the two foundlings, Daphnis and Chloe, and their initial inability (through ignorance) to consummate their love.

[3] See 1 Thessalonians 4: 4, 7.

seek thy commandments"[1] & the end of the evening lesson, (Augustine's) "make no provision for the flesh to fulfil the lusts thereof"[2] – [...]

The experience with M. *was* of course dangerous. I am not in fear for you – (but there *have* been so many cases of sex muddles connected with religion– people do deceive themselves) you were both in conscious control. I should fear more for her being so young. Has the man charge of the woman? or vice versa? I suppose it is fifty fifty. Does the experience make the battle harder for you, or easier? And for her? There is more in life than mating love – don't let that be all absorbing now. You must build up your strength first, mentally & physically. You know that. If you are both calmed & strengthened by your meetings good I should say, but if there be local physical excitement, not good. However I think you are quite aware of all this. Don't you think that now you know you are "en rapport"[3] as the French say – no English equivalent – in all-round sympathy with M. it would be good ascesis to refrain from this delight till the marriage stage – marriage we look on as a sacrament, to be prepared for by vigil, so that you may both be *free* when that time comes for utter intimacy. [...] It is perhaps presumption on my part to offer any comment. But look at your situation coolly, as a looker on – "Patience is willing to wait" – I have to learn that in my different situation, and when all that is disturbing you now has ended for me. I have faith that God will give you what is good for you. If you are going to be a helper in this world, you mustn't take more than he gives.

[...]

Don't think that I am insensitive to the reality & beauty of your experiences – you have written it well for me – (lots of mistakes in grammar & spelling I ought to correct, but let them pass for the moment!) I wish dear child I could share some of my experience out of the past with you – but anyhow I doubt whether one person's special experience helps another very much. You would not write if you were not sure that I should understand. It is certain that we must endure hardness without always seeing why – or even knowing surely that there *is* a why – yet we do know.

[...]

With so much love & thanks.
F.

Private collection.

---

[1] See Psalm 119: 45.

[2] See Romans 13: 14.

[3] As Bethell notes, the phrase has no exact equivalent, and is sometimes used euphemistically to indicate a sexual liaison. I suspect Bethell wishes to preserve some ambiguity here; perhaps it might be translated as 'getting together.'

TO JOHN SUMMERS – MARCH 9, [1940]

St Faith's Webb St. ChCh.

[...]

Sunday

I am *very* tired – if I don't feel better in a few days I must go to a doctor. It was an effort to go to "early service" & I have been resting – it is now 10.30. While resting I have looked into Buber (I have a second copy) – it is a great little book – & re-read the preface – "There is one Thou which never becomes an It, the 'eternal Thou', God." This reminded of one of your letters, earlier in the year, which it seemed to me overstressed the *Immanence* of God – But you have since expressed the balance – the Transcend*e*nce (notice spelling). Von Hügel has a good deal about this.

[...]

The chief impression left on my mind by this hour (it was more!) of investigation was that of the amazing progress you have made. If I return the MS it must be by book post with a book (quite lawful!) letter postage is too heavy. I wish I had time to type them but I havn't.

When I see this kind of volcanic eruptions of M.S. or geyser playing all within a week or two (but some are not dated) I don't wonder that in your last letter your "studies had gone flat" – you needed a spell. I know this excitement of thought & then flatness – its like that when one writes poetry. You needed a good thriller or detective story perhaps! I am sorry I could not furnish the romantic Abailard[1] – (In the other one you will see an answer to your query about castration[2] – not being a pathologist I could not discuss that) – I have always felt an interest in Heloïse.

[...]

When I send books like Von H. Letters to a Niece you must wonder how I could, having known these truths, go so near to despair again[3] – The floods overwhelm one, John, & wash all the meaning out of words. But in the darkness one must hold on to what one *has* known & not give up. Remember that. You are very young & there are many trials yet to come. I think that I stayed at *enduring* the darkness – things you have said told me we must *accept* the darkness – use it. That's what St. John of the Cross said – one night he discovered that "Thou (God) art

---

[1] Bethell originally wrote 'Abelard;' in a postscript she added 'The solid book says Abailard unquestionably right spelling.'

[2] The letter containing this query is not extant.

[3] Bethell may be thinking of Von Hügel's reflections on the value of suffering, and on the relationship between suffering and joy, which occur in several places in the letters.

the Dark".[1] How often I said that to myself, hoping to understand it in time.

I believe there are things in yr. last letter left unanswered – I'll look at it again. It was a *very* nice letter – How your spirit has changed, darling Johnny, how you have changed! I think you see now, don't you, that I am taking your M.S. in the way you wd. like – I think we have come to a good understanding about it. I am glad you are not in a hurry. You are absorbing. Your light *is* burning. "Significance"? Well, you have that for me at any rate! But don't be in a hurry about that either – and when I wrote that things had been said before – why no-one is *quite* original – What I meant [was] that it is a reason for not printing, even as an article, unless one is sure that the matter is better expressed than heretofore, or in a new context, applied to a new situation. A badly written article does not *commend* its thesis – makes people impatient of the view that's being presented. I've known that happen! Please note that I have *not* destroyed any of your M.S. (except ephemeral notes) in the first place I kept them in order to observe progress. You should be working under a competent "Professor" John – not listening to me! But this is *some* good in the meantime.

(I think you are right about leaving the matter of "chastity" out of our discussions[2] – only this I wd. say, that in the case of bad habits, as well as – or sometimes instead of – "wrestling" – it is useful to "make no provision" – that is so to dispose proceedings that there will be the least opportunity (compare putting gloves on children who suck thumbs – or getting them interested in other things) – & then to commit the whole problem to God's grace. There *have* been cases of an obsession being suddenly taken right away – e.g. craving for alcohol etc. You need not make any comment on the foregoing – it may be quite beside the mark. What you say on the subject is very sound & true, especially about freedom, & living under the shadow of the law – you don't need any remarks of mine.) [...]

I hear the St Faith's dinner-bell – must go & see about some lunch – you are first on a list of *15* pressing letters I wanted to write today – (not possible of course!) and I must go on to No.2. Anyhow I feel all the better for my quiet morning with dear Johnny – who in some sense I take to be a special charge these days! 'Surfeit of godmothers' indeed! Which of us are you going to get rid of?

---

[1] The idea of finding God in darkness is central to John's mystical theology. See also Bethell's 'Evening Walk in Winter,' where she refers to John of the Cross as the 'night-initiate Spaniard' to whom God says 'I am the dark.' (*Collected Poems*, p. 76.)

[2] Summers wrote a series of 'cogitations' including one on the nature and practice of chastity.

Monday

I started another letter instead of finishing this one. I am feeling *much* less tired today & so I hope really getting over the adventure. I must post this & not say any more till next time.

God bless you
love from
F.

Private collection.

TO CHARLES BRASCH – MAY 28, 1940

47 Webb St. ChCh. N.Z.

Dear Charles

I look with such gratitude on two letters in your shapely, legible, pleasing handwriting (Jan 16 & Easter) unfortunately tinged with vexation that I've been – had to be – so silent. To think that Day & Night even arrived without its covering letter, to say that I did *not* expect you to like it! I know that my utterances are *not* your "cup of tea" – but its your usual kindness to take an interest & thank you so much for comments.[1]

This last week's news has of course put all such matters into the background & one does not know what the next morning may bring.[2] I forbear to comment. We were warned long ago what it would be like, & now it is here. N.Z. is going totalitarian, in the wake of England – when Parliament meets this week. It had to be. There are difficult hours coming for some of my young friends – One of them, a Quaker, not known to you I think, writes that though his convictions of what is right & wrong do not change, he begins to feel that his love of his fellows will take him with them, against those convictions. There are sharp divisions of opinion in this small land. My nephew goes with the 3rd echelon – he is a farmer, not a soldier, but sees it as his duty. He is such a good fellow & had been so thoughtful for me, I shall miss him. Looking at it – or trying to – dispassionately – I think that it wd. be wiser for him to be kept on the farm – providing food. Already the production has gone down there & the work is too much for my brother. One moment we are told that every ounce of food must be produced & the next that every fit man

---

[1] The last half dozen words have been added as an afterthought.

[2] In May 1940 the Government passed the Emergency Regulations Amendment Act, enabling it to introduce conscription. The necessary powers were taken in June, and the first ballot was held in October 1940.

must enlist. Perhaps the new move will bring co-ordination. To me it all looks very confused. [...]

I'm not a "pessimist" because I believe that good is stronger than evil, & that this has been shown to us. But it seems that we must all suffer a great deal – I hope to learn to do better – & we shall need all our faith & courage. A smashing victory on either side would surely make a shallow peace. But I am very ignorant. I always feel that I have my share in the evil, in the measure of my own selfishness & bad tempers of my career.

[...]

I forget whether you know Dr. Helen Simpson. Her Centennial book on the Women of N.Z. came out last month & is very well done. "Incidentally" as they're so fond of saying out here – my name appears publickly for the first time – under "Occupations" with some, you wd. think I am sure, too warm praise.[1] It has had the useful effect of impressing my family. To revert for a moment again to Day & Night. You are the first who has not approved of the get-up![2] I like it very much myself – the instructions were to make it as like The Garden as possible. There wasn't much choice for binding, as you will understand, under the circumstances. Only the dust-jacket was done by Denis without interference.

[...]

I do hope you will write again & keep me in touch – for I'm *not* ungrateful however it may seem – & letters mean a great deal. I agreed with what you said about the situation. Freedom. I read very little, except papers. The New Statesman is passed on to me, & the New English Weekly – *and* the Revue des Deux Mondes! And I see a "Christian Newsletter" copied from King Hall – & a good small magazine "Theology" – and so far The Christian Pacifist, but am expecting that to be banned, though I do not think it is really "subversive".[3]

[...]

---

[1] Helen Simpson's *The Women of New Zealand* was the seventh of the Centennial Surveys. It included an account of women poets, ending 'Last and greatest, Miss Ursula Bethell need fear comparison with none. Her spacious scholarship, wide humanity, and delicate perceptiveness have been, with exquisite craftsmanship, transmuted into poetry at once rich in content and finely austere in form. Hers is the most individual voice in New Zealand literature today' (p. 165).

[2] Brasch had written: 'I find Denis' production of this disappointing – not a patch on Time & Place. His taste must be erratic.... Of course I always remember that he likes Leo Bensemann's execrable drawings.'

[3] Originally published in London as *Reconciliation*, *The Christian Pacifist* continued publication until 1951.

And the price of books. D.G. thought of yours as an Edition de Luxe I think – I wanted mine to be cheaper – but we thrashed it out – and even at 5/- it won't pay. I think he is getting his 1/2 share of cost back – but I shall not get mine. There are not enough people in NZ who want to buy poetry – it was agreed that those who would buy mine would pay 5/-. Oh, and comparing D&N, as a *collection*, with T&P, *I* think you are right in thinking the latter the better – tho' other people have said the contrary. I chose T&P very carefully – Above remarks made with the feeling that its all a thing of the past now. About yourself I won't speculate – the Divine Wisdom has you in charge. I do not *worry* about my sister – only I hope that if she has to be a victim, it will be death for her & not other suffering – she would be quite happy to die. Those of us who have lately lost people dear to us must be thankful that they are taken away from this trial. Sometimes I have thought that I would like to introduce you to my old friend Arthur Mayhew at the Colonial Office. He is "a lovely person" as Toss has it. A scholar – educational administrator – a humanist – a practising Christian – He did a great work in India, where I stayed with them. He holds with the war of course – but is quite liberal – He was to be retired, but has been called back – His two sons will now be in the army, no doubt. What a terrible time for all my friends there – & by the time this reaches England what may not have happened!

[...]

Now I really am getting up – should have put out my reading lamp long ago. It rains & rains.

With my love to you
Ursula Bethell.

Hocken Library. MS-0996-3/19.

TO ERIC MCCORMICK – JULY 27, 1940

47 Webb St. ChCh.

Dear Eric

Saturday evening.

I now make a beginning of commentary.[1] I fear it will be lengthy – what takes but a moment to say, takes many lines to write! First, thank

[1] Bethell was asked to read and comment on the manuscript of McCormick's centennial survey, *Letters and Art in New Zealand.* She asked Helen Simpson to assist her and together they provided almost 40 close-written sheets of comments, written over several days. The extant material begins directly with the commentary; there are no introductory remarks.

you for a most interesting & enjoyable morning today! Helen S. – husband obligingly gone to the Races – came over & we were so sorry that she had to go home directly after lunch to receive an afternoon visitor. This sounds as if we had embarked on an elaborate critique – but its really that we enjoyed reading & talking about your MS. First she read so far & made her notes, & then I went over it with her & produced my notes. She made the same comment as I on Chap I "How interesting this is! & a new view to me" – It delighted & fortified me to find that she agreed with me on all points, & had noted many of them herself. You will see that they are small & unimportant details – You may think it worth while to adopt one or two of the suggestions, but *we don't expect you to*, and shall not be disconcerted if you resist. (H. said *she* had felt obliged to resist most of the suggestions made to *her*!) I only hope you won't think it impertinent & bumptious of me to put down all these trivial points. Its a sign of zeal & interest & gratitude & affection.[1]

[...]

Don't for a moment think please that our little cautions detract from our recognition of your success. Miraculous success, we feel, knowing the hindrances of your overburdened days.

[...]

Tuesday afternoon

[...]

How queer, dear Critick, to be borrowing your role!

We think the book is *very good* & see what a colossal labour it must have entailed. You'll have to imagine our pleasure in the parts we *havn't* questioned – our exclamations of "How good" "That's excellent" "All that's extremely well put" "Now isn't that interesting" etc. etc.

Some day I'll show you the MS. with our V.G.'s in the margin.[2]

Some corrections are attempts to make the sense clearer where we have been baffled at first reading, (sometimes are still uncertain).

Others for the sound. My inclination has been to make it move along more *quickly* by removing perhaps unnecessary epithets, or turns of phrase. [...]

And there are some words you use too often – of course because you havn't the time, or have been too tired – to look for others. A few we object to altogether – we know we are old-fashioned.

And as a couple of Victorians we have a slight grievance – you despise us, we feel, too much! You re-iterate the reproach, but as H. S. said It's *his* book! & if he feels like that, I know I must lump it!

---

[1] The last four words appear to have been added later, as an afterthought.

[2] The typescript is still in Bethell's papers – but with surprisingly few 'V.G.'s in the margin.'

[...]

Wednesday

Helen S. has been talking to me over the telephone & says she's in a panic about the impertinence & daring – and so am I of course – only worse. We ought to be sending *praise* – but *that's* not wanted for the printer! You said your book wd. be *dull* – & I came to it expecting that because of the *subject* – (such unknown country to me) but it isn't – its interesting & very often entertaining – & gives a very good view over the whole – I've gained a lot from it – we are longing to see the last 2 Ch's – (I'm surprised that there is enough left for *two*.)

Its been a "labour of love" and *gratitude* on both our parts – you've been *so* good & helpful to us – so we *hope* our impoliteness won't offend – & that it *may* be of a little use here & there. We wish we'd had more time to do it calmly. (I told H. *she* needn't worry because it was *my* responsibility, calling her in.)

Good luck to the last lap & my love & any apology that may be fitting

M. U. B.

Alexander Turnbull Library. MS-Papers-0166-14.

TO PAT LAWLOR – AUGUST 12, 1940

As from 47 Webb St Christchurch
At Timaru.

Dear Mr. Lawlor[1]

I am sorry that my thanks for your kind note have been so long delayed – the reason is, you see, that I was away from home. It is always a pleasure to hear that one's writings have found a new reader who likes them – that you propose to write an article to make them better known adds to the pleasure, & this partly because, as you know, books of verse are not best-sellers! I am afraid, however, that I have an incurable aversion from emerging from private life, & had rather you dwelt on the verses, & not on the writer's history. And I hope you will excuse me too from sending a photograph – in fact I have not one to send. My shyness was such that the first book – "From a Garden in the Antipodes" – was published under an assumed name (Evelyn Hayes) but I agreed with Dr.

[1] Pat Lawlor (1893-1979) is best known as a journalist, but also wrote poetry and fiction, was an avid and discerning book-collector, and became, in 1934, the central figure in the establishment of the writers' organisation, PEN. His innate conservatism and staunch Catholicism, however, sometimes had him at odds with younger and more radical writers from the late 1930s.

Simpson that the time had come when it would be more sensible to call me by the real one, now that most people who are interested in the poetry know who the author is.

About "From a Garden." It was published in London by Sidgwick & Jackson about 1927 – Whitcombe & Tombs are supposed to stock it. I don't know whether the Wellington branch still has it, but there were a couple of copies in the ChCh shop not long ago. Until lately I have kept a few copies by me to give to friends, or sometimes sell to people who found the 7/6 or 8/- charged by shops too much for their purses – (the book was published at 5/- & discount is allowed to authors). Because of an illness & then the war I have neglected to send for more & must attend to this, but it will be many weeks before they can arrive. I could lend you a copy but several people in Wellgn have it – for instance Miss Duggan whom you must know – and it is in the Parliamentary Library & the Turnbull.

I would gladly answer any questions or give any details for your own information, to explain the verses for instance in The Garden – which were written from the point of view of a new-comer – & if you know Sydney it might amuse you to connect the pseudonym of Hayes with Vaucluse.*[1]

For the public I could furnish some rather interesting facts relating to the publication of The Garden – but these are noted in ChCh – where I expect to be at the end of the week.

With many thanks for your letter

Yours sincerely
M. U. Bethell

(*Some of the pieces in The Garden were first printed in a Sydney magazine called 'The Home' or something like that.)[2]

Alexander Turnbull Library. 77-067-1/2.

TO PAT LAWLOR – SEPTEMBER 2, 1940

St Faith's. 47 Webb St. ChCh.

Dear Mr. Lawlor

Please forgive this tardy answer – I have been getting over influenza.

---

[1] Now a heritage property, Vaucluse House in Sydney is most commonly associated with William Charles Wentworth, perhaps the most prominent politician in 19th century New South Wales. However, the original (very modest) Vaucluse was built by Bethell's ancestor, the Irishman Sir Henry Hayes, who had been deported for abducting and forcibly marrying a young heiress.

[2] For details, see the letter to Sidgwick, Nov. 4, 1929.

I will give you my biography, tho it doesn't seem to me to have much bearing on the poetry, and, if I am not being too tiresome, would ask to see, before you print it, what you pick out for the Public.

I was born in 1874 & my first book (The "Garden") was published in 1927.[1] So you see I am not "a Writer" – it was without any thought of publication that the Garden verses were written.

Born in Surrey, England – brought to N.Z. as a baby, childhood in the country – (Canterbury) – After some schooling in NZ educated in England & abroad. Returned to N.Z. end of 1892. Returned to England end of '95 or early '96 (I forget). Lived abroad for 2 years to study music & painting – then to England – worked (at Boys Clubs etc) in South East London & in Dundee, Scotland from '98 till 1902 – broke down in health & convalesced in California & N. Z. Back in England 1904 – out to N Z again 1908 – Lived in ChCh – Returned to England 1913 (5 months in India en route) Was in Switzerland when the "Great War" broke out & returned to London for the duration – occupied in "social work" & some "war work" with rests in the country. To N.Z. again 1919 & have remained here, but for 6 months in England in 1926. (These journeys were not restlessness – there were reasons for the migrations.)

For 10 years from 1924 I shared a home on the Cashmere Hills with a dear friend who died suddenly in 1934. During these years all my verse was written. I made & enjoyed a lovely garden & some of the poetry was prompted in the garden, & some while we were driving out in our car, or walking on the hills. If I could get out of this town, where I have lived since I sold our home, I might write again – I don't know – I am growing old. This last paragraph may explain the books to you, but you will readily understand that it relates to my *private* life.

With regard to "From a Garden" etc. the facts I thought would interest you are in the following paragraph taken from the Publisher's Preface to "A Faggot of Verse" published by Sidgwick & Jackson 1930.[2]

"The MSS of poems from which selections have been made for this book were submitted at various times during the past few years by the five authors. One by one the publishers rejected them – for economic reasons – but with unceasing regret that so much good poetry should be suppressed; and thus the present venture, a cooperative anthology, was evolved.

One of the five MSS was the 999th of 1000 poetical MSS (exclusive of those of poets of known standing) received, registered, and read by the publishers in the decade which ended 31st December 1929. Of the

[1] Corrected to 1929 in another hand, presumably that of Lawlor.

[2] Bethell has already alluded to this volume; see her first letter to Schroder, July 21, 1931.

1000 MSS. the publishers have accepted & published fifteen, by twelve authors. Two of the fifteen volumes have paid their way. The twelve authors have shared £73.4.4. The publishers have lost, on the fifteen books, a little more than double that sum."

You, with your experience, will recognize the bearing of that notice upon my little book. I did not, however, share in that £73! – not enough copies were sold to bring me any royalties, & so far I'm afraid the venture has been a loss to the publishers. They are not an advertising firm, & Mr. F. Sidgwick (who, alas, died last year) did not envisage a NZ "market" – which I now think was the one to be appealed to!

The verses were written for pleasure. A friend who was in N Z at the time, remarked when I read some of them aloud, that they were "good enough to be printed" – and nine of them appeared in an Australian Magazine in 1926 or 1927. Afterward I sent the whole set Home to an old friend, scholarly & distinguished, who would know what to do with them. He passed them on to Sidgwick & Jackson[1] – (personal friends) who replied *in a private letter* "We feel that we cannot afford to give the go-by to anything as good as this, & we should like to publish it this autumn. It is our duty to do so, but it will also be a pleasure – and it may or may not be a burden. As you say the author is aware that poetry as a rule is not remunerative, we should propose that, while we of course bear all costs of publication, the author should not receive a royalty until the sales have covered the costs – if they do!"

I paid for the production of "Time & Place" & 1/2 share of "Day & Night" – sales of the former came near to reimbursing me & I had hoped that "Day & Night" would bring back enough to justify bringing out a better done edition (the first being exhausted) of "Time & Place" but so far I have received nothing myself, though I believe the Caxton Press has almost recouped its outlay. However I still wish to reprint "Time & Place" in a format to resemble the other two – the pieces in "Time & Place" were – for obvious reasons – carefully chosen.

I have written the foregoing (in some haste!) for your personal information & not for publication.

Thank you again for your interest. Hoping to meet you later on.

Yours sincerely
M. U. Bethell

Alexander Turnbull Library. 77-067-1/2.

[1] Initially, Mayhew submitted the manuscript to his own publisher, Faber.

TO JOHN SUMMERS – OCTOBER 6, 1940

As from 47 Webb St. Christchurch.

Dearest John Summers,

I wanted so much to write to you before leaving town yesterday – in answer to 2 letters from you – but could not manage it – Everything takes me much too long these days – First I must tell you that I wrote to you at the first Taranaki address & am afraid missed you – (You don't say why you moved on?) I told you in that letter why I had been silent for so long, having been pretty poorly again since Influenza early in August. Now I have escaped from that dismal town, & feel a different person already. Its the most gorgeous day here. I am sitting out of doors – blue mountains with snow on them – & all the pastures vivid green – & willows still brighter green. I am at my brother's farm for the weekend & then going on to cousins above Waiau. I must have told you that my brother has been in hospital in ChCh for a month – had an operation on the very morning his son went off to the war! I used to go along to see him most days, & that was all I could manage on top of my house jobs. He is getting on very well now & I think it has given him a fresh start for his task of running the farm again. He is a very nice man & much beloved & respected in the district.

[...]

I don't think I have turned warwards as you said – The more I read of it the more I loathe it and the growing spirit of hatred. Of course one must admire the skill and daring of our sailors and air men – but alas, its the fruits of the skill and daring one has to think of and only time shows the whole horror. But now it seems of little use to study the rights & wrongs of warfare – we are *in* it & we can't be out of it do what we will – what a young man's duty is – that is too difficult for me. My turn wd. come if I were conscripted into a munitions factory – the case is not impossible. I don't believe I could ever throw myself wholeheartedly into the cause as my sister could & does. *She* has never had any misgivings – to fight Hitler is a Christian task to her eyes – She has no fear & writes calmly & cheerfully & says I'm not to leave off telling her trivial things, since we must keep life as natural as possible in the face of pandemonium.

The reading I've done lately (& not much of that) is more on the line of how to make the world better in the future. The Archbishop of York is saying that if we don't do that – if we only mean to put things back where they were before, then we have lost the war. I should like to show you some of this literature. I am sorry you have strayed so far away! I suppose its of no use to send you books just now unless you have some time on Sundays – or would you like some small ones? I have that book on verse you asked for, put aside. I am sending some newscuttings on subjects you were interested in. I suppose they might as well come back some day. I have Burnaby's Lectures on The Love of God – mostly about St Augustine's religion.[1] You wd. like them. A big book – Eros & Agape again. (I don't much care for the phrase in one of those cuttings "mystic riches of death"! Death is a horror, an enemy – only welcome in Christ.)

[...]

It is now afternoon. My brother is resting, my sister in law has gone off to play golf, which seems to me to be such a waste of this lovely day! I am sitting out in the garden she made very cleverly – There are glades with drifts of narcissus under the trees, lawns, & on the other sides of the creek a bit of the swamp has been turned into a rose garden, with great trees behind it – beyond is the plain & the mountains & the clearest blue sky. I feel here how miserable it is to be mewed up in ChCh – never to *see out*. I wish I could see my way to a move, but never get any light on the problem. Anyhow I must get away from ChCh next winter.

I think I have been rather selfish & *aloof* so far about this war, but there will be plenty of time yet – it will spread. As far as "war effort" goes the government can *take* all the money it wants – but refugees e.g. must be helped. I am sending a contribution to student relief. I worked hard in the last war.

This is my 66th birthday – it is going by unnoticeably, as I should wish, with just good wishes from my people. In town there are friends who bring me flowers etc. My 60th birthday was the last festival one – what a day that was – we kept up the celebrations all the way. And the little one in *such pain*. She wouldn't show – I often think she must have had a sense of what was coming. Just a month to her death – I live those days again. The heartache never goes – *the world's pain does not diminish one's own private grief, does it.* The loveliest thing today is that the special bird has been singing – I have never heard him at this place before – There are many other birds – magpies, thrushes, & some I don't know, but riro is the best. Its a concert.

I think the hard physical work is probably the best thing for you just now. By the way I suppose your letter wd. have told me if your name was drawn in this ballot. No one I know so far was drawn.

[...]

Now darling Johnny I must get on to another letter. I do like to hear from you – so try to send a few words. I never forget you. As you

---

[1] John Burnaby, *Amor Dei: a study of the religion of St. Augustine* (1938).

say, what can we do but love one another, & those who loved before, as [the] poet said, let them love more now[1] –

So I send you mine & a kiss.
F.

Private collection.

TO ERIC MCCORMICK – OCTOBER 15, 1940

As from 47 Webb St ChCh.

My dear Eric

Helen's comments should have gone to you direct – I have contributed nothing.[2]

These short instalments leave one hungry for more! I came across country in a Bus from Waiau today – wild & magnificent & have just had dinner at a Kaikoura hostelry & am sitting on a sort of terrace with the ocean lapping below – such an exotic scene. I feel its Italy – or some stranger place. A very mild air & what I think are Norfolk Island pines at intervals along the shore. The mountains are snow topped – rosy sunset glow on them & on the sea & in the sky – colours one can only call "opalescent" I think.

I expect to be back in ChCh about the end of the week.

[...]

So nice to think I may be seeing you quite soon!

Meanwhile love from
M U B.

Alexander Turnbull Library. MS-Papers-0166-14.

TO PAT LAWLOR – OCTOBER 18, 1940

As from 47 Webb St. Christchurch.

Dear Mr. Lawlor

I am very much obliged to you for letting me see your article[1] – long in getting to me because I am far away in the country & mails are slow –

---

[1] Bethell had recently been re-reading *The Prelude* and may be recalling these lines from Book IV: 'I loved / Loved deeply all that had been loved before, / More deeply even than ever.' Alternatively, she may have in mind Mary Coleridge's 'To an Old Friend,' whose friends 'Vowed that love should not grow colder / That we would love as we loved before, And the years should make us love the more.'

[2] Included with the letter were several more pages of notes on McCormick's *Survey*, many of them in Helen Simpson's hand.

However I remember you said there was no hurry about printing the notice – so I hope the delay won't matter. I am even going to suggest a further delay:– I am making a short visit to Wellington at the end of the month – could you hold over publication till after that, so that we might have a little conversation first? I should be glad if that could be.

Meanwhile I find that I should still prefer to have even so much of biographical detail withheld. I could not I think be called "timid" or "bashful" – but personalities in print set my teeth on edge, & I would rather let the books make their way, or fail to do so, on their merits or demerits as books. Let it be granted that the sentence you quote from Dr. Simpson is overpraise[2] (I am to be sure a little sorry that you cite it) even so it is a critical judgment, & to point out that the poetry is bad & why, is a critical judgment, & criticism either way helps to place a book, but I don't think that chat or surmise about a writer does that. (Rather a different case when its an established author to be dealt with?)

Again it is not quite the fact that my verse has not had recognition – there was a good notice about "The Garden" in the London N. Z. paper on its publication,[3] & later a long review in the "Press" (ChCh) by Mr. Schroder. And there was a very good article by D'Arcy Cresswell in 'Tomorrow' when 'Time & Place' appeared. And Mr. Schroder gave the whole of a book review broadcast to 'Day & Night'. And Father Walsh in Wellington has noticed the verse in broadcast & reviews. And there have been other references to the books beyond the circle of my friends, but as I said before, I should be glad, if only for the sake of the Caxton Press & related financial considerations, if the books had more attention drawn to them.

I write in a hurry to catch a mail, or would like to touch on one or two other points (G. M. Hopkins e.g. – I had not read him when most of the verse was written!) I count, however, on your kindness to allow me to discuss them with you shortly – and thank you for what you have said – I was so pleased that you turned mostly to 'Time & Place' which is least known I think.

With kind regards

Yours very truly
M. U. Bethell

---

[1] A typescript of the article is still in Lawlor's papers, though there is no evidence it was ever printed. Intended, no doubt, for a South Island paper, 'ML's Undiscovered Poet' was lightly revised, both to take account of Bethell's reservations, and later to acknowledge her death.

[2] See the letter to Brasch above, May 28, 1940.

[3] The book was reviewed anonymously in *New Zealand News*, Dec. 3, 1929.

P. S. In case I forget – may the garden *not* be called "homely" it wasn't at all that! I must have failed to convey it to you rightly!

Alexander Turnbull Library. 77-067-1/2.

TO ERIC MCCORMICK – [LATE 1940 / EARLY 1941]

47 Webb St. ChCh.

Oh Eric darling,* what a splendid letter! For that's how I must take it – a chance to thrash out a better understanding? otherwise it might depress me dreadfully – for I do think you "take me up wrong."[1]

[Added below] (* Note well – this adjective = spontaneous – unthinking – and addressed-to-a-contemporary – to-an-Equal. *Not* a Babe = expression-of-affection. Often on my lips before 1934 – seldom now!)

How *obstinate* you are! Did you not believe me when I told you some time ago that I did *not* mix you up with others, but kept you entirely separate? Or have you forgotten?

Of course, 34 = Prime of Life – (you might have added to your historical instances, the age of the Crucifixion – "it is finished"[2] – it should be the Greek) but *relatively* young. (I shall have to run on to pages of exegesis like the DD's expounding the scriptures!) When I said (I remember) "young important friends" not expected to write to me, I was quite candid & humble *not* patronising (*Stupid*!) It was partly an admonition to myself – *You* are old & on the shelf & out of it – You are getting on for seventy – Why should you be written to by a busy young man doing important work? He counts in the world. He's making his life. Yours is finishing up. *Never* let them think "Tiresome old woman, I suppose I ought to write to her" – (Stupid fellow can't you *see*?) When my interest or my affection's roused I am afraid of forgetting this old age stage, & have to put myself in my place. (I *am* old, I am lonely, I am tired, tired, *tired* – but I know I must go on, & learn more things – entsagung sollst du!)[3]

My query about yr. social criticism, therefore, had nothing to do with *age*. Have you "got that"?

This [was] what was in my mind when I said that "*perhaps* you didn't *really* know" (I remember that). In letters I think aloud – (that is, I write unthinkingly! –) but this is what was in my mind:- You know that women

---

[1] McCormick's letter has not survived, but its general content can be gleaned from Bethell's rejoinders.

[2] See John 19: 30.

[3] Ger. Although these words occur, just so, in Genesis 3: 17, as part of the curse visited on Adam ('with suffering shall you feed yourself), they do not really make sense here.

are proverbially "personal" – They *are*. I don't think in terms of classes, and civilisations etc. I think of this person, & that, & that – (Oh I dare say a young woman university graduate today thinks easily in terms of classes, social history etc. – but I am a Victorian.) My thought was: if he *knew* this person & that – my brother for instance – knew them really well – he would not only like them, he would love them, & there wouldn't be this bitter tone of *resentment* about England etc.

Good of their kind (I am going through your attack line by line!) You mustn't take me as a *sample* of a Country (England) or a Class! I wouldn't be a good specimen – I am too variegated. Now my brother *is* a good specimen of his sort, all of a piece – and a very nice person indeed. So is my nephew – but not such a good *sample* – belongs to a more mixed generation. That's one of the sad things about me! – I don't belong anywhere in particular – I've dodged to and fro – my friends are of all sorts of classes & countries – I'm not a fair *sample* – I have not been able to settle, always there was some event, some frustration – "no road". So please don't ticket me like that, – "*tag*" the Americans say.

I didn't know that I talked so much about England, and the past. I must "watch out" – I suppose I cast about for something interesting to tell! There's not very much to be said about my actual life of domestic toil! (Apart from Wellington "debauches"!) Yes, I suppose I do dwell on the past. Isn't it a characteristic of advancing years? No, I don't judge N. Z. or "take up an attitude of superiority" – I don't really think about it! But if I *sound* as if I did, I must be more careful. (Do you, Sir, take up an attitude of superiority about N. Z.??? Oh its ridiculous) I believe its *you* attacking England who are the "Aggressor"!

I did not (*intend* to, at all events) "indignantly repudiate" the suggestion of NZ as a birth place. I don't recall the occasion – but it wouldn't have been meant seriously.

You say that I ought to know more about N. Z. I daresay that is true. But up on the hill we had our hands pretty full, & were so happy in our little life, we didn't *want* to move round in ChCh. I'll admit that I have always disliked ChCh as a place to live in – (not the Hill). After Effie went I began to realise that I ought to throw myself more into life out here – since I wasn't going back. And I've tried to – tho' my life down here is in a narrow groove of course.

No, I don't look back to England thru' "rose-coloured haze" – I look at it through tears, that's all.

"Indulgent patroness" – well, there must be some grave fault of voice or manner if that's how I strike you! I should like to amend it – but how can it be done if I am unconscious of it? I was tempted to exclaim "Good heavens, does he really dislike me all that much?" – but surely there must be some love or liking or you wouldn't bother to write all these reproaches! No, I will trust my first intuitions, & believe that we are meant to be friends, really – Oh no, any imagination about "patronage" is *very* much beside the mark – I wd. admit having "humoured" you perhaps at times – because such a sweet-natured person couldn't (There, I used up all that writing block & must take some of the cherished Rise Cottage residue) *couldn't* be so irritable if he were not utterly over-tired. (But teased, too, sometimes I am afraid, for one of my nasty qualities has been (less, now) the tendency to tease – even to the verge of cruelty.)

It was a mistake to tell you about those reasons for not marrying – he was so pathetic I thought – but it was the *nobility* of his attitude as well as the pity that struck me – & that was bound up with the whole of his character & his surroundings – (And in relation to that I might well fit *you* with blinkers dear – you don't understand *everything*!) The same boy (so I think of him tho' precisely your age I believe – & this is a good opportunity of reiterating that I *don't* think of *you* as a boy!) [so] disliked & despised the 'gilded youth' of the Oxford Col. he was sent to that he refused to stay more than a term!

And now we come to your crowning query – "What do I make of the Beatitudes?" And what is the bearing of *that* query? You know well enough that here are the laws professing Christians pray every day to have written on their hearts! Now dear porcupine, throw away those spikes! Be sensible. Don't be smart. I *accept* your prods, because I know very well that if you've an *impression* of artificiality, pose, pride there's something in me to give rise to that impression, there *is*, & those laws are not written deep enough in my nasty, stony heart. You are a particularly sincere & real person, as well as kind and sympathetic, and so I know that you have reason to scold – that there really *is* something rotten in me that corresponds – (tho' I am not sure that you give the right names to it.)

On the other [hand] why are *you* so touchy and suspicious? *Are* you really mature?

I have just [been] reading over the Beatitudes Sermon – Luke's narrative.[1] Blest are you poor, for yours is the Kingdom of God – blest are you who hunger now, for you shall be satisfied, blest are you who weep now, for you shall laugh, blest are you when men shall hate you ... for the Son of Man's sake – Love your enemies, bless those who curse you (- - - so I bless you for *your* curses Eric!) Luke hasn't the one I love best: Blest are the pure in heart – they shall see God.[2] (And *that* has a

[1] See Luke 6: 20-23.

[2] See Matthew 5: 8.

long ago remembrance of St. Mary's Oxford! – an occasion you'd probably scoff at). Poetry it is. But if you rake up the Sermon on the Mount where do I stop? – Presently it goes on to motes & beams.[1] Shall I take a microscope & look for some motes? For instance, why do you – no, no you have plenty of time to work it out! I have so little *Time* left. My sister I recollect wrote to me when I was getting to my forties "I see that you are getting middle-aged – I notice that you are more *tolerant*." I'll stop. There's one going into town who will take my mail to G. P. O.

Please Critick (de Moeurs!)[2] try to love my good points (if any!) as I love yours.

MUB

Alexander Turnbull Library. MS-Papers-3381.

TO MONTE HOLCROFT – MARCH 16, 1941

St Faith's House. Webb St. Christchurch.

Dear Monte

(or used you to end it with 'y' – it is so long ago, I forget)

At long last I am writing to you about your book. Ill-health was the reason I did not write congratulations when the Prize essay was announced[3] – and then I thought I should like to read it before writing & wondered how & when it wd. appear. Then when I was in Wellington, Denis Glover sent me the notice of its publication & finally I acquired it & have been trying to write to you ever since – I'm not very strong now & I "do for myself" & the daily round leaves me so tired I can't write in the evenings as a rule & I get 'all behind' with overseas letters – my sister & friends in England, my nephew with the army in Egypt. But no more excuses!

Even now I write at a disadvantage, without the book beside me. I lent it to a man in hospital I thought wd. appreciate it & his daughter carried it off without asking my permission – & lent to her vicar & then rang & asked whether I knew your address, as he liked it so much he wished to write to you. Not knowing her vicar, I do not know whether you will find him an acceptable correspondent. I have been struck by the different kinds of people who do like your book.

[...]

---

[1] See Luke 6: 41-42.

[2] Fr. 'of manners, behaviour, morals.'

[3] Holcroft's *The Deepening Stream* was awarded first prize in the essay section of the Centennial Literary Competition.

The man in hospital is, or was, a carpenter – he likes my verse & I felt sure he wd. like your essay. But how tiresome people are about not buying books! – they always want to borrow them & it comes to this, that one needs to buy a desirable book in duplicate. I see that I shall have to get a lending copy of yours. For the result of lending it is that I have not read it *thoroughly* myself – only one chapter has been dwelt on by me – about the forest. I think myself that the colonists came with too strong a sense of acquisition & possession to be sensitive to those influences of which you speak. A few of us may have experienced the forest in that way, but we are not making a living from it! My relations & friends in the country look at the land thinking what it will produce per acre & with more or less respect. My own family do respect it & feel a tie between them & their acres (English tradition?) & would not work it to exhaustion, but I hear of really ruthless farmers who have not that respect. We've lost not only the animistic shudder, I think, but the biblical sense that "the earth is the Lord's"[1] – (I had some thoughts of this kind which were to be the burden of some more verses but my present mode of life leaves no vitality for writing.)

You must in this work, I think, feel that you have come nearer to your ambition as an author – it is a serious & solid achievement – & I am glad to find that your present post must have afforded considerable leisure in which to express & formulate your thoughts. Perhaps another time I may be able to tell you something of how the other chapters strike me, but today I must be content with offering a general congratulation. And I want to say that I was touched by your reference to my poetry, & much pleased, & I think I do understand what you mean about that (tho' others have said that they don't.)[2] I am glad that you think the best are in 'Time & Place' – the pieces were very carefully chosen for that collection. (The 'Garden' comes into a different category I think.) I should like to have another edition done when I can afford it – the first one is out of print.

With good wishes for *more* writing

from yr. old friend
M.U.Bethell

Alexander Turnbull Library. MS-Papers-1186-03.

---

[1] See Psalm 24: 1.

[2] Holcroft commented on the diffidence of recent poets 'in drawing attention to the hills and bush,' contrasting them with Bethell 'whose contacts with an older culture allowed her to discover an essential beauty while remaining apart from the intellectual difficulties of the native school of writers' (p. 20).

TO CHARLES BRASCH – MARCH 16, 1941

47 Webb St. Christchurch NZ.

Dear Charles

I wonder how many half finished letters I've torn up – the last to you is dated Feb 24 – while I was spending a few days at my nephew's farm near Waikari – something prevented its being finished. At home I am nearly always too tired, lately, after the day's jobs, to put pen to paper. As I think I said before, it seems difficult, increasingly so, to write to England – impossible to rid one's self of the feeling that one's small antipodean affairs must be an *intrusion* – Yet I do see that it may be pleasant to hear from a corner of the world where things are – so far – fairly peaceful & really more or less as usual. The tension for the onlooker is at the moment severe – raids renewed over England – the Balkans – the far East. However I've just been listening to Roosevelt's speech – & he sounds as if he were confident that U.S.A. has the matter well in hand!

[...]

I must tell you first what a comfort the gramophone is – very refreshing to have that music when I am tired, & I hope that my letter about the investment of yr. present was not sunk en route.[1] [...] Music certainly is a cordial for a mewed up life when one can't get out to see the land & hear the silence as I did on those Waikari hills. It really is aggravating, in this country, not to be able to go out & buy what one wants! [...]

March 20

Interruptions – & it was too wet yesterday for my char. to come so I have had more to do. A wild southerly & floods everywhere – the break up of our long lovely *drought* – ChCh has settled into its bog for the winter – but the land needed the rain.

Tension has been growing daily – indeed one cable in the Press today says the invasion of England may be a matter of *hours*. It is very terrible to think of. By this time we have had descriptions of the over-running of Holland & France. I think the growing *hatred* and suspicion is so awful – but we knew it would be like that. I believe it is true, as you say, that there *is* a core of peace in me – tho' I am far from being conscious of it always – I think that at the bottom of my *heart* there is fear – a legacy from childhood the psychologists wd. rightly say – but at the bottom of my *mind* there is confidence. Nothing that one can see or prove but a conviction & its not one that experience stultifies. Do you

---

[1] Bethell had purchased the gramophone with money sent by Brasch.

remember where it says in Pilgrim's Progress "Courage, my brother! I feel the bottom & it is good" – one of the characters, might have been Mr. Fearing who turned out so well after all, was crossing the last river.[1] But the present time *is* very dark.

You ask for news of Toss & his circle. He has an all the year round job now & I am afraid his painting has gone into the background. But the younger son must compensate for that. He is said to be very lively. I refuse to call him Paul, so ugly with the surname. Peter Paul is the nearest I can get. A room *with glazed windows* has been added. Rodney says its a vast improvement. He is not at Mapua but at some distance on a tobacco farm with his friend Colin O'Cahon[2] who is a C.O. & in the last ballot for overseas – Toss as the father of 2 *and* a Quaker is out of it for some time. I don't know about Rodney – I think he will be a firm C.O. John Summers has resigned from the Friends & says he will ask for Ambulance but will fight if forced to. Lawrence Baigent was in last ballot & took a firm stand & was let off unconditionally. His friend Leo's case stood over, but I gather that he is left undisturbed. George & Paul are in camp – G. driving ambulance or transport truck in North Is. – P. hospital orderly – neither called overseas yet. E. McCormick is just going or may even have gone, with medical unit. I shall miss him very much. Another Quaker, you don't know I think, an electrician came the other evg to tell me of his engagement at Xmas & that he is in this last ballot. He thinks he will lose his job – doesn't want to be let off easily. He wd. like to copy the Toss way of living – it *is* a foundation for a good society. Very much exercised about the question of bringing children to this troublous world. I said go on, go on! This planet never has been *secure*!

[...]

I must have told you already that I read – in fact *bought* in order to read! the novel Man Alone & thought it as good as you said.[3] Its praised, you'll see, in the Survey.

[...]

I am carrying on here – in fact I suppose it will be Webb St "for the duration". I have been getting the premises into better order, within & without. The kind Schroders came to help out-doors – cut up wood &

---

[1] Quoted in an earlier letter to Kennedy, Oct. 16, 1936.

[2] Bethell knew his name to be McCahon, but preferred O'Cahon as more euphonious. See her letter to Kennedy Jan. 14, 1944.

[3] Brasch had described it as 'a good whole, economically written in a very toned-down style, & well told, with some fine description (*not* purple passages, but well woven into the narrative) of wild country in the North Island. I doubt whether you'd *enjoy* it; it is as arid & little rosy a story as possible – arid like the appearance of our time; but a good book, I think, one of the very very few good N.Z. novels.' (Aug. 10, 1940)

made a bonfire. But when I was roaming about the limestone hills near Waikari the other day I shuddered to think of ChCh. The air is so light there – filled me with vitality. I thought of a cottage at Waikari – but oh dear, on the other hand, I should never see any *people*! One of the letter-beginnings I've destroyed (un-finished so long, out of date) was to you, written under an aromatic gum-tree on my nephew's land. Do you remember the blue gum stand just beyond Amberly? It was in never such full flower when I went by at Christmas, which I spent at my brother's. Its hard for him without the soldier son's help, but the younger one divides his time between the 2 stations, 25 miles apart, & he's tired too. Its getting harder for farmer's wives – girls all going to 'patriotic' jobs.

I still read once a week to Miss Allen. Her brother was there the other day. I confess to finding him very heavy going! those self-absorbed people are so exhausting & he knows so little, in reality, about his chosen "line' – English literature. He is the exact opposite of his sister, who is always a tonic. But he's a kind, good fellow. Pity he did not persevere with being a parson & mix up with "life" not "letters". I meant to tell you about an English schoolboy aged 17 (= N.Z. 25) a classic! who's come out for 2 yrs & spent 2 Sunday afternoons with me but there's no time & space. This must be posted today for I'm sending by Pacific Air – its been so absurdly delayed. With every good wish, wherever you are.

Yrs affectly
Ursula Bethell

Hocken Library. MS-0996-3/19.

To J H E Schroder – [late March, 1941]

47 Webb St. ChCh.

Dear Mr. Schroder

Many thanks. I like it very much – I like its *warmth*. I did not know that the Press one was yours[1] – & had thought that perhaps disproportionate space had been given (as in the case of the Women Survey) to limitations that couldn't be helped. But in the light of the broadcast I understand that you were defending our author from & explaining him to detractors – I had heard one such hostile review which this must have adequately answered. I hope that Mr. McCormick heard yr. review or has had the script from Mr. Duff (who sent me, you may remember, yr. kind remarks about myself.) I think I am within my rights

[1] In addition to giving a broadcast review, Schroder also reviewed in print McCormick's *Letters and Art in New Zealand* in *The Press*, March 15, 1941.

in typing a copy to tuck into the Survey? At any rate I've written to offer a copy to the surveyor in case he hasn't it – tho' its possible the contingent may have left "so sudden at the last"[1] they go. I have a deep regard for him personally & that is why I enjoyed the 'warmth' as well as a great respect for his critical judgement, & will not myself question his dicta, – certainly not those respecting the author of The Garden etc – *And* I was *well* content with what he said[2] – having been uneasy about my dear friend's passage in the Women – personal partiality I'm afraid & needing counterpoise – But I have to thank you incidentally for another little – what my family call "write up"! When I read such approval I feel a desire to get my residual fragments out of their drawer & work on them. But I'm always washing up.

I am to view the Art Exhibn[3] in company with Helen Simpson tomorrow & will give her the M.S. I expect she will want to carry it home, & return it to you herself.

Again thank you – & *If*, on a balmy day, you feel an uncontrollable urge to open air employment, I could offer wood chopping.

Yours sincerely
Ursula Bethell

Alexander Turnbull Library. fMS-018.

TO KATHLEEN TAYLOR – [JUNE 18, 1941]

c/- Mrs. McIver. Ludstone Terrace, Kaikoura[4]
Wedy. 8.30 am. Still abed

Well my darling new treasure Katya,[5]

How are you this morning I wonder – I am rested & cosy. A wild & bitter wind blows without – but its a different kind of cold, rousing, not withering like ChCh clammy cold. I went to bed by a wood fire wh. smells & looks nice, but takes a deal of stoking to make it at all effectual. Neither railway, bus, or landlady in the least impressed by amount of

[1] This phrase occurs in *Rose Mather: A Tale of the War* (1868), by the American domestic novelist Mary Jane Holmes.

[2] McCormick wrote that 'Evelyn Hayes ... has written nothing that does not bear upon it the marks of a distinguished and sensitive mind, and she has shown New Zealand that the work of a woman poet can be refined without sacrifice of strength or complexity' (p. 185).

[3] The annual exhibition of the Canterbury Society of Arts.

[4] Bethell spent almost two months on extended holiday here, in rather spartan conditions: she described it to Brasch as 'a camping sort of life' (July 11, 1941).

[5] Bethell provides, on several occasions, an account of her meeting with the young schoolteacher, Kathleen Taylor, and of the development of their friendship.

luggage! (wh. has neatly disappeared under the second bedstead in this room) in fact I could have done with yet another box, containing jugs, kettles, saucepans, tins etc – landlady seems rather short of such commodities (Goodness! a military march has just begun on a fine loud wireless – preparatory to news no doubt – yes, L explains that she only listens once a day – sensible woman – This means there will be a chance of music sometimes). *But* (re luggage continued) the panic at the Ry Stn. still causes rankling shame. I have reviewed the occurrence – a clear case of mental aberration & nervous inadequacy – & cause of needless fatigue, worry & upset to others – Deplorable – I KNEW perfectly well that the back verandah was left a blank & that the black case was on the taxi! – I'd *seen* it there – & yet, when I could not see it in the van, my brain froze & I could only go back to the pre-taxi situation. Such is panic! It frightens me rather that I should lose my brain control in this way – am I fitted to manage my own affairs? But I must say that I have become so used to seeing myself off, that I am much more *composed* by myself, & concentrate on the job – instead of chatting to you etc. (I *loved* having you dear don't mistake me) – knowing that I alone am responsible. Of *course* I should have seen all the bits on to the train before going to carriage. I shan't feel any better till I hear how you got on – not late for school – not too tired – but I'm afraid you *must* have been very tired & hungry – I hope that some of the P.C.s notes & telegrams – handed to postal employees at stations – *did* arrive!

I say nothing about needless expense – that's part of my punishment! Besides, the luggage wasn't weighed! I usually arrive covered with "EXCESS" labels.

Next I want to say that you weren't thanked enough my dear for all you did – it all seemed so *natural* – I am afraid I just accepted it – but its delightful to look back on – People are so kind – but you know it makes all the difference when its the *right* person doing the things & the naturalness is part of the charm. Dear me, how *very* surprising its all been! Miraculous in fact. [...]

Journey thru' lovely country & much to be preferred I thought to all the way [by] Bus. More beautiful in spring, but the snow made it unusual. Wish you were coming *here* for next Mondayish weekend! – it would be fun. Nice walks.

You'll guess that I did not make much impression on the lunch packet wh. continues to feed me here – (I meant *you* to have one of those h.bd. eggs – another aberration). At Waipara about 9.30 I fetched a cup of tea & made a good Breakfast sandwiches etc. Before getting out at Hundalee about 12. Banana & sip of sherry – Landlady had large plate of hot mutton & vegetables ready for me here about 1.45 – "my guest today"

– I was quite right about her. Have learnt more – she's not strong – gastric – peptonised milk diet – but tireless. Clad in old fur coat & cap dashes about premises for wood etc Has a cat & a dog & boards 3 sheep – goes to W.E.A. class one evening a week – Is very generous – Not military thank goodness – (comes of Quaker stock) – but supports war – Her war work ambulance classes, one took place here yesterday aftn. in kitchen. "Poisons" followed by tea. I was safe on my bed.

I am taking a firm line about my arrangements – no shilly shally – This to give her an impression of strong-mindedness!

She has quite a sense of humour.

I am only missing two things: 1. Heal's box-spring mattress. 2. Katya.

Have made preliminary list of 30 letters to be written. There will be more.

[...]

Porte toi bien chèrie[1] – want you to be in that Play. All's well here, except ruefulness about Panic.

With the special love belonging to you
M.U.

Macmillan Brown Library. MB 572. A.

TO KATHLEEN TAYLOR – JUNE 25, [1941]

c/- Mrs. McIver – Ludstone Terrace Kaikoura.

[...]

Its 4.45 & a clear sky & I am beside my wood fire, having just consumed far too much (new) bread & butter – (such a beguiling crusty viennese loaf!). I went for a walk – town-wards – & found yr. letter on return – I was looking out for one today – what a nice long one – Yes, I think a little more of you – but still I have to conjure you up – it must be the absence of the smile my landlady talks about still.[2] [...] Anyhow I am very glad to know all about it – poor little dear you must have paid for the weekend with too much fatigue. No breakfast! That *deadly* ChCh! – how blest I am to be here. I came away just in time [...] Yesterday blew up a rainstorm again & fresh snow on our mountains last night. Sunday *was* a miracle.

[...]

Having tried it, I now am happy to announce that I *don't* mind sharing a room with you! With *you* mind. (Not but what I'd choose a room to myself normally!) Its curiously *natural* to have you about, Katya,

---

[1] Fr. 'Look after yourself, darling.'

[2] Kathleen Taylor had visited and stayed with Bethell on the previous weekend.

I felt it almost from the first – And there'll always be a shakedown at least for you if required.

To think that something bad must happen to counterbalance the good is much too Celtic & primitive for you! – No, *no*, NO. (I cry this "no" because of the struggle in my own mind between faith and unfaith) more than ever we must, mustn't we – trust and pray to the God who is love or we shall be done for – we women, especially – & more especially must a woman who's got a bit past active works exercise herself in these matters.

[...]

A birthday letter but only my love & blessing go with it – you are such a nice present to me perhaps in course of time I'll prove to be a nice one to you. [...] Many happy returns darling. Now it seems to be time to look towards bed, tho' I wanted to make a hanky for the Deaconess [for] her birthday.

A kiss for Katya
from M.U.

[...]

Criticism again: there *are bits* of yr. letter which are *you*! Don't let yourself *congeal* on paper – if you feel yourself stiffening swear loudly and ask Would I *say* this in hot blood? Cling to the one syllabled – I always feel a little ashamed of my underlinings! Every other word almost of my great aunt's letter underlined. Sometimes I think of resorting to capitals instead when I care to emphasise. How I hate italics in printed matter – especially poetry. I think its Coventry Patmore who emphasises with them.

In former letter darling you said you'd cried over some letters. That touched me that you could do that. Its all we *can* do sometimes.

Macmillan Brown Library. MB 572. A.

To Kathleen Taylor – July 2, 1941

c/- Mrs. McIver – Ludstone Terr. Kaikoura.

I've been *panting* for a letter from you dear (understudying Paul[1] one might think!) & what a satisfying one was handed to me just after I came back from the first pleasure walk I've taken since the one we took together! I settled down to it at once, before the hot bath I was looking to – highlight of the week's arrangements! (Has to be in the afternoon –

---

[1] Paul Gabites, brother of George, had originally introduced Kathleen Taylor to Bethell. Bethell's desire for a romantic relationship between the two is a regular theme of ensuing letters.

pipes frozen till noon – boiler cools down after 4 P.M!) Yes! I've got you in this letter, got you nicely – No conjuring required – I was quite depressed about it, do you know, thinking, how could you & P. become better acquainted by letter if you could not get yourself on to paper better than that! No doubt, however, its easier to write to a contemporary – and such a devoted one! I am so pleased with all that detail, so good of you darling – but also naughty – for you must have been up to all hours to get so much written – And while I think of it, you mustn't try to write to *me* on Fridays. No, I am reminded of a French hairdresser in ChCh 45 years ago, who would cut ladies' hairs in the morning, but explained that in the afternoon "Je me consacre aux messieurs."[1] You must consecrate yourself to the monsieur on Fridays mustn't you – I am not quite used to the misleading associations of your script yet! I think a more *shapely* page could be got from you by begging for a wider margin on the left of it!

[...]

I am glad & sorry about the Play – it might have been too much of a tax on you this term & yet if it would have given you a chance of seeing something of more young men its a pity. Your "contacts" just now are too exclusively feminine! Much as I covet you for Paul (as I've never ceased to make plain) I know you ought to experience alternatives – especially now that you know what kind you *don't* want. But all this must be left to Divine Providence – (Presently when we've killed off all our young men there won't be much *choice* for girls!)

[...]

Yesterday I took my lunch out towards the mountains. Missed Katya dreadfully at first, & then fell back to the other miss, which is always there, & always will be. Whether revisiting an old together-place, or investigating a new one, I long for my little dear all the time, & with such a pain. But it was a most beautiful day. Great blobs of yellow gorse against the icy blue ranges, & *such* air – I am afraid however that its too good farming hereabouts – They are beginning to hack away the great gorse hedges & soon they will be bonfires.

[...]

Poetry – So glad you like Time & Place – think my best are in that – very carefully chosen for Effie. I remember how thankful I was to find that I *could* write the Envoy – There are one or two in Day & Night I have a special feeling for, but weren't so suitable for Effie's – I don't know whether there's any poetry left in me now – She used to say "Don't flood the market! Poetry's always *there* you know" – but, I think perhaps

[1] Fr. 'I devote myself to the gentlemen.'

its gone away now together with my heart's Treasure. But when I've done the letter writing job, I'll see. If I were 'getting poetry' & you came up you'd have to settle yourself several yards off as Effie did – at our picnics. No, we must not *scheme* for that. All your appearances so far have been so sweetly miraculous – we must leave it to Providence – If we *schemed*, they might all be wet days & we might get on our nerves each other's I mean & quarrel!

[...]

I must STOP & set off for P.O. It won't do for me to [be] going on writing to Katya at *this* length! Holds up the 30 letters schedule – I should get on so much better with it if I hadn't lost my perfect pen in Wellgn but you don't know about that disaster. [...] Farewell pet. Have a nice evening & give my best love to the Monsieur – I wonder would you care to pass on this letter? Might save me repeating myself to him – & show him we havn't quarrelled *yet*. & a kiss for Katya.

Love
M.U.

Macmillan Brown Library. MB 572. A.

TO KATHLEEN TAYLOR – JULY 10, 1941

[c/- Mrs. McIver. Ludstone Terrace. Kaikoura.]

ANGEL!

I've just carried out another successful smuggle![1] Went to the wash house & into a state of vague disintegration before landlady dashed out to see that my wet coat didn't come into the house. (I didn't mean it to!) How perfect! Everything's there for utter comfort now (perhaps poetry will follow on???) Coffee – just ready for it. Delighted to have own knife & fork & spoon (saves trips to kitchen when I wash them myself). Cake – very glad of it all [...] Good idea walnuts – for picnics when weather clears again – steady rain today. [...] Duster & gloves good – and ersatz button hook o.k. – but you havn't kept a pair of gloves for your own coaling dear? – oh yes, there is another coal glove somewhere – And pencil, as you know, is bought – That little cushion will be a great comfort – can't think why I didn't bring it – Also nice on hard chair when I'm typing! I could have done without blue coat, as already stated, but have a feeling that its going to come in handy tho' since you've sent it! And finally (I think its finally!) Michael. I *adore* that picture of him –

---

[1] Bethell received a number of parcels, and an increasing supply of goods, which she contrived to hide from her landlady.

he used to sit there every evening watching the sunset. (What happy days they were, what happy days.) Beautifully packed darling – you are very good to me, aren't you? I couldn't think why the package was so heavy! (but didn't quail). The apples explained. I shall be able to allow myself two a day now. (Landlady's are pathetic – she presses them on me!)

[...]

Think that's all I have to say so will boil kettle & give you several imaginary kisses my poor, victimised, indefatigable, little Katya.

M.U.

Post just in. & yr. note – such a surprise! [...] My Darling if anyone's to blame (& after all it was mostly a series of contretemps beginning with my blindness!) it was *me* – & that is what my Effie wd. have said I know – my fault for *wanting* things & not sensibly doing without! She always used to say to me:– "Now, don't *complicate*!" (That's what I've done & no mistake!) Let us end it up by agreeing that there are no misunderstandings & couldn't be I think, between us. As I told P., there has been (to my intuition) a curious sense of harmony from the outset. The practical moral is – how careful one has to be when composing telegrams![1] [...]

Macmillan Brown Library. MB 572. A.

TO CHARLES BRASCH – JULY 11, 1941

As from 47 Webb St. Christchurch. NZ.
At Kaikoura.

My dear Charles

And today, I said to myself this morning – when I turned on my reading lamp at 6.45 (summertime) – today I shall begin that letter without fail. *That* letter was *this* – & now here is your airmailed one of June 11th despatch – Exactly a month. Would that be what we call the Clipper Mail? I think so, but we have more to pay for it – your stamps add up to 4/6 I see – what a handsome one is the 2/6. If I go on at this pace I shall never get all I have to say written! No doubt it is the effect of easy chair in front of manuka wood fire – coming after a walk in southerly rain. I dug myself well into these '41 winter quarters (& I never use that expression without thinking of my early excursion into Caesar –

---

[1] The incident referred to here concerns Bethell's desire to have with her a particular photograph – which in fact was already in her baggage. She sent a telegram to say 'Found photograph,' but it was transmitted as 'Find photograph' and interpreted by Kathleen Taylor as a somewhat peremptory command, causing a prolonged and fruitless search. Bethell attributed the mistake to the telegraph boy's accent.

How I wish I'd kept up Latin. How I wish I knew Greek. And how I wish I knew German better) about three weeks ago – feeling very limp after Influenza & at once made a list of more than 30 overdue letters to be dealt with in this valuable solitude – Every day there are local letters to be dealt with first – but they *can* be written at once – & that's *so* soothing to the nerves I find!

[...]

I must tell you that I have a new friend – a charming girl of 23, who is teaching in ChCh this year. She is in a lodging & has been lonely & out of her element – We only met about three weeks before I left, but got to know her very quickly, quickly enough to be delighted to arrange that she should spend an evening in my Parlour at least once a week, make a fire, cook a meal and *play the gramophone*. It airs the room & refreshes her. [...] It makes quite a difference to the prospect of going back to have that young creature on the look out for me – (ChCh is always a sad place to me). We get on very harmoniously together & have planned some outings for Sat. or Sun.s [...] A wonderful thing for an old lady like me suddenly to acquire a young friend full of life & zest, & possessing the same tastes. She helped me pack up & get away – I do need help of that kind nowadays – & then came up for a weekend, being offered a lift. Her escort had to start back at 4 a.m. for them to be at their respective employments on the Monday. We had a most perfect Sunday (it was just about Shortest Day) sunshine, & snow on the mountains, we made a walking (& resting) picnic of it, lunch & tea. That's what's so good in N.Z., brilliant days in the middle of winter. Not brilliant in ChCh! I think Kaikoura is destined to be the fashionable winter health resort of the South Island – it won't be so pleasant then! Nights are however extremely cold. I daresay you know the place en passant – mountains & pastures & sea shore – magnificent breakers – I hear them at night. [...]

July 18

I had to break off to cook evening meal on open fire (its a camping sort of life) & then make dispositions towards getting to bed. [...]

Looking over the beginning of this letter I thought "What *prattle*!" Now, to quote my brother's favourite author, I'll cut the cackle & get to the 'osses – (it *was* Jorrocks wasn't it?)[1] The first horse shall be my subsistence – on which you seem to be putting your nice blue shirt (cannot help being glad it has not been exchanged for a khaki one!) – but there, if I try sporting similes I shall go hopelessly wrong – my mental background is *not* that of my country family! I think I'll assume that

[1] John Jorrocks, the sporting grocer, was the creation of the English novelist, Robert Smith Surtees.

you've had my Clipper letter – (enclosing one from Toss) dated June 4th which contains the Surprising Revelation of my wealth – Surprising to me too, for I never know where that £300 a year *is*, & do not believe in it until I make my income tax returns. [...]

(I wish I *could* have been your Beneficiary Charles, you do it so nicely!)[1] The question of the disposal of my annual fortune (it has varied a good deal of course – slump years very low – but there were relations who helped then who are dead now) is indeed a puzzle – especially when I remember that its been not only *income*, but the monthly instalments of Rise Cottage sale – which *ought* to be there (as Richard said) for my Old Age Home. Lavish, lavish – that's what I've been. If a young man wanted to read a book, why, I would buy it forthwith to lend to him – Handing over my furniture – all my *carpets* – to St Faiths! (But then I thought I was going to England – or to *die*) Holidays! My Wellington 3 weeks would run into £20 easily. Clothes! – I *must* buy the same sort as I used to get at Home which cost three times as much out here – And so on. But all that is a thing of the past. Must be. The war means contraction all the time. We shall stay put & wear our old clothes. I should think so indeed. Richard – my nephew – does not handle my affairs (the lawyers who make my returns "know all"!) – unlike my sister, who wished to be rid of all responsibility, I have kept my small affairs in my own hands – but knows my resources pretty well – (the main part comes from the farm, wh. he manages, or *did* manage –) & takes the kindest interest. Once he made out a budget for me, on a basis of what I need per ann. So much for rent, so much for food, so much for Help, holidays, doctors (not enough!) So much (not much!) for "pocket money" but nothing I noticed for Church, Presents, Books, such recreation as a picture-show – oh *that* would be pocket money! – periodicals, to say nothing of Gramophone records – or *postage* – which looms so large for me (during these 4 1/2 weeks in Kaikoura I have spent £2.14.5 on stamps but thats a bit out of the ordinary). Well, I suppose my list *does* mean luxuries! My rent is very small – only £1 a week – but I have spent so much every year on improving the premises – e.g. verandah room £30, shed £20 & do all my own repairs, & have a gardener. See what a deal of rather confidential information you have drawn down on yourself! It was the only way to meet your kind thought, dear Charles. Do you know that although I clearly see my guilty extravagance, I am not sure that I feel *really* conscience stricken! I feel that I have enjoyed my money's worth – If I am short in Old Age it may come home to me. [...] My attitude to my

---

[1] In response to an earlier letter about financial difficulties, Brasch had offered a substantial annual allowance of £50 or even £100.

extravagance reminds me of what one of my young friends said (not one you know). "I am so happy that I even thank God when I know I am doing wrong"! Richard still advises me to make Webb St my H.Q. & to put away any thought of a cottage for the present – & go away in the winter. But its not very easy to arrange that going away in the winter. I could not hear of any boarding-house where one could have bedroom fire – I simply *cannot* sit in the small parlours & listen to bridge-playing & Z.B. radio! – hotels are too expensive. This place suits me but wd. not suit everyone & its quite laborious. Shortage of water – one hot bath a week. No meals provided, but landlady brings me early tea in bed. I go to the Pub. for mid-day meal. I don't think she will be here next year. But something is sure to turn up & I am not worrying. What I ought to worry about more is trying to get some help at Webb St. I am growing less "active" now.

Quite enough about *that* horse – my small affairs. But I thank you again so very much for the thought – I am afraid I must have *grumbled* – to make you think it! So I shall not be writing to your father (– by the way I hope *you* won't be moved to delete the "c' – your name is much handsomer just so I think.)

[...]

Kierkegaard – yes, I have 2 smaller translations & have ordered another – very laborious to read. These translations so often are. But one *must* read him – he has had such a wide-spread influence – and anticipated things to come as great men do. [...] I expect K. is one of those writers one should read masses of, & then feel the influence! (What a sentence!)

[...] Tutira – I hope you will enjoy that.[1] I thought it quite a fascinating book – about the first book on N.Z. I came in touch with, when I came out after the war. Bought it for a present to an old gentleman who didn't care a bit about it – in fact didn't read it I expect. (More than once I've regretted giving away an inapplicable present.)

[...]

Nov. July 24th

Interruptions – even in Kaikoura. I am just going "up the coast" for a night perhaps 2, so decided to send this off (on account of the financial question) & carry on next week.

With my love
M.U.B.

Hocken Library. MS-0996-3/19.

[1] H. Guthrie-Smith's *Tutira: the story of a New Zealand sheepstation* had been published in 1926.

TO TOSS WOOLLASTON – JULY 12, 1941

c/o Mrs. McIver. Ludstone Terrace. Kaikoura

My dear Toss

I'm breaking off from my "overseas" list (at the moment its a long one to Charles Brasch) to write you a few lines. All these NZ letters, including your yellow one (date 25th May & it seems yesterday) look at me so reproachfully. [...]

Since 25th May I've had Flu – now forgotten – but it weakened & made it seem almost impossible to pack up & get away. But Heaven has sent to me such a delightful new friend of 23 years – tell Edith – she is teaching in ChCh this year – but may be off again I think after this – Anyhow she's been wonderful – came to spend weekends & helped me get ready & finally saw me off at station. *Not* finally, because, being offered a lift, she came up for my first weekend & we had a gloriously fine Sunday & took our lunch out. Kaikoura has a splendid winter climate & I am more thankful than I can say to be away from ChCh. I have a bedroom *with fireplace* in cottage of retired district nurse – got in 1/2 cord wood – find dinner in township. Getting slowly thro' a list of some 30 letters – have some books – whether poetry making will follow I don't know. In this wartime one has to pray & ponder so much about the world & one's fellow men. Sometimes I go to the daily war prayers – or rather peace prayers – I like the Presby. minister's way of taking them very much – Such services have too often hurt me. I get The Christian NewsLetter from Home & other helpful periodicals.

I've just had another airmail letter from Charles – He *is* a good person! He had been Fire-watching in London (not passed medically fit for army) & was likely to change over to another civilian job. [...]

I have heard twice from Eric McCormick. In the last he had been taken away from his hospital (menial jobs of course – which however he was happy to do) & made an archivist again. Public Relations, its called, at H. Q – which would be in or near Cairo. I thought they must in the end make use of his brain.

Yesterday I had a short letter from Johnny who tells me briefly about having been to Nelson, & the influence of your "Uncle Frank" – who must be a saint. I am so thankful that J. has come back to prayer. I agreed with you about his "spiritual means" theory – & so did Archdn Whitehead – What he must have meant was that he had come to feel that war was *not* too bad a thing for a Christian to take part in. The grace of God is not doled out, so much per week!

Your house sounds very nice – the "capital value" will be considerable when you've done with it! I *should* like to come & stay there again – but *do* sheep-dip the maori-bugs first. […]

I do like your way of life, Toss; its building the 'Christian Civilisation' my papers talk of – not that civilisation will be christian all through, even after this breakup. But we ought to be able to show a pattern, surely, & your simplicity & toil sound right.

Any painting? I often look at your Taranaki drawing & wonder whether you have ever done anything better! […]

Basking in the sun after Southerly – mountains opposite snow covered – must go forth & seek lunch.

With love to Edith & all.
from M U

Hocken Library. MS-0996-3/225.

To Charles Brasch – July 31, 1941

As from St Faith's. Webb St. Christchurch NZ.

My dear Charles

Too many letters from this correspondent for you I'm afraid! But I have found myself sending off one after another with (to me) the most important things left unsaid – If you *will* make such interesting observations about current events & ask such provocative questions, what can I do but respond?

Its the war of course. You say, as I have read it said before, that your generation has never known a stable world,[1] but you are my only friend who has said it of himself, very conscious of that background. I suppose the world of my youth *did* appear stable – Wasn't I handed gilt-edged "securities" when an aunt died – didn't the lawyer talk about "settlements"? Did I not fit into the social scheme of things spending school holidays among relations in the country with landed estates? (Yorkshire was particularly solid.) Used we not make plans imperturbably for a distant future, for travel in the meantime, sure of moving about befriended in any country? Have I not looked on at both of Victoria's Jubilee processions? (Ah but at her funeral too!) Yet there *were* disturbances of thought you know. My schooldays were under the shadow of Darwin & Huxley. When I recall the undergraduates who

[1] In a letter of Nov. 23, 1940, Brasch wrote: 'I find that in some ways those who knew the pre-1914 age of stability endure better the strain of this war, because their lives seem based on something firm, than some of my generation who have never known a stable world.'

were my contemporaries there certainly were upsets & dismays. Mechanical forces were coming into play. But you know all about that & it can't have been comparable with the quaking of the 1920s & 30s.

You say truly that pacifists should have a core of peace in themselves, & that I for my part must have such an inner source of strength – you put it as half a question. From my soon to be seventy years I ought to be able to look back & give an answer to that, yes or no. But its not so simple & I think the answer must be yes *and* no. Its one thing to have an intellectual notion of the universe which is satisfying, & another thing to be possessed by a conviction.

I had a bad start – an unhappy childhood. Unhappy in respect of human relationships, though happy in my country surroundings & pursuits. ("Nature" *was* the consolation – no wonder I took kindly to Wordsworth later on! but I never *personified* Nature.) There was as early as I can remember one of those conflicts between mother & daughter. She was an unhappy person. She must have "chosen her parents badly." Later on one learnt all about it from the Psychoanalysts & I've no doubt that a great deal of my nervous fear & disability could have been dealt with by a skilful psychologist. But by the time that science – hardly a science even now? – came to the fore I must have been too old to be dealt with in that way! Even so, I believe that short of illness, it is far better to take oneself consciously in hand. Religion as imparted by that mother, a sort of evangelical calvinism, was gloomy & alarming – but it did touch up the conscience! When I got to my school in England (childhood had been N. Z.) in my teens & was boarded with a lively & outspoken family of young people, life took a different turn. And presented then by what may be called the Catholic Faith it appealed to me strongly. In particular the notion of a world-wide society, into which the nations were to bring their various glories took hold of my imagination (as I said my prayers I seemed to see the world or globes revolving in the background) that vision kept me I suppose from being bitten later on by ideas of imperialism & nationalism. I recall, too, Charles Gore's Bampton lectures at St Mary's (you were Oxford, weren't you?). I heard at least one of them – (he was then held to be a daring innovator, later a stiff conservative – but he *was* a saint with a clear mind) & I still have a picture of him hanging over that pulpit, totally unselfconscious, & gazing round that congregation, mostly of youth, at the conclusion of a disquisition & the words "Blessed are the pure in heart, *therefore*, for they shall see God"[1] – Quite undeniable I felt! – but did not know the difficulty of being really pure-in-hearted – as I know

[1] See Matthew 5: 8. Bethell refers to the Bampton lectures on several occasions.

now! Yes, the doctrines of the Christian creed had a fascination for me from my youth up – the doctrine of the Trinity for instance – dazzling but elucidating – and the mysteries of the Gospel narratives – the Agony in the olive garden, the resurrection meetings – those startling conversations before the end. Later I studied other religions to some extent, but they did not make the same impression. And philosophical considerations (tho' I might not quite grasp them – how amused Dr. Popper[1] was the other day, to find Wittgenstein on my shelf!) such as "Time & Eternity in Christian Thought"[2] (a book I have with me) always absorbed me. But "inner peace"? When, after a homesick for England space of 3 years back in NZ, I took myself abroad to go on with music & painting the uneasy conscience was not satisfied, & at 24 still uneasy – partly on that account & partly because Public Service was instilled into us at school – I took myself to south east London to go on with the Boys' Club job which had been such a consolation in the homesick NZ days.

I seem to be embarked upon an autobiography! That's impossible – but a question about inner peace is a question about religion – & religion seems to depend on – have its roots in everything that has happened to one – as I said to the silly fundamentalist parson with whom I argued once (quite uselessly!) when he asked "If your faith is not founded on the infallible rock of Holy Scripture, what *can* it be founded on?" (I'm not sure that he didn't expect me to say "An infallible Church" –) Faith I felt had a hundred legs like a centipede & if the legs at times seem all to be lifted in the air at once (what a feat for centipede!) they do come down again.

In South London – to go back to it – I used to be very depressed during those years which ended in serious illness at 29 – the conditions were depressing & exhausting of course, & I became aware then I suppose of the offences of our social & economic arrangements, & I remember the boys' argument that Christianity was impossible for them because everyone outside their own families was an enemy – (competing for their jobs) but I also became aware of the fact that I really cared a doubtful twopence about my fellow-creatures & my prayer was (I well remember that moment before my crucifix!) that my heart might be

---

[1] Austrian-born philosopher, Karl Popper took up a lectureship at Canterbury University College in 1937, partly in flight from Nazism and anti-Semitism. He was known as a brilliant lecturer, not only in the university, but also in public and adult education programmes. A profoundly influential thinker, he found the intellectual climate at Canterbury cramping, and eventually took up a post at the London School of Economics.

[2] F. H. Brabant, *Time and Eternity in Christian Thought* (1937) – another in the Bampton Lectures series.

cured by *any* means. I went on with my religious & liturgical studies mean-while as my chief interest.

I must cut the story short – – it has been one of sadness underneath – blow after blow – persons I cared for removed by illness, death – the other war. (I was then in London after 4 years in NZ) some terrible experiences – the Cashmere ten years of happiness – of inner peace? no; always that early conflict to [be] reckoned on, waking to dread – ending in the last shock, the too sudden death of the nearest & dearest companion – & the bitter knowledge, always the worst sting of death, of how much more I might have done for her. Death! I cannot forget that last week of suffering. She died just a month after my 60th birthday, which we celebrated with great pomp. The seven years since I should call purgatory. For we *were* happy – & the things that made our life amusing – the cottage – the garden – the car – the *cat* – the view – *all* gone with her. Still to wake to dread – still to reach for the weapons. For I have battled on. All this does not sound like "inner peace" does it? – and YET. I think I have never, even at worst times, lost the sense of purpose. "This is either *cruel*, or *good*." – I did not come to think that there was no meaning at all. And when my prayer was at a minimum, I knew there must still *be* prayer, however wild & despairing – some conscious relationship with the invisible Will. (But my prayer is better than that now.) I was pleased to find a saying of an English mystic "Faith is a desolate thing"[1] – and of a Jesuit "The Catholic Church has always allowed her children to cry their eyes out." I think that in the end one must come to security through despair & desolation. And I think that at last my religion has become less *oblique* – (Have you read I wonder the Jewish writer – philosopher or theologian – Martin Buber – I have noticed his influence in other writings – a short book of his "I & Thou" I have in translation wd. probably be better in German – You might like it – the bit about the cat appealed to me very much.)[2]

I think there has always been a *tension* – perhaps in the history of our race & its struggles, there has always been a tension? Is the soul's faith & peace a tension?

Have I conveyed *anything* by all this! You did not expect to draw upon yourself such a torrent of words. But as I get older I feel its "up to me" to say (and to see for myself) where I stand, when questioned.

---

[1] See the letter to John Summers, March 12, 1939. I have not found the quotation attributed to the Jesuit.

[2] The translation Bethell used was one supervised and approved by Buber, although *I and Thou* is sometimes said to be virtually untranslateable. The 'cat' passage occurs in the third part, and speculates on the eloquent glance of the cat and its communicative potential.

Lately I have [been] thinking about *Hope*. One of the people in Bernanos' novel – wasn't it called Journal d'un Curé de Campagne? – said to the curé "For thirty years I have been sinning against Hope"[1] – & I felt that I must add that to *my* list of sins. (I do enjoy a French book sometimes – but feel obliged to order translations for the sake of N.Z. *borrowers*. I know French much better than German.)

Do you know, although it does not sound like a 'core of peace' I think it may be so after all. Was it Mr. Fearing, at the end of Pilgrim's Progress, when they came to the deepest river, who called out "Courage, my brother, I feel the bottom, & it is good"[2] – I still have dreads, but I think I shall know *that* when the worst comes – The curious thing is that it is easier to know & feel dearly for others. The young friends who are going now, I have faith that the Divine purpose is being fulfilled in them. I am very thankful for those young friends, to be interested in their lives has taken me out of my private griefs. Sometimes they say wonderful things – (Toss, for instance, said that it was the intensity of my grief had shown him what the depth of love is). It has been consoling to me that a sensible & lively girl of 23 should find me good company & someone she can be fond of – if I were truly unsettled & unsure & unhappy at the core, I think that she could not feel that. Though I should wish to be able to say that I *have* inner peace, I would prefer to make an understatement than a presumptuous one. I think it is difficult for a woman to sum up, or to generalise – we take things one after another intensely – each event, each mood, makes its own strong impression – we can't see the wood for the trees. (I believe I read something like that about Virginia Woolf – have seen in a paper now that she took her own life not because of the war but because she feared insanity – & I have seen her portrait – what a beautiful woman!)

So, looking at the war – (dazing to me, an ill-informed person,) as it goes on, I see that it is horribly evil, but how much more evil than our so-called Peace I don't know. & I do believe that good is stronger than evil, & that good can & will come out of evil – (the Christian faith). Even now one sees some good by-products of the war! I saw that one London vicar, carrying on services in the crypt after destruction of the church – had to warn his people against being too pleased with these good by-products, lest they forget the hatefulness of war. Did I thank you for

---

[1] The character is Mme la Comtesse who, just prior to her death, writes to the Curé an admission that she has wilfully sinned against hope for eleven (not 30) years, since the death of her infant son. Bernanos' novel was published in French in 1936, and in an English translation, *The Diary of a Country Priest*, in 1937.

[2] In addition to quoting this to Brasch just a few months earlier, Bethell cites it in a letter to Kennedy, Oct. 16, 1936 (q.v. for identification).

those two bits from Rilke's Letters?[1] (I saw the review of that translation.) I have copied them out. I am afraid it was true of the last war that it did not bring us "face to face with God" (& hence the "peace") but surely there is much more general searching of heart & mind this time? That is what makes one afraid of a too quick & easy peace – though my pacifist paper says that a long war *cannot* make it better. It does not look as if it were going to be quick & easy (but a *great* tribulation). If I read the newspaper aright we are being warned that it may now come to this country.

You ask about criticism of the conduct of the war. (Greece e.g.) As far as I know very little has been published in NZ. I fancy there is a stricter censorship in NZ than elsewhere & have seen complaints about it. I am not in the way of hearing much *talk*. So far my brother has said nothing to me showing dissatisfaction that his son should have been sent to fight in Greece. (I think I told you that my nephew came out safe, but having lost *all* his possessions.)

Monday Aug. 4. a.m.

[...]

These are my last days – I go back to town on Friday. We have had a run of southerly storms, rain & snow – but last night it cleared – & today is more dazzling than ever – mountains whiter. I must get up! [...]

I cut out bits about C.O. appeals for you & the easiest way is to put them inside a copy of the Press, which I will do. Apparently L. Bensemann is not [out] of the wood yet. I wish Denis wd. stop using his drawings which repel me so much – but Denis admires them. This reminds [me] to ask you about something that occurred to me the other day. "Day & Night" is out of print[2] & I see that Caxton Press is asking for a copy. It was paper covered & I have wished that it could be done again in stiff boards like "Day & Night". If D. wd. do it, I suppose it ought to be considered before long – before he's called up (no children come first). But he doesn't like doing my work because our tastes differ about print & binding – mine are old fashioned. Prices are going up all the time. D.&N. cost £50 & I paid half. D. said afterwards that £50 did not make it worthwhile. T.&P. might cost £30 or £40 I suppose & I

[1] Brasch wrote (June 4, 1941): 'Two things ... I must quote to you – one phrase about "those proofs of consecutive inner transformations that in the last analysis constitute being alive." and "Fearful as the war is in itself, it seems to me still more dreadful that the pressure of it has nowhere contributed to bringing man out more distinctly, to forcing him – the individual or the mass – face to face with God, as great tribulations in earlier times had the power to do."' Both can be found in Rilke's *Wartime Letters*; the first from a letter to Countess M. ((June 25, 1920), and the second from a letter to Bernhard von der Marwitz (March 9, 1918).

[2] A mistake – Bethell means *Time & Place*.

don't think I ought to undertake it. Till lately there seemed to be no hurry & I put off thinking about it. Now, I wonder whether you would feel that to help with that enterprise (if D. considers it) a suitable outlet for your generosity? I chose the 12 for T.&P. so carefully I think it must contain my best things.

[...]

I am sorry to leave this beautiful Kaikoura to go back to foggy ChCh – but there are things calling me. The work at the flat is becoming a bit much for me & I suppose I shall have to face a move – but I can't let myself worry – Perhaps the solution will be Evacuation, before its an immediate problem? There is a lovely spot seven miles "up the coast" where the post mistress keeps a primitive boarding house. She's very nice & I'd like to try it another time but doubt whether I could put up with the conditions. I'm *soft* – a pity because it wd. be "echt-Neu Zeeland".[1] Hapuku its called. Mostly dairying country about here – such milk & cream & butter, & I can only send a tiny bit to England! I was delighted to hear that the butter I sent to my sister arrived in perfect condition – better methods since the last war. She is so good to me. I want to pay it – some of it – back in parcels. She gave me this holiday. What makes me sad in the country is the useless destruction of mountain bush – I could start another hare by talking about that! Subject based on a paragraph in the Press about "development" of South Westland Forests to Mill, & gold to be dredged by biggest dredge in NZ – have you seen the fiendish work of those dredges? *That's* what is at the root of our troubles – greed & impiety. It wd. be the burden of my verse now "The Earth is the Lord's"[2] & not to be exploited.

I shall send as much of this letter as weight will allow by the 2/6 air & anything over by surface. And I think its safe to promise that never again shall you *receive such a deluge of confidences from me! What I have said is very incoherent & inadequate – one is learning all the time & I feel that I am really only at the beginning. I think that at the core I have *patience*, if not peace.

With my love & many thanks again for your thoughtful kindness

Ursula Bethell.

[Added in margin] * & I expect I've taken you too heavily!

Hocken Library. MS-0996-3/19.

[1] Ger. 'Old New Zealand.'

[2] See Psalm 24: 1.

TO KATHLEEN TAYLOR & PAUL GABITES – AUGUST 31, [1941]

St Faith's. Webb St. ChCh

Darling Paul & Katya

It seems natural now to write to you together. First, today's bulletin – Still heavily colded, but on the mend. What I am thankful for is to know that its not going to be anything worse, this time, than a "common cold"! This time I've been quite "*and*amant" (Effie's word) about staying in bed [...]

Wonderful to lie here in *sunshine* & just see the sun on snowy mountain tops between the rooves.

Thinking about my dears, it seems to me that this affaire de coeur has been bowling along pretty briskly! I shouldn't be a bit surprised to hear that the hesitations were melting away – (as the snows soon will if this sun stays out). What with moonlight walks and so on – – but then of course one must remember Glamour. When K. comes back to the "C.Major of this life" in Webb St, she may begin to analyse again. Paul darling has been marching round & round Jericho & is probably longing to blow a blast on the trumpets.[1] But now I am going to dare to ask something – that is if the walls havn't already collapsed – I was so touched by Paul's inscription "Ursula's room" – When he comes to put the decisive question – could it be done right there?* It would please the old lady no end & does seem rather fitting. The Christian tradition of troth-plighting is something very different from the modern "engagement" which gets put in the papers – & means so little & ends so easily as you know, dears. (Shall we ever get back to the consecration of every stage of physical life?) I can see the parlour tidy and candle-lit for the ceremony! (Quite incorrigibly romantic old bird.) I don't *at all* wish to hurry things – to 'let them evolve' is the surest – but circumstances *are* "extra" – as the Londoners used to say & if my dears feel by that time that they wish to, & *can* settle it – I should like Paul to break his journey north – (That would be the 13th or 14th to 15th eveng. wouldn't it?) & come in for all the time he can spare. (And I may add that, to *my* view, it would be quite unfair to his family, who are devoted to him, especially his mother, to leave before the last moment, unless for *serious* affairs, but "a marriage to be arranged" does take precedence!) There are one or two questions I should like to ask, before the decision, if there is any doubt, for it is much more than romance – & that wd. give the opportunity.

---

[1] See Joshua 6.

[Added along side of page] * If the answer be in the Negative, the parlour can take it & so of course can "His Impetuous Male Augustness"[1]

And now I will run on much too fast – and anticipate. I never had an "Engagement" & a Ring – & if I were Katya I'd rather wear one on a ribbon round my neck (sounds rather uncomfortable perhaps) – but she may think quite differently. The fact is I was wondering whether expense could be spared by my looking in my trinket box (stock-pot!). I forget what is left there. (If that doesn't make you laugh nothing ever will.) I suppose however that conventions *are* socially sound.

[...]

I ponder upon my future – some change there must be – outlook not hopeful for old woman small means no strength, no relations handy, hates a boarding house – So much the simplest to pack up & get off from this planet – but if the Lord doesn't intend that, I must carry on somehow – I come of healthy & longlived stock on both sides and have always supposed there might be 80 years to go. Little Effie used to say "We'll be two merry old ladies of 90" – Not so easy to be merry by oneself but I mean to try. Bombs may be the solution.

The problem is: if I don't live within my income at a rental of £52 per annum, how should I manage with rental of £75 to £100 a year (any move wd. mean that) *and* Help? Richard said it could be done & made out a Budget – but allowed *nothing* for books, music, outings, garden, presents, church & not enough for food & warmth as things are & not nearly enough for clothes *then*, but shan't need them *now*. Of course it can be done when I stare it in the face, leaving out Effie's "little amenities that make life amenable", & it *shall* be done, when it comes to the point.

[...]

Such a lovely day & such lovely *peace* – now that I have stopped sneezing!

Visions I have of little E. arriving with trays of delicacies, *and* wearing herself to death – Thank God she is not here to see me "failing" – Its because I allowed her to do too much that I have a horror of depending on other people now – It was, tho' wonderful – & recalled the past when you & P. ministered to me – so different from old, *stupid* people! – Nasty thing to say, that! After Effie went away, *everyone* else seemed so *stupid*.

[M.U.]

Macmillan Brown Library. MB 572. A.

---

[1] No doubt a private joke. The name is a rendition of the Japanese Storm-God, from Shinto creation stories.

TO KATHLEEN TAYLOR & PAUL GABITES – SEPTEMBER 3, 1941

47 Webb St. ChCh

I've found some of this blue paper to write on to my dearest dears this morning – easier for my crippled pen & something like the snow blues I can just see over the rooves. Since their bulletins – as Paul calls his (& good, that!) – came I've been gazing awhile at the white & blue & thinking of them – & want to put some of the thoughts – a few, I fear, inadequately – on to this paper before Laura & sordid-food considerations intervene[1] – I like it so much that *they* were gazing at "my mountains, all snow," when the 'two hearts' – at last – 'beat as one'! (bulletin!) How happy & thankful I feel about it all I think I needn't say. But I must write to you separately – you are more not less individual now that you both know! And the best bits in both letters would not have been said by the other.

First, on this page, I'll get *my* bulletin (not really called for now) out of the way. Almost, not *quite*, free from cold, to an observer, but *feeling* free from cold. Feeling, however, *reduced* – and the stairs rather a bother – It wd. be absurd to go away again just as I've come back – tho' that might be the best thing – and anyhow nothing wd. induce me to go away from K. I must be content to be idle & by Sunday no doubt the hue of health will again mantle the cheek[2] – Laura, (very sketchy) will see me over – I'm quite attached to Laura & shall recompense her rather handsomely because she is going to save up for a plain tweed skirt & for wool to knit a cardigan to go with – its right to encourage sound ideas about clothes.

[...]

(L. has intervened – Kind contribution of curried steak from Mum – To be postponed – *not* curry yet! Now washing up with goods arranged under my direction – I get quite hoarse trying to bring some precision to Laura's operations – Thank Heaven she laughs when I attack her! – doesn't Take the Huff. We should get on. All very well to say "Muddler yourself" – I *have* my ideals & but for Failing – – – What a first class washer up you have in dear Paul.

Now I'm back to Paul via Laura I needn't close parenthesis! I said it had been *unifying* darling – this courtship – even more so now – You will understand more of me, I think, for example. Oh yes, I know about those eyes – havn't I had that look, and from more than one – but in farewell & renunciation – "l'éternel adieu" – I know now its not "éternel"

---

[1] Laura was the daughter of Bethell's 'daily,' who came to help out with meals and cleaning while her mother was sick.

[2] Bethell may be remembering the maiden's song from Book IV of *Endymion*.

– I may offer my sorrows dears, for *your* happiness – We're allowed that, in Western Orthodoxy – Because of the Cross – its poetry I think, & hard to understand – (Eastern Orthodoxy seems not to think that way). Looking at the snows I begged to be purged from thinking of myself & what I've missed – thinking of you – And I *have* had such riches.

Dear Paul's eyes are so expressive (– really you shouldn't go telling him all I say! –) I have never forgotten one day I went to Timaru & he stood at the door looking *welcoming*. It sure did one good.[1]

Macmillan Brown Library. MB 572. A.

To Kathleen Taylor & Paul Gabites – September 5, [1941]

47 Webb St. ChCh.

I really must send one more wave of the hand to my dears – because its a Friday & because (therefore) its the last one – I am, truly, pleased that there is nothing from them today, because not a moment of their precious & running out time should be given to letter writing. I havn't – since Tuesday wasn't it? – had any cause to worry further about those adventure ships putting safely out to sea – for its rather that than making a safe landfall – the first metaphor to occur. I think of those dears as two happy people in bright sunshine.

[...]

There was a ring from Johnny Summers this morng. Coming off the Ferry. Could the Wayfarer's Room (*I* never called it that!)[2] receive him for a few days – Lucky for me term begins officially tonight & bars the way, for I couldn't have coped with him, & it might have seemed unkind. The child is rather exhausting with all his eager talk, without having to feed him. As it is, he may come in very useful, domiciled elsewhere! I shall pay off Laura today. It occurs to me what a suitable girl-friend she wd. be for him! Let them meet over the coalbuckets therefore! Sketchy housework & sketchy erudition. Dear little John, I am *very* fond of him really – & he has great insight spiritually – & unusual insight into people – souls I was going to say but mustn't be too St Faithy.

How fortunate that it is St F's role to furnish Katya with bed & board, not mine! For I can't get up any interest in food for myself or any one else & even if there were vast enthusiasms about it, I couldn't carry them out. But an old hen may spend tomorrow afternoon in a Turkish bath preparatory to Sunday supper for K. Dinner I'm afraid, she must absorb at the common table.

---

[1] The letter is unsigned; a page or more may have been removed.

[2] She does do so, in a letter to Eileen Duggan, Jan. 30, 1938.

[...]

Its lovely upstairs in this weather – that's where I live, wandering with trays. I'm not bothering to dress beyond underclothing – much more comfy for lying down – besides I want to impress J. with being ill, so as to subdue him a bit.

Well, darlings, have a heavenly last day there (is moon still holding out?) & then lets hope for some lovely moments, if too brief, for you here. Well-fuelled, weather won't matter in the Parlour.

Au revoir Katya *soon* – Au revoir Paul anon – I kiss them both.

U.

Macmillan Brown Library. MB 572. A.

TO MONTE HOLCROFT – SEPTEMBER 9, 1941

St Faith's House. Webb St. ChCh.

My dear Monte

My plans for writing to you at some length about 'The Deepening Stream' have so far been frustrated. At Kaikoura I worked through a long list of overdue "overseas" letters – but since my return have been laid up with another attack of Influenza & am not quite over it. I am "getting on" in years & do not, I think, find myself on recovery quite where I was before each of these recent attacks. And now I hear that you have another book in hand. I have a lending copy of 'Time and Place' – & will post it. I should like to have another edition printed with a stiff cover – it is sometimes asked for – & as a memorial I wish it might have a more protecting binding. But it is costly. Only a very few people like to read my verse – but those who do, don't tire of it, & that satisfies me. Not a hundred of Day & Night have been sold.

I was wishing to write to you, about now, about a young friend to whom I sent 'The Deepening Stream'. Working on a dairy farm he has been educating himself by wide reading & has great ambitions in the direction of authorship, but I am afraid is a long way yet from writing good English. He sent me among other papers an essay which he called a Ripple from (or on?) The Deepening Stream, & he talked much of your work when he was here the other day. His home is in Invercargill & he was on his way there, to await being called into Camp for overseas. I think he is about 23 now. You say that you are specially busy just now & I don't know whether you would have time to see him, but he would much like to meet you & I shall venture to give him an introduction. He is an interesting person & I have a good deal of affection for him. He will be *something* some day, but whether it will be a writer, I don't know. My friend Archdeacon Whitehead of Selwyn College thought highly enough of his abilities to offer him a scholarship there – but for various reasons he did not take it up. His *name,* by the way, is John Summers. He reads quite difficult books, & some of the kind that used to interest you.

I have heard several times from Mr. McCormick in Egypt – he is now in the Public Relations Department there.

Referring to your previous letter: did I say that Charles Brasch is a friend of mine – but I don't think there wd. be any "influence" altho' he likes my verse & I like his.[1] He reads a great deal of the younger school of poets in England (went back two years or more ago) & writes most interesting letters. He is a great admirer of R. M. Rilke.

I hope that I shall be able to write a better letter than this one some day. With best wishes for progress of yr. new book

Your old friend
M.U.Bethell

Kaikoura is a most lovely place & the winter climate should make it *the* winter resort of the South Is. surely someday.

Alexander Turnbull Library. MS-Papers-1186-03.

To Edith Woollaston – September, [1941]

St Faiths. Webb St. ChCh.

And now, Edith dear, spring time in Webb St is coming back, after all the wild wet weather & snow, & your pear tree, what's left of it rather, will soon be in flower & I have been thinking of you a good deal as you will presently understand. I do not remember which of us wrote last, or when, but it must have been before the winter in Kaikoura. [...] I came back quite able to look after a young friend convalescing from mild mumps, who stayed with me – in spare room. But when she went away well, I began to do too much with my fresh energies & got tired, & then one day stupidly ran to catch a tram, which made me feel queer & shaky – & on top of that caught another Flu germ – which seems to have been rather a poisonous kind. I was so exhausted after doing a *very* little cooking & tidying last week that I have taken to bed again. The Dr. says that the heart is all right but needs rest. I feel I just *can't* be active & am thankful to "stay put" with some milk & oranges beside me – & it gives me the chance to do some letter writing. (I sent more than 60 from Kaikoura – but there are always more to be answered – & now English

[1] Holcroft thought he detected 'traces of your influence in the poetry of Charles Brasch.... he has something of that feeling for the anatomy of the land which I find in your own work' (March 24, 1941).

Christmas.) I have been getting older these last two years – I don't think that I am back to where I was before, after each of these Flu attacks. My nephew advised me to stay here until he comes back, & go away for the winter, but it is difficult to find a place, & altogether I have been finding the work too much & yet dreaded the thought of another move.

Now, however, new life & hope has come in the person of a new girl friend (& with her I come nearer to the chief reason for this letter). She was introduced to me by Paul G. who had been seeing something of her last holidays & learnt that she was lonely in her ChCh lodging. Her profession is school teaching & she has a post in ChCh for this year. We took to each other at once & she helped to get me off to Kaikoura (help I badly needed) & came up at the weekend shortly afterwards to see how I was getting on. It was she who was recovering from mumps & we got to know each other very well during that week here. And this term, there being no students, I have been able to institute her as a boarder – she has one of the little bedrooms opposite this. This relieves me of food responsibility, but she spends her evenings with me, or in my parlour, if I've gone to bed. She is out all day, & eagerly I look for her return! She is only 23, but in some ways very mature, & is really well educated, & such good company. Her affection has changed my life here completely, & I cannot tell you how thankful I am to God that the years of loneliness seem to be ending.

But better than that – Dear Paul has seen more of her these last holidays & now they are engaged. For the present they want it to be known only to intimate friends, but I am allowed to tell you – Indeed I *must* tell you. He was in ChCh from Sun. evening till yesterday evg, when he went back to the School, for it may be a very short while before he goes into camp, for overseas. That makes it all so *very* poignant. I love them both very dearly, & *feel with* them. They are not to be married before he goes, so I think that I am to be allowed to take care of her till he comes back (*if* he comes back, one does not say, but it might have to be said) & she will take care of me. We don't see further than St F's yet, but what I should like would be to get some little place where we could be together. She hopes for another post in ChCh next year, and the difficulty would be ways & means, for I should need hired help. But all this has been so surprising, miraculous indeed, that I believe what is needed further will be provided. Sometimes I think that my little Darling has sent her to me – just when my strength is beginning to fail. I feel now that I should like to be allowed to live, in order to stand by her. This news about Paul is for you & Toss only, & now comes a bit that specially concerns *you*. I am so glad to feel perfectly certain that you will be glad about what I have done. They feel that their betrothal is something special & so do I – (doesn't everyone perhaps feel that!) & they were not content with the idea of an ordinary engagement ring. Kathleen & I were looking through my trinket-box one evening when I gave her a pear & crystal pendant (which was made for me in India & not a family thing) as a remembrance of these last weeks & of their betrothal – she saw your opal & was completely fascinated by it. She loves opals & had never seen such a bright one – I told her the story of it, and gave it to her for her ring, if Paul should agree. He likes the stone & likes the *story* & I gave it to him yesterday & they took it to the jeweller. It is to be set "à jour"[1] with a diamond on each side of it. The sun & the moon & 2 stars. Paul & I think the opal is so like her, she is full of light. I told them both that you would love to be in the giving. You know dear I have looked at it again & again & not known what to do about it. Nothing I had was suitable for a setting & I could not somehow think of the expense of having something made. So there it has been shut up in the dark. And now the time has come when I do not need trinkets – but it is a time of spring & resurrection for me as you foretold, & the opal has been caught into a very great love & one in which I have my share. No one else is to know the story of their engagement ring (its to be ready in a fortnight) – you may wish Toss to know, but no one else is to know. I felt there was a benediction upon that stone, & K's eager attraction to it dispelled any hesitation about parting with it. *Not* "parting with" – its just been given a further meaning. You agree, don't you? And I shall see it on her finger, instead of, perhaps, on mine.

[..]

Yesterday's post brought a letter from John S. announcing his forthcoming marriage to Connie Jones on the 27th. She should make him a very good mate. He was here on his way home – I wasn't quite well enough for his exuberance – he was going to see her in the evg. & I suppose it was fixed up then.

Today's post brings a letter in very small writing which on examination proves to be from Toss' "Uncle Frank." I can't cope with the tiny script today with this head & I don't think it looks quite like "my cup of tea". (Nearly every sentence ends with three or even four exclamation marks!) If he is still with you would you thank him on my behalf & say that I hope he will forgive me if I do not answer it for some time – I cannot deal with all present accumulations of correspondence.

---

[1] Fr. 'up to date.' The significance of this stone is further explained in the ensuing letter to Toss Woollaston (Feb. 16, 1942).

The enclosed snap will show you what has happened to your pear tree (the big dark pine has gone altogether). Its not a very good likeness. The ones of K. no good at all.

Any new snaps of the bairns? Hope you are enjoying the improvements to dwelling house I heard of.

With my love to you & T. & J. & P. P.[1] from
M. U.

Hocken Library. MS-0996-3/225.

[1] The Woollaston's second child was called Paul, but Bethell objected to this, too, and insisted on calling him Peter Paul.

VI: 1942–1943

To Paul Gabites & Kathleen Taylor – January 4, 1942

Pahau Pastures, Culverden, Amuri.

Darling – or darlings indeed,

This in reply to your letter & note enclosed of yesterday* – (written on Tuesday) – such a pleasant surprise! & my only letter because I'd told St F's to cease sending on. And by the way if you did go so far as to address another here I shall get the mail tomorrow in Culverden before leaving. Such a glorious morning but now clouding over again. It was chiefly devoted to hoeing the drive while my sister[1] opened up & decorated the unused drawing-room.° Some ChCh people are coming to tea – I should say Afternoon Tea – en route Hanmer-ChCh (official petrol) & since they havn't been here before the place must be shown off! I am dashing off a few lines hoping to get this posted in ChCh by them – Otherwise I might as well post on arrival in ChCh – Your news is very nice – the "we' comes so naturally now! [...]

[Added in margin] *My sister in law rode over to get her horse shod.

[Added in margin] °We sit in smoking room en famille.[2]

More & more rain. Stump[3] came up on Friday prepared to work here for 3 weeks – but went home yesterday rain having set in again. It cleared up however beautifully in late afternoon – & I slipped out for a solitary ramble & did not come back till just in time for dinner at 7. It was so beautiful & *silent*. One can't see the mountains until one gets outside the homestead demesne – its all shrouded by big trees – necessary because of winds. There's just one gap towards Kaikoura where one looks over from the verandah. [...] Physically I am extremely well & feeling like a prize ox after all the good living – 3 square meals a day – but not much of me beyond the flesh is active here! Not just my "spiritual home" – much, however, to admire if one looks out for it.

[...]

Wartime Pahau is so different. I should have brought working clothes – breeches even. So odd to see my brother driving off in the old buggy, as I saw him 40 years ago!

The visitation hour draws near! – I have put on that new silk frock – don't like it very much I think – but it will be very *useful* I am sure – It

---

[1] I.e. Bethell's sister-in-law, Thyra, not Rhoda, who was in England.

[2] Fr. 'as a family.'

[3] A note attached to the archive identifies this as Christopher Bethell.

was very dear of our Paul to put in a word for the New Year – please kiss him for me.

Glad I did not go back yesterday – there [were] 65 passengers booked from Culverden to say nothing of surrounding places, besides the Kaikoura passengers already on the train! How different going back wd. be if you were not to be there again in the not distant future!

Your loving
U.

Macmillan Brown Library. MB 572. A.

TO KATHLEEN TAYLOR – JANUARY 8, 1942

47 Webb St. ChCh.

My *precious* little Katya

What a nasty peevish letter – letters in fact – I must have sent off yesterday! I must run along to the pillarpost with this repentance, hoping it may somehow catch up. After all the scramble I was too late for St Albans so went to the G.P.O. – was determined to get them off because it seemed so ungrateful – But I should have done better to wait till I was in a better mood. Darling it *was* terribly disappointing to begin again here with headache & exhaustion – the old state over again – instead of country vigour! (Morning headache again, I have one now, even after my tea! not one decent cup of tea while I was away! It was not in the train I had this headache – it began half an hour after I'd settled in here – must be ChCh atmosphere.) That's *no* excuse for snapping at you about anacins! How *could* I? (Aspirin was in a case downstairs I hadn't unpacked & I wasn't well enough to clamber down in the blackout – wh. I hadn't effected.) The spectre of lonely old age asserts itself – and then, when I come back to our familiar things, there's an intolerable longing for my little Effie, & our home – the air, the view, the garden – Michael – all that's lost – it hurts so much – but it drives me to take refuge in the holy will of God, which is ultimate reality & truth. I rebelled against this suffocating gaol, against toiling up and down the institution staircase, against the fatigue-for-nothing! – but now this clear morning I see Mt Grey, & trees, & a streak of snow, & I think what a very nice room it is & anyhow how *wicked* to be peevish about trifles in war-time! Things *are* a tiny bit tidier since yesterday & some washing done.

[...]

I expect the border will be battered by rain. When this room is really tidy I shall pick one of the lilies to scent it sweetly – no flowers so far, except a rose bud for Effie. I'll put something for Katya today – a geranium I think. The minute I saw my border I felt that it had poetry about it! even this. The Pahau garden IS beautiful (about 7 acres of it) but there's an absence of poetry & spirituality wh. I found so *arid*, too you know dear (a few moments for musing before I must get up). About two years ago it must be, yes, just before the war – I ventured to put in my prayer – seeing that life was going on – that, if it were possible, three things might come to me again – love, & poetry, & a home. And then how strangely and unexpectedly your dear little love came! It was something like my Effie coming (thirty seven years ago) because before I knew her I felt sorry for her being lonely & désoeuvrée,[1] & Rhoda & I planned a home & occupation for her. Similarly, I didn't take you in at all the first evening – I asked you to come again because Paul said you were lonely in yr. lodging & I asked him whether you wd. care to come – The second time I remember seeing that you were a very right-minded young woman! & then I was charmed by your being hungry! – like a boy. [...] There remain poetry & a home! One may depend on the other, because my poetry only seems to happen in peace & quiet. But at the moment I am only afraid the Japanese may shoo me out of this *ersatz* home!

I wonder whether I shall hear today what is to happen to dearest Paul. A nuisance the post coming in so late. Tell him I've been reading Karl Barth's (the Swiss neo-Calvinist) Letter to Great Britain – booklet sent to me from England. He is one of those happy people who are perfectly clear in their minds about the war – & it is an excellent piece of writing.[2] He doesn't believe in the Natural Order of Catholic Theology – but he does believe that the State "wields the sword" rightly for justice sake. (Must discuss the difference with the Rev. Merlin who must be the latest from theological school.)[3] "What then, is this war? It is a large-scale police measure which has become absolutely necessary in order to repulse an active anarchism which has become a principle."

9.30 Have meanwhile grasped that its useless to post early! & so you'll be thinking of me as a nasty old woman for 24 hours! I deserve it. Garden has liked rain, esp. beans – Sky looks like more rain – possibly storms – wish we had a cellar! [...]

---

[1] Fr. 'at a loose end.'

[2] Barth had been explicitly invited to write an open letter to his 'Christian Brethren in Great Britain,' providing a Christian justification for the war. It was published in The Christian News-Letter Books series; the passage Bethell quotes can be found on p. 21.

[3] Merlin Davies came to New Zealand as chaplain to the Student Christian Movement in 1940. The following year he became Precentor at Christchurch Cathedral, in addition to teaching theology and Scripture at College House. Later, he and Kathleen Taylor were married.

Later. No Pauline news today. He forgot "The Brothers" – perhaps now will wait for camp. May post to you (if you are not coming up with him) 'House of Prayer' & small collection of children's verse just come from Home.[1] Must broach my N.Z. Claret (Thank you Paul) & see what that will do for me. Perhaps this headache has something to do with thunder. But I did not have it at Pahau when it thundered! Hope I shan't forget the little bits about P. to tell you. The impression that remains now is the last sight of my brother, one of the very, very nicest men on the planet! Goodbye my Darling treasure & au revoir – When will that be? XX to the nth degree (wasn't that how we put it?)

Your U

Macmillan Brown Library. MB 572. A.

To Toss Woollaston – February 16, 1942

47 Webb St. ChCh.

My dear Toss,

[...]

About D & N. I must tell you that many things in it are much *truer* for me now, than when I wrote them. They were notions then – now experiences. I can follow all you say about the morning, and the arising. There *are* many "dark nights" in life, and mornings. Your words remind me of Edith's encouragement & hope when she was staying here that first time. I felt paralysed – done for – & she said she felt that there was spring in me! That's what the opal stood for. (Paul said in a recent note that his happiness in having found Katya, is like the opal "full of new lights & lovely colours every time I look at it") In this connection, truest of all perhaps for *me* is a bit in Time & Place called Warning of Winter.

Some people havn't liked "The Spirit of Beauty" but surely its true – The Holy Spirit *must* be the Spirit of Beauty?[2] Perhaps it doesn't express well what I meant, but I did not think of any other way of expressing the joy ("adoration"?) I felt. *My* desire, do you know, is to write more & better poetry – but I am so old it seems very unlikely! (The barren

---

[1] 'The Brothers' is Dostoyevsky's novel; the 'House of Prayer' may refer to a book (so called) by a minor novelist and poet, Florence Converse, which was popular in the early 20th century.

[2] Woollaston had written (Feb. 11) of his 'intense joy' in reading *Day and Night*, and particularly 'the repeated mention of the name, "Spirit of Beauty" which I noticed from poem to poem.'

woman in the Bible who thought she was past child bearing?)[1] If you are not chosen to write verse Toss – your prose is, to my mind, vastly improved – in this letter especially.

[...]

About the war & yourself. What can I do but think of you in my prayer? As I do.

Forgive this poor scrawl, dear Toss – & inadequate thanks for such appreciation & sympathy! I must dress now & go to read to my blind friend – & post on the way. We have to post by 3.30 now – the last collection & that at the branch post office.

I think the Quaker expression for such a letter as yours was "heart-tendering".[2] I hope Edith is very well.

Much love to you both
M. U. B.

Hocken Library. MS-0996-3/225.

TO MONTE HOLCROFT – FEBRUARY 19, 1942

St Faith's House. Webb St. ChCh.

Dear Monte

[...] Like you I am 'desperately busy' – tho' in a very different way. The daily business of providing food, & other domestic calls, attention to visitors, the details of everyday life press upon me so much, that I have [been] driven, with acute reluctance to set aside letter-writing, even to my oldest friends. My sister in England gets fairly frequent letters from me, but very illegible ones I'm afraid. I've been in rather poor health for two years & more – at last a few weeks ago I began to feel really well again & set about all kinds of postponed occupations.

My young friend Miss Taylor, whom you saw here, came back after the holidays, & was helping me a good deal pending a new post – but *she* began to be ill last week. I took her to a specialist yesterday & he thinks its a case for an operation (not a severe one) & that's going to keep me busy, visiting her in hospital. This by way of explanation of my silence. My "call" seems to have been to relationships with human beings during the last four years – little reading or writing, & less communing with nature!

[...]

---

[1] Bethell may be thinking of a number of figures here: Sarah, Rebekah or Rachel (see Genesis 11: 30; 25: 21; 29: 31), or Elisabeth (see Luke 1: 7).

[2] Bethell probably found this in Woolman's Journal (see, for example, Chapters 9 & 12), but it also occurs in other Quaker writing.

The MS looks exceedingly interesting![1] I have only glanced at it, but hope to make some time to read it carefully during the week end. The chapter headings are promising, & I like the *title* particularly (you wd. know that!) & the bit from Charles Brasch (That will please him – its some time since I heard from him & I think a letter must have been lost. A copy of the 'Dublin Review' came from him a few weeks ago with interesting articles.)

In your letter of Jan 28 about the book you say that you see flaws wh. could have been avoided if you had been able to give more time to it. If there's no success at present about publication could you use the delay for further revision & enrichment? or perhaps its too late for that & the impetus spent. That's all for the moment about "The Waiting Hills" – except to say what an honour it is to have it sent to me! I shall respect what you say about its being withheld from perusal before publication, although I know there will be temptation to read tit-bits to the young friend aforementioned, who is extremely intelligent & good critic! I shall however hope to withstand temptation.

[...]

Mount Grey! I gaze at it (my only Mountain here) from my balcony – & wonder whether I shall ever be nearer to it again![2] Even the distant view is a solace. There seemed to be a chance when Miss Taylor, who has a ticket, discovered Rental Cars, & we did go for one picnic, to some of my old familiar spots Tai Tapu way, – but now petrol shortage & her health have upset our plans again. Perhaps I shall be taken to the country by Evacuation!

I was at my brother's farm for Xmas & New Year – but too busy to meditate to my distaste – so short-handed everywhere.

A disgraceful little brochure called The New Triad[3] has been sent to me from the Caxton Press – I don't know what Denis G. (who as I expect you know has gone to the British Navy) wd. say to it! The perpetrator has joined the Caxton Press. In it I read a notice of the new publishing project at Wellington, with which I see D.G. associates himself.

---

[1] Holcroft had submitted the manuscript of 'The Waiting Hills' for comment. As an epigraph, he quoted the first four lines of 'Land and People (i),' the opening poem of Brasch's volume.

[2] Holcroft had been encouraging her to undertake such a trip, exhorting her that Mt Grey's 'genius loci requires poetic expression' (Jan. 28, 1942).

[3] *New Triad* was a monthly periodical published in Wellington, 1937-1942. Its editor was Noel Hoggard.

Martin Buber – yes, I read it as poetry I think[1] – there was much that I hailed in the light of my own experience. (I wonder whether you noticed the bit about the *cat*). Bosanquet wd. be beyond me.[2] I read reviews of the stiffer books as they appear – & somewhere I have I think a study of the Meeting of Extremes. I should like to sit under Dr. Popper.

The War! Tremendous. If one could forget the horrors. What a drama! It looks now like the humiliation of British Imperialism? Locally we are concerned with black outs and trenches & sand bags etc more last straws in the daily routine – but in the meantime, apart from the roar of Wigram flights – it has brought some quietness as you say.

Now I must break off & see about cooking some lunch. Then plant some bulbs (for the Japanese to pick?) & write a few lines to a young C.O. in prison – & we have to post by 3.30 instead of 5 p.m.

[...]

Yours very sincerely
M. U. Bethell

P.S. Have I ever said what a pleasure it was to see you again! One of the rewards for growing old (besides our nice *pension)* is to see *maturity* come to our juniors. Or should I say to see them attain it?

Alexander Turnbull Library. MS-Papers-1186-03

TO MONTE HOLCROFT – MARCH 1, 1942

St Faith's. Webb St. ChCh.

Dear Monte

I don't know whether I am keeping yr. MS too long. This week my friend has had her operation & with that & other pressing tho' minor matters, I've had no un-tired time since last Sunday when I spent some time reading you. First I dipped into each chapter here & there & then read more of the last three chapters, to which you drew my attention, & then – unashamedly! read all of your words about my writing. After that I began Ch.I. reading systematically & making some notes. I *hope* I may be able to finish reading carefully this evening – if my head doesn't give out. Meanwhile I'll clear the ground so to speak by telling of my pleasure in

[1] Holcroft had written: 'I enjoyed it in much the way that I can enjoy a somewhat obscure poem – taking delight in the occasional flashes of insight, but withholding judgment for the lack of a complete understanding' (Jan. 28, 1942).

[2] In the same letter Holcroft suggested that Buber's attempt to bridge idealism and realism had been done '20 or 30 years ago ... in one of Bosanquet's lesser-known books, "The Meeting of Extremes in Contemporary Philosophy."'

your view of my verse. You are I think the *only* reader who has seen what I owe to the English Bible! Constant attendance at the Liturgy & the Offices during my years in the poorer parts of London had that influence. To that influence, to the good education I had in my teens, & to the suppressed desire to paint, I attribute whatever I have achieved in expression – And you do understand – and share – the influence of this land.

That's all I can say now, as I want to take advantage of an offer to post my mail. (One of the difficulties of wartime is getting letters off from anywhere but the city.)

With my thanks – and an apology for hurry

Yours sincerely
Ursula Bethell

A confession – I *did* read some of your words to the friend aforesaid. But she is very discreet & honourable & I think no harm is done.

Alexander Turnbull Library. MS-Papers-1186-03

TO TOSS WOOLLASTON – MARCH 7, 1942

As from 47 Webb St. ChCh.
At Rhodes Convalescent Home. Cashmere

Dear Toss

[...]

We wanted to thank you for sending the drawing – K. does like it & says she *has* seen me look like that & thinks its a good drawing – Yet not comprehensive enough to be a portrait.[1] She wd. like you to have another shot at it, but I don't see how that can be! I will return it when I get back to Webb St.

[...]

For about a year, I think, I have wished I could begin writing again, but the impulse does not seem to be strong enough to break me away from the trivial, Martha occupations[2] that have enslaved me – Partly, bad health has inhibited such impulses. And it has seemed that I must have to do with human beings instead of thought & language – So the years have passed – You have revived the wish by writing so feelingly about "Day & Night" – and now Monte Holcroft has sent me the M.S. of an essay he wishes to publish which has a chapter about NZ poetry, & a

---

[1] This probably refers to the charcoal portrait that Woollaston drew in 1938. See the letter to Kennedy, July 6, 1938. He also painted a portrait of Bethell in oil nearer the time of this letter, c. 1940 (now housed at the Museum of New Zealand Te Papa Tongarewa).

[2] See the episode in Luke 10; 38-42.

long notice of my own which gives me much pleasure – He is one of the few who have recognised what I owe to the Bible – Perhaps the time has now come when I should attend to this impulse – but it wd. mean some quiet & solitude & release from the fatigue of domestic toil. And since the Japanese are expected so soon & we are all in a fuss about blackouts & trenches & evacuation, it doesn't seem the likeliest moment for devotion to art! But, as you say, its a question of what is *given* to one to do.

March 8

I want Edith to know what a joy that opal is – I see it more & better than if it were set in something of my own! We were at a jeweller's about a watch & the ring attracted his notice & he said what a good "fire opal" it was, & then proceeded to show us a treasure of his own – a very large stone which he called a 'sunset opal' & thought it might be unique – it was found and polished by a man digging in the Queensland opal fields – very beautiful – like a landscape – very dark in the lower part, then a line of fire running to & fro – & above, clear bright pale colour – the sky. It reminded me of sunset from the Cashmere Hills, & there was just such a sunset last night. Katya is so much my own person, & seems to have brought Paul nearer too, it is a sort of miracle – one of those Mornings – sometimes I feel that my little lost darling has been allowed to send her to me. [...]

Thought about the war has become too difficult – its too vast – when I listen to a good pacifist – I feel, yes you are right. Or if to one who decides that it is right to take part in this war, I feel, yes this war must be fought. I know that I am a coward. Perhaps the preservation of life becomes too important to a woman. My own attitude won't be put to the test at my age, & I might feel it being let off too easily, but I shall not worry about it. I must be a looker on, & try to keep peaceful within myself.

[...]

Well, now I must get on with the M. H. manuscript. I feel much less tired & clearer headed up here. There's something *wrong* with my life in Webb St!

Love to you both.
M. U. B.

Hocken Library. MS-0996-3/225.

TO MONTE HOLCROFT – MARCH [8-10], 1942

As from 47 Webb St. ChCh.
At R C H Cashmere[1]

Dear Monte

Here I am under the pinetrees – a norwester roars high overhead & I lean against a sheltering bank – & it must be confessed that there's a strong temptation to give oneself up to listening to the lovely sound & to dreaming. But here also is your MS on my knee, & your words about what it cost *you* to deal with *my* verse spur me on to mental effort! The more I dwell on the subject, the less of value I feel there can be in my opinion of your work! The first reflection I made was that your prose struck me as being an advance on The Deepening Stream, terser & more vigorous. Unfortunately I hadn't it with me, to look through again with this idea in my mind (I rounded up things for my patient's need, & hadn't time to think of my own requirements.) My next "reaction" was to feel baffled by the complexities of the subject. I recognized that the themes of the last 3 chapters were particularly your own – you appeared in a new rôle in the first four, the observant journalist well versed in current affairs, intellectual & political ... What I asked myself is this? Is the whole welded together, proportionately into a *book*? Is it not rather a case of a series of Essays? one could almost say articles for a monthly Review?

[...]

Looking back over it all I still have the same impression, & wish that the book were all in the same key, that it were made about the same length as The Deepening Stream ... but that is an absurd remark! It probably *is* the same length! Typescript bulks so much larger. Anyhow I would like to have more emphasis laid on your theme, more of your own summary, your own deductions made from the facts given in the first pages, less of the facts. Even in the 6th Chapter[2] I feel that there is too much *information* about the Bible, facts which would be commonplaces to an average, educated person! I hope & think that you will not set much store on my impression, I am probably *utterly* astray, but that is how it strikes me. Or could the first chapters be put under the same heading, as a preliminary – somehow or other the book ... fails in unity?

March 10 I had to go to Webb St yesterday to inspect the shelter trench – a horrible object really, but apparently demanded of us. John Summers has been at work on it, between other 2 employments – (& by

---

[1] Rhodes Convalescent Home.

[2] This chapter, 'The Awakening of Poetry,' included Holcroft's comments on Bethell's poetry.

the way he has more than once dwelt on the pleasure he had one day at your house – a meal al fresco. He spoke of your home quite wistfully.) I brought back with me 'The Deepening Stream' & now think I was wrong about the prose – the style is quite as succinct, no doubt the difference in subject matter in the first chapters made a different impression. I must admit that here & there I found a slight hint of journalistic language which didn't happen in the case of The Deepening Stream.

[...]

For the rest I have a list of references to points it would be nice to talk about, but which wd. make a letter too long. For instance, how interesting to see how the word "forest" recurs again & again! Its a symbol deep in your consciousness. (Its riverbed that haunts me, but a much less musical word !) [...]

For instance the Syrian hills[1] – have I ever told you how the country passing through Utah, by Salt Lake City, put N.Z. in mind? & how I read that the landscape there was supposed to resemble the biblical scene? [...] I like the passage – p. 170 beginning "religion in its widest sense" but I should not have to *contrast* that with religion "expressed in the dogma & ritual of a church". It is precisely the Church of England service wh. made me familiar with Hebrew poetry *in my bones*! I am bound to say that this was in England & that they were intelligently & perfectly chanted.

Out here I'm very conscious of the "gulf fixed" (apparently) between the church-goer & those who care for art, poetry, music. It is deplorable. Sometimes my verse has, in sort, made a bridge between church & non-church!

I mustn't however ramble on – I want to say that I don't actually *expect* you to *recast* your book as a result of my remarks![2] You will give it to New Zealand as you yourself have seen it, and I wait with the greatest interest to see what N.Z. will say to it.

Forgive me if I have been presumptuous & too outspoken, as well as, no doubt it will become apparent – mistaken. Thank you again for sending me the M.S. which has given me some very interesting hours – I've valued the privilege. I hope that the appearance of your work won't be long delayed, and that it will do a great deal of good.

Your old friend
M. U. Bethell

P.S. Don't you think that *some* of The Garden pieces (tho' the collection was to be sure written largely in homesick mood) have a N.Z.

---

[1] See her 'Appel' (*Collected Poems*, p. 22).

[2] In fact, Holcroft did substantially revise it, in part at least along lines she had suggested.

flavour?[1] For instance, 'When I am very earnestly digging'. To me most of it is quite New Zealandy.

I have made a resolution to read Mason, Curnow, Fairburn – I tried them & did not find them easy. Sometimes I found it hard to *believe* in them – their sincerity – but doubtless was mistaken.

Alexander Turnbull Library. MS-Papers-1186-03

TO MONTE HOLCROFT – MAY 10, 1942

47 Webb St. ChCh.

Dear Monte

You have rightly guessed I hope, that physical & mental disability have kept me silent. To go into detail wd. fill up a letter, but the short of it is, I have been too exhausted after daily duties to write to you & many others who *should* be written to. I could only lie on my back & rest. After a short stay with a kind niece who kept me mostly in bed I have had some busy days, & now this Day there is a pause – with no visitors expected & a friend kindly seeing to the meals – I do hope to pay one or two of my most serious debts.

Looking back to your book I think that on the whole my impression remains the same. But what I have been feeling most strongly is that some more competent critic should read the M.S. – some one with a better knowledge of the audience you wish to address. Two people I have in mind who are most competent – E. H. McCormick who is back in NZ but writes that he began work immediately & I think might not be able to give attention to it. The other L. C. Webb might also be too busy – but I wish you would allow me to ask him whether he could give time to reading it. (I have not forgotten your saying that you don't like your work to be read by many before publication, but his opinion would be so much more [worth] having than mine.)

[...]

I don't move about enough to know how most newspaper readers see things, only I do know that when I go to stay in the country I perceive that music art & letters don't exist there.

[...]

And I am aware, of course, of how much "good stuff" there is in yr. work – & I only wish there were a chance of discussing with you some of the questions you raise in one's mind.

---

[1] In a footnote, Holcroft suggested that the Garden 'lacks the unmistakable New Zealand flavour which was to come later' (p. 84).

(I wish you wd. write an autobiography – the story of your own thought.)

I am afraid you must miss a good deal, situated where you are. I myself am tied to the house far too much, yet now & again I meet an interesting person or hear a stimulating speech -- such as was made by Prof. Sinclaire last week on Capping Day – I hope it will be printed. His Press articles have appeared in book form, no doubt its been sent to your paper.[1]

I must tell you that on the day I went to Waikari – at the beginning of the last spell of hot N.W. weather – I was quite overpowered by the beauty of the country I passed through (even as seen from the Motor Bus!) Never before surely has there been such an autumn blaze of red & gold, willows & poplars with scarcely a leaf fallen all lit up, and Mt Grey in the background. Words began to come – but there's no leisure, as you say, & no solitude – And I think I have too tired a brain, Monte. (On my return journey trees were almost bare.)

It was a relief to get away from the besieged looking city. I daresay that down there the invasion question looms near, & preparations, even for such a one as myself, have taken up, & still do a great deal of time. (And I tore a muscle in my leg trying to shovel earth when the shelter trench was made in the garden!) I do hope that by the end of the year we shall know whether we belong to the Japanese or not.

I hope you will consider my suggestion – you might easily get a quite contrary opinion. You wish yr. book to make its mark both as propaganda & as a work of art, & I can't tell whether it is successfully conceived in either respect. I hope earnestly that it is.

With my best wishes as always
Yours very sincerely
Ursula Bethell

Alexander Turnbull Library. MS-Papers-1186-03

TO CHARLES BRASCH – MAY 10, 1942

47 Webb St. Christchurch. N.Z.

My dear Charles

I've already destroyed several attempts in the way of a letter to you – the last one (dated April 12) had run to five sheets – but now reads so dull & out of date that it must feed the fire.

[...]

---

[1] Published by Caxton Press as *Lend Me Your Ears*.

John has withdrawn I think from the Friends, at any rate he has found himself free to serve with Medical Unit & is in camp at Trentham. (Having previously married a C.O. who was in gaol for 3 months & feels that she has made her witness. Her account of her experience made me think that she should take up prison work – or should have. She is now expecting a baby. I encourage marriages & families – spinsters *do*!)

[...]

My nephew [is] in Syria, transport officer, now a Captain & safe so far – but of course we all live with bated breath waiting for what will happen next. He was in the thick of that Libyan business.[1] The other nephew will be in the next round up & will not appeal – it will come hard on my brother. My niece says she can manage the smaller farm having a good shepherd. Two farmer friends near here are in camp & their wives carrying on.

Rodney is in the Defaulter's Camp near Rotorua. He would not appeal as a Quaker (they are let off without parley) & stated his own case, which was not allowed. [...] I think you will have seen Denis Glover who left about Christmas to join the British Navy & he will have told you about Lawrence & the others. Basil Dowling was turned out of his parish on account of his views & works in an orchard at Heathcote – I wonder whether you have seen his book of poems (Caxton Press) – good I think – Simple but good.[2] I like his choice of words. (Not specifically New Zealand.)

[...]

I confess that its a temptation to look up & gaze at mountains, meadows, sky. Its a blazing southerly (dry & still southerly) day & such a different world from our ChCh. Its hardly believable – we are perched on some steps – the cottage is well up above the country road & commands the view. The sea's deep roar – there have been storms – is somehow soothing. So different from the mechanical grind of the aeroplanes! Its a clash of pleasures, that & this letter – besides I *owe* it to you – I am deeply in your debt. Debt makes me think of money [...] I know that everything is in the melting pot & that your circumstances as well as mine must have changed in the meantime – but I am now wondering whether, if they have not changed too much, it *would* be right for me, this year, to accept the generous help you offer? [...]

Some of my little investments are fizzling out – Japanese Bonds! Greek bonds! can't be hoped for – and an Argentine Railway had thrown

---

[1] The New Zealand Division was involved in Operation Crusader in Libya in November and December of 1941. It was a field of particularly intense fighting, with very heavy casualties. The Division had a few months rest in Syria before returning to Egypt in June.

[2] Dowling's first volume, *A Day's Journey*, had been published the preceding year.

up the game pro tem. [...] And it came my way to help a friend with a loan, the repayment of which I should like to postpone indefinitely – And one or two extra comforts provided against the winter – such as a larger electric heater. Hitherto I have "felt a stop in my mind"[1] as the Quakers say about accepting a present from you, but now I am thinking that perhaps it would not be wrong to do so this year, if you are still in need of an object for your benefactions. To put back £50 into the Savings Bank against the future would be quite enjoyable but you *must* understand that mine is *not* a state of penury. & I don't quite know whether it really matters that one should 'take up capital' at my advanced age! I believe it would give you pleasure as you say, to do this, and few are the people, I must say, to whom I should feel able to allow such a pleasure! Please take it as a *testimony of esteem*! And on *no* account think of it if circumstances have changed.

[...]

How nice of you to write as you do about my rigmarole from this place last year. I do not remember very well what I said, but I was afraid of having bored you. I have made some progress I think in the spiritual life since then – not trying to count gains, but a sense that the way is clearer. I am still far from S. Teresa's "My prayer is solid like a house"[2] but my prayer is much better. That saying about Faith was either Hilton or Matt. Weyer.[3] I have not books with me – It was the latter I think who wrote "The essence of a thing is too worthy to be said."

Monday Early

I was beside a driftwood fire in the evening to finish up this letter, but sleep supervened. Nice of the landlady to give me bedroom fire – I specified it last winter, but not this time. It makes us a private sitting-room – something hard to come by in N.Z. travel. We lived with the mountains yesterday – this morning observed. They impose themselves, yet are not so near as to be oppressive – Certainly they *do* seem to say when evening comes down upon them "Warte nur, bald[e] ruhest du auch".[4]

I was going to tell you about the course of lectures upon religion the W.E.A. asked for this year. [...] Dr. Popper, the Viennese philosopher, is giving several & Archdeacon Whitehead came up from Dunedin for the

---

[1] Quoted in an earlier letter to Kennedy, Oct. 26, 1937.

[2] This comes from Ch. 24 of *The Life of S. Teresa of Jesus* (i. e. the Spanish Carmelite, Teresa of Avila), first published in 1558.

[3] See her letter of July 31, 1941, and the footnote there.

[4] Ger. 'Only wait. Soon you will rest as well.' These are the concluding lines of a short poem ('Wandrers Nachtlied II' c. 1780) written by Goethe while in the mountains near the town of Ilmenau, and inscribed by him onto the boards of a hut set in the hills.

opening one & asked "What is religion?" He refused to give a definition tho' that is exactly what the W.E.A. faithful crave for! This "concern" about religion is very noticeable to-day. Prof. Sinclaire put it to the forefront in his discourse – & you know what a revolutionary *he* is. And Leicester Webb in the address I mentioned turned his expectation to the Church, in considering our Present Situation. Many revisions of thought during my life-time. It seemed to me that L.C.W. had arrived at what has long been intellectually convincing to me. My task in the years that may remain to me is I think so to resign myself to these convictions that the facts of religion are as near & natural & undebateable as the air and the sun at Kaikoura. I live, I think, increasingly in this spirit – *and* increasingly aware of my own dreadful failures! There is a sense of the wards of a lock turning – quite silently. It is a comfort to have come to this point now that I have this eager, spiritually alive little girl beside me – we can travel together.

I've lately read a striking book by C.S.Lewis – The Problem of Pain I think it was called. No doubt you have seen it – perhaps too easy for you. Have you ever read Buber's "I and Thou"? I've had the translation for years – since it was published in fact & it amuses me to see it at last "featured" in Xtian News Letter & even in the pulpit!

The list of books you were reading or about to read makes me envious. So did Arthur Mayhew's list of what he worked through during convalescence (by the way he is my contemporary). He always turns to the classics. I must get out my Wordsworth & read that bit of the Excursion. I was wont to read Wordsworth as a girl – and have studied him from time to time since. My copy of Matt. Arnold's selection dates from school days. Paul has left a splendid edition of Donne with me 'for the duration' – But alas how seldom comes the space of uninterrupted, unfatigued leisure needful for absorption in such literature! There must be a margin of time round such reading – The war is a boiling surging *mental* Rotorua!

Having at last achieved this letter, I feel quite anxious that it should reach you! – too bad if it were lost, because it shows that I *was* grateful for yours – dull & rambling as it *mine* I mean – is. I should like to be more succinct. I think it will be easier to write to England when this anxious winter is past with its suspense & waiting. Now please, please pay no attention to my monetary passages unless you are really in need of an object for your kind intentions. [...] Remember that I'm *not* indigent & rather a spender as you may have observed. But, Charles, I *do* try to *trade* with my talents as the parable bids[1] – especially by keeping things

[1] See Matthew 25: 14-30.

moving for young & hopeful friends. It amuses me how I confide my circumstances to you! Actually a compliment & I hope you think it so.

[...] Now space has run out. So goodbye, & may St Nicholas or whoever has charge of mails speed the passage of this one.

Yours affectionately
Ursula Bethell

Hocken Library. MS-0996-3/19.

TO JOHN SUMMERS – JUNE 25, 1942

St. Faith's. Webb St. ChCh

My dear John

I have been wanting to make time to answer your excellent letter of last week dated "Monday" & now today comes another, just as good, dated "Sunday". I'll deal first with No 1. It is quite remarkable, Johnny my dear, how, suddenly, you seem to have got a grip of the English language! Its as if some chemical had been thrown into your expression & caused a precipitation of the rubbishy parts. Merlin was here last Thursday & I knew you wd. not mind his reading it all through, as well as the message sent to him. He was just as struck as I was (& so was Miss Taylor) by the advance. He said that your remarks about Bro. Every's book were quite just, & apply not only to the Newsletter book, but to Every's writing in general.[1] He said that if your criticism were filled out a little & expressed in rather more precise English, it wd. be a perfectly adequate review. However that may be, I fancy that your note-book should come first just now – I agree that its important. I didn't mean to oppose your writing things down, dear, only doubted the wisdom of "rushing into print". (There are still mistakes in English – which I suppose a course of class-work wd. correct – Miss Taylor's work of preparation for her English classes reminds me of all the rules there are! I have forgotten *them* & am left with merely the conviction that this is right, that, wrong.)

[...]

I am deeply interested in your paragraphs about the tension between passionate conviction & openminded tolerance. No doubt you are right about prayer & inward humility – the intellectual fruits of that mental life wd. result gradually – as your mind clears & steadies itself – the surer you are yourself the better you can understand others. I daresay

---

[1] From Summers' letter, the book can be identified as George Every's *Christian Discrimination*, part of the series 'The Christian News-letter Books' (1940).

I've quoted Von Hugel's saying before – that one should be convinced at the core – & then can afford to shade off to the twilight of opinion at the periphery – *not* his own words, I forget them.

[...]

I value that letter, Johnny, & shall keep it by me for the thought it contains.

As the world outlook grows darker (and it does, this Axis advance means prolongation of the war, and that means more suffering & more shattering of the things that *can* be destroyed –) I feel more and more strongly the summons to Christian thinking – there is no real principle of cohesion in the world but the Christian faith. And I think how it will be for such as you to help build up the community long after I'm dead. I said that to K Taylor this morning – for she is spiritual, & ready to study religion, & has a bright young mind. Yes, we must have something to offer to all who ask & the call to do so comes in most unexpected ways. [...]

Do you not find that many men say "Oh you can't do any thinking in the army" "you can't be Christian in the army" "religion must wait till the end of the war" etc. But *now is* the time to think – & to find faith.

[...]

I think its necessary for you to have arguments to meet – how else can one reach solid ground? Not that sound arguments & *opinions about* religion are all ones requirement, as well you know. It's the spiritual *life* – the inward honesty – the prayer – but intellectual work "mental strife"[1] is urgently needed today & I often wish this institution, sound as it is no doubt, were the more advanced theological college of my former dreams.

I am reading a good book to my blind friend – Oliver Quick on the Creed.[2] You wd. like it I think.

I am so pleased with what you say about your marriage[3] & hoped that it *would* turn out like this – Connie is a true *woman* & able to give you what you need. It is grievous indeed that you have to be away from her, & find it too difficult – but that is what war does – & we know all the defective & dangerous ways of escape from the situation the men on service resort to – I pray that the grace of God may strengthen you in your difficult situation & give you a victorious way out at last – until you are able to start your *home* together – One longs for this for many another, John, but we are all involved in the responsibility for this world

---

[1] Bethell may be thinking of Blake's 'mental fight' (from *Jerusalem*).

[2] Perhaps the book in question is *Doctrines of the Creed: their basis in scripture and meaning today* (1938).

[3] "Marriage is and forever shall be the most merciful & beautiful gift that God has given to me ... it is as it were rooted in the earth." (June 22, 1942)

at war. I hope that you may have some leave soon & be able to be with her for a few days – but even so you will need patience until the child is born – wasn't it to be July or August – I can't without looking up my last year's diary recall when you were married! I think it was late winter?

Offer to post this, so must close.

With my love – & cheers
M.U.B.

Private collection.

TO RODNEY KENNEDY – OCTOBER 17, 1942

As from St Faith's House. Christchurch.

Dear Rodney

A short letter – because I must get on with English Christmas – So many of my friends there have not been written to since last Xmas – – if then –

Your letter is dated Aug 26th. I am sorry not to have written before now – it has been such busy time. I rather think that my last to you can't have got to you before you wrote it. You had had the book parcel & I am glad to know that some of it was useful. I hope soon to make up another packet – I am not sending any that need to be returned – I had a spare copy of Poetic Experience[1] – so do what you like with it, won't you – I must send more dates too, if I can get them. I found that hot water run over them made the rough ones quite soft again.

At the moment I am in a country school-room supervising a Red Cross written exam. The silence & tense concentration are delightful to me & I wish that the ordeal went on for several hours instead of only one! It is a most lovely day and looking out of the window I see the soft contours of the limestone hills. I am spending a few days at a nephew's farm – there is a young great-niece, and the home does *not* offer silence & concentration – my time is so short there I don't want to absent myself & wander about the fields.

But I must get on to any news I can think of about your friends. The only one I have seen is John Summers, who is on his way north today from Final Leave – He spent Monday evening with me & our friend Merlin Davies of S.C.M. joined us. The christening of Faith was on Thursday & I missed it – at the cathedral, & M.D. the officiant. [...] I think that John has now decided to belong with us anglicans, but he has only lately come to that. He has thought his own way through to it –

[1] Thomas Gilby, *Poetic Experience: An Introduction to Thomist Aesthetics* (1934).

there has been no pressure as you suggest. He liked the Anglican "padré" at Trentham & studied the prayer book with him. Of course I am glad that J. has come back to the catholic tradition – but I am glad too that you have found your spiritual home with the Friends. I feel that anyone who comes back to the C. of E. in N.Z. must come by means of the burning fire of thought of wh. Wm. Blake wrote[1] – there is no visible attraction. We are very badly staffed & in a poor way altogether & far too complacent.

[...]

The hour is running out. I must tell you before I close how much I enjoyed your bits about your natural environment – they are very vivid – & the animal life. It wd. be worthwhile to keep a diary with such notes – but I suppose you have to put all your writing-time into letters. I shall look forward to your next but I know that I must wait some time for it. I am glad that you have found as many as three fellow internees who could be real companions – I don't quite know where you are situated geographically. Summer coming should make the life easier – but I know you don't want it to be *too* easy.

Goodbye for the present.

Your friend
M. U. B.

Hocken Library. MS-0741-001.

TO EDITH WOOLLASTON – DECEMBER 16, 1942

As from 47 Webb St
Written from Ballantyne's Lounge, Dunstable House.

My dear Edith

I am posting a packet of printed matter for Christmas – please distribute according to taste – I thought Joseph for Joe wd. be good. The hanky is for Anna (shop-soiled – & I had not time to wash it – so sorry).

This "Christmas rush" comes suddenly. I have been going through a troubled time. Dear little K. has felt obliged to end her engagement. I can't tell you the ins & outs. Its just that Paul has proved not to be the companion for her – as she put it "if I married him I should have to seek elsewhere for spiritual companionship." She is more mature in mind than he, & I think the Army has not helped him. The good thing is that she has had time to think the thing through calmly. I have seen it coming for many weeks. He has asked her to keep the lovely ring – its meaning

[1] The phrase occurs, in one of the cries of Los at his anvil, in Ch. 4 of *Jerusalem*.

hasn't been what I hoped & believed – but some kind of blessing is with it, I am *sure*.

I mustn't write more now. I hope you will have a very happy Christmas. I am well but find a tendency to old-age varicose veins rather trying! (That's between ourselves)

Please tell Toss that I can't say anything more about his vase I'm afraid. He must choose a younger & more modern critic – I'm sorry. In any case I've so little time nowadays for anything but material jobs – vegetable garden the last straw!

Much love from
M. U.

Hocken Library. MS-0996-3/225.

TO CHARLES BRASCH – [APRIL 18,] 1943

Palm Sunday 47 Webb St. Christchurch. N.Z.

My dear Charles

If I could keep this letter within bounds I would make it a – Airgraph is the word! (they say *much* quicker)[1] but fear I cannot. Am not at all good at compression.

I had hoped to say: "*Yesterday* your note in Little Gidding arrived" – but alas it is already two weeks since Saturday Ap. 3rd when that pleasure came – Of course I should have sent a postcard at once – but waited to read the poem again – a Douglas Credit cousin had lent me the number of the New English Weekly in which it was printed. [...] And a nice thing is that Burnt Norton was given to Katya by a Dunedin friend (where she says there is a *real* bookshop) so I was able to read both together. I read Dry Salvages too in N.E.W. & so far that one had said most to me – but now I find Burnt Norton most rewarding. I have not seen East Coker.[2] Little Gidding is difficult – *un-musical*, so far, to my ear? It must be full of allusions I don't grasp. Of course the bits from Julian of Norwich are familiar to me. Will poetry in the future have to be increasingly built up

[1] The Airgraph Service had been developed by the British Post Office in 1941 in response to the closure of the Suez Canal, and the consequent delay to seaborne mail. It involved the micro-photography of standardized letter-cards, and despatch of the film rather than the actual letter. Originally provided for the military, the service was extended to the public in 1942.

[2] The individual poems making up Eliot's *Four Quartets* were all published separately at first: 'Burnt Norton' was included in the *Collected Poems* of 1936; 'East Coker,' 'Dry Salvages' and 'Little Gidding' were published in *New English Weekly* in 1940, '41 and '42 respectively.

of quotations? The fire & the rose would be Dante. Yes I know about Little Gidding & have a picture of "the secluded Chapel" which I like much as a building. (I know about the Ferrars apart from 'John Inglesant'![1] did you ever read that?) No 4. in Little Gidding I recognise as Dante having just re-read T.S.E. on Dante & the quotation from the Inferno. The theme of *time* always fascinates me. One should read all 4 together, I suppose, from the 'children in the foliage' of B.N. to 'the children in the apple tree' of L.G. Yes, I do find T.S.E. worth grappling with, but some of it very dry – at any rate at first. [...]

And oh dear! its *Whitsunday* now! – What a hopeless business my letter writing seems to be now – and yet there's nothing I'd rather be at if I had the time & strength. Today I'm in bed getting over a fierce head-cold & that is the chance to seize pen – the question is, which is the most urgent letter? Have just finished one to a lad in Egypt – begun on Easter Eve – think those soldiers have the first call?

Meanwhile, on May 27th, my first airgraph arrived – quite an event! You are *such* a good friend, dear Charles! [...] Back to your airgraph – written on Easter Day – delightful to hear of those bells – & very interesting about the pacifist players. You observe that darning socks & thinking of me "don't go together" – but they do! It was most harmonious that darning should suggest me – do I not spend many golden moments on making *pre-war* stockings last? *Any* domestic occupation should now harmonise with me, alas! Sometimes I feel that this régime *can't* go on much longer – I can't cope with it. And just as that conclusion is forced upon me it is announced that this Institution may be wound up! The Head of it is going to Australia at New Yr. to take charge of a much bigger one of same sort to wh. NZ girls could go. I havn't been at all satisfied with St F's – but could say nothing. Now there will be a chance of trying something quite different – & plans are being hatched of which you shall hear later on. If they eventuate, they may include me still, but more comfortably.

And *now* its *June 25* & we are passed La Trinité – and Midsummer day. My cold grew worse & before I was quite over it I had to look after my little Katya whose [cold] was worse still. So I brought her for just four days, before she must if possible begin work again, to the Roman Catholic Lewisham Hospital's Convalescent Home, right at the crest of the Cashmere Hills. Very comfortable indeed, & the Sister in charge most kind. Yesterday we were imprisoned by a wild sou'west storm – but today is brilliant, & my patient well on the mend. We went for a little

[1] A Victorian romance, which is at the same time a novel of 'faith and doubt,' by Joseph H. Shorthouse (1880).

turn, as far as the view upon Governors Bay & Lyttelton Harbour – on the other side lay Lake Ellesmere & the Ocean to the West. Its most exhilarating but at times I have sharp pangs of homesickness for the past & for Rise Cottage.

Meanwhile I *have* sent you an Airgraph which I hope has been in your hands for some time. I have been looking back over the weeks since I began this letter – my diary records *mostly* cooking, washing up, & fatigue, – and yet how interesting & absorbing my obscure life actually is to me! Its quite a puzzle – so little change of scene, so little to relate to the likes of you! It is of course the young friends, & the interest of *their* lives – though to be sure they are very obscure too! I think I agitate myself a little *too* much about their ups & downs! I had to see a doctor about tiresome headaches I've had this year (tho' otherwise in good health) & he pronounces me to be about 20 years younger mentally than I should be at my age, & it seems that its rather a strain on my physical brain! Anyhow he has provided what appears to be quite a helpful remedy to be taken three times a day!

I shall now tell you about my most recent visitor – you must know him I think – Denis Glover's friend Allen Curnow.[1] Mme. Dronke (the refugee jewish actress, convert to Catholicism, about whom I told you)[2] is coming down to give 2 W.E.A. Lectures in August and wanted me to see this Curnow about a proposed poetry recital in ChCh. I've always thought that he (judging from his I think earlier poetry) must despise one living under the shadow of the Anglican church – & fancied that I for my part should not like him very much – But I do like him, & I think he liked me – anyhow we had an interesting talk, & he promises to come again. Among other things he told me that Monte Holcroft's second book is ready – I don't know whether the Caxton Press did it[3] – forgot to ask – I must certainly buy that – I wonder whether anyone is sending it to you.

I had to pause to look at the sun going down & the thick white fog spreading over horrible Christchurch – We shan't like going down again on Sunday! Have you ever been as high as this I wonder. It struck me just now that it wd. be lovely to dive into my P.S.B.[4] & bring Maria Dronke

---

[1] Perhaps New Zealand's foremost poet, Allen Curnow (1911-2001) initially trained for the Anglican ministry, before working as a journalist, and later teaching English at Auckland University. He was also an enormously influential anthologist, beginning with the 1945 *Book of New Zealand Verse*, which he had just begun to compile.

[2] For a fuller note on Maria Dronke, see the letter to Kennedy, Sept. 1, 1943. See also *DNZB* IV, 143-44.

[3] It was published by the Progressive Publishing Association in Wellington.

[4] Post Office Savings Bank.

up for two days rest between her lectures. She works so hard & is so tired. This peaceful atmosphere wd. be just the thing – & the right religion too – tho' I must say hers is a more liberal, instructed, & modern kind of it.

I brought your September 1942 letter up with me, remembering that it has never been *properly* answered – & since I did write something in acknowledgement I have read Eric Gill's autobiography – liked it immensely – have you read it?[1] I mention that because of your stay at Llanthony of course.[2] Your descriptions of your holidays & the richness of all that is still to be seen in England makes me *restless*, reading them. I was saying to Katya just now – how do we manage to subsist in this country with practically *no* human works to gaze upon & be enthusiastic about – not even the animals & the wild flowers. A. Curnow said how unhappy he was as a child about the gap between his picture books & the actual scene around him – K. had felt that too, she says. N.Z. is all background! But there is certainly a glorious sense of space (up here!) & possibilities in the future. Curnow & I were speaking of the Eric Gill sort of life – only possible after all for the few artists. And N.Z. is to be more & more industrialised.

[...]

Another book I've lately read, all but the last chapter for it had to go back to the lender – is C.S.Lewis' The Allegory of Love. Having read his theology I wanted to read his professional subject. The theme was not altogether unfamiliar – magazine articles I think. I must get it again to read the chapter on Spenser. [...] I now have Forster's Rede Lecture on V. Woolf. They charged me 4/6 for it out here! – I brought with me here an account of Boethius – references to him and quotations have teased me for many years, & now I shall *know* about him. But I have not read it – I *must* write letters in this quiet.

[...]

I must think of bringing this rambly letter to a close. I had such a conscientious feeling since your wonderful Benefaction happened that I must render an account of my stewardship! I don't think there has been anything "extra" lately to record – except *this*, the Con. Home I mean, & that my little girl is having riding lessons at my suggestion – Its the only

---

[1] Eric Gill (1882-1940) was an English engraver, sculptor, typographer, and writer, with a particular interest in workers' rights and community living. His ideas on art and philosophy were influenced by Jacques Maritain.

[2] An Augustinian priory was established at Llanthony in Wales in the 12th century, but later destroyed during Owain Glywndwr's rebellion against the English. Privately owned in the 19th century, it became home for a while to Gill (whose *Autobiography* was published in 1940).

form of exercise that won't tire her back – standing all day teaching makes her too tired for walking. As I expected she has taken quickly to horseback – I have advanced the money for the jodhpurs – she couldn't possibly have got them herself. It was the last length of material the tailor had – so I felt it was "meant"!

The white cerements now hide the city entirely from us – for ten minutes I watched that happen! Above is our clear sky & rosy sunset clouds. How dreadful to live under such a pale. I am always conscious of it. Nearly time to descend to the sixth of our seven nourishments a day! They bring 5 out of the 7 to our rooms – and oh, what a relief not to have to cook them, still more not to have to wash up after them!

And I have not said one word about the Tunisian victory![1] My nephew was having his leave –

Thank you again for everything.

Yours affectionately
Ursula Bethell.

Hocken Library. MS-0996-3/19.

TO RODNEY KENNEDY – MAY 9, 1943

St. Faith's House. Webb St. ChCh.

Dear Rodney

Its a real grief to me, this silence on my part – all my oldest friends in England, Canada, Australia, asking for letters for months, years even, & I too tired by my daily jobs, & people coming and going, to take up my pen in the evening. Today I decided on a Sunday morning in bed – hoping to do something about letters. The holidays are here & all but one of the residents away. I have never got used to living with those restless noises – they really hinder me & "get on my nerves" – (Plenty to get on your nerves in your present life I don't doubt). Today a letter to you must be one of the first, because to my great surprise & pleasure a case of winesaps has just arrived – I am so touched – so very much touched. I have just written to Toss asking him to convey my gratitude for the thought, & for my daily breakfast thro' the coming winter. (In fact its come, but we have had a lovely autumn after wet summer.) Still the only apple I can eat raw is a wine sap. Thanks to you in the first place, Rodney. It is so good what you can effect in spite of those bonds!

Your Christmas letter was very good & it is that I am 'answering' now of course – must try to be succinct or others will have to wait But it

[1] This letter was written over two months, and completed in late June. The 'Tunisian victory,' achieved on 12/13 May, marked the end of the campaign in North Africa.

is difficult for me to compress & it takes time to do it – as in verse. [...] I have been reading Eric Gill's Autobiography & like it so much that I have bought it – & the price out here is 22/6. [...] I wonder whether the R.C's you have in camp wd. think Gill a wild man (he has such a beautiful, easy style). I get the Pax papers[1] from Home although I do not belong. They are a small body but very zealous – some seem to be devoted to Gill's way of life (small rural communities) & some wish to be only against war – He joined the Dominican Third Order, feeling the need of some rule of life. I rather think the English Dominicans are not in favour in NZ – I have taken their magazine 'Blackfriars' for some years, and it was interesting to find them in the autobiography.

[...]

I think I've mentioned nearly all the people we both know & now come nearer home. The Deaconess has accepted a post in charge of a new institution – like St F's but much bigger – in Melbourne & leaves N.Z. at the New Year, *for good*. She plans to go back to England after Australia. There will be an interim here & I hope a total reconstruction. It hasn't been quite what my sister & I had projected. I don't know how this will affect me – I may have to take charge of the house (with some one to board) for a time – later may have to move. I have grown to be quite fond of *my* gaol but not of the town & have made improvements & done things in the garden – but its when the rest are away that I am really at home. I shall be 70 next year, and shall be thinking of a home for the last lap. I should like one, however humble, with a view of mountains, & with native birds about. I feel quite envious of the nearness to a Bird Sanctuary of which you speak in your letter.

[...]

Sunday afternoon – Very hard to get on with letters. I had to go a long way to church this morning – so as not to be upset by sub-christian prayers & sermon! I knew what to expect, but was safe at S. Michael's – Mass with plainsong & incense – very "High Church" – rather sectarian in fact *I* think – prefer prayer book rite intact, but I do like incense. Then had to get a meal, & then alas, telephone rang & could a lad from Wigram come? "When?" "Well, *now*?" Had to put him off till this evg. Have been looking out your packet & have done *no* wash up. I had hoped to have the eveng for letters – but its always like this & in the vacn. friends from a distance turn up unexpectedly.

Now before I end I must tell you where your little painting is at the moment – you wd. never guess. I lent it & the Russian picture & a

---

[1] A number of journals have this title; Bethell is probably referring to a quarterly begun in 1939 by the Benedictines at Prinknash Abbey.

photograph of early gothic sculpture to the SCM Chaplain friend I spoke of. His rooms are of course furnished for them & on the walls the most deplorable "chocolate box" school of pictorial art. Persuaded him to remove them & substitute my War collection. I wished I could afford to present him with one of the two lovely T. McCormack watercolours at the autumn exhibition – There was nothing else one wished to look at! [...]

There have been lilies of one kind or another in the Chinese jar most of the summer – But all over now. In fact most flowers gone but I have some blue & green hydrangeas, rather lovely.

Must now prepare for my visitor. Its getting to be rather much for me to keep an open door to youth – but if they want to come, come they shall –

You are in my prayers Rodney

Goodbye today with love
M. U. B.

Hocken Library. MS-0741-001.

To Monte Holcroft – June 26, 1943

As from St Faith's House. Webb St. ChCh.

My dear Monte

At last I've a chance of writing a few lines to friends near & far! I am spending 4 days at the Rest Home right at the top of Cashmere Hills (Roman Catholic Sisters – very well run) getting over a severe cold – I've only half *rested*, because of the score at least of letters I had on my mind to answer. Yours is dated Dec 21st and some are much longer ago than that. I've wanted particularly to write to you since Allen Curnow came to see me a few days ago – the first time we've met. He told me that your Waiting Hills is out. I suppose his wd. be an advance review copy. We had a bit of business to discuss & I did not even ask him whether the Caxton Press had printed it. But he is going to call again & then we shall be able to talk about your book. I've been very un-literary all these months. My time & strength is spent on cooking & washing up & the like & my day seems to grow shorter & shorter. Eyesight failing a bit too. And yet I *don't* find life uninteresting! Lots of young friends to sympathise with keep coming along.

There wd. be more to tell you than I've time to write, even here – but it must keep for our next meeting. Even you will have to have a holiday sometime – I was very glad to hear that you are exempt from serving in the army, for all your newspaper life is so laborious.

[...]

The landscape here makes me feel homesick for the past! I don't think I could *live on it.* I don't even feel moved to write about it now – but I should like to do my Rangiora memories book. L. Benseman didn't seem able to cope with a new edition of Day & Night just now, but promised to keep paper. They are very busy with "commercial" work.[1]

I can't read much now – glance at the daily paper & at periodicals & am amazed to see in the T.L.S. how many books are being published in wartime. I've read most of C. S. Lewis "Allegory of Love" but had to return it before I'd read the last & Spenser chapter wh. is said to be very good. And Eric Gill's autobiography – which I found absorbing. And small things like E. M. Forster's Rede Lecture on Virginia Woolf. I've been given her Death of the Moth – but it was immediately borrowed from me. And oh yes, TSE's Little Gidding – and the new Penguin – not so new now Religious Anthology.[2] And always some theology of course. You know, Monte, I felt after you were here last time that the next thing *you* must get is a theology! Bones to your thought – organisation – or foundation – or what is it I am trying to say?

I've never found stray bits of a letter to you so I don't know what happened!

My health? Thank you, I should say it has been better & I've felt quite lively in between times – but I have to be careful not to get tired & that restricts me a great deal. I have to remember that I *shall* be 70 next year!

I gave Miss Taylor your message thank you – it is a great help to me having her companionship. We shall be reading yr. book together no doubt & I foresee that I shall be writing to you again, about it. But oh, when? It may not be for months & months! But be sure of my interest. I daresay you are already started on something else!

Yr. friend
M.U.Bethell

Alexander Turnbull Library. MS-Papers-1186-03

TO RODNEY KENNEDY – SEPTEMBER 1, 1943

47 Webb St. Christchurch.

My dear Rodney

I have wished to answer before now your letter of "the shortest day" which touched me very much – but I have been intermittently, & mostly,

---

[1] Bensemann was running the Caxton Press while Glover was serving in the Royal Navy.

[2] *An Anthology of Religious Verse: designed for the times*, ed. Norman Nicholson (1942).

ill since then. At that time I was getting over my first influenza cold – a few days at the Convalescent Home away on the top of Cashmere Hills (the R.C. one) seemed to set me – but ChCh on my return was too cold, & I took to my bed again with a touch of pleurisy – I was able to get someone to come in & look after me luckily, & was quite well again by Aug 4th when Madame Dronke came to ChCh & stayed with me. I think I must have told you about her before – I met her in Wellington when she arrived there just before the war. She was a distinguished actress before her marriage – at one time understudied Bergner – & acted with Moissé.[1] A Jewess by birth, convert to Catholicism & very spiritual. She saw much of the Liturgical Revival, & RC Youth movement. Her husband is "Aryan" & Catholic – it was safer for them to leave Germany & they got out to England early in '39 & finally obtained permit to come to N.Z. Their possessions all went down in a german cargo ship, scuttled off Brazil when the war broke out – Grand piano, cello, and household goods. She teaches voice-production & verse speaking & Mr. D. works in a factory! (he was high up in legal profession & a noted cellist). She gave 3 WEA lectures at Cant. Coll. on religion – the second one was crowded, & it must have been there I caught my present chest-cold germ which developed the next day. I was *tired*, – rather too much for me having to do for a visitor. There was also a poetry recital at Begg's. [...] She read a very good unpublished poem by A. Curnow & 2 of mine (The Long Harbour & Warning of Winter) [...]. She thinks there is a great deal of talent in N.Z. but standard of taste low & the "public" content with mediocrity.

I enjoyed her visit very much & am so thankful I was well for it. Now I am trying to be well enough to go to the country next week – I have heard of a Convalescent place near Waiau – & that's country I love. I can't stay away very long – there will be meetings to attend about St Faith's future – I hope that these affairs will be settled up, at least temporarily, in October, & will let you know then what is to be done about this house. I feel that I can't go on as I am another year – the up & down stairs is too much for me. I should like a little *home* but don't know whether I am meant to have one in *this* world.

As I said before, your letter touched me very much. Thank you, Rodney, for saying those things. If I do have a home, you will be a welcome caller there, when this trouble is overpast. And your letter was a remarkably interesting one to come from a camp, cut off from the world. [...] I am including the Forster Rede lecture in a packet for you – the

[1] Elisabeth Bergner was a German-Jewish actress, prominent in Berlin in the 1920s until she fled to London. The slightly older Alexander Moisse was also a prominent actor in Berlin prior to the First World War.

injunctions are to keep it clean & not keep it too long! I wish I had duplicate copies of Blackfriars – It has such interesting short articles – but is too useful to part with.

Connie sends me on things of John's – It is particularly hard for *him* to be cut off there – he flies to writing as an outlet.

The sun is coming out nicely & I must get up. You shall have another letter before long to make up for this rather short one –

My love to you & every good wish
M. U. B.

Hocken Library. MS-0741-001.

TO CHARLES BRASCH – OCTOBER 24, 19[43][1]

47 Webb St. Christchurch N.Z.

My dear Charles

Just two weeks ago I was pleased to [dis]cover one of your succinct, informative little letters enclosed with a welcome 'Dublin Review' – (I'm never succinct – the less I have to relate – the more protracted the relation!) I'd had it in mind just about then to write you a short interim news-letter – I forget about what! I think about Allen Curnow's visit bringing Douglas Lilburn (I hope you know about him "young N.Z. composer" – of course you do from F.P.[2]) & telling me of his oeuvre – anthology of N.Z. verse – to include you of course – he was going to write to you about it – & no doubt has. It will be better than anything of the kind so far I've no doubt.

I have a rule – which is almost worse than no rule in the absence of observance – that despatch of "overseas" letters shall be noted in my diary – my last note of such, in your case, was June 25. but I'm certain I have written since then . . . Yes, of course – when I thanked for Péguy.[3] Have I told you that it was almost at once borrowed for sending to a reader of French in C.O. Detention Camp? (I sent it with "Prière et Poésie") Nearly all I know about Péguy comes from an account of him in a Sheed & Ward book called "Wrestlers with Christ". It is I suppose journalism but it afforded information about several other v. interesting writers – Soloviev e.g. & Léon Bloy. I have Bloy's Lettres à sa Fiancée in

[1] Bethell actually dated the letter 1934; it is corrected in Brasch's hand.

[2] Fred Page. See the letter to Brasch, April 16, 1938.

[3] Bethell received a volume of Péguy from Brasch in late July. She wrote soon after to thank him, commenting on Péguy's 'original style – a sort of incantation – this after he is hastily parcouru' [Fr. 'skimmed'] (Aug. 3).

translation, which is a good one, by Maisie Ward.[1] I always used to obtain French books in the original – (English versions seldom satisfactory don't you think?) but these are of so little use for lending in N.Z. that of late I have tried for the Englished. And, à propos, if you *could* find a translation of Bernanos' Country priest's diary I should be very glad, altho' the reviewers said it was very bad. I read a friend's French copy – but there are one or two people who wd. be glad to read it, who don't know French. Reverting to Léon Bloy – I happened to look at those Letters again after reading Eric Gill's autobiography – two men, "co-religionists" (dreadful expression!) but what poles apart in temperament! E.G. such a happy man – knowing what he wanted – and attaining to it! "Lived happy & hoped to die happy" – & one felt how right that he should! And this L.B. – his passion for suffering – for its own sake one might think. One knows what the psychologists call *that* – but his religion lifted it above being *merely* that? [...]

Yeats – I havn't read nearly enough of the later Yeats – I put off buying the collected poems till all books became too expensive to buy. I'm sure A. Curnow – who seems to have a well-furnished library – wd. lend it. Its the *sound* in Yeats I attend to – it is fascinating as you say – and I have not attended much to the sense. I think poetry is quite the least easy thing to read when one is tired, overbusy, & likely to be interrupted! usually my case.

Your bit of personal news is very interesting – that you are now planning N.Z. 'fin 1945" – (With a shock I realised how long it is since I looked ahead for as much as *two* years & I don't suppose I ever shall again.) That is good reading. But more & more do I feel that if you mean to *stay* in N.Z. you must prepare for dullness – You have yr. friends of course, & the means to move about, & procure for yourself alleviations in the realms of the arts & literature. But more & more am I conscious of the limitations within which one labours here – and, if I am not mistaken, the declining standards of taste according to which the population is nourished – Don't deduce from this that I myself am bored – only seldom do the limitations press upon my mind. I've had my life, & now, limitations wd. be making themselves felt, I suppose, in any surroundings. And of course, always, contemplating the war, how thankful one must be for a negative peace, an unshaken mediocrity! No doubt the war seems to accentuate the limitations, cuts us off from

---

[1] The books referred to here have all been identified elsewhere except for Bloy's *Lettres à sa fiancée* (Paris, 1922), which was translated, not by Maisie Ward, but by Barbara Wall, for Sheed & Ward (1937). Léon Bloy (1846-1917) was a French novelist, critic, and social reformer. A convert to Roman Catholicism, he preached spiritual renewal through poverty and suffering.

foreign sights & sounds, denies us books – cuts *me* off from natural beauty – but as I talk with my many (thanks be!) young friends who don't know anything but N.Z. I reflect What it is like *not* to have seen an ancient building – (or an ancient meadow!) not to have seen one classical masterpiece of art – never to have heard a first rate orchestra – never to have seen a first rate play? Not to have in memory my Ravenna, my Chartres, my Rothenburg, my Wells, my villages? The liveliness of their interest in photographs of the like is reassuring – still more the liveliness of their interest in what lies around. Come out and add your encouragement & sympathy! I would say – but be prepared to contribute, not acquire! One *does* acquire, however, against all likelihood! There *are* riches. For more than two years now I have enjoyed the freshness & intelligence & spirituality of the little girl who is to be married to her Welsh parson at Christmas – now that I know him well I am altogether delighted about it. But who will take her place if they move away I don't see, & sometimes shiver a little. But its still probable that they may be in ChCh next year – & possible even that they may rent this house, leaving me in my "flat". I certainly can't stay here another year as I am – must have easier conditions. I have "failed" a little these latter years – a good deal worn (am in my 70th now) & have been mostly engaged in having Influenza (3 different types in succession) since June.

[...]

Hoping daily for my nephew's return on furlough – he has been given M.B.E. but according to his batman, who was beside him all through – he deserves something far more glorious than that!

Prof. Sinclaires book of Essays (Lend me your Ears) has gone into a second edition – you know what a "phenomenon" *that* is in N.Z.!

I didn't mean to flow on to another page – but here is an example of what I mean by these deprivations in N.Z. – these things one can't go out & get. I thought suddenly of a drawing I used to be very fond of – a rather romping Holy Family – the Virgin's Mother is in it – lovely lines – it must be Milanese School – ?Leonardo – & the version at B. House was either better or worse than the ?Louvre one I saw – or was that a painting?[1] I gave away most of my photographs of pictures when I left Rise Cottage – & now can't go out & buy one to refresh my memory as I could in London – and you see how vague my memory has become? This is as good as asking you to do something about it! but I don't really mean that. And I imagine that the stores of such photographs have run out in London, or the shops bombed – near the B.M. they were. But I do ask

[1] Bethell is thinking of two works of Leonardo illustrating the theme of the Virgin and Child with St. Anne. The earlier (charcoal on paper, c. 1499-1500) is the Burlington House Cartoon; the Louvre oil on panel was done c. 1508-1510.

you, if you are hovering over book-barrows, not to pass by a Ralph Caldecott[1] picture book without thinking of me – I was reminded of those books by a charming Menander article in the T.L.S.[2] I wonder whether I could find it, called "Under the Apple Tree" I think. I really mustn't run on any longer so goodbye & thank you again for Review & for letter.

M.U.B.

Oct 28

Reading over foregoing I see that I did not complete my remarks about you as an émigré – or rather repatrié[3] – I'd been thinking of all the plans, small & big, I had read about – for the re-making of Europe & how you are near at hand & likely to be enlisted for these. Your knowledge of languages would be so valuable. I am afraid NZ would not have much chance! To read about such plans consoles one for reading about the war – The Student Christian Movement papers in particular give one an insight – its truly international – the Quakers too. [...]

Butter rationing announced this morning – & begins today 1/2 lb a week – Handsome compared with my allowance in the last war – but my amateur cookery of today is all done with butter. *No cream of course* & *no margarine* for civilians. And because I've been ill I've neglected the catering & am *not* a pound ahead as usually I am!

Hocken Library. MS-0996-3/19.

TO MONTE HOLCROFT – DECEMBER 8, 1943

St Faith's House. Christchurch.

My dear Monte

You must have been wondering at my silence. I have been ill all the winter, but am picking up now warmer weather has set in. Not much strength however. Any letterwriting I do (& that is little) is done before I get up & this morning I began my day at 5.30. It is such a heavenly morning, with Mt Grey delicately clear, & streaks of snow on the more distant ones.

I did not at once buy your book, because it is expensive, & I hoped that someone might give it to me for my birthday in October! But no one did & I have it & have read it rather hastily. I see some changes &

---

[1] Randolph Caldecott was a highly successful illustrator of children's books in the Victorian period, particularly known for his Christmas books and nursery rhymes.

[2] 'Menander' was a pseudonym for the novelist and critic Charles Morgan.

[3] The term seems Bethell's invention, suggesting that Brasch is not an emigrant, but one returned home.

improvements. I like *very* much, as you know, what you say about me ... you are my best, what shall I call it? Appreciator! I have a letter from E. H. McCormick, returned to Egypt. He says that he read you on the voyage & was "deeply impressed by parts of it." – "The section on your own work I thought extremely good – the best interpretation of you so far". He says he was going to send you a note – perhaps he has already done so.

I think I warned you there might be a change of address for me next year – the institution as such has closed down "for the duration" & perhaps longer & anyhow I could not have gone on as I am. But friends of mine who are to be married at Xmas will occupy this house next year. I shall have more rooms & they will take some care of me.

[...]

Perhaps next year I may have some time for books!

Perhaps I'd better include in this hurried note my good wishes for Christmas & New Year. I may not be able to write again. There is a good deal to do about this place before Xmas & as I said, not much strength for to do it – I hope you may be coming north for a holiday during the Summer. (I am planning to be away a week or two in January.)

Always yours sincerely
M. U. Bethell

Allen Curnow tells me he is engaged on an anthology of NZ verse.

Alexander Turnbull Library. MS-Papers-1186-03

TO KATHLEEN DAVIES[1] – DECEMBER 30, [1943]

47 Webb St. ChCh.

[...]

Well darling you know of course that I miss you & that the old bitter pain of loneliness wells up in solitude & overwhelms me with its tide. Its always there, waiting, underneath. Its my lot, & must be accepted – part of the pain of the world – & will be put off I hope with the mortal vesture.[2] I suppose more people (those who *do* feel) are desolate than not, on this planet! When I get un-tired enough to attend to jobs pain will recede into the background & heaven knows there's enough occupation for more than January in coping with the squalor &

---

[1] Kathleen Taylor had married Merlin Davies on Dec. 27.

[2] The phrase had some currency in 19th century verse, and can be found in a 19th century translation of Augustine's *Enchiridion*, but it perhaps occurs here as a conflation of the phrases 'mortal flesh' and 'human vesture' from the hymn 'Let all mortal flesh keep silence', found in *Hymns Ancient and Modern*.

dirt of my own apartments here – The common sense part of me says how valuable this time of solitude (& I'm sure I hope there *won't* be many interruptions!) will be for tackling it. Not envy, pet, now, not envy! I am *heartily* in agreement with the Creator about bringing you two together! – & now you are joined, its my Nunc Dimittis.[1] There must be few marriages so perfect – I delight in thinking of the joy, comfort, & completion you are appointed to bring to our precious Merlin after his years of hardship, loneliness & deprivation – And you my child – I should say "godly matron",[2] now! Now you have what I've longed for you to have, & so perfectly (do you remember how we talked about Annus Mirabilis?[3] And this one after all so much more mirabilis!) Now you know what those dear little soft breasts are for – & the dear little small-of-the-back is no doubt appreciated even more than by me! For touch. And for sight I think sideways on getting in to the bath one catches the best of both curves. Are those beautiful grey eyes being stung to sight of more earthly beauty everywhere than they've dreamt of? Everything should *mean* more to those eyes than to the un-purged ones – don't you think so? (Dear me I *am* letting myself go!) Do you both feel that the fields & the mountains are the right setting? and I hope that the air has life & sparkle in it still, in summer. The air here is so lifeless – If I could get out to my field, the trees & the grassy earth, it would be an alleviation – but I can't make the effort yet.

[...]

Looking over this letter – a bit of it sounds as if I thought the experience was all *senses*! You know me better than that! Gates – but to less than nothing without the spiritual – but they *are* the gates swinging open now – "pas vrai"?[4]

[...]

I may address a few remarks to M. now – Sometimes I think that what I prize most in his character is his *courage* (which is one with his faith?) so hold on a bit pet – – –

To Merlin: Darling – do you want my Newsletter, Theology etc or are yours being sent on to you or don't you want to be bothered with them? There is a v. good article on Religion & Art in Nov. Theology. You & K. wd. like to read it.

[...] I do hope you dears are finding Kaikoura restful – I think of you asleep most of to-day. Think I shall sleep this afternoon, but there are a heap of odd jobs. You know my gnawing pain (as mentioned to K. She

---

[1] Lat. 'Now, you give leave.' Otherwise known as the Song of Simeon (see Luke 2: 29-32).

[2] See Acts 9: 39-43.

[3] Lat. 'Marvellous year.'

[4] Fr. 'Isn't that so?'

wd. not have to be told – in fact it wouldn't be any good pretending!) is my thorn-in-the-side – & the heart that puts up with it is now a very *thankful* heart. So thankful for you, darling.

What I said to you about addressing the human Christ was true – but I can't say that I make a success of it. Too like speaking to a character in a play, taken like this, i.e. as a human person (I know that I skate on thin ice on this question, so to speak, theologically.) Easier the Paternoster. Easier to approach to that "Not alone because the Father"?[1] Approaching from the other side, the Trinity is everything for religion. But more must be learnt by me & I've long known it. I don't find your second Xmas sermon left for me to read? I wish to apprehend your experience in this matter! And shall have some questions to ask about it when you return. Whether there's any difference made in the consciousness by a new, merely human, relationship for example. I expect you don't want to be reminded of sermons & such just now – so let this pass –

[...]

Too much haste & now I stop. So much love, darlings – not rationed.

U.

Macmillan Brown Library. MB 572. A.

[1] See John 16: 32.

VII: 1944–1945

TO MERLIN & KATHLEEN DAVIES – JANUARY 1-4, 1944[1]

47 Webb St. ChCh.

Jan. 1. Early. Saturday.

A wonderful morning for that fiction of New Year – Happy New Year, darling. It promises well for another "ann. mir."[2] for you doesn't it. I can't see out much because of headache.

[...]

Head was BAD last night – odd how this affliction has revived – think it must be Nature's revenge for too much emotion during latter days! I have a fancy that if I could *cry* it would ease this headache! but I cried so much when Effie died. I can't any more – except for something very piercing like Xmas Eve [...] I looked out at the stars – a clear night for ChCh. & thought how much brighter they wd. be at Kaikoura. Perhaps you sleep on the verandah. Slept till 2. head still bad – fell asleep again later but not refreshing sleep – & head's all buzzy this morning. Eyes, too, affected – wearisome not being able to read. Prayer too is difficult.

Sunday evening.

Such a change since I put aside this "cronocle"[3] Established myself in garden [...] suddenly, (I'd been there about an hour) a sort of whirlwind struck the garden & soon declared itself as a cool southerly with soft rain – the heavy throbbing in my head stopped, everything lightened [...] I had a lovely rest on my bed after that, quite free from pain & very happy & thankful. [...] These days have seemed like a hundred years – For you no doubt they have gone all too quickly. [...] You have come alive again now, my darlings, but rather far away. I have been looking back over the past months & thinking how rich & wonderful it has been. Yes you are alive in my prayer & I shall be near you tonight I believe. I don't want to start the head again & will now close my eyes.

---

[1] Bethell began a long letter to the Davies on Dec. 31, adding to it over several days before posting on Jan. 4. The various 'notes' are sometimes addressed to one or the other, or to both.

[2] Annus mirabilis. Lat. 'Marvellous year.'

[3] The spelling recalls Effie Pollen; see letter to Sidgwick, Dec. 30, 1934.

Jan. 3. Monday Morning

[...]

To come back thus to our intimate affairs – this is the "week's mind" of the wedding-day! I wished there had been some opportunity of speaking about it – There hardly was – It was all so beautiful, simple – inevitable – I have never felt so deeply the drama of a marriage. Deep to the roots of creation & the purposes of God! And the benediction of the Holy Spirit of God. Can't put it into words. Queer that it should be thought of as something to be funny about! A way of dodging the awe, perhaps.

[..]

Since the pressure in my head lightened you have become alive & near again, both of you – and you especially my precious treasure – Never, never, never shall I forget you nestling here early last Monday – & your little yawns – you seemed so *small* & so dear – so truly my child. And all so *easy* – nothing catastrophic about the ceremony to come! All easy & natural – just a seal on the acceptation & betrothal – But I must say that veil did frighten me a bit! I have been thinking over the last six months. I believe that Merlin must apprehend better now my anxious cares for you. Perhaps I should have taken him in more rapidly! But I had much to impede understanding. Not that I ever really *obstructed* him! I'm quite clear about that. On the contrary! When I longed for marriage for you how little I could know how it would come about – "Made in Heaven" – how little I knew that it would bring a shattering revelation of what I had missed in life – all the more devastating because so perfect. Not for one moment could I wish to have been spared that knowledge – (I have *looked on* sympathetically at courtship & marriage before but not been drawn right within the orbit!) It is part of Beauty & my transient pain will I believe be merged in your experience. Oh no, I prize that revelation! But how mysterious it all is. I was so angry with A.[1] when he said he couldn't forgive himself for having "spoilt my life" – (a current Victorian phrase). It just wasn't going to be spoilt! But now I wonder *was* it? Not that any sort of marriage would have made things right! Of course not – a part of one's nature might have been satisfied at the expense of so much else – But I have never realised so clearly before the fundamental deprivation. (There's *no envy*, darling! be sure of that.) Not that its *everything*, this two sided sexuality. I think my poetry shows that pretty clearly, don't you. There was peace & happiness (for all the blemishes) at Rise Cottage, and *fun*, *such* fun! & you don't have fun without peace – Lots of anxiety too, & therein perhaps the maternal

---

[1] Bethell does not name him in any of her letters. See Introduction.

constituent was having its day. The haves and have nots – one must accept that – Perhaps the parable of the wages has some bearing – 'Shall I not do what I will with my own?'[1]

I came upon these lines in my Commonplace book yesterday, in fact I looked them up, to see how far they were true:–

Desiderium
It is to sit & want & not to have,
To sit & want with the whole heart & soul,
To know that what you want & only that
Will make you happy, & yet not to have.
To think of what you want & have it not;
To see it in your thoughts & not to have it,
To hear it always, whosoever speaks,
Whatever sounds there are, yet not to have.
To dream you have it, happy, then awake
And call to it & know you have it not.
And other things you might have – and at times
Can wish for, and the other wish seems dead.
And when you have them, & should be content,
Back comes the other wish and speaks to you,
And you are bound to hear, and in your heart
All liking dies away for what you have,
And you are dead, alive, for what you have not,
And where you were before, there you are now,
Captive and miserable, and again you sit,
And want with all your heart and have it not.

That is only true part of the time – & I don't know whether the writer was thinking of *mating* – it might have been some other satisfaction! – (He was ordained at age 64 & vicar of St Mary Magdalen Oxford when he died.)[2] It is a good description of *flatness* and apt for a good deal of my time in my thirties. "Other things" loom much larger than he reckons in reality – anything active & 'creative' to use Johnny's

---

[1] See Matthew 20: 15.

[2] I have not found these lines in any published form. However, the author may be Arthur Gilkes, who had retired as headmaster of Dulwich in 1914 and fretted at being inactive during the war. He was ordained in 1915, and became vicar of St Mary Magdalen's in 1917, where he died in 1922. There is no record of his having written verse (though he did publish prose works), but he is the only likely candidate given the very advanced age of ordination. I owe this suggestion to Rev. Hugh Wybrew and Alan Palmer of St Mary Magdalene's, Oxford.

word. (This diary-letter is uncommonly like him! but unlike him I do *not* look for an answer to it! It shows however that its an outlet to put down one's vagrant thoughts when one can't do much else.) No, its not *quite* everything on this planet & one has a fumbling sense that in some way, one can't think how, the miss will be made up "afterwards". According to this bit of Emily Dickinson's (who could not righteously have the man she loved) which I have just transferred to the said common-place book – from a scrap of paper.[1]

"Renunciation
Is a piercing virtue –
The letting go
A presence for an expectation –
Not now.

The putting out of eyes
Just sunrise,
Lest Day Day's great Progenitor
Outshow.

Renunciation is the choosing
Against itself
Itself to justify
Unto itself;
When larger function
Make that appear
Smaller, that sated vision
Here.

In the worst darkness of deprivation God is still there, & even when He seems to be cruel, & even seems to be gone, & the body seems to overcome the Spirit, that turns out to be a lie. But when the body, the vehicle of the Spirit, has been dissolved – how can the losses & the misses of the bodily life be fulfilled – In the Resurrection does that oracle "in heaven no marriage"[2] proclaim, not a doom, but a glorious emancipation? I should say an *inclusion* "that nothing be missed". On the

[1] Almost nothing of Dickinson's poetry was published in her lifetime. Bethell is quoting here from an early edition. The version included in most modern editions (see Johnson, No. 745) shows some differences of wording and lineation. The 'man she loved' is often identified as a married clergyman, the Rev. Charles Wadsworth.

[2] See Matthew 22: 30. The other quotations in this paragraph may be from their letters to Bethell (which have not survived).

other hand one can't feel that St John of the Cross or St Teresa *missed* anything! Its all very difficult. They too were bounded by the body – could they yet understand everything by sympathy, not experiences? Its true that those saints were enduring hideous physical sufferings & illnesses most of the time – they were all engaged in *killing* the body! Should one say that sexuality is available for spiritual growth, not essential? Its essential for life on the planet! the "bringing of more love into the world" – Are some, not all, meant to be drawn into that dance of matter – and spirit! I do feel that for Merlin the experience *was* needful, that he should "understand the world aright" – I feel that you darling K. were given to him just in time (how perfect he is for you was only disclosed bit by bit!) And sometimes I feel that you two who have, on this planet, been the instruments of such pain, as well as joy, to me – (holding the last dregs of that cup of individual loss to my lips as it were!) – may also be, on this planet, the instruments of pacification.

Tuesday. Jan 4. 1944. 8 a.m.

[...]

Enclosed are fragments of a sort of diary-letter which has been a relief to my feelings but wearisome reading for a voyage de noces![1] I couldn't read or sew, or make the effort to write other letters, and the summary of the days since Thursday is that I've been laid low with a very bad head & on my bed mostly. *Now quite on the mend.*

[...]

Saturday evening must have been my gloomiest hour! I had been rather disappointed that there wasn't a postcard from my dear vampires on Friday & knew I must wait till Tuesday (to-day) Were they too tired by journey – was everything at Mrs. McI's all right etc etc. After the headache came on I seemed to lose touch with you (tho' I know you are there all the time really). The gates of the senses swung to! I could not hear your voices or see your eyes or feel your touch –

Just like Effie I felt you K. were being absorbed into happiness a great distance away. So often I've lifted up my eyes being in torment & wondered what her happiness is! Can't imagine her disembodied – couldn't *picture* her. I could picture you to some extent & I know what your happiness is! Comforted, I thought, while I was tormented! (& longed for little Effie to put a cold rag on my forehead – then remembered *her* pain & thanked God I was beside her then, tho' I couldn't do much – so much worse to watch another suffer than to be hurt ones-self –) Often you dwindled to little pinpoints on the horizon –

[1] Fr. 'honeymoon.'

or moving about the village – figures without significance! & M. almost a myth! These were waking nightmares & the result of the headache I know. I could not make that leap of the Spirit which kept me near you on Monday night. A sort of identification with you both – should I say that God had withdrawn that liberty of happiness? It was so good that you used the word "holy" speaking of it Darling K – it was a holy night for me too.

Not the headache but the ensuing desolation *mattered*. The mystical books say that desolation is God's chief discipline – "we must kill our senses & be stripped of them, their destruction means the reign of faith" (That's S. François de Sales) – "God instructs the heart by means of sufferings & contradictions not by ideas." "It is only by mortifications of all sorts, by trials & deprivations of all kinds, that we can be established in pure love.' "It is love which entering into a soul to make it happily die to itself alive to God, bereaves it of all human desires." "To detach ourselves from creatures & abandon ourselves entirely to God."[1] I have perhaps a *notion* of this – but those saints *chose* it as their way. Perhaps they had a much stronger love of creatures to start with – I had to discover love of creatures as individuals – always loved *creation* I think!

I remembered when little Effie went I suddenly realised I could never now do anything more for her again – were you K. darling being detached from me like this? Common sense said that there wd. still be scope to be useful to you but was it fundamentally the same event – you were given to another to cherish according to my prayer! Out of work so to speak, 'désoeuvrée'[2] is a good word. I found myself wondering whether God would send another to be cherished now that you are fixed up & then remembered that my strength is spent now. Rather I should pray for someone to cherish me! Unreasonable. The end is solitude in the nature of things. But I could do with someone to put a hand on my forehead & rest me to sleep – to wake *refreshed* – out of the body perhaps would it have to be? The Creator taking the creature back – Then I thought: this notion of resting in strong arms is too like the psychologist's "back to the mother's womb"! Better to be revived to individual activity! You must pray, Merlin – I thought – for me to "recover some strength before I go hence"[3] so as to clear up all this litter of letters etc – I should hate to go leaving a litter behind – but Katsy no doubt would push all those letters into the incinerator & no one would

[1] The quotations are drawn from *The Treatise of the Love of God* (by St. François de Sales) and Jean-Pierre de Caussade's *Abandonment to Divine Providence*.

[2] Fr. 'at a loose end.'

[3] See Psalm 39: 13.

know that all the love & wit I had withheld from burning was now consumed!

I wondered, again, whether these days were a sort of rehearsal for when you go away to England. It won't be easy & I must be better prepared by then.

Such were my gloomy thoughts & I want you to know them – but they are better in the past tense! I am better enough now to post this without making you anxious. There is a good deal of neuralgia about the eyes still & I must not use them when I get tired or in the evening but head pressure stopped. Nose has been bleeding freely – it had conveniently almost stopped on Mon & Tues! *Is* there any connection I wonder? If so, I wouldn't use Dr O.B's adrenalin ointment I havn't begun yet. Such a collection of gory hankies to be washed! Tooth ached with the rest but that is easing too & I am not so *tired*. The inactivity has been very trying, but I can pick fruit today.

Later

This letter flows on like Johnny's! I quite see what a resource it is when you can't do much else. There was another from him last week – dated still well before the airgraph in reply to news of engagement. He plans to buy typewriter on return & keep the family by his pen! I fear there will be a downfall. I told Connie to say that I am not well enough to write, wh. is more or less true – but I don't know *what* to write!

[...]

Oh what a lovely day – perhaps I shall be able to *enjoy* it? Mt Grey is clear again – yesterday veiled. Certainly that mountain says something!

I feel free to post this, whether I hear from you or not, because I am certainly better – the first day I have felt *really* on the mend – but I am going to be oh so cautious. Now it can be a good *Retreat*, that I have a clear head. I feel you both there & its the more remarkable, this conviction that M. is always close interiorly – that it hasn't come slowly as with you my treasure – *we* had time to *grow* together, hadn't we?

Oh Merlin what volumes I could write to you about our darling! – but you don't need to be told. (May I say "our"? I don't think I have yet, tho' I've often said "our M." to K.)

End of letter at last! I'm afraid a great deal of my talk herein would sound very extravagant & absurd to the 'outside world' – but not to you. But its quite rational! There may be discrepancies & contradictions, with the vibrations of feeling & in agitation – like any picture in the making – but the fin des fins[1] is quite rational!

---

[1] Fr. 'final outcome.'

Darlings what rows of symbols there wd. have to be to be adequate! You must sort them out xxxxxxxxx!

U.

Macmillan Brown Library. MB 572. A.

TO MERLIN & KATHLEEN DAVIES – JANUARY 7-8, 1944[1]

47 Webb St. ChCh.

Darlings

Back on my bed after the Return of Richard episode.[2] I meant to be silent for a bit – even for the rest of your holiday – felt I had been *selfish* in my outpourings. But I have now read yr. missives & 'feel free' (as the Quakers say) to respond. [...]

Well, my little Katsy darling I take up the Jan 5. letter – in which you beg me not to be ruthless with myself! Oh darling, I'm collapsed – *done for* – (pro tem) & am not attempting *anything* in house. You say it must have been hard for me to write to you when I felt ill – but it "takes my mind off" that's what Effie said when she had her "new pain". [...] I don't think I've ever had such a pain as this in my eyes – except after operation & the time seems so long. [...] Thyra[3] was *extremely* kind today – said she would gladly take me back with them (her car) & keep me in bed, as she has cook and housemaid. But more of family anon.

It was an immense relief to know that you are both *well* – I did not doubt your *happiness*! It was all from expecting that P. Card. I could *see* it – signed "K&M", & just saying arrived safely, & all well! – I was so disappointed when *nothing* came (do remember how tired you both were) & my morbid imagination got to work, fearing the worst, as it always does. (I told Richd. how I never expected to see him again & how I always expected the worst – & he said, Oh I go in for expecting the best!) It all sounds most satisfactory & just what I'd hoped – before I began to be fearful. You must always remember how easily I am made sad & fearful, & give some little tangible sign to reassure me! – I don't know how much of my despondency is physical & how much mental – but I know that everything is harder when I am exhausted physically – And remember that I am *alone* – (not that I'm wanting Outside World!) You have each other. "Nothing matters" little Effie exclaimed once, when

---

[1] This too is in the form of a diary-letter, written at various times over two days.

[2] Bethell had sent a postcard earlier that afternoon relating a lunch with her nephew.

[3] Marmaduke's wife.

outlook was bad – "nothing matters so long as we have each other" It was not very long after that – – –

[...]

I have been addressing myself mostly so far to my own darling K. but now dearest M. I am looking at you! And first I want to say, don't please (you *or* K) feel that you've got to write (altho' these letters today *have* been such a comfort.) I know you have duty letters – & you'll never again have such a chance as this to let time flow by un-noticed. Above all don't write as Chaplain! only from yourself, if later on you are moved to do so again. 'Going thro' the vale of misery use it as a well' – I *was* able to use this pain last night for 'costing'[1] prayer & thus used, this time will bring me nearer to God. I was thanking Him for you & K & for you, for you Merlin – you are very important to me as well as very dear! What you write about your happiness is lovely, comforting, profoundly precious for our darling's sake – and is like talking about heaven to one in purgatory. Last night my purgatory was superseded for a while (tho' the physical pain in head went on) by what I must call a mystical sense of the reality and *inclusiveness* (so to speak) of God. The intellectual question I was coping with (when eyes did not ache *too* violently) what is this separateness of individuality? *Why* is it not enough for me, more than enough, for you & K to be completely happy in each other? – I don't *ask* for such happiness – its passed me by – But why can't I identify myself (I asked last night) so perfectly with them that their joy is my joy? Its what I desired for them – why is there this undercurrent of desolation? Perhaps the ingrained sense that everything is transitory & for a short time[2] – like flowers, has some part in the sadness. I fight all that, of course, I know well its not the truth – any more than the pain in my eyes belongs to sight! I see no other way out than *one-ness*. And by this time, when you are both with me – bodily presence I mean – I do feel that one-ness – with K. completely I believe, & with you beloved Merlin, "more & more". But now that you are removed from sight & touch I lose that sense of one-ness. Last night, however – but then, as you say – it won't go into a letter.

[...]

9 P.M. I felt pretty good when I went down after the rest chatting with you – but the effort of seeing to the jobs I did there was too much & started the burning, searing pain in the head (not so much eyes today – they are *2* pains!) Sheer tiredness. I used to think "If only I can keep

---

[1] Bethell may have borrowed this word (meaning spiritually exhausting) from her reading of von Hügel. The *OED* cites its first occurrence in his letters.

[2] See her poem 'Response' (*Collected Poems*, p. 1).

going till they are married." Now I think "I must keep going till the hospital"[1] – One can be suitably animated & chat brightly on demand, but when I looked in my glass tonight such a tired, sick old woman I saw there! Its a very oppressive NW evening & I have been lying with wet rag on forehead for an hour – no relief – & then remembered that bathing with *hot* water was said to be good for headache & I've had a scalding hot sponging – & its certainly easier. [...] Darlings you are experiencing the *usual* bliss of honeymoon days! – I've heard it & read of it over & over again! but better than usual because you are better quality people! & you were already much further on than most. I hope you liked the little monkey fairy tale – Katya – such a *choice* touch with words it made me shiver with pleasure – I'm afraid M. would not relish a fantasy – he must be *serious* – or does he now enjoy the notion of "avin' a gime"? – Do you remember the days when we used to laugh & giggle with fun, Katsy? They seem far away. Everything has been such *stress* – Shall we ever be amused like that again? – or have you put away childish things? You'll have to get them out again when you have *your* children!

I'm glad you had flowers in your room, K. I've had yellow roses – at last that bush flowered [...] but its really too hot now for flowers in water & my eyes seem to be too tired to enjoy them. I keep them shut (when not writing to you!) I'd better shut them now – but its so hard to think of anything but headache. My prayer will be nothing but the whimpering of an animal! As a matter of fact my prayer is often Merlin much better than you'd think from these meandering letters! The prayer of the church, you know.

You must imagine eye-shut pauses between my remarks.

Tonight I am haunted by the words (probably misquotation) "when this mortality shall have put on immortality, THEN – –"[2] I think I can get at Eternity best by way of the mountains – geological time – so immense – so irrelevant to humanity! Calm. Then a *sense* of the everlasting Now.

This has been a great day! I was very much touched by Richard's kindness – it *rested* me – we really seemed to *meet* – I hope not an illusion! He has grown up now. Very reticent. I think he's very tired in reality. His eyes look strained.

[...]

Its cooler now – You know what I am hoping will NOT happen while you are away – a thunderstorm!! I feel a bit easier & rested, perhaps I could sleep. I like the little touches in yr. letter, pet – about "my wife"

---

[1] About a week later, Bethell entered a private hospital in Riccarton, where she remained for a month.

[2] It is a slight misquotation: 'when ... this mortal shall have put on immortality.' See 1 Corinthians 15: 54.

etc. I like those little details – And Merlin I love what you say about "our darling" – how nice that you said that too, just when *I* did in *my* letter – Now I am peaceful. Now I will go to sleep. I am contented that you exist! It is an over-plus that you love me & don't let go of me.

Saturday 6.30 am

Went to sleep – suffocating night – heavy pall of clouds woke 3 am. with head – Now the wind is round gently to Souwest – such a relief – Clouds are banked up beyond Mt Grey. So freshness has not reached *you* yet. These are certainly brain headaches, but since they occur when I am overtired best dealt with thro' the body I think.

[...]

These voyage de noces[1] babblings – (you two certainly do know me at my very weakest! – but remember my poor tormented head & my exhaustion) put me down plump beside Johnny! I understand the ease he gets by writing. [...] Did I tell you that his magnum opus is to be a complete "Christian philosophy" of sex. It *will* be convenient to have my speculations set at rest! "The volume of this stuff is surprising" says Johnny! – not so surprising to me when I look at his packet of letters! (I must remind him that the Catholic Church is *not* Puritan.) I shall be interested to see what he has to say to virginity! – not much does one find. Usually a spot of 'sublimation' is recommended – with warnings against 'repression' – go and work in an orphanage – paint a picture – (yes, that suits *me* better.) On the other hand, the erotic Christ-worship of the convent, which I find so repulsive. As a matter of fact, in the living, free and independent life *is* worthwhile, and we are *not* all crazed as some of the dissertations appear to suggest. I do admire the way in which Johnny, driven away from newly discovered hearth & home, has not been 'downed' – He *is* at work constructing – or as he prefers to say – 'creating' – but oh dear what downfalls are in store? [...] I think Wm. Blake must be very bad for him – I have thought that Blake tended to hasten my cousin's madness. Oh what a relief to have such a fresh morning – I feel much better. But longing for fields & trees. (Pause).

[...]

Johnny's right. One does adore through creatures – mountains, flowers animals people – but God is there first, or one sticks. [...]

Later What a nice 'surprise' letter as you say – and quicker. I couldn't come to Kai. dear – tho' its sweet of you to plan it. Couldn't do journey – nor "do for myself" there. (Worse than here without conveniences.) If well should love it of course.

---

[1] Fr. 'honeymoon.'

You don't seem to have taken in how 'done finish' I am ! I was afraid I'd said too much & you might be alarmed. But evidently I have not offended in that respect! (Richard seemed pitiful – no doubt sees a change in me since 1940.) No, a week in bed is the thing for me & then I hope for a fresh start [...].

I *was* surprised dears, that you did not understand how much I *needed* a SIGN - a wonder should I say, a p.c. from a "honeymoon couple"! Blest are they who don't need signs![1] Of course I understand – You were Rapt – but I'm not rapt! I have been bereft, & in pain – well, well, you are not Superhuman! – still less am I – But I love you – all is well –

You may say – She can't be so very bad, writing all these tiresome rigmaroles – & that's true – but you see don't you, that it "took my mind off" – Today is MUCH *easier*. [...]

Goodbye. I kiss you darlings – many many times & thank you.

U.

Macmillan Brown Library. MB 572. A.

TO MERLIN DAVIES – [JANUARY 9], 1944

Epiphany I. 47 Webb St. ChCh.

Dear

I've usually addressed myself to K. – force of habit. Your turn to-day. This letter was made in the watches of the night, but only gets on to paper now.

[...]

This letter is not however another instalment of complaint but an apology for the former ones. Please destroy, forget, & forgive them (I am so sure of yr. forgiveness!) I must surely have been in a fever all last week (did not think of taking temp.) They were so wild & foolish, & so unfair to the holiday. I do regret them. Yesterday evening, (although the pain was not gone, only less) my brain seemed to clear, & I was able to think lucidly, & was above my consciousness, as it were, once more! It was a (small!) torment before, & the time has seemed very much longer than it really was. Time's so relative! I suppose I am beginning to be rested (altho' when I got up this morning I felt *deadly* tired) & that would account for the blessed state of lucidity – (*and* your prayers?) Once more I know that there is *really* nothing to be desired but the will of God (&

[1] See John 20: 29.

how pleased I was to meet with today's Epistle which I had forgotten.)[1] I find the steady beat of the rain very helpful these "nuits blanches"[2] – like the ticking of a clock, to say that the hours are surely passing by & pain with them.

It was possible between 7 & 2 to do some self-examination & to review this strange, lovely, triple relationship. And Merlin, dearest Merlin, I found, still [illegible][3] traces of that doubtfulness, that fundamental mistrust, which has hampered my religious life, to be still affecting the bond with you. Not with K – its faith there, & it is her doing. And I recalled the discovery of her intense wish that all should be clarity & confidence between you & me – (I often think of little Effie's "Our Third" – that was Michael & he certainly was a sort of *glue*, the beloved (but *not* befooled) animal!) I want to tell you that, because I think that discovery is going to be valuable, and herein I desire to thank you, as I think I have never done before, for the most beautiful 'declaration of love' I've ever had in my life, except I think little E's "wonderful love" & I did not take that in completely then because the most heavenly K. will remember that, and knows what an impression it made upon me – I think perhaps because of my fault you don't know how deep the impression was. But I saw last night that I've never *fully* accepted it – or should one say – never *fully* believed it. Always fearing & doubting & preparing for the worst! (Not an irrational habit, *humanly* speaking, in the light, on the whole, of events!) But now I believe that I *have* begun to accept it without reserve – *entirely* (now) without reserve – – – You know I've counted on it a great deal already, and its part of the Divine Mercy – You know, I do believe in the tender mercies of the *past*! The fear is that they won't come again!, tho' I love that line "My trust is in the tender mercies of God, for ever & ever".[4]

[...]

After this I should like you not to bother about me any more. The time will go too quickly for you & you mustn't have anything to interrupt it. I confess that I have been rather frightened this last week – it was so like Effie at the end & the doctors not guessing – but *her* pain went on for months. I am glad to have shared her experience. I recall the night when the pain was at its worst & she was too ill to get to me – & the sick terror I felt when I found her like that in the morning when she'd gone,

---

[1] The Epistle for the First Sunday after Epiphany is Romans 12: 1-5; Bethell may be thinking of the 2nd verse, containing the injunction to be 'transformed by the renewing of your mind, that ye may prove what is that good, and acceptable, and perfect will of God.'

[2] Fr. 'sleepless nights.'

[3] A word here is illegible; it may have been smudged, or erased later.

[4] See Psalm 52: 9.

one of my first thoughts was – "you can't be hurt through your body any more my darling".

[...]

Now let me talk to our darling, having kissed you both – Her last two missives read queerly because she adopts your wording!! Oh Merlin, you're not going to "*mould*" her I hope! You once accused me of doing that – I liked her own quaint words – tell her to stop it! But after all they're very good words & meet the case, so why worry? The interesting thing is that you *have* now your own words to be borrowed! – Merlin the inexpressive is certainly no longer that! After all many's the word of mine she has adopted in the past – tho' I protest that I did *not* mould her.

[...]

So good to read that I am "close" (Merlin's word) darling. I havn't been able to feel it always – the pain has got in the way. But that is better. I ought to leave off writing now or eyes will play up. Longing for the hospital – must wash some nighties etc. first. This one's blood spotted down the front – 'orrible! – nose bleeds so suddenly.

[...]

Using best note paper for this letter because its supposed to be an improved letter! – as explained to M. Thank him for staving off painters. I'm not surprised at his house-craft. He's very intelligent you know & when he does get something into focus, nothing will budge him! There should be a whole sheet of these XXXXX

Your U

Macmillan Brown Library. MB 572. A.

TO KATHLEEN & MERLIN DAVIES – [JANUARY 13, 1944]

147 Ilam Road. Riccarton.

Darlings

I feel much nearer you here! Perhaps the wind in the pine-trees (Macrocarpa, mark you, like Kaikoura, not insignis) & the fresher air – I can smell hay. At Webb St I felt that you were up in the sunshine far away & I struggling along in a dark valley full of pain – Its still a little like that, but the contrast is not nearly so acute!

I was a bit disappointed in this place at first – a small house, & pokey I thought. But Mrs. O'C[1] has pushed another patient into the small dark room she spoke of & put me on a sort of (glazed in) open air

---

[1] The nurse who ran the private hospital (St. Francis Hospital) is identified later as Mrs. O'Connell.

balcony about the size of Mrs. McI's front one I think.[1] Upstairs. Looks on to trees – I don't see Mts – (but not by way of looking at anything yet!) & I don't see rooves – Fields all round & some houses, not visible. I have to come thru' another patient's room to this sleeping porch – & the door's open between us at night wh. I don't like – but one must put up with something. An old*er* lady. Very quiet. Seems to get up in the day-time – I think she may be daft. Its an *unspeakable* relief not to have to get up & make efforts – just got back into bed after bath, instead of crawling down to kitchenette to scratch up food. [...] Everything very clean tho' shabby & bed most comfortable – I feel as if I couldn't have held out at Webb St for another 24 hours! [...]

I can see you clearly this morning dears – wish I could go walking with you up that country road – Don't really wish to walk – only to lie still with eyes shut. (Should enjoy this open to light porch more if they were stronger.) Last night was obscure & misty – but I think it may turn to heat today. On Tuesday night I saw the clear moonlight & thought you wd. be enjoying it – but I could not take an interest in it – Went to sleep cleaning saucepans (tired Martha-mind) & woke up making a piece of verse about warm, living love having gone away out of sight & I dead & spent like the moon & Should I be content with reflected brightness etc. Very commonplace (sad, ebb-tide mind).

Can it be only a fortnight since you left – It seems like many years. I reckon that the corner of yr. holiday won't be turned till the 16th – & then you will have begun to come back as it were. For that last ten days you must be *completely* segregated into ecstasy – no post in or out (only you must send me that post card on safe arrival at camp) so it behoves us to come now to an understanding about your home-coming. You have not told me whether or no you are dining out with your Young Friends that evening. If I may venture to put my oar in for once I suggest too tiring Merlin after that long journey for yr. young wife but you may think otherwise. I recommend bite of food & bed [...] It seems unlikely that I shall be able to cook anything nice for you, but I hope I'm mistaken about all that.

There is another possibility I have been considering – i.e. that I should not be here at all when you come back. I have looked, in the glass, such a hideous, puffy, flushed old woman, that I wd. rather be gone than that you should see me like that – I don't want you to remember me like that. But I look less flushed this morning (tho' eyes queer) & I think I've come away just in time.

[...]

---

[1] Mrs McIver was the landlady where Bethell stayed in Kaikoura.

The "Retreat" had to be called off Merlin darling – too much pain – But here I think prayer will be easier. I have had ringing in my head the last line of that poem (not hymn) of Wesleys about Jacob wrestling with the angel, which I like very much. A favourite of A's – he read it to me first – probably that week we "parted company" – I wonder whether you know it – Its in the Oxford Treasury (or is it Golden Treasury) of religious verse – "Through all eternity to prove, Thy Nature & Thy Name is Love."[1]

[...]

I was thinking that the "closeness" about which you wrote so sweetly, & was lovely to read of – wasn't very *practical*! since it did not correspond with *my* feeling *you* "close"! – (I've lost you for long lapses, but today you are near) and it did not convey to you any sense of what I was going through at the time.* It belongs to the region of faith I suppose. What treasures you both are. Bodily pain does obscure things – (besides the sudden shock of absence & solitude when you went away) I have been glad to know more of what my darling endured – but hers was so much worse – And I have raised it up with what's going on in Europe – More prayers please, darlings, I *do* want to get well you know. I've been thinking how soothing & lovely you will be now that you are perfectly rhythmical & melted, I am longing to see you, & if I'm here still, you must come *next day* & see me here. Its pleasant to come where one's known. Rachel beamed & said "Its nice to see you again Miss B." She's very tickled because I call her Martha instead of Rachel[2] (I always did) but this frightens me because my mother did that towards the end "Thwaites" for "Rafferty" e.g.

* [Added in margin] Just as well! It might have clouded your Bliss a little and that wouldn't do at all!

[...]

You may be *quite* easy about me here, dears. You said "Take care of yourself" but what I need now is someone to take care *of me* – I'm quite all right with Mrs. O'C. whatever happens. And I can rest, & presently, relax – When this letter goes there'll be *nothing* more to think of for the rest of the day! My head aches, of course, not surprising after yesterday. I mustn't be left alone at Webb St again you know – that's a fact. (Merlin, you "asked for" it!)

This will be a *first-rate* place for writing & meditating when my head clears. I know *feelings* are *no* guide – but twice in my life I've ignored

---

[1] The poem is John Wesley's 'Wrestling Jacob.' The last line Bethell quotes recurs through the final 5 stanzas of the poem.

[2] Bethell's misnaming is no doubt suggested by the Gospel figure of Martha; see Luke 10: 38-42.

feelings & struggled on, consequently all but dying on friends' hands, & giving such trouble – And I can't forget those episodes. So you will understand if I seem to have made too much of this break-down, children? M. said a Mother but I've been thinking Grandmother or nice sort of Greatauntie wd. be nearer the mark! – But I'd prefer something more contemporary if I've life enough in me to survive now! But you *are* my darling children all the same.

[...]

Darlings, if I write again it will be to tell you that I am really better. I do feel better already! The spirits have risen, but *not* hectic-ly! As I said, *More* prayers please! You *do* want to see me again, I know. The absence of strain, not having to think & plan, is *heavenly* – And there's been, all through, the solid fact that you are happy, that you, K. are fixed up for good. Nothing can deprive you now of what you've had, my darling.

I might choose the wedding snap today – eyes a bit stronger – Merlin's quite good but does look tired – but K. darling – you are disappointing – how can you be so stodgy! I'd like to *paint* your portrait while you are looking illuminated – I believe it could be done. M. wd. be impossible – & K. you will agree with *that*!

I've been filling in time till they come for letters of course – now for complete – what shall I call it – negativeness – (I've written quite enough – head's heated). Goodbye dearest dears

XXXXXXXX
U

Macmillan Brown Library. MB 572. A.

TO KATHLEEN & MERLIN DAVIES – [JANUARY 13 1944]

St Francis Hospital. Ilam Road. Riccarton.

My darling

Your letter (Tuesday's) was handed to me after Church & I think I will carry on with "answering" – its positively the *only* occupation I find easy! I can't begin on outside world yet – and everyone, just now, is "outside world" compared with my own darling Young Couple en voyage de noces![1]

[...]

[1] Fr. 'on honeymoon.'

So glad you don't appreciate Hervey! I do not, & I've been so afraid that it was professional jealousy![1] Loose construction of Xmas Eve stanzas? I thought they followed the In Memoriam formula pretty closely[2] – I suppose they could be boiled down but the thing didn't seem to call for terseness. Eric doesn't like any of my rhymed things (*nor* religion of course) Too facile – its extraordinary how rhyming runs away with one. Look at Whim Wham.[3]

[...]

And now darling – Elect Lady! (It is an election indeed to be given what you have, isn't it?) I think the rest of my chat must be addressed to our precious Merlin direct, not obliquely. His footnote has given me quite a shock. I must have expressed my best-notepaper letter[4] very badly – or else it had not arrived. I feel that you understand so perfectly about him & me - - - and I have told you every new phase as our relationship progressed – his & mine I mean – Do you really feel that I *still* havn't "accepted him completely"? – Of course he did not *rest* me as you rest me – I realized that I hadn't yet accepted him to the point of *rest*. In confidence, esteem, love, I havn't faltered. You know that. But there was the vestige of 'too good to be true' & the fear of being a bother etc – Also, I fancy that in the meantime he's been growing up – and I shall *feel* a difference – Do believe that in mind & heart I'm his just as I'm yours. You know I think its rather like the bits of glass or needles working to the surface – my scepticisms! Did you read his foot-note, I wonder? – truly I havn't "wobbled" about *him*, the angel, I love him intensely – Perhaps I put it badly on paper. Wait till I see you again. (I began to think I *shouldn't* see you again.) Remember that you are *both* quite unusual. What other young man absorbed in his passion for you wd. have thought or heart for an old woman like me? What other girl would be able to include in her heart the love of such a lover, *and* mine?

And now I must rest eyes & head before addressing myself to *my beloved* Merlin – I wish I could *telegraph* it to him!

[...] I have qualms sometimes about writing so much, & so egotistically, to you at such a time! But I *will* try not to have these fears.

---

[1] Bethell's disdain for J. R. Hervey (1889-1958) is somewhat surprising, as they might have been imagined to have much in common. He was an Anglican clergyman from 1914-1938, and at the time his verse was well regarded. Like Bethell, he shows a fondness for unusual Latinate words, and his language rhythms are much influenced by scripture and liturgy.

[2] This refers to a poem of Bethell's, 'In a Hospital: Christmas Eve, 1932,' first published in *The Press*, Dec. 23, 1933, which employs the stanzaic form of Tennyson's *In Memoriam*.

[3] Whim Wham was a pseudonym used by Allen Curnow for satirical verse he published in *The Press* and later in the *New Zealand Listener*.

[4] See the letter of Jan. 9.

It has been a relief. Oh darling K. I do *want* you! (That is a very *weak* thing to say.)

Your U.

Merlin darling

I really can't 'settle down' tonight (that's a hospital expression) without talking to you a little about your bit of today's letter. I havn't thanked you & K. half enough for writing to me [as] often as you've done – & at this too precious time – it has been a great comfort to me – sick old woman that I am. [...]

Dear, I took a bit of my *expensive* notepaper on Sunday I think it was – to write to you after some quiet thought in the night, what I hoped was a *progressive* letter – but I must have expressed myself badly – it can't have sounded as I meant. Please, please, I havn't "wobbled" about *you* – that was my word applied to the reactions – not always to be anticipated by me! of shall I say my nervous system to the developing relationship between K. & yourself. I won't go into that again – I think you do understand & I'm sure K. does. The "I & Thou" relationship of you & me is Something other. I believe it has gone on deepening all the time. And, truly, K. hasn't had to "sense" where it may have faltered – I have told her all my thoughts & feelings about it as time went by, & that I felt I couldn't be happy, as I discovered she wouldn't be happy, until you & I had a *perfect* understanding – Her own words say it right, "I must accept you as completely as I accept her" – but darling, what's such a shock to me – (& my poor head thumped & throbbed like anything when I read the word!) is that you speak of "rejected" love – oh no, *no*, NO! accepted, but with trembling. I will clasp that sharp word to my bosom like the asp & see whether it will teach me something, because you would not have used it carelessly – Is *that* how it has seemed to you? – I can hardly believe it – but oh, please think better of me than that, quickly! Of course it "drew" me – beautiful! Of course it did, and does. But it is so wonderful, & my doubts & fears have gone on cropping up, & hindered peace. I saw more clearly that night how my fundamental lack of trust has crept in everywhere. Not doubts of *you* – dearest Merlin – but doubts I suppose about what such love could imply. Its just the same in religion. I've never had peace & rest in faith – (& I've been dubious about the authenticity of what people profess on that point.) Its like your boils – the poison comes out & out. If one can detect the virus & deal with it direct, good – next to that, you must poultice *my* blains of fear! The last instance was on the wedding day when I thought you were in haste to get rid of me – and it seemed *so* natural and right! but I simply could not hurry & was feeling rather agitated & over done – And then horrified at being a bother, when *you* were so tired. But afterwards we met so very closely & completely, it seemed to me, the morning we said goodbye. Don't you think so? I was very happy about that. Its not wobbles darling it really isn't, but a trembling exploration & *progress*. Surely you don't look on that as "rejection"? or do you? If so I must indeed "think again", & with a different dread. I ended my bit of this letter to K. with the exclamation "I do want you" & said it was a weak cry – & so it was because I can't have her just now – but at the risk of sounding weak I'll repeat it to you beloved Merlin – I want you – and I need you – & I'll try to be cured of fears!

And yes – dear, I'd love to be "taken care of" by you – I do so *long* to be taken care of! A "*but*" tried to come in there saying: he can't take on an old crock as well as a not too tough young wife! but I won't be *too* crocky & you & she will share it? This job was new to you & cost you far more effort than – say Richard who was trained to it & finds it "as easy as falling off a log" as the boys used to say – tho' to be sure, he can't have had much practice lately! But now you have been exercised in it & in *noticing* – That's splendid – I'm so comforted that you are being "alert" about her getting tired. Oh, Merlin is it possible that I've *still* been hurting you? Do ask K. how I *really* think of you! – All she knows. The trembles of my doubt will surely evaporate, now that they have been stared at boldly by me! Oh, darling – "rejected" – my poor head doesn't like it at all – please withdraw *that*.

Friday

I do hope this letter will convey what its meant to convey – my love in short. And more faith. I am so much better this morning. [...]

Adieu darling M. I kiss you trustfully.

U.

[To Kathleen]

Do hope my enclosure to M. doesn't sound too 'emotional'. I *was* rather upset by that "rejected" & am anxious to have the shock pacified. You will help won't you. But I am quite calm & collected today [...] M. is so unlike everyone else! Not in E.P.'s way I think with any number of extra antennae, long & tenuous, playing about other people – & recording things I hadn't observed – more like the sea creatures with short sensitive filaments being played upon – He is a most precious treasure, your husband, take *great* care of him & *don't* let him be hurt by any inadvertence of mine ever.

Et maintenant ma petite je t'embrasse et te quitte.[1]

XXXXXXXX for both of you.
U.

Macmillan Brown Library. MB 572. A.

To Rodney Kennedy – January 14, 1944

As from 47 Webb St ChCh

My dear Rodney

I had relapses of Influenza almost up to Christmas & at the same time was obliged consistently to overtax my strength. For I had undertaken to board my delightful young friend, now Mrs. Merlin Davies, who was teaching full-time & overtime at St Andrew's College, when St F's ceased to provide meals for residents – that was in October. I managed to keep going till after the wedding on Dec 27th, but since then have been quite exhausted & have now come to a hospital for a rest-cure. One of my troubles has been severe headache, & with that, great pain in my eyes, so that I have not been able to use them, & even now, not too much, or it sets up trouble – They were weakened by that recurring influenza which affected the eyes in a great many cases. So now you know the reason for my silence at Xmas, & the reason why I have not already replied to your delightful Epiphany letter – (you put 1943 but had Jan 6th correct!)

[...]

I had a bad year in many ways, but the outlook for this one is after all very bright. Sometimes, (not always!) one can SEE providential care for the sparrow shining out![2] Your Sep 23 letter was so sympathetic and *understanding* about a probable uprooting that I know you will rejoice to hear that I'm not to be uprooted – yet. I've no love for the Webb St house, (though appearance has been deceiving I must admit) but it is *people* who make a home – 47 Webb St is no longer St Faith's, but still belongs to the Church of course – and they don't yet know what use to make of it. So it has been arranged that Merlin Davies (very few people seem to call him Mister!) is to occupy it during 1944 & be my landlord. He has become as great a friend as his young wife has been for more than

[1] Fr. 'And now, my little one, lots of love.'

[2] See Matthew 10: 29. Bethell alludes to the sparrow image again in subsequent letters to Kennedy.

two years, & nothing could be happier for me – they are eager to "take care of me" – I need that now. I dare not look further on than the end of this year, because I am afraid it is too likely that they will go to England – I can't afford a servant & can't live alone, so it may end in a room in some kind of nursing home. But remembering the "tender mercy of God" at this crisis, I need not fear the next one, need I? There has been a crisis, or big event in my life every ten years so far, & I am now in my 70th, & was quite expecting some new turn of the wheel. Miss Pollen died in 1934, & that changed everything for me as you know. The companionship of a charming girl has brought back some of the Rise Cottage atmosphere – "Cabined & confined"[1] I've always felt myself to be at Webb St, but the new circumstances should give it a different feel. Its not settled yet what rooms I am to have, but [at] any rate I am to have *more* & not be so cramped. It was such a beautiful wedding – at 8:30 in the morning because the newly married pair made their Communion according to old & good custom – now mostly forgotten in the Church of England I'm afraid. By beautiful I mean happy & peaceful & full of faith.

[...]

Its high time I made you another packet of literature, but I have been so disabled & so pressed for time to do aught but struggle with domestic work. I have read very little. Rilke has so far baffled me, & I feel the translations are bad, but M Dronke is a great admirer, & I must persevere. I've been given A. Curnow's new book of poems for Christmas[2] – they look good to me. Its so nice the way you relate to me anything concerning my poetry – I almost forget nowadays that I ever wrote any! But they do still mean a great deal to me –

When I last wrote I think I was planning to go to a Convalescent Home near Waiau. It rained all the time, but I was so comfortable that didn't matter – But a week wasn't long enough & I could only stay a week for reasons aforesaid. Not long ago I heard that the nurse who ran it so well, had given that up, & opened this small hospital in Riccarton. Its really quite in the country & so pleasant. I look on to green trees & love the sound of the wind in them – I can't look long at any detailed or coloured thing – a new experience for me. Its called St Francis Hospital, but I have not put the address because I am not sure how long I shall be here. I should like to be back to prepare for the new inhabitants when

---

[1] 'But now I am cabin'd, cribb'd, confin'd, bound in / To saucy doubts and fears.' *Macbeth* III. 4. 23-24.

[2] Curnow's *Sailing or Drowning* was published by the Progressive Publishing Society, 1943.

they return from the wedding journey. I do not lament the close of St Faith's – because it has not turned to be what my sister planned.

[...]

John Summers lately complained that my letters were flat! I'm afraid they *are*. I can't praise his writings as much as he expects, but I have to remind him that I *never* set up to be a literary critic. I wonder whether he writes to you. I fear Connie is very lonely – but she has her little Faith to tend, happily.

I am passing on to you one of my Xmas cards where you will find the chief Feasts noted – One still cant get the sort I used to send you – This one looks very ecclesiastical or should I say "Churchy"! – Did you know that Epiphany is a favourite day of mine – I landed in India on that day in 1914. Have I quoted to you before those lines:

"Wise men all ways of knowing past
To the shepherds' wonder come at last" – [1]

Balthazar – Melchior – and what was the 3rd? Nice names. (That splash is my drinking water – *not* tears!)

I am interested in what you say about Colin – I wish he would change it to *O*'Cahon – so much more euphonious & natural sounding. That settlement will be "quite a place"!

Now that I think of it, I have read one novel within the last 6 months – Phineas Finn,[2] lent to me by Prof. Sinclaire. I enjoyed it very much. I recall the remnants of that society. And Charles Brasch sent me the 4 last TS Eliot poems.

My eyes are saying that I'd better stop. I hope that in the meanwhile you have not been snatched away from yr. coloured garden to another camp. Thank you, dear Rodney, for all your kindness, & for your courage in living. And for New Year good wishes & you have mine. Your Xmas sounds like mine this year. There seemed to be no time for it! And through looking at the wrong page in the Tram timetable I only got to the 11o'c mass at the Cathedral half way through. But I did hear the carols there on Xmas Eve.

My love to you
M. U. B.

Hocken Library. MS-0741-001.

---

[1] From 'Lord when the wise men came from farr,' by the Cavalier poet Sydney Godolphin. The name Bethell forgot is Gaspard.

[2] By Anthony Trollope.

TO KATHLEEN & MERLIN DAVIES – JANUARY 18, 1944

147 Ilam Road. Riccarton. ChCh.

Darlings

How lovely you are! Back from dentist,[1] there lay yr. letter on my dressing table – best possible Restorative. I read it while gustating cautiously [...] & gratefully swallowing the broth Mrs. O'C. had specially prepared for me.

[...]

Merlin, dearly beloved, your letter finds me much further on than even yesterday (I have many quiet spaces, you know, here). I think indeed already *there*. So ready to assent to whatever you propose. I have been finding out by degrees all that you mean to me – it was too noble & gracious to take in all at once. [...] I think I meant some of what you say by my "deep reconciliation" – Will you depend upon me while you are away? and set it all in order when you come. This is a very poor inadequate attempt to say what's in my heart & will, darling – please accept it, please 'read through the lines' written under rather hampering circumstances! A miracle, at the latter end, has befallen – "The good wine until now"[2] – You & K. seem to be the epitome, as it were, of all my affections in the past. Darling K – [...] would you give your – our– Merlin one of your very tenderest & most thankful kisses as from me? You know he has been too wonderful for me to take in, "& that's the truth." You'll understand what I mean when I speak of being awestruck. It is like an arithmetic sum when it begins to come out & you know it can't help going on. And it touches the whole of life. I'm afraid that's very nebulous, but later on I'll explain better.

This is my line, dear, as I wrote it:

"Past all *debate*, all hazard, *still* and sure"[3] – & a pretty good line, too tho' I say it as shouldn't – It was so rejoicing & satisfying to see my own line coming true that early morning of yours! (Yet that's what *I* wanted to be – a Bride. A fig for all this mothering! I wd. say – Well, well, patience & perseverance & a bottle of sweet oil & that Jerusalem of stillness & assurance mayhap is reached by another gate – "Right through the gates of wrath!")[4] Your wedding, darling, how I dwell on it all – How well everything fell out! – Providence *was* about.

[...]

---

[1] Bethell had just had two teeth extracted at another hospital.

[2] See John 2: 10.

[3] The line comes from 'Candour' (*Collected Poems*, p. 44).

[4] A proverbial saying suggests that with patience, perseverance and a bottle of sweet oil the snail at last reached Jerusalem. The 'gates of wrath' are from Blake's 'Morning.'

You can't imagine the profound thankfulness I feel about *everything*, and especially you, my own dearest dears.

U

Macmillan Brown Library. MB 572. A.

TO KATHLEEN & MERLIN DAVIES – JANUARY 30, [1944]

147 Ilam Road.

So grieved that after all dears – I can't welcome you Home. Its ordained that I'm to go straight to Lewisham to-morrow to have Xray & Dr. Robertson to see me Tuesday, there.

[...]

I shall send written notice to Lewisham office NO VISITORS – except Rev. Merlin Davies & Mrs. Davies whenever they are able to call. If anyone rings about me please say *no* visitors – Richard will ring you from Pahau (tomorrow) i.e. Monday evening. Went home yesterday – Is afraid I'm going to impose upon you – have tried to reassure him. Is terribly masterful! but so kind. Mrs O'C. VERY kind too & has nurse she will lend me when & if I come home after op. who wd. cook for me etc. too – Richd. brought huge bunch gladiolus yesterday I'll take to Lewisham – so don't bother about flowers – only scented verbena when you come – I do hope *soon*! Could you bring one copy The Garden & one Day & Night to me to inscribe – lowest shelf behind blue armchair – my thank offerings to Mrs. O'C & Nurse.

[...]

Miraculous to feel so well today – I've had a bad time.

All love.

U.

Macmillan Brown Library. MB 572. A.

TO RODNEY KENNEDY – MARCH 19, 1944

47 Webb St. ChCh.

My dear Rodney

I liked your Ash Wednesday letter – especially the sparrow epithet. Yes I *have* been cared for. Left Lewisham Feb 11th & by "luck" heard of a semi-nurse to look after me – & since then a club-boy's (of 50 years ago) widow has kindly come to the rescue. I have had a great deal of pain & still have to take dope to sleep, but am beginning to feel stronger. Eyes too are stronger, tho' I can't use them much. [...]

Everything here is changed – for the better certainly where I am concerned. Workmen only just out of the house (sent by Church Trustees) but I have been "above" *that* "battle" – I have all the upstairs floor now & a nice little sitting room there. Books distributed about the house. Its a private house now – I have no separate entrance. Quiet is delightful now that the workmen have gone. Religiously I am being helped. Three times we have had Holy Communion in my room – & we often have prayers together. Naturally I long for the time when I shall be able to use my eyes to read again, as I am obliged to be inactive still, though feeling stronger in myself. I am beginning to see a few visitors (singly if possible) but hitherto it has been too tiring to talk to people much. And they don't understand that my head is so weak that loud voices are painful! I have been much prisoned into myself all this year & no doubt it is a good discipline – but people have been very kind indeed & I am thankful.

[...]

Marie Dronke seems to have had a very successful time at Auckland. She tells me she recited (or read) Long Harbour 5 times – it will become quite familiar at that rate. But A. Curnow, who is editing a new anthology of N.Z. verse writes about his choice of me & I do not find that one. I am rather surprised at his list – most from Day & Night & none from The Garden. Its as follows: from Time & Place – Warning of Winter; By Burke's Pass; Envoy – (but is it good to detach that from its place?) From D & N: Spring on the Plain (wh. *I* have never thought of as one of my successes!) Night Rain, (wh. a scholarly friend in England told me was inadmissable – the product of high fever & irrational!) October Morning (OK. I think) Morning Walk, Southerly Sunday, 9th July 1932, The Small Hours, Norwest Evening, Winter, Waves. (I am glad he chose this one)[1]

Lady Day.[2]

My head has been too tired to finish this – I should have posted it "tel quel",[3] as I do now. I could not listen to V.M's broadcast – too much pain in my head. Three months it will be on the 29th since it began!

With my love to you & good wishes for endurance & hope.

M. U. B.

Hocken Library. MS-0741-001.

---

[1] Curnow's final selection included, in addition to all these, 7 other poems: 'Pause,' 'Time,' 'Fraicheur,' 'Trance,' 'Dirge,' 'The Long Harbour,' and 'Forest Sleep.'

[2] i.e. the feast of the Annunciation, March 25.

[3] Fr. 'as it is.'

TO CHARLES BRASCH – APRIL 27, 1944

As from 47 Webb St. Christchurch. N.1. N.Z.
(In hospital)

My dear Charles

I've just stamped an airgraph to you in which I promise to begin on a surface letter at once – & so I do. My eyes are much stronger, but I dare not use them for long at a time. It has been a strange experience to be cut off from reading all these months, & not to be able to bear music, radio or gramophone. I've discovered that most people have terribly piercing voices! (Thank heaven, my house-mates have *not*.) Its strange that the head & eye pain is so much better, while the swollen cheek remains & has a little corkscrew in it – not *always* turning, though, as it used to do. I have some hope that it may not be the worst thing threatened, but am prepared for it. Singular mercy that, with the illness, I've been provided with my domestic chaplain's spiritual help. I could not have come through it all without that.

Your letter of Feb 16th is so interesting. When you write about your country sojourns it always makes me feel that England *is* still there.

Ap 28.

Eyes gave out. "Undisturbed nights" in Gloucestershire is corollary to my sister's account of the return of blitz on London. There are so many one is anxious about there.

[...]

I shall write to you later if & when I'm able to read the Nativity Play[1] – & look forward v. much to the other one which you say is better verse. Merlin D. reads a little verse to me now & again & that is a treat – but he has so little free time & he has far too much demanded of him for his strength – so that, when there is a spare hour, he is usually played out. K. does not read aloud well, tho' she has a very pleasant voice – & her domesticities use up all *her* spare strength. (My picture for this year was that I was to be a help not a burden – however by Holy Luck as Ch. Williams says a char. was secured for 3 times a week & we shared her & I had personal help as well for some time.)

I wonder whether the American trans. of the Alcestis you wd. like the Adelphi Players to do would be by "H.D." (whoever *that* is – do you

[1] None of Brasch's letters after 1941 has survived, so it is not possible to identify this play with any certainty, but two plays by Charles Williams deserve consideration: *The House by the Stable* (1938) and *Seed of Adam* (1939) are both verse Nativity plays, and Brasch might well have sent work by one of Bethell's favourite authors.

know?)[1] It wd. be a fine thing if such a troupe could exist in N.Z. & I've often thought that there Rodney's true place wd. be. But I can't at all imagine drama being considered a work of National Importance in N.Z.! There are entertainments for the troops & there is a great deal of effort about drama in a small way – "community centres" for instance. They are just going through one in ChCh, at Opawa – Old house & grounds given for it. A scheme is afoot something like Adelphi – but not like enough I'm afraid – led by Ngaio Marsh & friends. She certainly has a great deal of ability – her Hamlet at Cant. Coll. last year was a 'notable achievement' but I've come to feel artificiality there – & its the Noel Coward touch I think.[2] They fraternised when he was in N.Z. doing patriotic pushing over the air – dreadful I thought it. On the other hand there's Maria Dronke, who had a successful Auckland season in Feby. Did Cradle Song[3] & a Yeats Play and five crowded poetry recitals – (800 Training Col. students at one). She wd. be a good one to lead such a venture & has a business like husband – & a small stage & props, but she *is* a bit passionate for N.Z. perhaps! & they don't like refugees v. much. "Art in NZ" is surely negligible? I havn't seen it for ages. There were some good illustrations, but letterpress bad, & the "short stories" lamentable. Toss, you ask about. My impression is that he has shot his bolt, tho' he goes on working at painting as far as he can. There were things of his at the Group Ex. but I wasn't well enough to stay long or take them in. One of Edith by lamplight was striking. His breadwinning takes it out of him, & he has to help Edith. They are having a fourth child this year. Their children must be starting their lives under v. good influences – the house I'm told is much enlarged & improved.

[...]

Next yr. questions about Allen Curnow – but again my eyes have given out – & Pain start up in cheek. I don't know why.

Ap 29

I sat up most of yesterday & spent my eyesight at intervals on a mending job. (My chaplain's braces in fact!) Sewing in large stitches or easy knitting is the easiest eye-task just now. But I find that it takes

---

[1] 'H.D' was the American Imagist poet, Hilda Doolittle. Although she did translate some of Euripides' work, the *Alcestis* was not among them. Bethell may be thinking of the 1930 translation by Richard Aldington.

[2] See Chapter 10 of Marsh's autobiography, *Black Beech and Honeydew*.

[3] Although there are numerous short poems with this title (by Blake, Tennyson and Yeats, among others), the context suggests a play. The only drama I have discovered with this title is by the Spanish playwright, Gregorio Martinez-Sierra (trans. J. Garrett Underhill). Moderately popular in the 1930s, the play is set in an enclosed Dominican convent in Spain.

more arm & neck energy than lying back & using a pen. In bed this morning keeping quiet before the move – my nephew coming for me after dinner – the married one – he's in town & has the farm truck, which is family motor car in front. Most country people seem to use these now. It will be wonderful to escape from the racket of this Hosp. Its real torture – but I suppose that people who have *not* my head wd. not notice it. Beside the noise there is the trial of some young woman dashing in to the room on some errand – at least every half hour for most of the day – & usually either leaving the door open (leaving me exposed to cross draught) or slamming it, the door closed does make a little difference to the din without. And so many different girls! – I can count at least 20, without stopping to think, in my 11 days. Some are man-powered to the job. Oh well, I shall soon forget it & the place is no doubt efficiently run. Its a C of E institution – they bring Communion to one's room on Sundays on request – at first I believe they were over zealous & rounded people up to be taken to chapel when not feeling like it! – or so the story goes. When the bell rings in front of the little procession (a tiny nun tinkles the bell & carries a candle) its the only quiet time in the place – then it feels something like the catacombs. I don't know why & anyhow not a very cheerful suggestion for a hospital!

This afternoon I shall see Mt Grey instead of the doctors' cars (I'm ground floor wh. I hate) & have 2 hours complete quiet & solitude while my house mates repair to his Pacific Area intercession service at Christ's Coll. Chapel. He's very good at arranging such things. I daresay you know that the Chinese & Jap Xtians have gone on with their prayers for each other & get messages across. I don't think many in this country wd. realise that there are such people – its rather the Daily Mail view that all Japs. are sub human – (if *they* were our allies I suppose the chinese wd. be the sub-human ones). The small hosp. I'm to go to this day week will be as quiet as the trams permit & I don't mind that sort of noise – regular & impersonal.

I was starting on Allen Curnow & what I say must please be strictly between ourselves, because I really know him very little & I must not be influenced by what I hear from others. Did you know that his father is a parson (I'm told a prosy bore, but I believe not completely stupid as so many of ours alas are, here) & that he was reading for Holy Orders at Auckland, when the influences you refer to were at work. There seems to have been nothing for the intellect to bite onto in the training – in fact I don't see how it could be called a training at all – all the same he persevered & it wasn't till he came south to seek for a "title" that he was finally put off & took to journalism. I'm sure he must have said many things offensive to the clerical world, but when I listen to broadcast sermons or "devotions" they seem to me to be quite fatal to the spread of religion. We're in a real quagmire of mediocrity or worse than mediocrity. (But there's always the vision, & the remnant.)[1] This background accounts for the choice he's made of my things to go into his book, which rather surprised – and pleased – me. He's not put off by archaic scriptural echoes. (Eric McCormick on the other hand queried "convenient food"!)[2] Allen says he's been driven to church from 5 years old & the rhythms & phrases of the prayer-book remain, as they do with me, & that in his journalism he often finds himself on the point of using a biblical phrase. He's outgrown, you see, the anger & bitterness of the revolt from his beginnings. But what he has to stand on now, I'm sure I don't know – in his talk with me he was sympathetic with & in agreement with one's ideas, but its mostly negative I feel. He's not a 'virile' person – I think he's below par physically & always overtired by the nature of his work – but that lack of conviction is not characteristic of his type alone – all these young N.Z.ers are afraid of committing themselves, giving themselves away. They wrap themself round with phrases & catchwords they hear at the university – they don't take their stand on anything. Whether they will go on through life like this one doesn't know. Take Denis Glover – he has such a good heart, such a fund of good sense & generosity – if he could be really serious what a force he might be. Allen is very fond of Denis – that's evident in the verse of course. I like Allen – perhaps "if I'm spared" I shall get to know him better. He's a really sensitive critic of verse I think – at any rate I saw the justice of what he said about mine! I think making this anthology will "buck him up quite a lot" (as I hear them say). His domestic arrangements, as related to me by others, don't sound very helpful – – a sort of slovenly bohemianism I greatly dislike. But now I am getting into the region of gossip. He's fond of his children! And perhaps that's all I can say about Allen Curnow.

Monte of course is *serious* enough – but he's never thought through his view of life – he has smatterings of self-taught philosophy. Last time we had a talk I said I thought he ought to get on to a *theology*. He did not feel it to be impossible. But the editor of a daily is in a very tight place! I do value his sincerity & seriousness – he's not afraid of giving himself away. I must have told you how I knew him as an earnest little boy of 10 yrs, bent, even then, upon being "an author". And did I tell you that he

[1] The phrasing here suggests another Biblical allusion; perhaps she is thinking of the vision in Revelation 12: 1-17, in which the remnant of the woman's seed are persecuted by the dragon.

[2] Bethell uses the phrase in 'Nor'-West Evening, Winter' (*Collected Poems*, p. 54); her allusion is to Proverbs 30: 8.

cut out a good deal from the MS of Waiting Hills wh. Katya & I criticised in 1942. I feel with him about the Canterbury country. And à propos of that, thank you, kind sir, for what you say about me & my attempt at rendering that country. Lately I've been reading over some of the not-so-landscape pieces I'd rather forgotten – and what I said in my haste, being happy, is turning out to be true!

[...]

I wish I could comment on literature with your ability – put my vague impressions into words! I don't get much further than Punch's "I know what I like" – K. can do it. In my young days we were not taught to criticise! We were trained to accept the correct thing!

I'm glad you are fully aware of NZ narrowness & the sterility – But do come! There are so few equipped to do what you could do here. One has to choose in the end. And give oneself to the given, without wandering glances! When one commits oneself, then one starts. As K. said, after her marriage, "*Every* thing I do now has a *meaning*." I've thrown those glances towards England, & Europe generally, many a time, but on the whole I've *lived* in N.Z. these latter years – and the war has arrested many a wandering glance! I noticed the following inspiration in one of my periodicals "that a growing band of people may take their stand, burn their boats, & without looking back, dedicate their lives to changing the basic assumptions, temper & outlook of our time" – It might be better expressed, but its more needed in NZ I think than where you are. So you will be welcome at wasn't it Christmas 1945? But shall I be here?

[...] The war news now is so appalling, the bombing I mean, I can't read it.

And now I put this away, to be finished at home.

May 4th

Today I see snow Mts from my bed after the 1st really winter southerly wh. has lasted since Sunday when I came home to peace & quiet & affection.

No news from Lab. yet. The waiting is hard. Sometimes its hard to believe that something serious is going on. I feel so much better in myself – but when the pain in the cheek tunes up & has to be quelled with drug – then I wonder.

[...]

But what I've most wanted to write about (& now am getting tired!) is your N.Z. periodical project[1] – I was quite stirred up about it! There

---

[1] Brasch intended returning to New Zealand and beginning a literary periodical. *Landfall* was the result.

wd. be room for the right one, and as sketched by you. Do come back & try it. It wd. have to be very, very different from anything yet attempted. Rubbishy schemes crop up one after another. Dr. Helen Simpson has just refused to be a party to the latest one – (you wd. have to rope her in). Standards are deplorably low – in fact none. "If I'm spared" I'd love to know about it, as the idea evolves. Oh dear, I'd like to stay on this earth a bit longer – but *not* to be a burden. M & K have made all the difference. [...]

Before this illness I was talking with Lawrence Baigent[1] about new edition of Time & Place & Day & Night – both O.P., & still enquired for it seems. I thought perhaps I should put a codicil to my will, but my sister wd. see to it. In this letter you speak of Vita Nuova for me – so it is – but where to be continued I don't know.

On Sunday I go to small hospital not far off, perhaps for sometime. I can't return here till adequate help in house can be secured. I think I'm to go to Public Hosp. several times a week for ray treatment. At least that was the surgeon's last forecast. [...]

This has been written in bed, sun coming in. Now I rise to go downstairs so that K. may not have to carry food up. This house is transformed & all my old shabby furniture polished up looks quite dignified. What a letter! It really wd. be sad if it were lost! Better finish up & let it go. Au revoir, good friend. Come back & do your best for this cut off little country.

And my love to you.
M.U.Bethell.

Hocken Library. MS-0996-3/20.

TO RODNEY KENNEDY – MAY 6, 1944

47 Webb St. ChCh.

Dear Rodney

This is to thank you for your letter of Ap. 26th – rather out of your turn – but I want to pass on something from Charles Brasch before putting his letter away.

First let me tell you that I went back to Hospital on the 19th & had my operation next day – the surgeon cleaned out antrum & sent some tissue to the Lab. about which we have not had report. I still hope it may

---

[1] Lawrence Baigent (1912-1985) was at this time working with Glover at the Caxton Press, having been suspended from Christchurch Boys' High School in 1942 because of his conscientious objection to military service.

not be the worst thing threatened, but have been prepared for that for some time. Its such a wonderful thing that with this illness I have been given the spiritual help I needed – I have often thought it has been worth the illness! This morning we had one more Communion service in my room. A piece of furniture from Rise Cottage has made a perfect little altar, my crucifix hanging on the wall behind it – & brass candlesticks from the parlour & a little jar of flowers underneath the crucifix – That picture will stay by me in the small hospital I go to tomorrow I don't know for how long. My dear friends here go for 10 days holiday on Monday, but I can't return here unless more household help can be secured.

I got over the operation well & was able to come home for this week – a great mercy. The noise & racket of the big hospital was torture to my painful head. I thought the surgeon might do more than he did, & during the very few days notice I had of the op. I made haste to settle up some things "in case" so Mrs. Davies was duly advised of your claim upon the white jar.[1] If I have a slow illness I shall be able to think over possessions calmly.

What you say about the anthology is interesting – in the end I saw that The Garden was best left alone. A. Curnow told me he had decided to include The Long Harbour & Forest Sleep – I don't know whether he left out any of the others. I was surprised & pleased that he chose some of what I might call the more Christian pieces. He is familiar with prayer book language – his father's a parson & once he meant to take Holy Orders himself.

[...]

I'm so afraid I may not have strength to do your packet of literature before I go – today I must repack – but the raisins wh. were for your Easter Egg are being posted. The Southerly has finished up our garden but there was a fine decoration of chrysanthemums dahlias snapdragons etc when I came home. (To be able to say "home" once more is so heavenly – strange that it may only be for a short time)

[...]

A more important thing – To my great surprise, & it touches me so much, the case of apples arrived while I was in Hospl They are beauties this year – better than last – Being without teeth at the moment I can't sample them, but have told K D to eat some for me – she loves apples & we have only pears in the garden. She has laboured so hard for me in my distress – thankful she's to have a holiday.

---

[1] A 17th century Korean vase Bethell had acquired in London.

Goodbye dear Rodney – from the perhaps-falling-to-the-ground sparrow – but meanwhile my eyes are stronger & pain less thank God.

My love
M. U. B.

Hocken Library. MS-0741-001.

TO RODNEY KENNEDY – MAY 10, 1944

c/- Mrs. O'Connell 235 Papanui Road ChCh.

A postscript to my last to tell you, as I think I should, that it *is* the "worst feared" i.e. cancer. There cannot be an operation. I am to have deep x ray, but the result is quite uncertain & I don't know how long I shall have the use of my eyes. The sparrow has been provided for in great comfort & peace at the above address, good care in every way & opened on the very eve of the day the Davies were to leave for their holiday. I expect to be here for some time. That I am calm & happy is entirely the work of "my domestic chaplain" – he is *wonderful*. Sent to me *with* the illness. From the earthly side it looks like a sad blow to our plans for Webb St – but I know it must be good. Its possible that progress of the disease may be staved off, but the Dr. tells me to "live from day to day" – I am, strangely, in less pain. Its also possible dear Rodney, that I may not see you again. I know that you are with us in our prayers. Better not pass this on – I must write to people myself – the Woollastons for instance.

Love
M. U. B.

Hocken Library. MS-0741-001.

TO EDITH WOOLLASTON – MAY 10, 1944

Mrs. O'Connell's Rest Home 235 Papanui Road. ChCh

My dear Edith

Yr. letter before me is dated 28th Jan.! You will have guessed that ill-health has been the reason for my silence. I love the snapshots & am delighted that there is to be more family – Yes, I agree, a sister for Anna!

I must be brief – eyes not strong – giving my story. 10 days at Lewisham Hosp. for Xray & observation under specialist – many weeks of pain at home with my dears – still under observation. Knowing at last that it might be a growth. To hospital again for an operation (on antrum) of exploration on Ap 20. Suspense, hard to bear, waiting for report from pathologist. Last Sunday morning was told that it *is* cancer. Quite a relief to know – and that an operation is impossible – the thing I dreaded most. The Davies were to have their much-needed holiday on Monday & the little nursing-home I was at in Jan. out at Riccarton re-opened close to us on that very day! Never have I felt "providential care" to be more clearly shown. Here I have every possible comfort & *peace*. (The noise at the big hospital was terribly trying) I am to have deep ray treatment, but my doctor promises nothing & says I "must live from day to day." At the "best" I suppose it may be staved off for a while, at the "worst" (God's "best") I don't know how quick it may be.

That I am calm & happy is all the work of my "domestic chaplain" as I call him. It has been a miracle this help sent to me *with* my illness. I was such a *fearing* person, fearing & grieving, but Merlin has shown me what faith is, & upheld me by his faith & prayers. I thought I was going to *live* with them at 47, but he has prepared me to die. We have had such beautiful services of Holy Communion in my bedroom there, E. P.'s favourite tea-table just right to be an altar.

I have had to give up a lot of projects! My thought runs upon the disposal of possessions. Would Toss like to have his Taranaki drawing? It is so good & I am amused to think how long it took me to appreciate it! I want K. to have the Karori painting which I love. Is there any special book or other object you would like? K. will see to that.

I wonder whether you wd. like to have, *now*, the opal, wh. was taken out of the ring for me? – You might like to use it with the others. It's a lovely little stone.

This marriage of K & M. is a perfect one – a beautiful thing for me to have seen happen.

I have so much to be thankful for.

Eyes cannot be used much, & I may not be able to write another *letter*, but if there is anything to tell, you shall have a postcard.

My much love to you both & blessings on the children.

Mary Ursula.

Hocken Library. MS-0996-3/225.

To Eric McCormick – May 19, 1944

As from 47 Webb St. ChCh
At a Nursing Home

Dear Eric

This is to tell you that I have been ill since New Year, severe pain in head, eyes, & cheek. Last month I had an "exploratory" operation in the latter, & now the doctors tell me I can't get better. Yes, its cancer. I am having deep X-ray which may stave off a bit, on the other hand it may be quick, & its inoperable. I am not telling everyone in N. Z. but there are some people at a distance I should like to know, of whom you are one. It was a surprise, because only a few months ago a Dr. told me I was strong & might live another 20 years! Of course I'm leaving undone much I meant to do, but I suppose that happens to everyone. I do not suppose that I shall see you again, not here – That was a nice goodbye you gave me the last time I saw you ! Perhaps you were "averti".[1] I called it "chivalrous", but I think it was your real self. This is my 70th year & there has been a crisis in my life every 10 years – so I was prepared for *something*. (Rise Cottage began e.g. when I was 50 & ended just as I had turned 60.) St. Faith's closed down last Nov. for the duration, probably longer – & great friends of mine took over the house, me staying on. If you write, please address instead of St. Faith's c/- The Rev. Merlin Davies. I *may* be able to go back there for a little while. I had expected to live happily with them for a year or more (instead of on the edge of an institution!) but from them I've had the "loving care" my Doctor said I needed, & from him the spiritual help I needed still more.

You have heard I expect of the Anthology of NZ Verse Allen Curnow is editing – to be published by that Progressive Co. in Wellgn.[2] He is putting a good deal of me in. Someone is sure to send it to you or I might have one go as a parting present. Those lamps you gave me, 2 left, have been a comfort on wakeful nights, nice and low. No more to be got now.

Au revoir dear Eric with my love

M U B

Thank you again VERY much for all the help & encouragement & time you gave to Day & Night.

Alexander Turnbull Library. MS-Papers-3381.

TO LAWRENCE BAIGENT – MAY, 1944

c/- Mrs. O'Connell. 235 Papanui Rd.

Dear Lawrence

I think by this time you will have heard from Basil Dowling where I am, & why. Inoperable cancer. I have decided that there should be a new edition of T&P & D&N to be paid for by me (fully or in part) before I die. Could you put it through fairly quickly, as my time may be short?

[1] Fr. 'forewarned.'

[2] In fact, it was published by Caxton.

You promised to get the D&N a/c set in order & let me know – I have been ill since New Year & I daresay you have rung up without getting reply. Could you come & see me about this, with suggestions for paper & binding? I thought weekend wd. be best for you. I am too tired by the evening. How about Sunday morning – next one or next after? (Dinner is 12ish – hospital hours – so 10.30 or 11 wd. be good) Please ring & make appt. because my visitors are of course rationed.

Yours v. sincerely
M U Bethell

I should have liked to see you again in any case.

Macmillan Brown Library. MB 558. L4.

TO LAWRENCE BAIGENT – JUNE 2, 1944

235 Pap. Rd.

Dear Lawrence

Here's my airgraph effort. Will you post it if you approve. I havn't put stamps on in case you do not. And would you send one yourself simultaneous? Enclosed also the Contract. (I have other relevant matter to hand over later.) The correspondence with present management has not come to light yet, but I feel sure they will agree. I'm glad about that.

Enclose also the sad poems[1] – only for yr. eyes (& I feel shy almost sending them to you!) I was right in thinking them unsuitable – unless the Akaroa one with 1st & last stanzas omitted. You wd. be right if you said that I should have learnt to "transcend" that grief – but I allowed myself to give way once a year, thoroughly.

I am seeing A Curnow on Sunday morning & will consult him about unpublished ones which I have looked out meanwhile. Dr H S will be v. glad to do proofs & is so pleased that there is to be a reprinting. That's a big thing off my mind.

Yours affectly
M U B

My own name must appear *this* time.
"The grave's a fine and private place"![2]

Macmillan Brown Library. MB 558. L4.

---

[1] Bethell sent copies of the six memorial poems to Baigent.
[2] From Marvell's 'To His Coy Mistress.'

TO LAWRENCE BAIGENT – [JUNE 5, 1944]

King's Birthday 235 Pap. Rd.

Dear Lawrence

A P.S. with some oddments of verse. Should be v. glad of yr. opinion whether worth preserving. I should like the Kaikoura ones to go in. There are a few other bits still, but some unfinished.[1]

Another Sun. morning wd. be good if you have one to spare before I begin my Xray again.

M U B

Or is Sat morn perhaps better for you?

Macmillan Brown Library. MB 558. L4.

TO CHARLES BRASCH – JUNE 5, 1944

47 Webb St. Christchurch. N.1.

My dear Charles

This airgraph has been planned for some time. *First*, to say how clever of you to send me *pictures* now that my eyes don't serve me so well! [...]

Second. Airgraph 11.5.44 "wood anemone campion sponge" you won't see those in N.Z! Its all (magnificent) *background* yet to be filled in. (I had a notion of a poem about that once!) Sympathy – thank you v. much & yes, it *is* everything having M & K. Altho' I can't be with them now. Reference to Allen C. I'm seeing him about some unpublished verses to be included in reprint & T&P & D&N in one vol. Think I told you about that. I find him a sensitive critic – but he's rather what shall I call it – pathetic? Seems to have "missed the bus" spiritually? But the bus is caught some day. However I have had v. little talk with him really. Have seen Lawrence Baigent too – he is v. helpful. I gather that Caxton P. can carry most of the expense. Promised to have it done, whether I'm still here or not. I'll leave the matter (with much else) in M. D's hands. (If the bus was missed it was my church's fault. He was reading for Orders once. Church & culture generally out here much [in] need of help.)[2]

Third. Letter of 17.4 with promise of Dublin Review, and of money which has since come. I had been reflecting that you in yr. kindness

[1] It was some time before the *Collected Poems* was printed. In the meantime, Baigent showed the unfinished poems to Brasch; it was the latter's opinion that was influential in the final choice of poems.

[2] This last sentence was added as an afterthought in the nearest space.

might be concerned about expense when you heard of my illness, but as it is I'm free to use up Capital of course. (Inconvenient if a miracle happened or I "lingered on"!) Have had lots of nice ideas for your £25 – including the re-issue of poems. Also thought of old baby car for MD who is really not strong enough to bicycle about in all weathers. Comes (so convenient to flow on to second sheet) in chilled & exhausted. K. wd. soon teach him to drive. But I find they cost now more than £100 (sold our Essex for £50 in 1935!) Hope you will approve my having paid it meanwhile into P.O. for K. I was concerned about her having nothing of her own to fall back on in emergency. (He has v. small salary.) All this is between ourselves. Yr. cheque not known about by anyone else. You see how I treat you as close friend. K & M & I like the idea of *community* in goods, and yr. plans for NZ periodical we think v. sound idea. M.D. has just declined taking a hand in one of the sporadic propositions for NZ review – his reasons being no standard, no convictions, no point of view. It must be said that much NZ thinking is about 50 yrs behind the times. I meant to write about yr. plans by surface – but that letter might never be written. Some days can't make the effort. Had a good deal of pain yesterday & last night, but am seizing some clearheaded moments after dose of "A.P.C." this morning.[1] You wd. not find *many* contributors at first but there wd. be scope for editorials! Hope you will get in touch with my old friend Crawford Somerset, Feilding Community Centre. He has many plans [for] Adult Education & wants Church to be in touch with his work. If M&K are still here (do keep in touch with them, in any case?) M could suggest contributors. You've no idea how much constructive work he puts in behind the scenes. (I want you to know him well.) Sometimes I think wistfully that I could have been useful to him & others! But such thoughts don't hold me long. Have I told you already about F. Page leaving paintings of Eve's for me to look at. Such good ones. But it tires my eyes. I've told them I'm past looking at works of art now, as I've found I was past listening to music. All I want to look at now is my crucifix & the flowers friends bring & the bare trees against the changing sky, out of my lovely window. I wish you had been here to visit me – one a day now & 20 mins long (not counting M&K who come when they can, he about once a week). Au revoir again, dear Charles, & my love & so very many thanks. You know, I think you shld call me 'Mary Ursula' a fashion adopted by several of my younger best known friends. Hold on to that Review project – its the "proper idea" for NZ as outlined by you.

M U Bethell

---

[1] A commercially-available painkiller, combining aspirin, phenacetin and caffeine.

I get up for a bit indoors most afternoons – that's enough exercise! How unimportant my health is, when I think of Europe! Ought you perhaps with your languages to help reconstruct Europe? But I want you for N.Z! Recommend A. Buller. Darkness over Germany.[1]

Hocken Library. MS-0996-3/20.

TO CHARLES BRASCH – JUNE 22, 1944

As from c/- The Revd W. M. Davies 47 Webb St. ChCh. NZ.

My dear Charles

I'm still here & by way of "gathering up the fragments that remain".[2] [...]

It doesn't seem possible to tell you how I am – much weaker I think – but may be partly indoors & in bed. Mostly I get up for an hour or two & sit by my fire, but always glad to go back again. Dr. has told me this week not to wait to take Dope till pain begins, but carry on at regular hours – so that makes it more difficult to say. Pain sometimes bad when it sets in. I'm variable.

Saw A. Curnow last week about the reprinting & talked too much, whereby more swollen cheek & prizefighter eye & feeling good for nothing – some days can tackle a few postcards some days not even that – & today you see I feel I can scribble some words to you – I can't *make* myself do things – find it hard to remember things & have a pencil always at hand – difficult to *think out* anything now.

On the other hand went home in a taxi for a few hours one day! The Dr. thought it wd. be good for me & I don't think I was any the worse, and I saw to several matters good to get off hand. Want to decide remembrances for people. It was lovely to be in peace without nurses! & have the twain "around" – and to taste a cup of *real* coffee a.m. & *real* tea p.m. & a dinner thought out for me. Quite on this earth you see – but still don't know for how long. I believe I'm to have more Xray next month.

I do propose the funniest errands for you! Some day if you are in Bedfordshire I wish you wd. enquire at 8 The Brook Cottages *or* The Manor Farm Soulbury Leighton Buzzard for Sydney Parrott the farm hand.

My mother belonged to the Overseas League[1] – After she died in 1927 a letter came thru' the O.L. to her from this S.P. wishing to be a

---

[1] Ernestine Amy Buller's *Darkness over Germany* had been published the previous year.

[2] See John 6: 12.

correspondent. I answered saying I'd be glad to tell him anything about NZ. & there followed a series of what I think quite fascinating letters from him (I'm leaving them with K.) they have such a *flavour* & he looks so nice in the snapshot of himself & plough horses.

I answered his last letter in 1939 – either that went down (many did) or his reply may have been lost. I meant to write again & never have. I'd like him to know about me & that I did not forget him. Brook Cottages was his lodgings. Perhaps he has been killed in the war. Perhaps you could hear of him by means of a postcard. There, that's done, & my little burst of energy used up!

Now I sit back with eyes closed – No, I think I'll finish this up – always harder to begin again.

Papers pile up on my table & I've sent a P.C. to a new friend, D. G. Lilburn[2] – the music-composer (knows D'Arcy C.) who offered to read to me – asking him about Sunday & I'll get him to open all the papers & read me the headlines & then hand them over to K. I like him v. much. (He's one I talked too much to!)

I agreed with A. C's criticism of some unpublished verses & have actually been able to amend some lines.

If I *did nothing else* I might be spared to write my "By the River Ashley" after all!

Pain's beginning! Good bye.

With my love
Ursula Bethell

Hocken Library. MS-0996-3/19.

TO MONTE HOLCROFT – JUNE 26, 1944

As from c/- The Revd. W. M. Davies, 47 Webb St. ChCh.

Dear Monte

This letter must be as short as possible. My head is not good for much. I have been ill since New Year, with severe pain. Last month the doctors found that it is cancer – inside cheek bone – inoperable, thank God. It may be quick, or the deep Xray treatment *may* hold up progress of disease for a time – its quite incalculable. I think it must have begun a long while ago. I am growing slowly weaker. Pain is controlled by drugs. I am in a comfortable Nursing Home, not far from Webb St – every

[1] The Royal Overseas League, founded in 1910 by Sir Evelyn Wrench 'to foster international understanding and friendship.'

[2] Already mentioned to Brasch in her letter of Oct. 24, 1943.

kindness. A good illness to finish up with, because it gives one warning & time to prepare. I have now written all letters to a distance – & made most of the needful plans for reprint by Caxton Press of T&P & D&N both out of print – and they wish to include The Garden putting it under my own name. This will call for negotiations with England.

You will know about A. Curnow's forthcoming anthology of N.Z. verse (Caxton). It should be very good. He is a sensitive critic.

It looks as if I should *not* write my too long postponed "By the River Ashley" – always cooking & washing dishes these last years! No need to make those efforts now.

Please write to me if you can & tell me what you are doing about another book, (but I can't promise to answer. More of these announcement letters to be done.) I'm afraid there's little chance of seeing you unless Xray works its miracle, but you have all my good wishes. What you write is so *thoughtful* & so *honest*. It will be constructive for N. Z.

Au Revoir Monte
Your friend
M. U. Bethell

St Faith's closed down in Nov – M. Davies married my dear young friend Miss Taylor whom you saw & they occupy part of the house.

Of course I think you should go on to *Theology*!

You are well I hope.

Alexander Turnbull Library. MS-Papers-1186-03

TO EDITH WOOLLASTON – JULY 1, 1944

235 Pap Rd

My dear Edith,

Here is now the lovely little stone – between you & me – According to superstition it is I believe the right one for October when both our birthdays come.

[...]

Pain is worse and I am weaker. I don't think it can be very long. Best wishes for happiness in August.[1] Blessings on the children – Thank Toss for his letter.

Love to you all & au revoir
M. U.

---

[1] The Woollaston's fourth child, Philip, was born in August.

K. D. will send you a box of things from me – & consult with Toss about getting pictures to him.

National Museum of New Zealand Te Papa Tongarewa. CA 000457/1/5.

TO RODNEY KENNEDY – SEPTEMBER 12, 1944

235 Papanui Road

Please write. I should like it very much. Could even read it myself if in large, clear script.

With my love,
M. U. B. (dictated).

Hocken Library. MS-0741-001.

TO CHARLES BRASCH – SEPTEMBER 14, 1944

235 Papanui Road.

My dear Charles

This to thank you for two airgraphs (Aug. 1 & Aug. 11). They are wonderful. How odd that two people should become better known to each other upon airgraphs! & *one* can only mutter dictation in a rather dying sort of voice. I have long thought that 'Miss Bethell' sounded rather unsuitable, perhaps it's too late to do anything about that. But I hope you don't think of me thus. News is that M. and K. are going home sooner than they had expected. Nothing definite offered him in N.Z. but now just the right post in view. He feels he must go, anytime after January. I hope of course to be gone before then. They are anxious to meet you, & will have your address. Sometimes I think it was rash to advise you to come back, but I can't give up the conviction that it would be good for you & for this country, even if in the end you find you can't stay. I hope you will stand by the small committee who are fostering production of my book. It's possible a small loan might help, but Lawrence would tell you about that. Dr. Simpson, who is writing this, has helped me to get ready some unfinished ones, & beginning & end, & some other bits of my book to be called "By the River Ashley" are ready & may be included.

About my state of body, hard to say. Pain is sharper & I take less & less food. It has gone on much longer than they expected. It has been a hard trial, the noise & agitations of even a small hospital, & inefficient nursing in war-time, have counted very much. But I do not tell my sister about these things – no need to distress her.

You remember writing to me about faith. I told you how I lacked. Now, in this stress, when it's all or nothing I *am*, I believe, with M. D.'s help arriving at last.

It's wonderful having my old friend Helen Simpson to do this confidential writing for me, & read airgraphs to me. She comes twice a week for a short time.

This with my love.
M. U. B. [dictated]

Hocken Library. MS-0996-3/20.

TO CHARLES BRASCH – OCTOBER 2, 1944

As from 47 Webb Street.
235 Papanui Road

Dear Charles

Three good airgraphs from you. I am still here, going down all the time. Such cries of distress I could have sent all these months – such pain, and wartime difficulties at hospital. But must not distress friends so far away, least of all my sister.

(Merlin & Kathleen Davies expect to leave N.Z. for England any time after the New Year. He has been offered a good job – just the kind of work he likes & is best suited for, by the Bishop of Bristol – Ursula asks me to tell you this in parenthesis. H.M.S.)[1]

It would be sad if you missed M & K. You must get into touch with Helen Simpson, & weave her into your scheme. She reads letters to me – the greatest comfort helping like this.

In odd moments have put together bits of poems begun before and (this is Helen now speaking) the result is very lovely. *Most* of them are for the volume long ago projected, & to be called "By the River Ashley" – poems of her childhood, but a few are of the kind you already know in Time & Place & the other books. All will perhaps go into the Collected Poems that the Caxton proposes to print in January.*

[Added at end] * Ursula thinks I am wrong here, & that "By the River Ashley" is more likely to be a small separate volume. H.M.S.[2]

(Ursula again): Hope you will stand by production of book. It seems something tangible to leave behind, & there are some messages friends

---

[1] In fact, as Merlin Davies' memoir notes, the post fell through, and it was some time before he obtained suitable work.

[2] *Collected Poems* did not appear until 1950; it included 6 poems from the 'River Ashley' sequence, chosen by Charles Brasch.

will recognise. It's all or nothing now Charles – this faith we've talked about. I feel like the seagull in the Kaikoura poem.[1] Each message likely to be my last. So goodbye again.

With love,
M.U.B. [dictated]

Hocken Library. MS-0996-3/20.

TO RODNEY KENNEDY – OCTOBER 9, 1944

235 Papanui Road

Love for the narcissus poeticus and for the remembrance.[2]

Au revoir,
M. U. B. (dictated)

Hocken Library. MS-0741-001.

---

[1] See 'Winter 1941. Kaikoura' (*Collected Poems,* p. 77-78).

[2] Kennedy had sent flowers for her birthday 3 days earlier.

Bibliography

1 Unpublished sources: Letters from Bethell

Alexander, W. F.
ATL, MS-Papers-0423-1.
Andersen, Johannes
ATL, MS-Papers-0148-029B.
Baigent, Lawrence
MBL, MB 558, L4.
Bethell, Isabella
Private collection;
MBL, MB 558, C1.
Bethell, Richard
Private collection.
Brasch, Charles
HL, MS-0996-3/19 & 3/20.
Davies, Kathleen
MBL, MB 572, A.
Davies, Merlin
MBL, MB 572, A.
Duggan, Eileen
Catholic Archdiocesan Archive.
Gabites, Paul
MBL, MB 572, A.
Hall, Lady Rose
ATL, MS-Papers-1784
Hall, Sir John
ATL, MS-Papers-1784
Holcroft, Monte
ATL, MS-Papers-1186-03
Kennedy, Rodney
HL, MS-0741-01 & 02.
Lawlor, Pat
ATL, 77-067-1/2
Lillie, Mrs
Private collection.
Mayhew family
MBL, MB 558, L5.
Mayhew, Arthur
MBL, MB 558, C6.
McCormick, Eric
ATL, MS-Papers-0166-14;
MS-Papers-3381.
Mulgan, Alan
MBL, MB 558, L2.
Reader, Dorothea
MBL, MB 558, L5.
Schroder, J H E
ATL, fMS-018.
Sidgwick, Frank
Bodleian Library, Oxford, MS
Sidgwick & Jackson 142.
Skrine, Miss
MBL, MB 558, C8.
Summers, John
Private collection.
Taylor, Kathleen
MBL, MB 572, A.
The Press
MBL, MB 558, L6.
Tull, Emily
MBL, MB 558, C11.
V.I. R.
MBL, MB 558, L6.
Walker, Mary
MBL, MB 558, C11.
Woollaston, Edith
HL, MS-0996-3/225;
National Museum CA
000457/1/5
Woollaston, Toss
HL, MS-0996-3/225.

2 UNPUBLISHED SOURCES: LETTERS TO BETHELL

MBL, MB 558, C1: Lawrence Baigent, Blanche Baughan, Isabella Bethell, Marmaduke Bethell, Charles Brasch;

MBL, MB 558, C3: D'Arcy Cresswell, Allen Curnow, Denis Glover;

MBL, MB 558, C4: Sir John Hall, M. H. Holcroft;

MBL, MB 558, C5: Rodney Kennedy;

MBL, MB 558, C6: Arthur Mayhew and Frank Sidgwick, E. H. McCormick;

MBL, MB 558, C8: J. H. E. Schroder;

MBL, MB 558, C9-10: John Summers;

MBL, MB 558, C11: Emily Tull, Mary Walker;

MBL, MB 558, C12: Albert Wells;

MBL, MB 558, C14: Edith Woollaston;

MBL, MB 558, C15: Toss Woollaston.

3 BETHELL'S PUBLISHED WORK

From a Garden in the Antipodes. By Evelyn Hayes. London: Sidgwick & Jackson, 1929.

Time and Place, poems by the Author of "From a Garden in the Antipodes". Christchurch: Caxton, 1936.

Day and Night: Poems 1924–35, By the Author of TIME AND PLACE. Christchurch: Caxton, 1939.

Collected Poems. Christchurch: Caxton, 1950.

Collected Poems. Ed. Vincent O'Sullivan. Auckland: Oxford University Press, 1985.

Collected Poems. Ed. Vincent O'Sullivan. Wellington: Victoria University Press, 1997.

4 OTHER WORKS

Acland, L. G. D. *The Early Canterbury Runs.* Christchurch: Whitcoulls, 1975. (4th rev. ed. by W. H. Scotter.)

Aldington, Richard (trans.). *Alcestis.* London: Chatto & Windus, 1930.

Allen, C. R. Rev. of *Day and Night. Otago Daily Times.* Dec. 2, 1939.

Alpers, O. T. J., et. al. (ed.) *College Rhymes: an Anthology of Verse Written by Members of Canterbury College 1873-1923.* Christchurch: Whitcombe & Tombs, 1923.

Alverdes, Paul. *The Whistlers' Room.* London: Martin Secker, 1929.

Anson, Peter. *The Call of the Cloister. Religious Communities and Kindred Bodies in the Anglican Communion.* London: SPCK, 1964. (Rev. ed. by A. W. Campbell.)

Baigent, Lawrence. 'The poetry of Ursula Bethell.' *Landfall* 5.1 (1951), 23-30.

Baillie, Myra. 'The Grey Lady: Mary Lily Walker of Dundee.' In *Victorian Dundee: Image and Realities* ed. Louise Miskell, Christopher A. Whatley and Bob Harris. East Lothian: Tuckwell Press, 2000.

Barth, Karl. *A Letter to Great Britain from Switzerland.* The Christian Newsletter Books, No. 11. London: Sheldon Press, 1941.

Baughan, Blanche. *Brown Bread from a Colonial Oven: being sketches of up-country life in New Zealand.* London: Whitcombe & Tombs, 1912.

Baughan, Blanche. *People in Prison.* Auckland: Unicorn Press, 1936.

Belloc, Hilaire. *The Haunted House.* London: Queensway Press, 1936.

Belloc, Hilaire. *The Hedge and the Horse.* London: Cassell, 1936.

Bernanos, Georges. *Journal d'un curé de Campagne.* Trans. as *The Diary of a Country Priest* by Pamela Morris. London: Boriswood, 1937.

Bertram, James. *Charles Brasch.* New Zealand Writers and their Works. Wellington: Oxford University Press, 1976.

Bertrand, Louis. *Le livre de consolation.* Trans. as *The Art of Suffering* by E. F. Peeler. London : Sheed & Ward, 1936.

Binyon, Laurence. *The Flight of the Dragon: an essay on the theory and practice of art in China and Japan.* London: J. Murray, 1911, 1935.

Bloy, Léon. *Lettres à sa fiancée.* Paris: Stock, 1922. Trans. as *Letters to his Fiancée.* Barbara Wall. London: Sheed & Ward, 1937.

Bosanquet, Bernard. *The Meeting of Extremes in Contemporary Philosophy*. London: Macmillan, 1921.

Brabant, F. H. *Time and Eternity in Christian Thought*. London: Longmans, Green & Co., 1937.

Brasch, Charles. *Indirections: a Memoir 1909-1947*. Wellington: Oxford University Press, 1980.

Brasch, Charles. *The Land and the People and other poems*. Christchurch: Caxton Press, 1939.

Brémond, Henri. *Prière et Poésie* (*Cahiers verts*, 67). Paris: Bernard Grasset, 1926.

Brémond, Henri. *La Poésie pure; avec un débat sur la poésie*. Paris: [s.n.] 1926.

Brewer, Rosemary. 'A Pilgrim in the Library: the private letters and public poetry of Mary Ursula Bethell.' Unpublished M. A. thesis. University of Auckland, 1995.

Bridges, Robert. 'Humdrum & Harum-Scarum. A Lecture on Free Verse,' in *Collected Essays Papers &c.* London: Oxford University Press, 1928.

Bridges, Robert. *The Spirit of Beauty. An Anthology in English and French from the Philosophers and Poets*. London: Longmans, Green, 1925.

Bridges, Robert. *The Spirit of Man*. London: Longmans, Green, 1916.

Bridges, Robert. *The Testament of Beauty*. Oxford: Clarendon Press, 1929.

Buber, Martin. *Ich und Du*. Trans. as *I and Thou*. R. G. Smith. Edinburgh: T. & T. Clark, 1937.

Buller, Ernestine Amy. *Darkness over Germany*. London: Longmans, Green, 1943.

Bunyan, John. *The Pilgrim's Progress*. Ed. W. R. Owens. Oxford: Oxford University Press, 2003.

Burnaby, John. *Amor Dei: a Study of the Religion of St. Augustine*. London: Hodder & Stoughton, 1938.

Carswell, Catherine. *The Savage Pilgrimage: a Narrative of D. H. Lawrence*. London: Chatto & Windus, 1932.

Catherine of Siena. *The Letters of Catherine of Siena*. Ed. and trans. Suzanne Noffke. Medieval and Renaissance Texts and Studies 202-03. Tempe, Ariz.: Center for Medieval and Renaissance Studies, 1999-2001.

de Caussade, Jean-Pierre. *L'Abandon à la Providence divine*. Trans. as *Abandonment to Divine Providence*. E. Strickland. Exeter: The Catholic Press, 1921.

A Caxton Miscellany of Poems, Verse, Etc. Christchurch: Caxton Press, 1937.

Chesterton, Gilbert Keith. *Autobiography*. London: Hutchinson, 1936.

Coleridge, Mary. *The Seven Sleepers of Ephesus*. London: Chatto & Windus, 1893.

Converse, Florence. *The House of Prayer*. London: J. M. Dent, 1908.

Cresswell, D'Arcy. *Eena Deena Dynamo or the Downfall of Modern Science*. Christchurch: Caxton Press, 1936.

Cresswell, D'Arcy. *The Forest*. Auckland: Pelorus Press, 1952.

Cresswell, D'Arcy. *Lyttelton Harbour: a Poem*. Auckland: Unicorn Press, 1936.

Cresswell, D'Arcy. *Modern Poetry and the Ideal*. Auckland: Griffin Press, 1934.

Cresswell, D'Arcy. *The Poet's Progress*. London: Faber, 1930.

Cresswell, D'Arcy. *The Voyage of the Hurunui*. Christchurch: Caxton Press, 1956.

Cresswell, D'Arcy. 'Whence cometh our strength.' *Tomorrow*, 2.33 (Oct. 14, 1936), 19-21.

Cresswell, Douglas. *Squatter and Settler in the Waipara County*. Waikari: Waipara County Council, 1952.

Curnow, Allen. *A Book of New Zealand Verse*. Christchurch: Caxton Press, 1945.

Curnow, Allen. *Sailing or Drowning*. Wellington: Progressive Publishing Society, 1943.

Davies, W. Merlin. *Towards Spirituality Today: a Welshman's Response to Aotearoa/New Zealand*. Manurewa: College Communications, 1990.

Dene, John. Rev. of *From a Garden in the Antipodes*. *Art in New Zealand* 3.9 (Sept. 1930), 53-54.

Dickinson, Emily. *The Poems of Emily Dickinson*. Ed. Martha Dickinson Bianchi and Alfred Leete Hampson. London: Martin Secker, 1933.

Dickinson Emily. *The Poems of Emily Dickinson*. Ed. Thomas H. Johnson. Cambridge, Mass.: Belknap Press, 1963.

Dickinson, G. Lowes. *A Modern Symposium*. London: Dent, 1908.

Dictionary of New Zealand Biography. Wellington: Allen & Unwin; Dept. of Internal Affairs, 1990-2000.

Dowling, Basil. *A Day's Journey*. Christchurch: Caxton Press, 1941.

Duggan, Eileen. *Poems*. London: Allen & Unwin, 1937.

Du Maurier, George. *Peter Ibbetson*. New York & London: Harper & Bros, 1891.

Dunne, J. W. *An Experiment with Time*. London: A. & C. Black, 1927.

Elder, Charlotte. '"Dear Mr Schroder": an annotated edition of the correspondence between Ursula Bethell and John Schroder.' Unpublished M. A. thesis. Victoria University of Wellington, 1999.

Elder, Charlotte. 'Seeing the Light of Day: J. H. E. Schroder's Broadcast Review of *Day and Night*.' *Kotare:*

New Zealand Notes and Queries 3.1 (May, 2000), 10-21.

Eliot, T. S. *The Idea of a Christian Society*. London: Faber, 1939.

Erwin, Robert. 'Ursula Bethell and Evelyn Hayes : a misattribution?' *Landfall*, v. 31, no. 2 (June 1977), 156-162.

Every, George. *Christian Discrimination*. The Christian Newsletter Books, No. 8. London: The Sheldon Press, 1940.

A Faggot of Verse: poems by five women. [Aileen Barr, Isabel Butchart, Winifred Gill, Elizabeth Holmes, and Hester Marshall] London: Sidgwick and Jackson, 1930.

Forster, E. M. *Virginia Woolf*. Cambridge: Cambridge University Press, 1942.

François de Sales. *Traite de l'amour de Dieu*. Trans. as *A Treatise of the Love of God*. Miles Car. 1630. Rptd. Ilkley: Scolar Press, 1975.

Garner, Jean. *By His Own Merits: Sir John Hall – Pioneer, Pastoralist and Premier*. Hororata: Dryden Press, c. 1995.

Garrity, Tim, et. al. *The Kennedy Gift*. Dunedin: Hocken Library, 1990.

Gilby, Thomas. *Poetic Experience: An Introduction to Thomist Aesthetics*. London: Sheed and Ward, 1934.

Gill, Eric. *Autobiography*. London: J. Cape, 1940.

Gore, Charles. *The Incarnation of the Son of God*. Bampton Lectures 1891. London: J. Murray, 1892.

Gore, Charles, et al. *A New Commentary on Holy Scripture, including the Apocrypha*. London: SPCK, 1928.

Gore, Charles. *The Philosophy of the Good Life*. Gifford Lectures, 1932. London: J. Murray, 1930.

Gore, Charles. *The Religion of the Church. A Manual of Membership*. London: A. R. Mowbray, 1916.

Guthrie-Smith, H. *Tutira: the story of a New Zealand sheep station*. Edinburgh: William Blackwood, 1921.

Haynes, Renée. *Pan, Caesar and God*. London: Heinemann, 1938.

Hearnshaw, Vickie. 'R. N. Field, Mary Ursula Bethell and "The River and the Sea" : a note.' *Bulletin of New Zealand Art History* 18 (1997), 87-88.

Heeney, Brian. *The Women's Movement in the Church of England 1850-1930*. Oxford: Clarendon Press, 1988.

Herbert, A. P. and Nigel Playfair. *Riverside Nights: an entertainment*. London: T. Fisher Unwin, 1926.

Holcroft, M. H. 'The Ball.' In *New Zealand Short Stories*. Ed. O. N. Gillespie. London: Dent, 1930.

Holcroft, M. H. 'The Boundary Hut.' *The Press* (Junior Supplement) 17 Dec. 1936, 7.

Holcroft, M. H. *The Deepening Stream. Cultural Influences in New Zealand.* Christchurch: Caxton Press, 1940.

Holcroft, M. H. *Mary Ursula Bethell.* New Zealand Writers and their Works. Wellington: Oxford University Press, 1975.

Holcroft, M. H. *Timeless World: a Collection of Essays*. Wellington: Progressive Publishing Society, 1945.

Holcroft, M. H. *The Waiting Hills.* Wellington: Progressive Publishing Society, 1943.

Holmes, Mary Jane. *Rose Mather*. New York: G. W. Carleton, 1868.

Housman, Laurence. *The Love Concealed.* London: Sidgwick & Jackson, 1928.

von Hügel, Friedrich. *Letters from Baron Friedrich von Hügel to a Niece*. Ed. Gwendolen Green. London: J. M. Dent, 1928.

Hulme, T. E. *Speculations: Essays on Humanism and the Philosophy of Art.* London: Routledge and Kegan Paul, [1936].

Huxley, Aldous. *Ends and Means.* [London]: Chatto & Windus, 1938.

Hyde, Robin. *Passport to Hell.* London: Hurst & Blackett, 1936.

Innes, M. A. 'Songs from Quiet Places.' Rev. of *Time and Place*. *The Press*, 12 Sept. 1936, 17.

John of the Cross, St. *The Complete Works of Saint John of the Cross*. Ed. and trans. E. Allison Peers. London: Burns & Oates, 1946.

Jones, Lawrence. *Picking up the Traces: the Making of a New Zealand Literary Culture 1932-1945*. Wellington: Victoria University Press, 2003.

Julian of Norwich. *A Book of Showings to the Anchoress Julian of Norwich*. Ed. Edmund Colledge and James Walsh. Toronto: Pontifical Institute of Medieval Studies, 1978.

Kegan Paul, Charles. *Memories*. London: Kegan Paul, Trench & Trübner, 1899.

Lamb, Charles. *Elia and the Last Essays of Elia*. Ed. Jonathan Bate. Oxford: Oxford University Press, 1987.

Laura, Valerie. 'Ursula Bethell: Publishing the Poetry.' *Stout Centre Review* 3.3 (June 1993), 10-14.

Leon, Philip. *The Philosophy of Courage or The Oxford Group Way*. London: Allen & Unwin, 1939.

Lewis, C. S. *The Allegory of Love*. Oxford: Clarendon Press, 1936

Lewis, C. S. *The Problem of Pain*. London: Centenary, 1940.

Mace, C. A. *Psychology of Study*. London: Methuen, 1932.

MacCarthy. Desmond. *Criticism*. London: Putnam, 1932.

MacCarthy, Mary. *A Nineteenth-Century Childhood.* London: Heinemann, 1924.

McCormick, Eric. *Letters and Art in New Zealand.* New Zealand Centennial Surveys, 10. Wellington: Department of Internal Affairs, 1940.

McCormick, Eric. *An Absurd Ambition: Autobiographical Writings.* Ed. Dennis McEldowney. Auckland: Auckland University Press, 1996.

Mantz, Ruth. *The Life of Katherine Mansfield.* London: Constable, 1933.

de la Mare, Walter. *The Listeners and Other Poems.* London: Constable, 1912.

Maritain, Jacques. *Art and Scholasticism.* London: Sheed & Ward, 1930.

Maritain, Jacques. *Humanisme intégral.* Paris: Aubier, c.1936. Trans. as *True Humanism.* M. R. Adamson. London: G. Bles, 1938.

Maritain, Jacques and Raïssa Maritain. *De la vie d'oraison.* Trans. as *Prayer and Intelligence.* Algar Thorold. London: Sheed & Ward, 1928.

Marris, C. A. *New Zealand Best Poems of 1932.* Wellington: Harry H. Tombs, 1932.

Marsh, Ngaio. *Black Beech and Honeydew: an Autobiography.* Auckland: Collins, 1966.

Martindale, C. C. *The Difficult Commandment: notes on self-control especially for young men.* London, 1926.

Martindale, C. C. *What are Saints?* London: Sheed & Ward, 1932.

Martinez-Sierra, Gregorio. *The Cradle Song.* Trans. John Garrett Underhill. London: Samuel French, 1934.

Mayhew, Arthur. 'My Early Life: a personal memoir.' *Education Research and Perspective* 25.1 (1998): 61-104.

Molinos, Miguel de. *The Spiritual Guide which disentangles the soul.* Ed. Kathleen Lyttelton. London: Methuen, 1907.

Millar, Paul (ed.). *Spark to a Waiting Fuse: James K. Baxter's Correspondence with Noel Ginn 1942-1946.* Wellington: Victoria University Press, 2001.

Milner, Ian and Denis Glover (ed.). *New Poems.* Christchurch: Caxton Club Press, 1934.

'Modern Verse.' Rev. of *Day and Night*, by the author of *Time and Place. The Press*, 25 Nov. 1939, 18.

Mulgan, Alan. 'Notable N. Z. Verse.' Rev. of *Time and Place. Auckland Star*, April 17, 1937.

Murray, Stuart. *Never a Soul at Home. New Zealand Literary Nationalism and the 1930s.* Wellington: Victoria University Press, 1998.

My New Zealand Garden. By a Suffolk Lady. London: Elliot Stock, 1905.

Nicholson, Norman. *An Anthology of Religious Verse: designed for the times*. Harmondsworth: Penguin, 1942.

Nygren, Anders. *Agape and Eros. A Study of the Christian Idea of Love*. London: SPCK, 1932.

Oesterley, W.O.E. *The Sacred Dance: a study in comparative folklore*. Cambridge: Cambridge University Press, 1923.

Okakura, Kakuzo. *The Book of Tea*. London: Putnam, [1906].

The Oxford Companion to New Zealand Literature. Ed. Roger Robinson and Nelson Wattie. Melbourne: Oxford University Press, 1998.

The Passion of Perpetua and Felicity. Trans. W. H. Shewring. London: The Fleuron, 1929.

Pfleger, Karl. *Geister die um Christus ringen*. Trans. as *Wrestlers with Christ*. E. I. Watkin. London: Sheed & Ward, 1936.

Plomer, William (ed.). *Kilvert's Diary: selections from the diary of the Rev. Francis Kilvert*. London : Cape, 1977.

Quick, Oliver. *Doctrines of the Creed: Their Basis in Scripture and Meaning Today*. London: Nisbet, 1938.

Richards, Bernard. Rev. of *Henry James: A Life in Letters*. Ed. Philip Horne. *Essays in Criticism* (April, 20010, 271.

Rilke, Rainer Maria. *Wartime Letters of Rainer Maria Rilke*. Trans. M. D. Herder Norton. New York: Norton, 1940.

Schroder, J. H. E. 'N. Z. Literature and Art.' Rev. of *Letters and Art in New Zealand*, by E. H. McCormick. *The Press*, 15 March, 1941, 9.

Schroder, J. H. E. Rev. of *From a Garden in the Antipodes*, by Evelyn Hayes. *The Press*, 18 July 1931, 13.

Schroder, J. H. E. 'Robin Hyde: Struggle and Dream.' *The Press*, 14 Oct. 1939, 16; 21 Oct. 1939, 16; 28 Oct. 1939, 16.

Schweitzer Albert. *My Life and Thought: an Autobiography*. London: George Allen & Unwin, 1933.

de Selincourt, Basil (ed.). *Anne Douglas Sedgwick: a portrait in letters*. London: Constable, 1936.

Shorthouse, Joseph. *John Inglesant*. London: Macmillan, 1881.

Shove, Fredegond. *Dreams and Journeys*. Oxford, 1918.

Sidgwick, Ethel. *Laura. A Cautionary Tale*. London: Sidgwick & Jackson, 1924.

Sidgwick, Frank. *Ballad*. London: Martin Secker, 1914.

Simpson, Helen. 'The Bicentenary of William Cowper.' *The Press*, 18 July, 1931.

Simpson, Helen. *The Women of New Zealand.* New Zealand Centennial Surveys, 7. Wellington: Dept. of Internal Affairs, 1940.

Sinclaire, F. W. *Lend Me Your Ears.* Christchurch: Caxton, 1942.

Skeat, Walter W. 'An Unknown Poem by Chaucer.' *The Athenaeum*, 4 April, 1891, 440.

Somerset, H. C. D. *et al.* 'Ursula Bethell: some personal memories.' *Landfall* 8 (Dec. 1948) 275-296.

Spence-Jones, H. D. M. *The Early Christians in Rome.* London: Methuen, 1911.

Stovin, Harold. *Totem: the Exploitation of Youth.* London: Methuen, 1935.

Sturm, Terry (ed.). *The Oxford History of New Zealand Literature in English.* 2nd ed. Auckland: Oxford University Press, 1998.

Summers, John. *Dreamscape 1.* Christchurch: Pisces Print/Griffin Press, 1991.

Swann, Robert and Frank Sidgwick. *The Making of Verse: a guide to English metres.* London: Sidgwick & Jackson, 1934.

Taylor, Jeremy. *The Works of Jeremy Taylor, D.D.* Intro. T. S. Hughes. London: A. J. Valpy, 1831.

Teresa of Avila. *The Complete Works of Saint Teresa of Jesus.* Ed. and trans. E. Allison Peers. London: Sheed & Ward, 1946.

Thompson, Edward. *Cock Robin's Decease: an Irregular Inquest.* London: L. & V. Woolf, 1928.

Torlesse, Frances Harriet. *Bygone Days.* London: Harrison & Sons, 1914.

Traherne, Thomas. *Poems, Centuries and Three Thanksgivings.* Ed. Anne Ridler. London: Oxford University Press, 1966.

Trevelyan, Jill. '"Perfectly fairy-godmotherish": the friendship of Toss Woollaston and Ursula Bethell.' *Kotare: New Zealand Notes and Queries* 4.1 (June, 2001), 3-16.

Trevelyan, R. C. *Thamyris: or, Is there a future for poetry?* London: Kegan Paul, Trench, Trubner, 1925.

Underhill, Evelyn. *Worship.* London: A. R. Mowbray, 1929.

Waddell, Helen. *The Desert Fathers.* London: Constable, c. 1936.

Werfel, Franz. *The Death of a Poor Man.* London: E. Benn, 1927.

Whitehead, Clive. 'Introduction to, and original text of "My Early Life": Arthur Mayhew's memoirs of his Oxford childhood in the 1880s, and his life as a student at Winchester and New College, Oxford.' *Education Research and Perspectives* 25.1 (1998): 46-60.

Whitehead, Clive. 'The Nestor of British colonial education: a portrait of Arthur Mayhew, CIE, CMG (1878-1948).' *Journal of*

Educational Administration and History 29.1 (1997): 51-76.

Wickham, Harvey. *The Unrealists*. London: Sheed & Ward, 1931.

Williams, Charles. *Collected Plays*. London: Oxford University Press, 1963.

Williams, Charles. *A New Book of English Verse*. London: Victor Gollancz, 1935.

Williams, Charles. *War in Heaven*. London: Victor Gollancz, 1930.

Woollaston, M. T. 'Verse: a Poet's Second Book.' Rev. of *Time and Place*. *Otago Daily Times*, Sept. 12, 1936.

Woollaston, Toss. *Sage Tea: an Autobiography*. Auckland: Collins, 1980.

Woolman, John. *The Journal and Essays of John Woolman*. Ed. Amelia Mott Gummere. London: Macmillan, 1922.

Wright, Elizabeth Mary. *The Life of Joseph Wright*. London: Oxford University Press, 1932.

Index of Bethell's poetry

Individual Titles

Note: Poems marked with an asterisk are not in the *Collected Poems*, (1985/1997)

INDEX OF RECIPIENTS

INDEX OF BIBLICAL REFERENCES

General Index